ISBN 978-0-265-40589-5
PIBN 10504945

M.

<u>MARRIAGE RECORDS</u>

<u>MARION COUNTY, INDIANA</u>

Ministers' Returns

for

the Board of Health

reported to

the Clerk, Circuit Court, Indianapolis, Indiana

## Marriage Record for Board of Health
### To Be Returned by the Minister or Other Person Performing Ceremony

_____ and _____

Groom's name _Rolc Lumgrufurter_

His age _21_                                    1050666

" color _white_

" occupation _Truck Driver_

" Birthplace—City _Indpls_ State _Ind_

" Residence—Street No. _2318 - S. 25 th_ City _Indpls_

Single / Widower / Divorced } _Single_          { 1st, 2nd or 3rd marriage } _1 st_

Name of Father _Harry Bert Lumgrufirter_

Maiden name of Mother _Rolc Perue Enspecue_

Bride's name _Julia Baldwin_

Her age _18_

" color _white_

" occupation _Headress_

" Birthplace—City _Jackson_ State _Miss_

" Residence—Street No. _2318 S - 25 th_ City _Indpls_

Single / Widow / Divorced } _Single_          { 1st, 2nd or 3rd marriage } _1 st_

Name of Father _Harris Baldwin_

Maiden name of Mother _Anna Lee Baldwin_

Date of this marriage _April 1, 1942_

Place of this marriage _Indianapolis, Ind_

Name and title of person Performing this marriage _Harry C Emerline_

His address _4750 N. Illinois St_

_Indianapolis Ind_

Witness { Name _Helen J Stone    Winnie Lehman_
        { Address _Indianapolis, Ind_

### Return this Report to County Clerk with License and Certificate

# Marriage Record for Board of Health
### To Be Returned by the Minister or Other Person Performing Ceremony

_____ *Warne C. Holcombe* _____ and _____ *Harriet Davis* _____

Groom's name _____ *Warne C Holcombe* _____

His age _____ 24 _____

" color _____ White _____

" occupation _____ U. S. Army _____

" Birthplace—City _____ Newark _____ State _____ Ohio _____

" Residence—Street No. _____ Ft Benjamin Harrison _____ City _____ Indiana _____

Single / Widower / Divorced } _____ Single _____   { 1st, 2nd or 3rd marriage } _____ First _____

Name of Father _____ Charles (Reed Holcombe _____

Maiden name of Mother _____ Nettie L. Newton _____

Bride's name _____ Harriet Davis _____

Her age _____ 26 _____

" color _____ White _____

" occupation _____ Clerk _____

" Birthplace—City _____ Little Valley _____ State _____ New York _____

" Residence—Street No. _____ 721 So Branson _____ City _____ Marion, Indiana _____

Single / Widow / Divorced } _____ Single _____   { 1st, 2nd or 3rd marriage } _____ First _____

Name of Father _____ Floyd James Davis _____

Maiden name of Mother _____ Edna May Fording _____

Date of this marriage _____ April 1, 1944 _____

Place of this marriage _____ Marion, Indiana _____

Name and title of person Performing this marriage _____ Rev. Leon Shaefer _____

His address _____ 409 Highland Avenue _____
_____ Marion, Indiana _____

Witness { Name _____ Martha E. Davis _____
{ Address _____ Ellicottville, New York _____

## Return this Report to County Clerk with License and Certificate

# Marriage Record for Board of Health

### To Be Returned by the Minister or Other Person Performing Ceremony

*Lawrence Lent* _____ and *Frances L. Kirk*

Groom's name _Lawrence Lent_

His age _43 yrs_

" color _White_

" occupation _soldier_

" Birthplace—City _Dayton_ State _Ohio_

" Residence—Street No. _2910 Mildford_ City _Indianapolis, Ind_

Single / Widower / Divorced } _Divorced_ { 1st, 2nd or 3rd marriage } _2nd_

Name of Father _William J. Lent_

Maiden name of Mother _Jennie Hose_

Bride's name _Frances L. Kirk_

Her age _47 yrs_

" color _White_

" occupation _____

" Birthplace—City _Springfield_ State _Ohio_

" Residence—Street No. _2910 Mildford_ City _Indianapolis, Ind_

Single / Widow / Divorced } _Divorced_ { 1st, 2nd or 3rd marriage } _2nd_

Name of Father _George H. Rizer_

Maiden name of Mother _Ollie Mills_

Date of this marriage _April 1, 1944_

Place of this marriage _Indianapolis, Ind_

Name and title of person Performing this marriage _Guy H. Ford, minister_

His address _36 w Hancock a_

_Tipton, Ind_

Witness { Name _Cal Rizer_ Address _508 S. Wittenberg, Springfield, O_

### Return this Report to County Clerk with License and Certificate

# Marriage Record for Board of Health
## To Be Returned by the Minister or Other Person Performing Ceremony

_Jack E Prapst_ and _Grace Poole_

Groom's name _Jack E. Prapst_

His age _18_

" color _white_

" occupation _Pickens Co  Ala  Sailor_

" Birthplace—City _Pickens Co_   State _Ala_

" Residence—Street No. _Navy_   City _____

Single
Widower
Divorced } _Single_   { 1st, 2nd or 3rd marriage } _1st_

Name of Father _Lt. B V. Prapst_

Maiden name of Mother _Ernstine Bath_

Bride's name _Grace Poole_

Her age _19_

" color _white_

" occupation _Teacher_

" Birthplace—City _Lincoln Co_   State _Kans_

" Residence—Street No. _Garda_   City _Ala_

Single
Widow
Divorced } _Single_   { 1st, 2nd or 3rd marriage } _1st_

Name of Father _Thomas Poole_

Maiden name of Mother _Zerla Dick_

Date of this marriage _April 1 1944_

Place of this marriage _Indianapolis_

Name and title of person Performing this marriage _Summer L. Martin Minister_

His address _6234 Haurford ave, Indianapolis Ind._

Witness { Name _Earline F. Hester_
{ Address _221 E. Mich. # 501  Indianapolis Ind._

## Return this Report to County Clerk with License and Certificate

12

# Marriage Record for Board of Health
### To Be Returned by the Minister or Other Person Performing Ceremony

_Eugene Fred Schnell_ and _Ruth Louise Weiland_

Groom's name _Eugene Fred Schnell_

His age _23_

" color _whit_

" occupation _Machinist_

" Birthplace—City _Indianapolis_ State _Indiana_

" Residence—Street No. _2125 S. East_ City _Indianapolis_

Single / Widower / Divorced } _single_  { 1st, 2nd or 3rd marriage } _1st_

Name of Father _Albert Schnell_

Maiden name of Mother _Adele Herrman_

Bride's name _Ruth Louise Weiland_

Her age _19_

" color _whit_

" occupation _underwriter_

" Birthplace—City _Indianapolis_ State _Indiana_

" Residence—Street No. _2157 Brighton_ City _Indianapolis_

Single / Widow / Divorced } _single_  { 1st, 2nd or 3rd marriage } _1st_

Name of Father _Henry Weiland_

Maiden name of Mother _Henrietta Schmidt_

Date of this marriage _April 1, 1944_

Place of this marriage _Indianapolis, Indiana_

Name and title of person Performing this marriage _Ernst A. Piepenbok_

His address _902 Sander, Indianapolis, Indiana_

Witness { Name _Robert Schnell_ / Address _54 Jenny Lane_

### Return this Report to County Clerk with License and Certificate

# Marriage Record for Board of Health
### To Be Returned by the Minister or Other Person Performing Ceremony

Sherill R. McIntosh _and_ Virginia Lee Cooley

Groom's name _Sherill R. McIntosh_

His age _32_

" color _white_

" occupation _salesman_

" Birthplace—City _Cisco_ State _Illinois_

" Residence—Street No. _24 S. Davis_ City _Indianapolis_

Single Widower Divorced } _divorced_ { 1st, 2nd or 3rd marriage } _second_

Name of Father _William Edwin McIntosh_

Maiden name of Mother _Ora Alice Williams_

Bride's name _Virginia Lee Cooley_

Her age _22_

" color _white_

" occupation _stenographer_

" Birthplace—City _Crawfordsville_ State _Indiana_

" Residence—Street No. _2 N. Campbell_ City _Indianapolis_

Single Widow Divorced } _single_ { 1st, 2nd or 3rd marriage } _first_

Name of Father _Luther Cooley_

Maiden name of Mother _Ona Jackson_

Date of this marriage _April 1, 1944_

Place of this marriage _Home of bride's parents, Crawfordsville_

Name and title of person Performing this marriage _Reverend Hugh E. Cooley_

His address _Crawfordsville, Indiana R.R. #2_

Witness { Name _Luther Cooley_
{ Address _Crawfordsville, Ind._

### Return this Report to County Clerk with License and Certificate

# Marriage Record for Board of Health

To Be Returned by the Minister or Other Person Performing Ceremony

John H Austin and Lizzie Mae Pardan

Groom's name _John Henry Austin_

His age _33_

" color _Brown_

" occupation _Soldier_

" Birthplace—City _Hickory_ State _N. C._

" Residence—Street No. _Camp Atterbury_ City _Indiana_

Single / Widower / Divorced — 1st, 2nd or 3rd marriage _1st_

Name of Father _Archer Austin_

Maiden name of Mother _Cara Mahaffey_

Bride's name _Lizzie Mae Pardan_

Her age _22_

" color _Brown_

" occupation _Civil Service Worker_

" Birthplace—City _Covington_ State _Kentucky_

" Residence—Street No. _1066_ City _Columbus, Ohio_

Single / Widow / Divorced — 1st, 2nd or 3rd marriage _1st_

Name of Father _Eric Taylor_

Maiden name of Mother _Elizabeth Baldwin_

Date of this marriage _April 1, 1944_

Place of this marriage _1233 N. Arsenal Ave._

Name and title of person Performing this marriage _Rev. David C. Venable_

His address _2814 Highland Place Indianapolis Indiana_

Witness { Name _Mrs. Marian B. Caldwell_
{ Address _1733 N. Arsenal Ave._

## Return this Report to County Clerk with License and Certificate

# Marriage Record for Board of Health
### To Be Returned by the Minister or Other Person Performing Ceremony

_Morris A B_____ g__ and _____ '__ >

Groom's name _Morris_ _Burg___

His age _Twenty o_ _____

" color _White_

" occupation _U S Navy_

" Birthplace—City _Chatt____d_ State _Ky_

" Residence—Street No. _117 N._ _austin_ City _____

Single
~~Widower~~
~~Divorced~~ }  { 1st, 2nd or 3rd marriage }

Name of Father _Hiatt Burge_

Maiden name of Mother _Argel_

Bride's name _Miss Louise _____

Her age _16_ _____ _June_ _12_ _1943_

" color _White_

" occupation _Farmer_

" Birthplace—City _Ft Wayne_ State _Ind___

" Residence—Street No. _117 N. Austin_ City _Indianapolis Ind_

Single
~~Widow~~
Divorced }  { 1st, 2nd or 3rd marriage }

Name of Father _Elmer ____

Maiden name of Mother _Mer____t_

Date of this marriage _April 1 1944_

Place of this marriage _Zanesville Ind._

Name and title of person
Performing this marriage _Rev. G M Sill_

His address _Zanesville Indiana_

Witness { Name _____ ' __
{ Address _____

### Return this Report to County Clerk with License and Certificate

# Marriage Record for Board of Health
## To Be Returned by the Minister or Other Person Performing Ceremony

_Herron_ and _Macy_

Groom's name _Ross Herron_

His age _58_

" color _White_

" occupation _Retired fireman_

" Birthplace—City _Hamilton Co_ State _Ind._

" Residence—Street No. _5016 Orion_ City _Indpls._

~~Single~~ } _Widower_ { ~~1st,~~ 2nd ~~or 3rd~~ } _Second_
Widower    marriage
~~Divorced~~

Name of Father _James H. Herron_ (Deceased)

Maiden name of Mother _Amanda Felts_ ( " )

Bride's name _Flora Macy_

Her age _56_

" color _White_

" occupation _Domestic_

" Birthplace—City _Hancock Co_ State _Ind._

" Residence—Street No. _2970 Ford Mass_ City _Indpls._

~~Single~~ } _Widow_ { ~~1st,~~ 2nd ~~or 3rd~~ } _Second_
Widow      marriage
~~Divorced~~

Name of Father _Henry L. Bennett_ (Deceased)

Maiden name of Mother _Mattie Walls_

Date of this marriage _April 1, 1944_

Place of this marriage _59 N. Rural St_

Name and title of person
Performing this marriage _Geo. Trisdale_

His address _59 N. Rural St_

Witness { Name _Mr & Mrs E. F. Hinchman_
          { Address _2417 E. New York St_

## Return this Report to County Clerk with License and Certificate

# Marriage Record for Board of Health
## To Be Returned by the Minister or Other Person Performing Ceremony

_Murray Siegel_ and _Shirley Kristir_

Groom's name _Murray Siegel_

His age _21_

" color _white_

" occupation _actor_

" Birthplace—City _Brooklyn_ State _N.Y._

" Residence—Street No. _NW Harrison_ City _Europe_

Singe / Widower / Divorced } _Single_   {1st, 2nd or 3rd marriage} _First_

Name of Father _Harry_

Maiden name of Mother _Anne Pecker_

Bride's name _Shirley Kristal_

Her age _21_

" color _White_

" occupation _salesgirl_

" Birthplace—City _Manhattan New York_ State _N.Y._

" Residence—Street No. _2258 N. Meridian St._ City _Indianapolis, In_

Single / Widow / Divorced } _Single_   {1st, 2nd or 3rd marriage} _First_

Name of Father _Nathan Kristal_

Maiden name of Mother _Charlotte Glenn_

Date of this marriage _April 1, 1944_

Place of this marriage _2318 N. Meridian St. Indianapolis_

Name and title of person Performing this marriage _Rabbi Finechriso_

His address _3351 Ruckle Street Indianapolis In_

Witness { Name _Bernard Shapiro_  Address _E Harrison Indiana_ }

## Return this Report to County Clerk with License and Certificate

# Marriage Record for Board of Health

### To Be Returned by the Minister or Other Person Performing Ceremony

_Jardan Filowers_ and _Mary Carthans_

Groom's name _Jardan Filowers_

His age _38_

" color _C_

" occupation _Sailor_

" Birthplace—City _Greenwood_ State _Mississippi_

" Residence—Street No. _____ City _Ft. B. Harrison_

Single / Widower / Divorced } _Single_   { 1st, 2nd or 3rd marriage } _First_

Name of Father _Will Filowers_

Maiden name of Mother _Nervie Lang_

Bride's name _Mary Carthans_

Her age _25_

" color _C_

" occupation _Matron_

" Birthplace—City _Lexington_ State _Mississippi_

" Residence—Street No. _9910 West Chester Cleveland Ohio_

Single / Widow / Divorced } _Divorced_   { 1st, 2nd or 3rd marriage } _Second_

Name of Father _Albert Carthans_

Maiden name of Mother _Lillie Lago_

Date of this marriage _April 1, 1944_

Place of this marriage _Indianapolis, Indiana_

Name and title of person Performing this marriage _S. S. Thomas, Minister_

His address _702 26. Illinois St Indianapolis, Indiana._

Witness { Name _Mary Louise Hall_  { Address _2832 Indianapolis Avenue_

## Return this Report to County Clerk with License and Certificate

# Marriage Record for Board of Health

To Be Returned by the Minister or Other Person Performing Ceremony

Byron Neyle Fish _____ and _____ Phyllis Mary Johnstone

Groom's name __Byron Neyle Fish__

His age ____28____

" color____White____

" occupation____Soldier____

" Birthplace—City__Troy____ State __New York__

" Residence—Street No. __Ft. Benj. Harrison__ City __Indiana__

Single
Widower    } ___Single___    { 1st, 2nd or 3rd    } ___1st___
Divorced                        marriage

Name of Father__Ozro M. Fish__

Maiden name of Mother____Mary Lincoln__

Bride's name ____Phyllis Mary Johnstone__

Her age ____25____

" color____White____

" occupation____WAC____

" Birthplace—City__Chicago____ State __Illinois__

" Residence—Street No. __Ft. Benj. Harrison__ City __Indiana__

Single
Widow    } ___Divorced___    { 1st, 2nd or 3rd    } ___2nd___
Divorced                        marriage

Name of Father__Orville H. Johnstone__

Maiden name of Mother____Frances Sarah Durnam__

Date of this marriage____1 April 1944__

Place of this marriage____Fort Benjamin Harrison, Indiana__

Name and title of person
Performing this marriage____Albert M. B. Snapp,____ Chaplain

His address____Fort Benjamin Harrison, Indiana__

Witness { Name __Marjorie C. Braden__    Harry Graham
        { Address __Ft. Benj. Harrison, Ind.__    Fort Benjamin Harrison, Ind.

## Return this Report to County Clerk with License and Certificate

# Marriage Record for Board of Health
## To Be Returned by the Minister or Other Person Performing Ceremony

_Isaac E. Parker_ and _Lucille Vaughn Stanley_

Groom's name _Isaac E. Parker_

His age _74_

" color _White_

" occupation _Salesman_

" Birthplace—City _Arba_ State _Indiana_

" Residence—Street No. _647 East 32nd_ City _Indianapolis_

Single Widower Divorced } _Widower_ { 1st, 2nd or 3rd marriage } _Third_

Name of Father _Jesse F. Parker_

Maiden name of Mother _Amanda J. Thomas_

Bride's name _Lucile Vaughn Stanley_

Her age _36_

" color _White_

" occupation _Manager of Retail Coal Sales_

" Birthplace—City _Brazil_ State _Indiana_

" Residence—Street No. _647 East 32nd_ City _Indianapolis_

Single Widow Divorced } _Widow_ { 1st, 2nd or 3rd marriage } _Third_

Name of Father _Raphael E. Vaughn_

Maiden name of Mother _Goldah M. Rogers_

Date of this marriage _April 1, 1944_

Place of this marriage _Indianapolis, Indiana_

Name and title of person Performing this marriage _Herbert Hoffman, Minister_

His address _1241 No. Alabama St_
_Indianapolis, Indiana_

Witness { Name _____
Address _420 _____

## Return this Report to County Clerk with License and Certificate

# Marriage Record for Board of Health
### To Be Returned by the Minister or Other Person Performing Ceremony

_Carl J. Laufer_ and _Eva Marie Chambers_

Groom's name _Carl J. Laufer_

His age _41_

" color _White_

" occupation _Allison Eng._

" Birthplace—City _Indianapolis_ State _Ind._

" Residence—Street No. _1530 N. Dell_ City _Indianapolis, Ind_

Single
Widower
Divorced } _Divorced_ { 1st, 2nd or 3rd marriage } _2nd_

Name of Father _Albert Laufer_

Maiden name of Mother _Anna Jordan_

Bride's name _Eva Marie Chambers_

Her age _24_

" color _White_

" occupation _Allison Eng._

" Birthplace—City _Ellottsville_ State _Ind._

" Residence—Street No. _4977 W. 13th_ City _Indianapolis, Ind_

Single
Widow
Divorced } _Single_ { 1st, 2nd or 3rd marriage } _1st._

Name of Father _Ross Chambers_

Maiden name of Mother _Marie Fletcher_

Date of this marriage _April 1, 1944_

Place of this marriage _Indianapolis, Indiana_

Name and title of person
Performing this marriage _Norman H. Schultz — Ordained Minister_

His address _2117 Napoleon St._
_Indianapolis, Indiana_

Witness { Name _Mr. Robert Stevens_
{ Address _362 N. Capitol, Indianapolis, Ind._

### Return this Report to County Clerk with License and Certificate

# Marriage Record for Board of Health

To Be Returned by the Minister or Other Person Performing Ceremony

Ray R. Mock _____ and _____ Ruth Reichel

Groom's name _____ Ray R Mock

His age _____ 56

" color _____ White

" occupation _____ Foreman

" Birthplace—City _____ Coshocton Co. State _____ Ohio

" Residence—Street No. 4104 N. Capital City _____ Indianapolis

Single
Widower } Widower { 1st, 2nd or 3rd } Second
Divorced } marriage

Name of Father _____ Benjamin Franklin Mock

Maiden name of Mother _____ Martha Ellen Hanks

Bride's name _____ Ruth Reichel

Her age _____ 53

" color _____ White

" occupation _____ Druggist

" Birthplace—City _____ Indianapolis State _____ Indiana

" Residence—Street No. 4012 Boulevard City _____ Indianapolis

Single
Widow } Widow { 1st, 2nd or 3rd } Second
Divorced } marriage

Name of Father _____ O. D. Bales

Maiden name of Mother _____ Margarite Stumps

Date of this marriage _____ April 1, 1944

Place of this marriage _____ Francisco, Indiana

Name and title of person
Performing this marriage _____ Rev. James I. Carrico (minister)

His address _____ Francisco, Indiana

Witness { Name _____ Mrs. James I. Carrico
         { Address _____ Francisco, Indiana

## Return this Report to County Clerk with License and Certificate

12

FILED
42 APR 4 1944

CLERK

# Marriage Record for Board of Health

To Be Returned by the Minister or Other Person Performing Ceremony

_Earl Smith_ and _Dortha Mae Hawkins_

Groom's name _Earl Smith_

His age _28_

" color _White_

" occupation _Defense Worker_

" Birthplace—City _Duffield_ State _Va._

" Residence—Street No. _120 N. Penn._ City _Greenfield, Ind._

Single Widower Divorced } _Divorced_ { 1st, 2nd or 3rd marriage } _2nd_

Name of Father _D. M. Smith_

Maiden name of Mother _Alice Money_

Bride's name _Dortha Mae Hawkins_

Her age _18_

" color _White_

" occupation _Housekeeper_

" Birthplace—City _Greenfield_ State _Indiana_

" Residence—Street No. _120 N. Penn._ City _Greenfield, Ind._

Single Widow Divorced } _Single_ { 1st, 2nd or 3rd marriage } _1st_

Name of Father _Roy Franklin Hawkins_

Maiden name of Mother _Stella Mae Schutt_

Date of this marriage _April 1, 1944_

Place of this marriage _Rushville, Ind._

Name and title of person Performing this marriage _Ernest V. Kane, Justice of Peace_

His address _152½ E. Court St._

Witness { Name _Mary S. Kane_

{ Address _3741 College Ave._

## Return this Report to County Clerk with License and Certificate

# Marriage Record for Board of Health
### To Be Returned by the Minister or Other Person Performing Ceremony

*ichael Sicitra* and *Althea Embody*

Groom's name _Michael Sicitra_

His age _22_

" color _white_

" occupation _soldier_

" Birthplace—City _Elizabeth_ State _New Jersey_

" Residence—Street No _Butler University_ City _Indianapolis_

Single / Widower / Divorced } _single_    { 1st, 2nd or 3rd marriage } _1st_

Name of Father _John Sicitra_

Maiden name of Mother _Mary Lombardi_

Bride's name _Althea Embody_

Her age _28_

" color _white_

" occupation _saleslady_

" Birthplace—City _Dupuier_ State _Montana_

" Residence—Street No. _331 N. Delaware_ City _Indianapolis_

Single / Widow / Divorced } _single_    { 1st, 2nd or 3rd marriage } _1st_

Name of Father _Noyes Embody_

Maiden name of Mother _Agnes Coe_

Date of this marriage _April 1, 1944_

Place of this marriage _Indianapolis, Indiana_

Name and title of person Performing this marriage _Ernest F. Lane, Justice of the Peace_

His address _Indianapolis, Indiana_
_152½ E. Court St._

Witness { Name _Helen Irene Taylor_
{ Address _150 E. Troy Ave_

## Return this Report to County Clerk with License and Certificate

# Marriage Record for Board of Health
### To Be Returned by the Minister or Other Person Performing Ceremony

_Charles Riley_ and _Mildred Recker_

Groom's name _Charles C. Riley_

His age _41_

" color _White_

" occupation _Produc. Eng. Luckas. Harold Corp._

" Birthplace—City _Indianapolis_ State _Ind._

" Residence—Street No. _2217 N. New Jersey_ City _Indpls. Ind._

Single } _Divorced_  { 1st, 2nd or 3rd } _Second_
Widower }             { marriage
Divorced ✓

Name of Father _Hubert S. Riley_

Maiden name of Mother _Catherine McBroady_

Bride's name _Mildred J. Recker_

Her age _34_

" color _White_

" occupation _Lukas Harold Corp_

" Birthplace—City _Indianapolis_ State _Indiana_

" Residence—Street No. _1031 N. Pennsylvania_ City _Indianapolis_

Single } _Divorced_  { 1st, 2nd or 3rd } _Second_
Widow }             { marriage
Divorced }

Name of Father _J. B. Jackson_

Maiden name of Mother _Lena Bentley Hunt_

Date of this marriage _April 1, 1944_

Place of this marriage _Indianapolis_

Name and title of person Performing this marriage _Ernest J. Lane, Justice of the Peace_

His address _152½ E. Court St. Indianapolis_

Witness { Name _E. C. Seale_
        { Address _1031 N. Pennsylvania St._

### Return this Report to County Clerk with License and Certificate

## Marriage Record for Board of Health
### To Be Returned by the Minister or Other Person Performing Ceremony

*Howard Leroy Hollinger* and *Mildred Maxine Bennett*

Groom's name _Howard Leroy Hollinger_

His age _30_

" color _White_

" occupation _Welder_

" Birthplace—City _Waynesboro_ State _Penn_

" Residence—Street No. _Ft. Knox_ City _Ky_

Single Widower Divorced } _Divorced_ { 1st, 2nd or 3rd marriage } _2nd_

Name of Father _James E. Hollinger_

Maiden name of Mother _Maude Schildnecht_

Bride's name _Mildred Maxine Bennett_

Her age _2_

" color _White_

" occupation _defense worker_

" Birthplace—City _Saline City_ State _Indiana_

" Residence—Street No. _528 N. Ala._ City _Indianapolis_

Single Widow Divorced } _Divorced_ { 1st, 2nd or 3rd marriage } _2nd_

Name of Father _Virgil Jenkins_

Maiden name of Mother _Edna Clark_

Date of this marriage _April 1, 1944_

Place of this marriage _Indianapolis Ind_

Name and title of person Performing this marriage _Emmrich Lane Justice of the Peace_

His address _152½ East Court St._

Witness { Name _Mary Jo Lane_
{ Address _3741 College Ave._

### Return this Report to County Clerk with License and Certificate

# Marriage Record for Board of Health
### To Be Returned by the Minister or Other Person Performing Ceremony

William W. Hood and Marie Norris

Groom's name _William W. Hood_

His age _35_

" color _white_

" occupation _Cab Driver_

" Birthplace—City _Hutchison_ State _Kansas_

" Residence—Street No. _801 N. Penn._ City _Indpls._

Single / Widower / Divorced } _Single_ { 1st, 2nd or 3rd marriage } _1st_

Name of Father _Charles B. Hood_

Maiden name of Mother _Myrtle Oston_

Bride's name _Marie Norris_

Her age _24_

" color _White_

" occupation _Semi Driver_

" Birthplace—City _Indpls_ State _Ind._

" Residence—Street No. _122 W 18th St_ City _Indpls._

Single / Widow / Divorced } _Single_ { 1st, 2nd or 3rd marriage } _1st_

Name of Father _Samuel Norris_

Maiden name of Mother _Marie Asmus_

Date of this marriage _April 1—44_

Place of this marriage _Indianapolis, Indiana_

Name and title of person Performing this marriage _Ernest W. Lane, Justice of Peace_

His address _15½ East Court Street_

Witness { Name _Mary Jo Lane_
{ Address _3741 College Ave._

## Return this Report to County Clerk with License and Certificate

# Marriage Record for Board of Health

### To Be Returned by the Minister or Other Person Performing Ceremony

_Lester Riley Bowden_ and _Mary Louise Smith_

Groom's name _Lester Riley Bowden_

His age _37_

" color _White_

" occupation _Crane Operator_

" Birthplace—City _Huron_ State _Indiana_

" Residence—Street No. _315 N. Senate_ City _Indianapolis_

Single / Widower / Divorced _Divorced_ — 1st, 2nd or 3rd marriage _2nd_

Name of Father _Shelby Bowden_

Maiden name of Mother _Margreta Meyers_

Bride's name _Mary Louise Smith_

Her age _34_

" color _White_

" occupation _Nurse_

" Birthplace—City _Greensburgh_ State _Indiana_

" Residence—Street No. _315 N. Senate_ City _Indianapolis_

Single / Widow / Divorced _Divorced_ — 1st, 2nd or 3rd marriage _2nd_

Name of Father _John Smith_

Maiden name of Mother _Eldora McClain_

Date of this marriage _April 1, 1944_

Place of this marriage _Indianapolis, Ind._

Name and title of person Performing this marriage _Emerson Lane Justice of Peace_

His address _157½ East Court_

Witness { Name _Mary C. Lane_
{ Address _374 College Ave_

## Return this Report to County Clerk with License and Certificate

# Marriage Record for Board of Health
## To Be Returned by the Minister or Other Person Performing Ceremony

Harry Hively _____ and _Opal Louise Brown_

Groom's name _Harry Hively_

His age _37_

" color _white_

" occupation _Soldier_

" Birthplace—City _Kansas City_ State _Mo._

" Residence—Street No. _Ft McClelland_ City _Alabama_

Single / Widower / Divorced } _Widower_ { 1st, 2nd or 3rd marriage } _2nd_

Name of Father _Alva Hively ( deceased )_

Maiden name of Mother _Minnie Shoals (deceased)_

Bride's name _Opal Louise Brown_

Her age _24_

" color _white_

" occupation _none_

" Birthplace—City _Bicknell_ State _Ind._

" Residence—Street No. _2413 E Wash_ City _Indpls._

Single / Widow / Divorced } _Divorced_ { 1st, 2nd or 3rd marriage } _2nd_

Name of Father _Willard Kenneth Brown_

Maiden name of Mother _Ollie R. Miller_

Date of this marriage _April 1 - 44_

Place of this marriage _Indpls. Ind._

Name and title of person Performing this marriage _Arnett Lane, Justice of Peace_

His address _15½ East Court St._

Witness { Name _Mary Jo Lane_ / Address _374 College Ave._

## Return this Report to County Clerk with License and Certificate

# Marriage Record for Board of Health
## To Be Returned by the Minister or Other Person Performing Ceremony

_Harry W. Cowden_ and _Soldie M. Daves_

Groom's name _Harry W. Cowden_

His age _34_

" color _White_

" occupation _Boiler Maker_

" Birthplace—City _Columbus_ State _Indiana_

" Residence—Street No. _2810 College_ City _Indpls._

Single Widower Divorced } _Divorced_ { 1st, 2nd or 3rd marriage } _2nd_

Name of Father _James T. Cowden_

Maiden name of Mother _Martha Alice Payne_

Bride's name _Soldie M. Daves_

Her age _25_

" color _White_

" occupation _Bakery Employee_

" Birthplace—City _Truman_ State _Arkansas_

" Residence—Street No. _3870 Farnsworth_ City _Indpls._

Single Widow Divorced } _Single_ { 1st, 2nd or 3rd marriage } _1st_

Name of Father _James Daves_

Maiden name of Mother _Earle Evelyn Reed_

Date of this marriage _April 1 - 44_

Place of this marriage _Indpls. Ind._

Name and title of person Performing this marriage _Carl F. Tans, Justice of Peace_

His address _15½ E. Court St._

Witness { Name _Mary Jo Lane_ Address _3741 College Ave._

## Return this Report to County Clerk with License and Certificate

# Marriage Record for Board of Health
### To Be Returned by the Minister or Other Person Performing Ceremony

_Thomas E. Shaffer_ and _Harriett I. Geddes_

Groom's name _Thomas E. Shaffer_

His age _26 yrs_

" color _White_

" occupation _Factory - Machinist_

" Birthplace—City _Carroll Co._ State _Indiana_

" Residence—Street No. _____ City _____

Single Widower Divorced } _Single_ { 1st, 2nd or 3rd marriage } _First_

Name of Father _Harry W. Shaffer_

Maiden name of Mother _Dot Allen_

Bride's name _Harriett Irene Geddes_

Her age _22 yrs_

" color _White_

" occupation _Housewife_

" Birthplace—City _Green County_ State _Indiana_

" Residence—Street No. _____ City _____

Single Widow Divorced } _Divorced_ { 1st, 2nd or 3rd marriage } _2nd_

Name of Father _George Crites_

Maiden name of Mother _Bessie Blann_

Date of this marriage _April 1- 1947_

Place of this marriage _Harrison Ohio - Ministers Home_

Name and title of person Performing this marriage _Rev. Henry W. Cohagan_

His address _303 Park Ave. Harriso Ohio_

Witness { Name _Carol Horsley_
{ Address _Harrison Ohio_

## Return this Report to County Clerk with License and Certificate

# Marriage Record for Board of Health
### To Be Returned by the Minister or Other Person Performing Ceremony

Harold Sheets and Anna Takacs

Groom's name _____ Harold Sheets

His age _____ 28

" color _____ W

" occupation _____ Lucas Harold employ

" Birthplace—City _____ Lawrence Co _____ State _____ Indiana

" Residence—Street No. _____ 28 N Jefferson City _____ Indianapolis Ind

Single / Widower / Divorced } _____ single _____ { 1st, 2nd or 3rd marriage } _____ first

Name of Father _____ Joseph Howard Sheets

Maiden name of Mother _____ Nellie Hunsucker

Bride's name _____ Anna Takacs

Her age _____ 25

" color _____ W

" occupation _____ Krug aus employe

" Birthplace—City _____ Perth Amboy N _____ State _____ New Jersey

" Residence—Street No. _____ 254 N Tremont City _____ Indianapolis

Single / Widow / Divorced } _____ divorced _____ { 1st, 2nd or 3rd marriage } _____ second

Name of Father _____ Joe Takacs

Maiden name of Mother _____ Catherine Wanyer

Date of this marriage _____ April 1 1944

Place of this marriage _____ 523 N Beville Indianapolis Ind

Name and title of person Performing this marriage _____ Rev Charles L Haney

His address _____ 523 N Beville Ave Indianapolis Ind

Witness { Name _____ Helen Takacs
{ Address _____ 254 N Tremont St

## Return this Report to County Clerk with License and Certificate

# Marriage Record for Board of Health
## To Be Returned by the Minister or Other Person Performing Ceremony

_____ and _____

Groom's name _Gordon D. Ammerman_

His age _24_

" color _White_

" occupation _Riveter_

" Birthplace—City _Indianapolis_ State _Indiana_

" Residence—Street No _911 No Meridian_ City _Indianapolis Ind_

Single / Widower / Divorced } _Divorced_   { 1st, 2nd or 3rd marriage } _2nd_

Name of Father _William C. Ammerman_

Maiden name of Mother _Roberta Merle Baker_

Bride's name _Betty Jean Marsh_

Her age _18_

" color _White_

" occupation _Household_

" Birthplace—City _Indianapolis_ State _Indiana_

" Residence—Street No _6165 Rosslyn_ City _Indianapolis_

Single / Widow / Divorced } _Single_   { 1st, 2nd or 3rd marriage } _1st_

Name of Father _Charles H. Marsh_

Maiden name of Mother _Grace May Coles_

Date of this marriage _April 1st 1944_

Place of this marriage _Indianapolis Ind_

Name and title of person Performing this marriage _Rev. W E Gillett_

His address _____

Witness { Name _Charles H. Marsh   Dorothy Hoover_
{ Address _6165 Rosslyn Ave Indianapolis Ind_

## Return this Report to County Clerk with License and Certificate

# Marriage Record for Board of Health
## To Be Returned by the Minister or Other Person Performing Ceremony

*Herman H. Lloyd* and *Nina E. Shockeney*

Groom's name _Herman H. Lloyd_

His age _61_

" color _white_

" occupation _Laborer_

" Birthplace—City _Hamilton County_ State _Ind._

" Residence—Street No. _451 Ketchum_ City _Indpls_

Single
Widower } _Single_   { 1st, 2nd or 3rd marriage } _1st_
Divorced

Name of Father _Thomas C. Lloyd_

Maiden name of Mother _Martha C. Cottingham_

Bride's name _Nina E. Shockeney_

Her age _52_

" color _white_

" occupation _Clerk_

" Birthplace—City _English_ State _Ind._

" Residence—Street No. _451 Ketchum_ City _Indpls._

Single
Widow } _Widow_   { 1st, 2nd or 3rd marriage } _2nd_
Divorced

Name of Father _Wilfred J. Ellis_

Maiden name of Mother _Belle Martin_

Date of this marriage _April 1 - 44_

Place of this marriage _Indpls Ind._

Name and title of person
Performing this marriage _Ernest H Damp, Justice of Peace_

His address _157½ E Court St_

Witness { Name _Mary Jo Lane_
          { Address _3741 College Ave_

## Return this Report to County Clerk with License and Certificate

FILED
42  APR 3  1944

CLERK

# Marriage Record for Board of Health

To Be Returned by the Minister or Other Person Performing Ceremony

Garrett A Snodgrass _____ and _Violet Evelyn Courtney_

Groom's name _____ Garrett A Snodgrass

His age _____ 27

" color _____ White

" occupation _____ U.S. Coast Guard

" Birthplace—City _____ Frankfort _____ State _____ Indiana

" Residence—Street No. _1405 Pacific St_ City _Virginia Beach_ Va.

Single / Widower / Divorced } _Single_ { 1st, 2nd or 3rd marriage } _First_

Name of Father _____ Clarence Garrett Snodgrass

Maiden name of Mother _____ Ethel Lucille Fulkerson

Bride's name _____ Violet Evelyn Courtney

Her age _____ 19

" color _____ White

" occupation _____ Stenographer—Cashier

" Birthplace—City _____ Butlerville _____ State _____ Indiana

" Residence—Street No. _630 N Colorado_ City _Indianapolis, Ind._

Single / Widow / Divorced } _Single_ { 1st, 2nd or 3rd marriage } _First_

Name of Father _____ Allen James Courtney

Maiden name of Mother _____ Hazel Rosana Courtney

Date of this marriage _____ April 1st 1944

Place of this marriage _____ Indianapolis Ind

Name and title of person Performing this marriage _____ Rev L G Huddleston

His address _____ 1613 Fletcher Ave Indianapolis Ind

Witness { Name _____ Charles D Johnson

Address _____ 3524 Graceland Indianapolis Ind.

## Return this Report to County Clerk with License and Certificate

# Marriage Record for Board of Health
### To Be Returned by the Minister or Other Person Performing Ceremony

Virgil Johnson and Eugennia Hart

Groom's name _Virgil Johnson_

His age _33_

" color _white_

" occupation _factory worker_

" Birthplace—City _Alpine_ State _Ind._

" Residence—Street No. _34 S Euclid_ City _Indianapolis_

Single
Widower
Divorced } _____ { 1st, 2nd or 3rd marriage } _____

Name of Father _James Johnson_

Maiden name of Mother _Katherine Meridean_

Bride's name _Eugennia Hart_

Her age _26_

" color _white_

" occupation _Employee of a house wife_

" Birthplace—City _Indianapolis_ State _Ind._

" Residence—Street No. _195 Harris_ City _Indianapolis_

Single
Widow
Divorced } _____ { 1st, 2nd or 3rd marriage } _____

Name of Father _Turner Hart_

Maiden name of Mother _Hazel Hart_

Date of this marriage _April 1, 1944_

Place of this marriage _Indianapolis, Ind_

Name and title of person
Performing this marriage _Rev Charles M Armstrong_

His address _Indianapolis_
_Indiana_

Witness { Name _Robert Hart_
{ Address _2037 W Washington Apt., Ind_

## Return this Report to County Clerk with License and Certificate

# Marriage Record for Board of Health
## To Be Returned by the Minister or Other Person Performing Ceremony

_____ and _____

Groom's name _Alonzo George Fairbairn_

His age _22_

" color _White_

" occupation _Y.M.C.A Secretary_

" Birthplace—City _Pittsburgh_ State _Penna_

" Residence—Street No. _Garrett Biblical Institute_ City _Evanston_

Single Widower Divorced } _Single_    { 1st, 2nd or 3rd marriage } _1st_

Name of Father _Thomas Fairbairn_

Maiden name of Mother _Margaret Monteeth_

Bride's name _Bettie Ruth Hargrave_

Her age _23_

" color _White_

" occupation _Student_

" Birthplace—City _Elwood_ State _Indiana_

" Residence—Street No. _339 Lesley Ave_ City _Indianapolis_

Single Widow Divorced } _Single_    { 1st, 2nd or 3rd marriage } _1st_

Name of Father _Ellis Burton Hargrave_

Maiden name of Mother _Carrie Ethel Stitzel_

Date of this marriage _April 1, 1944_

Place of this marriage _Indianapolis Ind_

Name and title of person Performing this marriage _Guy O Carpenter - Methodist Minister_

His address _3559 Central Ave_ _Indianapolis Ind_

Witness { Name _Mrs. G. O. Carpenter_  Address _3559 Central ave._

## Return this Report to County Clerk with License and Certificate

# Marriage Record for Board of Health
### To Be Returned by the Minister or Other Person Performing Ceremony

_Alden A. Webber_ and _Ruth E. Knauer_

Groom's name _Alden A. Webber_

His age _24_

" color _White_

" occupation _Machinist_

" Birthplace—City _Daviess Co._ State _Indiana_

" Residence—Street No. _2126 S. Delaware_ City _Indianapolis, Ind._

Single / Widower / Divorced } _First Single_ { 1st, 2nd or 3rd marriage } _First_

Name of Father _Clarence Webber_

Maiden name of Mother _Finnie Mae White_

Bride's name _Ruth E. Knauer_

Her age _20_

" color _White_

" occupation _Assembler_

" Birthplace—City _Greencastle_ State _Indiana_

" Residence—Street No. _152 8½ Remberant_ City _Indianapolis, Ind._

Single / Widow / Divorced } _Single_ { 1st, 2nd or 3rd marriage } _First_

Name of Father _Christopher Earl Knauer_

Maiden name of Mother _Florence Edna Barnard_

Date of this marriage _April 1, 1944_

Place of this marriage _Indianapolis, Ind._

Name and title of person Performing this marriage _Rev. J. Ray Stanton_

His address _Indianapolis, Ind._

Witness { Name _Russell Knauer_  Address _1718 Rembrandt St. Indianapolis Ind._

## Return this Report to County Clerk with License and Certificate

12

# Marriage Record for Board of Health

### To Be Returned by the Minister or Other Person Performing Ceremony

*Robert N Lee* and *Dorothy Silverman*

Groom's name .... *Robert N Lee*

His age .... *24*

" color .... *White*

" occupation .... *Stock Clerk — Allison General Motors Div.*

" Birthplace—City .... *Indianapolis* .... State .... *Indiana*

" Residence—Street No. .... *1006 Shelby* .... City .... *Indianapolis*

Single, Widower, Divorced } *Single*    1st, 2nd or 3rd marriage } *1st*

Name of Father .... *William Mason*

Maiden name of Mother .... *Ella Warren*

Bride's name .... *Dorothy Silverman*

Her age .... *29*

" color .... *White*

" occupation .... *Continental States Co.*

" Birthplace—City .... *Columbus* .... State .... *Ind.*

" Residence—Street No. *1521 Kennington* .... City .... *Indianapolis*

Single, Widow, Divorced } *Single*    1st, 2nd or 3rd marriage } *1st*

Name of Father .... *Gilbert Marion Silverman*

Maiden name of Mother .... *Laura Janie Staggs*

Date of this marriage .... *April 1, 1944*

Place of this marriage .... *Indianapolis, Ind.*

Name and title of person Performing this marriage .... *N L Schulz — Minister*

His address .... *2417 Napoleon St*
.... *Indianapolis, Ind.*

Witness { Name .... *Gilbert Alvin Silverman*
{ Address .... *1520 Kennington St*

## Return this Report to County Clerk with License and Certificate

# Marriage Record for Board of Health
## To Be Returned by the Minister or Other Person Performing Ceremony

_Jess F Conatser_ and _Thelma C Stanley_

Groom's name _Jess F Conatser_

His age _47_

" color _white_

" occupation _Factory employee – Press man_

" Birthplace—City _Nashville_ State _Tenn._

" Residence—Street No. _19th & College_ City _Ind. pls._

Single
Widower } _Divorced_      { 1st, 2nd or 3rd marriage } _5th._
Divorced

Name of Father _Andrew Conatser_

Maiden name of Mother _Sandy Pruitt_

Bride's name _Thelma C Stanley_

Her age _41_

" color _white_

" occupation _Housewife._

" Birthplace—City _Dayton_ State _Ohio._

" Residence—Street No. _19th & College_ City _Ind. pls_

Single
Widow } _Divorced_      { 1st, 2nd or 3rd marriage } _Third._
Divorced

Name of Father _George Charles Shaw._

Maiden name of Mother _Etta Harrison_

Date of this marriage _March April 1, 1944_

Place of this marriage _1960 Broadway Indpls. Ind._

Name and title of person Performing this marriage _Rev. Edwin Gwaltney_

His address _1960 Broadway Indpls. Ind_

Witness { Name _Fred W Israel — Grace M Israel._
        { Address _Zionsville, Ind R.R. X 1_

## Return this Report to County Clerk with License and Certificate

# Marriage Record for Board of Health

To Be Returned by the Minister or Other Person Performing Ceremony

_Willis Nichols_ and _Bessie May Robbins_

Groom's name _Willis Nichols_

His age _47_

" color _White_

" occupation _Creamery Worker_

" Birthplace—City _Belding_ State _Michigan_

" Residence—Street No. _607 E Ohio_ City _Indianapolis_

Single / Widower / Divorced } _Divorced_ { 1st, 2nd or 3rd marriage } _Second_

Name of Father _Smith Nichols_

Maiden name of Mother _Julia Walker_

Bride's name _Bessie May Robbins_

Her age _32_

" color _White_

" occupation _Cream Tester_

" Birthplace—City _Indianapolis_ State _Ind_

" Residence—Street No. _870 Fletcher_ City _Indianapolis_

Single / Widow / Divorced } _Single_ { 1st, 2nd or 3rd marriage } _First_

Name of Father _Jesse Robbins_

Maiden name of Mother _Myrtle Keller_

Date of this marriage _April 1, 1944_

Place of this marriage _Indianapolis, Ind._

Name and title of person Performing this marriage _Howard C. Lytle, Minister_

His address _415 W. Westfield Blvd._
_Indianapolis, Ind._

Witness { Name _Lillie Dicken_
{ Address _605 E Ohio St_

**Return this Report to County Clerk with License and Certificate**

12

# Marriage Record for Board of Health
## To Be Returned by the Minister or Other Person Performing Ceremony

*Callaway* and *Carter*

Groom's name _Arthur Callaway_

His age _19_　　　　　　　　　　　　1960666

" color _White_

" occupation _Bookkeeper_

" Birthplace—City _Washington_ State _Ind._

" Residence—Street No. _1147 N. Ill. St_ City _Indpls._

Single / ~~Widower~~ / ~~Divorced~~ } _Single_　　{ 1st, ~~2nd or 3rd~~ marriage } _first_

Name of Father _Arlie Callaway_

Maiden name of Mother _Flossie Fay Madison_

Bride's name _Dixie Belle Carter_

Her age _16_

" color _white_

" occupation _Clerk – Grocery Store_

" Birthplace—City _Greensburg_ State _Ind._

" Residence—Street No. _230 S. Walcott_ City _Indpls._

Single / ~~Widow~~ / ~~Divorced~~ } _Single_　　{ 1st, ~~2nd or 3rd~~ marriage } _first_

Name of Father _Claude Carter_

Maiden name of Mother _Ellen Burgess_

Date of this marriage _April 7, 1944_

Place of this marriage _230 S. Walcott_

Name and title of person Performing this marriage _O.C. Trinkle_

His address _59 N. Rural St_

Witness { Name _Claude Carter_ | _Mrs. Ellen Callaway_　Address _230 S. Walcott_ | _1147 N. Illinois St_ }

## Return this Report to County Clerk with License and Certificate

# Marriage Record for Board of Health

### To Be Returned by the Minister or Other Person Performing Ceremony

*Alfred L. Barnett* and *Merry Ellen Harrell*

Groom's name *Alfred L. Barnett*

His age *21*

" color *White*

" occupation *United States Navy*

" Birthplace—City *Linton* State *Indiana*

" Residence—Street No. *Southwest ¼* City *Linton*

Single ~~Widower~~ ~~Divorced~~ } *Single*   { 1st, 2nd or 3rd marriage } *First*

Name of Father *Arreatus Barnett*

Maiden name of Mother *Clementine Vandeveed*

Bride's name *Merry Ellen Harrell*

Her age *19*

" color *White*

" occupation *Stenographer*

" Birthplace—City *Linton* State *Indiana*

" Residence—Street No. *Rural* City *Linton*

Single Widow Divorced } *Single*   { 1st, 2nd or 3rd marriage } *First*

Name of Father *William Harrell*

Maiden name of Mother *Edna Baker*

Date of this marriage *April 2, 1944*

Place of this marriage *Linton, Indiana*

Name and title of person Performing this marriage *Waldo S. Hoar Minister*

His address *130 H St. N.W.*
*Linton, Indiana*

Witness { Name *Mrs. Hurbert McHaley*
{ Address *Linton Ind.*

## Return this Report to County Clerk with License and Certificate

# Marriage Record for Board of Health
## To Be Returned by the Minister or Other Person Performing Ceremony

_Walter B. Kennaw_ and _Mildred Ruth Brown_

Groom's name _Walter B Kennaw_

His age _29_

" color _white_

" occupation _Seargeant US Army_

" Birthplace—City _Middleport_ State _O_

" Residence—Street No. _____ City _Ft Harrison_

Single / Widower / Divorced } _Divorced_ { 1st, 2nd or 3rd marriage } _Second_

Name of Father _Clopha L. Kennaw_

Maiden name of Mother _Melle F. Tipton_

Bride's name _Mildred Ruth Brown_

Her age _23_

" color _white_

" occupation _Secretary_

" Birthplace—City _Indianapolis_ State _Indiana_

" Residence—Street No. _4338 Broadway_ City _Indianapolis_

Single / Widow / Divorced } _1st_ { 1st, 2nd or 3rd marriage } _First_

Name of Father _Wesley O. Brown_

Maiden name of Mother _Ethel M. Pool_

Date of this marriage _April 2, 1944_

Place of this marriage _Indianapolis, Ind._

Name and title of person Performing this marriage _Sidney Blair Harry — Minister_

His address _Meridian Heights Presbyterian Church Indianapolis Ind._

Witness { Name _Lucile Brown_
Address _4338 Broadway, Indpls Ind._

## Return this Report to County Clerk with License and Certificate

12

# Marriage Record for Board of Health
## To Be Returned by the Minister or Other Person Performing Ceremony

_James E. Koble_ and _Jacquelyn Mitchell_

Groom's name _James E. Koble_

His age _22_

" color _white_

" occupation _musician_

" Birthplace—City _Indianapolis_ State _Ind._

" Residence—Street No. _1318 N. Penn_ City _Indpls_

Single · Widower · Divorced    {1st, 2nd or 3rd marriage

Name of Father _Benj Harrison Koble_

Maiden name of Mother _Lillian B. Kruse_

Bride's name _Jacquelyn Mitchell_

Her age _22_

" color _white_

" occupation _musician_

" Birthplace—City _Boise_ State _Idaho_

" Residence—Street No. _1512 N. Meridian_ City _Indpls_

Single · Widow · Divorced    {1st, 2nd or 3rd marriage

Name of Father _Thomas Howard Mitchell_

Maiden name of Mother _Florence Elis. Ruckdaschel_

Date of this marriage _April 2 1944._

Place of this marriage _Indianapolis_

Name and title of person Performing this marriage _Rev. H. Mc Jorrn_

His address _717 S. Keb Jorrn 2_
_Indianapolis, Ind._

Witness  { Name ........................
{ Address ........................

## Return this Report to County Clerk with License and Certificate

# Marriage Record for Board of Health

### To Be Returned by the Minister or Other Person Performing Ceremony

_____ and _____

Groom's name _Earl L. Vandrei_

His age _22_

" color _White_

" occupation _Welder_

" Birthplace—City _Carroll Co._ State _Indiana_

" Residence—Street No. _927 N. East St._ City _Indianapolis Ind_

Single / Widower / Divorced } _Single_   { 1st, 2nd or 3rd marriage } _1st_

Name of Father _Earl Levi Andrei_

Maiden name of Mother _Opal Marie Cain_

Bride's name _Mildred Ruth Reed_

Her age _18_

" color _White_

" occupation _Inspector Presto Lite_

" Birthplace—City _Marion Co._ State _Indiana_

" Residence—Street No. _Claremont_ City _Ind._

Single / Widow / Divorced } _Single_   { 1st, 2nd or 3rd marriage } _1st_

Name of Father _William Herman Reed_

Maiden name of Mother _Mabel Marie Boughton_

Date of this marriage _Apr. 2 - 1944_

Place of this marriage _Indianapolis, Ind._

Name and title of person Performing this marriage _W.B. Shullenberger - Indianapolis Ind._

His address _____

Witness { Name _Roxanna May_ _Walter Reed_
         { Address _Indpls, Ind_ _Pittsboro Ind._

## Return this Report to County Clerk with License and Certificate

# Marriage Record for Board of Health
## To Be Returned by the Minister or Other Person Performing Ceremony

*Paul Lester Shepherd* and *Leona Elizabeth Walker*

Groom's name — Paul Lester Shepherd

His age — 23

" color — White

" occupation — Truck driver

" Birthplace—City — Portland  State — Tenn

" Residence—Street No. 3104 Jackson St. City — Indianapolis

Single / Widower / Divorced — Single  { 1st, 2nd or 3rd marriage } — 1st

Name of Father — Abe Shepherd

Maiden name of Mother — Willie Mae Stewart

Bride's name — Leona Elizabeth Walker

Her age — 19

" color — White

" occupation — cashier

" Birthplace—City — Indianapolis  State — Ind

" Residence—Street No. 3104 Jackson St City — Indianapolis

Single / Widow / Divorced — Single  { 1st, 2nd or 3rd marriage } — 1st

Name of Father — James A. Walker

Maiden name of Mother — Reva McNealy

Date of this marriage — April 2, 1944

Place of this marriage — Indianapolis, Ind

Name and title of person Performing this marriage — Almon J. Coble

His address — 8 S. Warman Ave. Indianapolis, Ind

Witness { Name — Lewis A. Walker
         { Address — 3104 W. Jackson St. Indianapolis, Ind.

## Return this Report to County Clerk with License and Certificate

# Marriage Record for Board of Health
## To Be Returned by the Minister or Other Person Performing Ceremony

Robert Wood Moore and Katharine Marie Bates

Groom's name _Robert Wood Moore_

His age _20_

" color _White_

" occupation _Student — South Bend, Ind._

" Birthplace—City _Easton_ State _Pa._

" Residence—Street No. _Stone Harbor_ City _N. J._

Single Widower Divorced } _Single_ { 1st, 2nd or 3rd marriage } _1st_

Name of Father _Woodlane Moore_

Maiden name of Mother _Margaret Irene Heas_

Bride's name _Katharine Marie Bates_

Her age _19_

" color _White_

" occupation _Student_

" Birthplace—City _Philadelphia_ State _Pa._

" Residence—Street No. _Claypool Hotel_ City _Indianapolis_

Single Widow Divorced } _Single_ { 1st, 2nd or 3rd marriage } _1st_

Name of Father _Dr. Wm Bates_

Maiden name of Mother _Marie Alice Bergstresser_

Date of this marriage _April 2, 1944_

Place of this marriage _Indianapolis, Ind._

Name and title of person Performing this marriage _F. Marion Smith, Minister_

His address _4730 N. Capitol Ave._
_Indianapolis, Ind._

Witness { Name _Dr. Wm Bates_
{ Address _Ocean City, N. J._

## Return this Report to County Clerk with License and Certificate

# Marriage Record for Board of Health

### To Be Returned by the Minister or Other Person Performing Ceremony

*James Henry Batts* and *Myrtle Florence Smith*

Groom's name ___ Pvt. *James Batts*

His age ___ *Thirty five* ___ (35)

" color ___ *Negro*

" occupation ___ *U. S. Army*

" Birthplace—City ___ *Prospect* ___ State ___ *Tennessee*

" Residence—Street No. *1418 Yandes St* City *Indianapolis*

~~Single~~
Widower
Divorced } *yes*   { 1st, 2nd or 3rd marriage } *3rd*

Name of Father ___ *Rev. Albert Batts*

Maiden name of Mother ___ *Catherine Garrett*

Bride's name ___ *Myrtle Florence Smith*

Her age ___ *Twenty Six* ___ (26)

" color ___ *Negro*

" occupation ___ *Waitress*

" Birthplace—City ___ *Prospect* ___ State ___ *Tennessee*

" Residence—Street No. *1418 Yandes* City *Indianapolis*

~~Single~~
Widow
Divorced } *yes*   { 1st, 2nd or 3rd marriage } *2nd*

Name of Father ___ *Lacy Smith*

Maiden name of Mother ___ *Augusta Nelson*

Date of this marriage ___ *Apr. 2 - 1944*

Place of this marriage ___ *1305 Yandes St.*

Name and title of person
Performing this marriage ___ *Rev. F. E. Tisdale*

His address ___ *1305 Yandes Street*

Witness { Name ___ *F. E. Tisdale*
{ Address ___ *1305 Yandes*

### Return this Report to County Clerk with License and Certificate

# Marriage Record for Board of Health

### To Be Returned by the Minister or Other Person Performing Ceremony

*James E. C. Bell* and *Maude M. Raymond*

Groom's name _James E. C. Bell_

His age _61_

" color _White_

" occupation _R.R. Fireman_

" Birthplace—City _Philipstown_ State _Illinois_

" Residence—Street No. _2844 N. Gladstone_ City _Indpls_

Single / Widower / Divorced } _Widower_ { 1st, 2nd or 3rd marriage } _3rd_

Name of Father _David Albert Bell_

Maiden name of Mother _Selina Drunk_

Bride's name _Maude M. Raymond_

Her age _61_

" color _White_

" occupation _Housekeeper_

" Birthplace—City _Boone County_ State _Indiana_

" Residence—Street No. _2844 Gladstone_ City _Indianapolis_

Single / Widow / Divorced } _Widow_ { 1st, 2nd or 3rd marriage } _2nd_

Name of Father _Daniel B. Lee_

Maiden name of Mother _Martha Jones_

Date of this marriage _April 2, 1944_

Place of this marriage _2844 N. Gladstone_

Name and title of person Performing this marriage _Rev. Wm. O. Breedlove_

His address _2312 Stuart St. Indianapolis Ind_

Witness { Name _Roy Egbert_ _Elsie Egbert_
{ Address _2601 Roosevelt Ave._ _2601 Roosevelt_

## Return this Report to County Clerk with License and Certificate

## Marriage Record for Board of Health

To Be Returned by the Minister or Other Person Performing Ceremony

George James Phillips and Velma Vernita Porter

Groom's name George James Phillips

His age Thirty Six

" color Negro

" occupation Truck Driver

" Birthplace—City Gosport State Indiana

" Residence—Street No. 1551 Martindale City Indianapolis

Single / Widower / Divorced } Single    1st, 2nd or 3rd marriage } First

Name of Father Luke Phillips

Maiden name of Mother Sarah Edmonson

Bride's name Velma Vernita Porter

Her age Twenty one

" color Negress

" occupation Housework

" Birthplace—City Humboldt State Tennessee

" Residence—Street No. 1551 Martindale City Indianapolis

Single / Widow / Divorced } Single    1st, 2nd or 3rd marriage } First

Name of Father George Porter

Maiden name of Mother Julia Woodson

Date of this marriage April 2, 1944

Place of this marriage Bloomington, Indiana

Name and title of person Performing this marriage Rev. Moses J. M. Porter

His address 509 W. 6th Street, Bloomington, Indiana.

Witness { Name Sarah A. Phillips
{ Address Gosport Ind. R. R. 1 # 250

## Return this Report to County Clerk with License and Certificate

# Marriage Record for Board of Health
## To Be Returned by the Minister or Other Person Performing Ceremony

William Robert Jennings and Rose Mary Yount

Groom's name William Robert Jennings

His age 23

" color White

" occupation Seaman-Maritime Service-Merchant Marines

" Birthplace—City Indianapolis State Indiana

" Residence—Street No. 1742 Arrow Ave. City Indianapolis

Single Widower Divorced } Single | 1st, 2nd or 3rd marriage } 1st

Name of Father Raymond Jennings

Maiden name of Mother Mildred Gillespie

Bride's name Rose Mary Yount

Her age 22

" color White

" occupation None

" Birthplace—City Indianapolis State Indiana

" Residence—Street No. R.R. #1 City Carmel, Indiana

Single Widow Divorced } Single | 1st, 2nd or 3rd marriage } 1st

Name of Father Charles Wesley Yount

Maiden name of Mother Ruby Ethel Wilson

Date of this marriage April 2, 1944

Place of this marriage McKee Chapel-Tabernacle Presbyterian Church-Indiana-
Name and title of person polis, Indiana
Performing this marriage _Boydwarya Uall_ Minister of above Church

His address 418 East 34th Street

Indianapolis, Indiana

Witness { Name _Mary Jennings Rauh (Mrs. Frad E. Rauk_ Address _1742 Arrow Avenue, Indianapolis, Indiana_

## Return this Report to County Clerk with License and Certificate

# Marriage Record for Board of Health
### To Be Returned by the Minister or Other Person Performing Ceremony

_Willard R. Richer_ and _Bella Marie Davidson_

Groom's name _Willard R. Richer_

His age _23_

" color _White_

" occupation _Farmer_

" Birthplace—City _Greenville_ State _Tennessee_

" Residence—Street No. _Camp Atterbury_ City _Camp Atterbury_

Single / Widower / Divorced } _Single_    { 1st, 2nd or 3rd marriage } _first_

Name of Father _Coy Richer_

Maiden name of Mother _Nancy Hensaw_

Bride's name _Bella Marie Davidson_

Her age _24_

" color _White_

" occupation _Defense work (Allisons)_

" Birthplace—City _North Salem_ State _Indiana_

" Residence—Street No. _McKinley_ City _North Salem_

Single / Widow / Divorced } _Single_    { 1st, 2nd or 8rd marriage } _Single_

Name of Father _Harley Davidson_

Maiden name of Mother _Dolene Thompson_

Date of this marriage _April 2 - 1944_

Place of this marriage _Indianapolis_

Name and title of person Performing this marriage _Rev. Joseph N Grang_

His address _3469 N. Capitol Indianapolis_

_Leona Sutton - 302 N New York St. Indianapolis, Ind_

Witness { Name _Anna S Cantrell_
Address _429 M.P. E.G Camp Atterbury Ind_

## Return this Report to County Clerk with License and Certificate

12

# Marriage Record for Board of Health

### To Be Returned by the Minister or Other Person Performing Ceremony

---------- and ----------

Groom's name _Harold D. Huffine_ 35357772

His age _37_

" color _white_

" occupation _Soldier_

" Birthplace—City _Evansville_ State _Indiana_

" Residence—Street No. _520 N. Meridian_ _Indianapolis_

Single / ~~Widower~~ / ~~Divorced~~ { } 1st, ~~2nd or 3rd~~ ~~marriage~~ { }

Name of Father _Forest Huffine_

Maiden name of Mother _Frances Ann Dunning_

Bride's name _Mary L. Howe_

Her age _31_

" color _white_

" occupation _Interviewer_

" Birthplace—City _Jonesboro_ State _Indiana_

" Residence—Street No. _520 N. Meridian_ _Indianapolis_

~~Single~~ / Widow / Divorced { } ~~1st~~, 2nd or ~~3rd~~ marriage { }

Name of Father _Alvin H. Howe_

Maiden name of Mother _Annabelle Gillespie_

Date of this marriage _April 7, 1944_

Place of this marriage _Stout Field, Indiana_

Name and title of person
Performing this marriage _Chaplain Walter Karsch_

His address _Stout Field, Indiana_

Witness { Name _T/Sgt B.R. Santy — Mrs B.R. Santy_  35157192

Address _1655 N. Alabama_ _1655 N. Alabama_  362-4 }

### Return this Report to County Clerk with License and Certificate

# Marriage Record for Board of Health
### To Be Returned by the Minister or Other Person Performing Ceremony

Lynch _____ and Anderson

Groom's name _James F. Lynch_

His age _20_

" color _White_

" occupation _Sailor_

" Birthplace—City _Chicago_ State _Illinois_

" Residence—Street No. _Arms Navard Ce_ City _Brooklyn N.Y._

Single / Widower / Divorced } _Single_    { 1st, 2nd or 3rd marriage } _First_

Name of Father _Walter V. Lynch_

Maiden name of Mother _Mary Helen Pedersen_

Bride's name _Dorothy Anderson_

Her age _20_

" color _White_

" occupation _Stenographer_

" Birthplace—City _Indianapolis_ State _Indiana_

" Residence—Street No. _720 4 N. Pennsylvania_ City _Indianapolis_

Single / Widow / Divorced } _Single_    { 1st, 2nd or 3rd marriage } _First_

Name of Father _Dan R. Anderson_

Maiden name of Mother _Marie McCreadY_

Date of this marriage _April 2, 1944_

Place of this marriage _Indianapolis Ind._

Name and title of person Performing this marriage _Rev. L. C. Trent_

His address _411 N Arsenal Ave_ _Indianapolis, Ind._

Witness { Name _Dan R Anderson_ { Address _Indianapolis Ind._

## Return this Report to County Clerk with License and Certificate

# Marriage Record for Board of Health
## To Be Returned by the Minister or Other Person Performing Ceremony

Allon Richard Griffith and Margarite Elzbrete Jameson

Groom's name _Alton Richard Griffith Sr_

His age _23 Yrs_

" color _Colored_

" occupation _Truck Operator_

" Birthplace—City _Birmingham_ State _Ala._

" Residence—Street No. _1234 N 26_ City _Indianapolis 8 I._

Single / Widower / Divorced } _Divorced_ { 1st, 2nd or 3rd marriage } _Second_

Name of Father _Edward Griffith_

Maiden name of Mother _Beatrice Branchad_

Bride's name _Margarit Elizbeth Jameson_

Her age _18 Yrs_

" color _Colored_

" occupation _House Wife and Assorter_

" Birthplace—City _Indianapolis_ State _Indiana_

" Residence—Street No. _2107 Harvee_ City _Indianapolis_

Single / Widow / Divorced } _Single_ { 1st, 2nd or 3rd marriage } _First_

Name of Father _Benjamin Jameson_

Maiden name of Mother _Beatrice Register_

Date of this marriage _April 2 — 1944_

Place of this marriage _Indianapolis Ind_

Name and title of person Performing this marriage _Rev. Frank F Young_

His address _760 W 25 st_
_Pastor 1st Baptist Church N.S._

Witness { Name _Alberta Young_
{ Address _760 W 25th St_

## Return this Report to County Clerk with License and Certificate

# Marriage Record for Board of Health
## To Be Returned by the Minister or Other Person Performing Ceremony

_____ and _____

Groom's name _David Warren Reeves_

His age _20_

" color _White_

" occupation _Sailor_

" Birthplace—City _Indianapolis_ State _Ind_

" Residence—Street No. _103 N. Vine_ City _Indianapolis_

Single / ~~Widower~~ / ~~Divorced~~ } _Single_   { 1st, 2nd or 3rd marriage } _first_

Name of Father _Elmer Reeves_

Maiden name of Mother _Grace Michael_

Bride's name _Rosemary Long_

Her age _20_

" color _White_

" occupation _Inspector at Mallory_

" Birthplace—City _Helmsburg_ State _Ind_

" Residence—Street No. _607 E Lincoln_ City _Indianapolis_

Single / ~~Widow~~ / ~~Divorced~~ } _Single_   { 1st, 2nd or 3rd marriage } _first_

Name of Father _John Long_

Maiden name of Mother _Violetta Cain_

Date of this marriage _April 2, 1944_

Place of this marriage _607 E Lincoln St Judge_

Name and title of person Performing this marriage _Rev Wales E Smith_

His address _101 E Raymond St_
_Indianapolis 2 Ind_

Witness { Name _John Long_
{ Address _607 E Lincoln_

## Return this Report to County Clerk with License and Certificate

FILE

42 APR 4 1944

CLERK

## Marriage Record for Board of Health
### To Be Returned by the Minister or Other Person Performing Ceremony

_John D. Howard_ and _Alcida Daggs_

Groom's name _John D. Howard,_

His age _27_

" color _Negro_

" occupation _U.S. Army_

" Birthplace—City _Indianapolis_ State _Indiana_

" Residence—Street No. _U.S. Army_ City

Single
Widower } _divorced_ { 1st, 2nd or 3rd } _3rd_
Divorced marriage

Name of Father _John D. Howard_

Maiden name of Mother _Annie M. Everett_

Bride's name _Alcida Daggs_

Her age _22_

" color _Negro_

" occupation _none_

" Birthplace—City _Lavadieville_ State _La._

" Residence—Street No. _347-28th St_ City _Indianapolis_

Single
Widow } _Single_ { 1st, 2nd or 3rd } _1st_
Divorced marriage

Name of Father _Joseph Dagg_

Maiden name of Mother _Louisa Middleton_

Date of this marriage _April 3rd 1944_

Place of this marriage _Indianapolis, Ind_

Name and title of person
Performing this marriage _O.G. Calhoun, minister_

His address _2128 N. Capitol_
_Indianapolis,_

Witness { Name _Hattie Dunnington_
{ Address _2310 E. 24th St._

## Return this Report to County Clerk with License and Certificate

12

# Marriage Record for Board of Health
## To Be Returned by the Minister or Other Person Performing Ceremony

_Frederick W Lange_ and _Stella G Bauman_

Groom's name _Frederick W Lange_

His age _29_

" color _White_

" occupation _Bus Driver_

" Birthplace—City _Utica_ State _N. Y._

" Residence—Street No. _Camp Forrest_ City _Tenn._

Single / Widower / Divorced } _Divorced_ { 1st, 2nd or 3rd marriage } _2"_

Name of Father _Earnest W Lange_

Maiden name of Mother _Cathrine Witsler_

Bride's name _Stella G Bauman_

Her age _30_

" color _White_

" occupation _Clerk_

" Birthplace—City _Utica_ State _N. Y._

" Residence—Street No. _338 Burgess aven_ City _Indianapolis Ind_

Single / Widow / Divorced } _Divorced_ { 1st, 2nd or 3rd marriage } _2"_

Name of Father _Frank Rachubka_

Maiden name of Mother _Rose Gwaira_

Date of this marriage _April 3 - 1943_

Place of this marriage _Indianapolis Ind_

Name and title of person Performing this marriage _Minister, Summer W Martin_

His address _6235 Haverford ave, Indianapolis Ind._

Witness { Name _Earline J Hester_
         { Address _221 E. Mich #501 Indianapolis Ind_

## Return this Report to County Clerk with License and Certificate

# Marriage Record for Board of Health
## To Be Returned by the Minister or Other Person Performing Ceremony

Charles Tomescu and Rosemary D. Cambridge

Groom's name _Charles Tomescu_

His age _30_

" color _White_

" occupation _U.S.A._

" Birthplace—City _Roumania_ State _____

" Residence—Street No. _745 Spruce St._ City _Indianapolis, Indiana_

Single / Widower / Divorced } _Single_ {1st, 2nd or 3rd marriage} _1st_

Name of Father _John Tomescu_

Maiden name of Mother _Floarea Velesenu_

Bride's name _Rosemary D. Cambridge_

Her age _21_

" color _White_

" occupation _Clerk_

" Birthplace—City _Indianapolis_ State _Indiana_

" Residence—Street No. _1106 Prospect_ City _Indianapolis, Ind._

Single / Widow / Divorced } _Single_ {1st, 2nd or 3rd marriage} _1st_

Name of Father _Cecil E. Cambridge, Sr._

Maiden name of Mother _Anna Whitaker_

Date of this marriage _April 3, 1944_

Place of this marriage _All Saints Cathedral, Indianapolis, Ind._

Name and title of person Performing this marriage _The Rev. J. Willard Yoder, Priest_

His address _5325 Oliver Ave. Indianapolis, Indiana_

Witness { Name _Cecil E. Cambridge, Jun._ Address _1010 Central Ave. #35 - Indpls. Ind._

## Return this Report to County Clerk with License and Certificate

# Marriage Record for Board of Health
To Be Returned by the Minister or Other Person Performing Ceremony

Willie A Ross and Dorthella Vaughn

Groom's name _Willie A Ross_

His age _20_

" color _C_

" occupation _Soldier_

" Birthplace—City _Cuthbert_ State _Georgia_

" Residence—Street No. _____ City _Stout Field, Ind_

Single / Widower / Divorced } _Single_ { 1st, 2nd or 3rd marriage } _1st_

Name of Father _Jes Ross_

Maiden name of Mother _Frances Bell_

Bride's name _Dorthella Vaughn_

Her age _18_

" color _C_

" occupation _none_

" Birthplace—City _Indianapolis_ State _Indiana_

" Residence—Street No. _1027 N Elder_ City _Indianapolis_

Single / Widow / Divorced } _Single_ { 1st, 2nd or 3rd marriage } _1st_

Name of Father _Finnis Cward Vaughn_

Maiden name of Mother _Onetta Walker_

Date of this marriage _April 3, 1944_

Place of this marriage _Indianapolis_

Name and title of person Performing this marriage _S. S. Thomas, Minister_

His address _702 S Illinois St_
_Indianapolis_

Witness { Name _Deloris Vaughn_
{ Address _1027 N Elder_

## Return this Report to County Clerk with License and Certificate

# Marriage Record for Board of Health

### To Be Returned by the Minister or Other Person Performing Ceremony

George E Phillips and Cordia Sears

Groom's name _George E Phillips_

His age _61_

" color _white_

" occupation _Fireman_

" Birthplace—City _Allan County_ State _Ky_

" Residence—Street No. _RR 12 Bx 187_ City _Indpls Ind_

Single / Widower / Divorced } _Divorced_   { 1st, 2nd or 3rd marriage } _3rd_

Name of Father _James Phillips_

Maiden name of Mother _Etta Jewell_

Bride's name _Cordia Sears_

Her age _46_

" color _white_

" occupation _Farming_

" Birthplace—City _Warren County_ State _Ky_

" Residence—Street No. _Haddock_ City _Kentucky_

Single / Widow / Divorced } _Widow_   { 1st, 2nd or 3rd marriage } _3rd_

Name of Father _Dave Snodgrass_

Maiden name of Mother _Laura Cook_

Date of this marriage _April 3-44_

Place of this marriage _Indpls Ind_

Name and title of person Performing this marriage _Ernest Kane, Justice of Peace_

His address _158½ E Court St_

Witness { Name _Mary Jo Kane_
        { Address _3741 College Ave._

### Return this Report to County Clerk with License and Certificate

12

# Marriage Record for Board of Health
### To Be Returned by the Minister or Other Person Performing Ceremony

Frank Jagajewski and Lucille George

Groom's name _Frank Jagajewski_

His age _28_

" color _White_

" occupation _Soldier_

" Birthplace—City _Cicero_ State _Illinois_

" Residence—Street No. _Ft Harrison_ City _Ind_

Single / Widower / Divorced } _Single_ { 1st, 2nd or 3rd marriage } _1st_

Name of Father _Anthony Jagajewski_

Maiden name of Mother _Mary Gadulig_

Bride's name _Lucille George_

Her age _26_

" color _White_

" occupation _none_

" Birthplace—City _Ralston_ State _Illinois_

" Residence—Street No. _1117 S. Cheyane_ City _Tulsa, Oklahoma_

Single / Widow / Divorced } _Single_ { 1st, 2nd or 3rd marriage } _1st_

Name of Father _Charles George_

Maiden name of Mother _Della Keefe_

Date of this marriage _April 3, 1944_

Place of this marriage _Indianapolis, Indiana_

Name and title of person Performing this marriage _Ernest J. Lane Justice of Peace_

His address _152½ East Court Street_

Witness { Name _Mary J. Lane_ Address _3741 College Ave_

## Return this Report to County Clerk with License and Certificate

# Marriage Record for Board of Health
## To Be Returned by the Minister or Other Person Performing Ceremony

_Carl E. Emory_ _____ and ___ _Wilma J. Cuemyer_ _

Groom's name ___ _Carl E. Emory_ ___

His age ___ _23_ ___

" color ___ _White_ ___

" occupation ___ _Soldier_ ___

" Birthplace—City ___ _Springfield_ ___ State ___ _Ill._ ___

" Residence—Street No. _Hq + Supp. Det - 1530 + SCI_ City _Ft. Benj. Harrison_ _Ind._

Single
Widower
Divorced } ___ _Single_ ___   {1st, 2nd or 3rd
marriage } ___ _1st_ ___

Name of Father ___ _Edward E. Emory_ ___

Maiden name of Mother ___ _Bessie S. Chilton_ ___

Bride's name ___ _Wilma J. Cuemyer_ ___

Her age ___ _21_ ___

" color ___ _White_ ___

" occupation ___ _Factory Worker_ ___

" Birthplace—City ___ _Rochester_ ___ State ___ _Indiana_ ___

" Residence—Street No. _____ City _Ft. Benj. Harrison_ _Indiana_

Single
Widow
Divorced } ___ _Single_ ___   {1st, 2nd or 3rd
marriage } ___ _1st_ ___

Name of Father ___ _Benjamin E. Cuemyer_ ___

Maiden name of Mother ___ _Blanche E. Hanshaw_ ___

Date of this marriage ___ _April 3, 1944_ ___

Place of this marriage ___ _Post Chapel Ft. Benj. Harrison Ind._ ___

Name and title of person
Performing this marriage ___ _Chaplain Albert M. Bishop, Chap._ ___

His address ___ _Post Chapel Office Ft. Benj. Harrison Ind._ ___

Witness { Name _Edith Cuemyer_ ___ _Everett Fry_
{ Address _Ft. Benj. Harrison Ind._ ___ _Ft. Benj. Harrison Ind._

## Return this Report to County Clerk with License and Certificate

# Marriage Record for Board of Health
### To Be Returned by the Minister or Other Person Performing Ceremony

James E. Hightshue ___ and ___ Madge King

Groom's name ___ James E. Hightshue

His age ___ 24

" color ___ White

" occupation ___ Soldier

" Birthplace—City ___ Clermont ___ State ___ Indiana

" Residence—Street No. ___ City

Single / Widower / Divorced } ___ Single ___ { 1st, 2nd or 3rd marriage } ___ 1st

Name of Father ___ Christopher C. Hightshue

Maiden name of Mother ___ Addie Wilson

Bride's name ___ Madge King

Her age ___ 23

" color ___ White

" occupation ___ Social worker

" Birthplace—City ___ New Augusta ___ State ___ Indiana

" Residence—Street No. ___ City

Single / Widow / Divorced } ___ Single ___ { 1st, 2nd or 3rd marriage } ___ 1st

Name of Father ___ Raymond Lynn King

Maiden name of Mother ___ Grace Schwab

Date of this marriage ___ April 3, 1944

Place of this marriage ___ Salem Lutheran Church, New Augusta, Ind.

Name and title of person Performing this marriage ___ Rev. G. L. Kleespie

His address ___ Whitestown, Indiana

Witness { Name ___ Sherman King & Catherine Wagle

{ Address ___ New Augusta, Ind. ___ New Augusta Ind.

### Return this Report to County Clerk with License and Certificate

12

FILED

42  APR 4  1944

CLERK

# Marriage Record for Board of Health
### To Be Returned by the Minister or Other Person Performing Ceremony

*George R Sims* and *Violet V Rice*

Groom's name *George R Sims*

His age *19*

" color *White*

" occupation *Mantiance Dept.*

" Birthplace—City *Indianapolis* State *Indiana*

" Residence—Street No. *R 3 80 S* City *Indianapolis*

Single / Widower / Divorced } *Single*    { 1st, 2nd or 3rd marriage } *1st marriage*

Name of Father *William Andrew Sims*

Maiden name of Mother *Jo Ana Madden*

Bride's name *Violet V. Rice*

Her age *18*

" color *White*

" occupation *None*

" Birthplace—City *Camby* State *Indiana*

" Residence—Street No. *R.3 - Bx 80-R* City *Indianapolis*

Single / Widow / Divorced } *Single*    { 1st, 2nd or 3rd marriage } *1st marriage*

Name of Father *William Franklin Rice*

Maiden name of Mother *Ida B. Kemp*

Date of this marriage *April 3, 1944*

Place of this marriage *Indianapolis, Ind.*

Name and title of person Performing this marriage *Everett Atkinson, Minister*

His address *1049 King ave Indianapolis Ind*

Witness { Name *Helen Atkinson*

{ Address *1049 King ave Indianapolis Ind.*

### Return this Report to County Clerk with License and Certificate

# Marriage Record for Board of Health
### To Be Returned by the Minister or Other Person Performing Ceremony

_Stanley Louis Terrell_ and _Betty Lou Tibby_

Groom's name _Stanley Louis Terrell_

His age _22_

" color _White_

" occupation _Electrician_

" Birthplace—City _Bedford_ State _Indiana_

" Residence—Street No. _832 Park Ave_ City _Indianapolis_

Single / Widower / Divorced _Single_    { 1st, 2nd or 3rd marriage } _1st_

Name of Father _Walter Terrell_

Maiden name of Mother _Anna Mason_

Bride's name _Betty Lou Tibby_

Her age _18_

" color _White_

" occupation _None_

" Birthplace—City _North Vernon_ State _Indiana_

" Residence—Street No. _119 N. Bodley_ City _Indianapolis_

Single / Widow / Divorced _Single_    { 1st, 2nd or 3rd marriage } _1st_

Name of Father _J. F. Tibby_

Maiden name of Mother _Agnes C. Fisher_

Date of this marriage _April 3, 1944_

Place of this marriage _Indianapolis, Ind._

Name and title of person Performing this marriage _Ernest Lane Justice of Peace_

His address _152½ E. Court St._

Witness { Name _Mary Jo Lane_
          { Address _3741 College_

## Return this Report to County Clerk with License and Certificate

# Marriage Record for Board of Health
### To Be Returned by the Minister or Other Person Performing Ceremony

*George F. Heckman* and *Edna J. Heckman*

Groom's name *George F. Heckman*

His age *30*

" color *white*

" occupation *Soldier*

" Birthplace—City *Augusta* State *Indiana*

" Residence—Street No. *Ft Hunter* City *Virginia*

Single / Widower / Divorced } *Divorced* { 1st, 2nd or 3rd marriage } *4th*

Name of Father *George Heckman*

Maiden name of Mother *Ella Reed*

Bride's name *Edna J. Heckman*

Her age *30*

" color *white*

" occupation *Inspector*

" Birthplace—City *Indpls* State *Ind*

" Residence—Street No. *937 N Ill* City *Indpls*

Single / Widow / Divorced } *Divorced* { 1st, 2nd or 3rd marriage } *3rd*

Name of Father *Claude Johnson*

Maiden name of Mother *Bertie Wyman*

Date of this marriage *April 3 - 4*

Place of this marriage *Indpls Ind*

Name and title of person Performing this marriage *Ernest T Lane Justice of Peace*

His address *15 2½ E Court St.*

Witness { Name *Mary Jo Lane*

{ Address *3741 College Ave.*

### Return this Report to County Clerk with License and Certificate

# Marriage Record for Board of Health
### To Be Returned by the Minister or Other Person Performing Ceremony

Eddie Leo Robinson ——— and ——— Maxine Gammill

Groom's name ..... Eddie Leo Robinson

His age ..... 23

" color..... White

" occupation..... Grinder

" Birthplace—City..... Frankfort ..... State ..... Indiana

" Residence—Street No. YMC ..... City ..... Indpls Ind

Single / Widower / x Divorced x ⎱ ..... 1st, 2nd or 3rd marriage ⎰ ..... 1st

Name of Father..... John Robinson

Maiden name of Mother..... Mary Reed

Bride's name ..... Maxine Gammill

Her age ..... 19

" color..... White

" occupation..... Clerkial

" Birthplace—City..... Vienna ..... State ..... Ill

" Residence—Street No. 721 Cleveland ..... City ..... Indianapolis

Single / Widow / x Divorced x ⎱ ..... 1st, 2nd or 3rd marriage ⎰ ..... 1st

Name of Father..... Claude Gammill

Maiden name of Mother..... Maude Upton

Date of this marriage..... April 3, 1944

Place of this marriage..... 2608 West Mich St

Name and title of person Performing this marriage..... Walter Bradford Justice of Peace

His address..... 2608 W Mich Indpls Ind

Witness { Name  Paul K Gassel
        { Address  1025 Sharon Ave

## Return this Report to County Clerk with License and Certificate

# Marriage Record for Board of Health
## To Be Returned by the Minister or Other Person Performing Ceremony

Warren S. Fisher and Pauline M. Clouse

Groom's name _Warren S. Fisher_

His age _23_

" color _white_

" occupation _Soldier_

" Birthplace—City _Bedford_ State _Va._

" Residence—Street No. _Little Rock Arkansas, Adams Field_

Single
Widower } _Single_ { 1st, 2nd or 3rd marriage } _1st_
Divorced

Name of Father _Thomas E. Fisher (deceased)_

Maiden name of Mother _Lydia E. Abbott_

Bride's name _Pauline M. Clouse_

Her age _24_

" color _white_

" occupation _Defense Worker_

" Birthplace—City _Keo_ State _Arkansas_

" Residence—Street No. _1222 Congress_ City _Ralph_

Single
Widow } _Divorced_ { 1st, 2nd or 3rd marriage } _2nd_
Divorced

Name of Father _John Paul Cook_

Maiden name of Mother _Viola Bradford_

Date of this marriage _April 4, 1944_

Place of this marriage _____

Name and title of person
Performing this marriage _Amber T. Rape, Justice of Peace_

His address _152 E Court St_

Witness { Name _Mary Jo Lane_
          { Address _3741 College Ave._

## Return this Report to County Clerk with License and Certificate

# Marriage Record for Board of Health
## To Be Returned by the Minister or Other Person Performing Ceremony

_Renzo D. Huffer_ and _Mary J. Ohermiller_

Groom's name _Renzo D. Huffer_

His age _43_

" color _white_

" occupation _Laborer_

" Birthplace—City _Forest_ State _Indiana_

" Residence—Street No. _Frankfort_ City _Indiana_

Single / Widower / Divorced } _Widower_ { 1st, 2nd or 3rd marriage } _2nd_

Name of Father _Albert A. Huffer_

Maiden name of Mother _Daisy Simpson_

Bride's name _Mary J. Ohermiller_

Her age _41_

" color _White_

" occupation _Housekeeper_

" Birthplace—City _Clinton County_ State _Indiana_

" Residence—Street No. _____ City _Thorntown, Ind._

Single / Widow / Divorced } _Divorced_ { 1st, 2nd or 3rd marriage } _2nd_

Name of Father _Willard Harshman (deceased)_

Maiden name of Mother _Iva Marity (deceased)_

Date of this marriage _April 4-4_

Place of this marriage _Delphi, Ind._

Name and title of person Performing this marriage _Ernest Cline, Justice of Peace_

His address _1525 East Court St._

Witness { Name _Mary Jo Lane_ { Address _3741 College Ave._

## Return this Report to County Clerk with License and Certificate

# Marriage Record for Board of Health

To Be Returned by the Minister or Other Person Performing Ceremony

*Thomas P. Rejetik* and *Amelia Frances Anderson*

Groom's name *Thomas P. Rejetik*

His age 26

" color White

" occupation Soldier

" Birthplace—City Indpls State Ind.

" Residence—Street No. Ft Benning City Ga.

Single
Widower } Single    { 1st, 2nd or 3rd } 1st
Divorced              marriage

Name of Father John Rejetik

Maiden name of Mother Mary Dace

Bride's name Amelia Frances Anderson

Her age 33

" color white

" occupation Cake Icer

" Birthplace—City Indpls State Ind.

" Residence—Street No. 806 Yoke Ave City Indpls

Single
Widow } Divorced    { 1st, 2nd or 3rd } 2nd
Divorced              marriage

Name of Father Charles Anderson

Maiden name of Mother Elizabeth Ruddick

Date of this marriage April 4 44

Place of this marriage Indpls Ind.

Name and title of person
Performing this marriage Everett Frans Justice of Peace

His address 153½ East Court St

Witness { Name Mary Jo Lane
        { Address 3741 College Ave

**Return this Report to County Clerk with License and Certificate**

# Marriage Record for Board of Health
### To Be Returned by the Minister or Other Person Performing Ceremony

Oscar Murray _____ and _____ Betty J Trusty

Groom's name _Oscar Murray_

His age _24 yrs, December 25, 1943._

" color _White_

" occupation _Operator - Street Car Company._

" Birthplace—City _Indianapolis_ State _Indiana_

" Residence—Street No. _1018 Oliver_ City _Indianapolis_

Single
~~Widower~~
~~Divorced~~ } _Single_   { 1st, ~~2nd or 3rd~~ marriage } _First_

Name of Father _Wm Jerrell Murray_

Maiden name of Mother _Hineritha Chrietta_

Bride's name _Betty J Trusty_

Her age _22 - Nov 6 - 1943_

" color _White_

" occupation _Factory worker_

" Birthplace—City _Indianapolis_ State _Indiana_

" Residence—Street No. _711 N. Meridian_ City _Indianapolis_

~~Single~~
~~Widow~~
Divorced } _Divorced_   { ~~1st,~~ 2nd ~~or 3rd~~ marriage } _Second_

Name of Father _Virgie Fisher_

Maiden name of Mother _Bessie Terrell_

Date of this marriage _April 4, 1944._

Place of this marriage _1437 Blaine Ave_

Name and title of person
Performing this marriage _Rev W. E. Watkins._

His address _1437 Blaine Ave_

Witness { Name _Clarence E Metzger - Plaza Hotel,_
{ ~~Address~~ _Bittie J Bickers - 2334 Gilford Ave_

### Return this Report to County Clerk with License and Certificate

12

## Marriage Record for Board of Health
### To Be Returned by the Minister or Other Person Performing Ceremony

_Rollin B. Horner_ and _Clara M. Horner_

Groom's name _Rollin B. Horner_

His age _35_

" color _white_

" occupation _Sailor_

" Birthplace—City _Wabash_ State _Indiana_

" Residence—Street No. _Samson_ City _New York_

Single / Widower / Divorced } _Divorced_ { 1st, 2nd or 3rd marriage } _2nd_

Name of Father _Oscar Horner_

Maiden name of Mother _Elsie Smith_

Bride's name _Clara M. Horner_

Her age _35_

" color _white_

" occupation _Defense Worker_

" Birthplace—City _Ripley_ State _Tennessee_

" Residence—Street No. _1703 N. New Jersey_ City _Indpls._

Single / Widow / Divorced } _Divorced_ { 1st, 2nd or 3rd marriage } _2nd_

Name of Father _Charles Difenbaugh_

Maiden name of Mother _Mary Hill_

Date of this marriage _April 4, 1944_

Place of this marriage _Indianapolis, Indiana_

Name and title of person Performing this marriage _Ernest T. Henry, Minister of Gospel_

His address _15½ East Court Street_

Witness { Name _Mary J. Kime_  { Address _3741 College Ave._

### Return this Report to County Clerk with License and Certificate

# Marriage Record for Board of Health

### To Be Returned by the Minister or Other Person Performing Ceremony

Frank R. Chapman and Mary Evelyn Carpenter

Groom's name _Frank R. Chapman_

His age _27_

" color _White_

" occupation _U. S. Marines_

" Birthplace—City _Hancock Co._ State _Indiana_

" Residence—Street No. _Greenfield_ City _Ind._

Single / Widower / Divorced } _Single_ {1st, 2nd or 3rd marriage} _1st_

Name of Father _Lee Chapman_

Maiden name of Mother _Alice Roberts_

Bride's name _Mary Evelyn Carpenter_

Her age _28_

" color _White_

" occupation _Telephone Operator_

" Birthplace—City _Argos_ State _Ind._

" Residence—Street No. _1116 N. Capitol_ City _Indianapolis_

Single / Widow / Divorced } _Single_ {1st, 2nd or 3rd marriage} _1st_

Name of Father _Byron Carpenter_

Maiden name of Mother _Carrie Thompson_

Date of this marriage _April 4, 1944_

Place of this marriage _Central Avenue Methodist Church, Indianapolis_

Name and title of person Performing this marriage _F. Marion Smith, Minister_

His address _4730 N. Capitol Ave. Indianapolis, Ind._

Witness { Name _Mrs. Edgar Benson_
{ Address _1116 N. Capitol Ave., Indpls._

### Return this Report to County Clerk with License and Certificate

# Marriage Record for Board of Health
## To Be Returned by the Minister or Other Person Performing Ceremony

John Fey _____ and Lura Louise Sanders

Groom's name _John Fey_

His age _66_

" color _white_

" occupation _Contractor_

" Birthplace—City _Rush County_ State _Indiana_

" Residence—Street No. _581 Ind. Ave._ City _Connersville, Ind._

Single
Widower } _Widower_ { 1st, 2nd or 3rd
Divorced ____ marriage } _2nd_

Name of Father _George Fey_

Maiden name of Mother _Catherine Metzger_

Bride's name _Lura Louise Sanders_

Her age _59_

" color _white_

" occupation _Nurse_

" Birthplace—City _Decatur County_ State _Illinois_

" Residence—Street No. _716 Central_ City _Indpls._

Single
Widow } _Widow_ { 1st, 2nd or 3rd
Divorced ____ marriage } _2nds_

Name of Father _Joseph Richard Reed_

Maiden name of Mother _Sarah Collins_

Date of this marriage _April 4, 1944_

Place of this marriage _Indianapolis, Indiana_

Name and title of person
Performing this marriage _Ernest V. Lane, Justice of Peace_

His address _152½ East Court Street_

Witness { Name _Mary Jo Lane_
         { Address _3741 College Ave._

## Return this Report to County Clerk with License and Certificate

# Marriage Record for Board of Health
## To Be Returned by the Minister or Other Person Performing Ceremony

Frank Gibson and Mary Hampton

Groom's name _Frank Gibson_

His age _58_

" color _Colored_

" occupation _Memphis Power & Light Co_

" Birthplace—City _Sumner County_ State _Tennessee_

" Residence—Street No. _635 W Delma_ City _Memphis_

Single / Widower / Divorced } _Single_    1st, 2nd or 3rd marriage } _1st_

Name of Father _Wash Gibson_

Maiden name of Mother _Jane Phipps_

Bride's name _Mary Hampton_

Her age _44_

" color _Colored_

" occupation _Penn. Freight House_

" Birthplace—City _Grace_ State _Mississippi_

" Residence—Street No. _330 Blackford_ City _Memphis_

Single / Widow / Divorced } _Widow_    1st, 2nd or 3rd marriage } _2nd_

Name of Father _Stew Jenkins_

Maiden name of Mother _Alice Green_

Date of this marriage _April 4, 1944_

Place of this marriage _Memphis, Tenn._

Name and title of person Performing this marriage _Lindett Kane, Justice of Peace_

His address _151½ E Court St_

Witness { Name _Mary Jo Lane_
          { Address _3741 College Ave._

## Return this Report to County Clerk with License and Certificate

# Marriage Record for Board of Health
### To Be Returned by the Minister or Other Person Performing Ceremony

Russell Brown and Ruth Allen.

Groom's name _Russell Brown_

His age _Thirty Six_

" color _Brown_

" occupation _United State service_

" Birthplace—City _Adel_ State _Georgia_

" Residence—Street No. _un nown_ City _Adel_

Single / Widower / Divorced } _widow_ { 1st, 2nd or 3rd marriage } _Second_

Name of Father _Major Daniel Brown_

Maiden name of Mother _Josie Brown_

Bride's name _Ruth Allen_

Her age _Twenty Eight_

" color _Brown_

" occupation _House wife_

" Birthplace—City _Hopkinsville_ State _Kentucky_

" Residence—Street No. _RR 2_ City _Hopkinsn_

Single / Widow / Divorced } _Divorced_ { 1st, 2nd or 3rd marriage } _oneel_

Name of Father _Melin M Allen_

Maiden name of Mother _Ellen Watson_

Date of this marriage _April 4, 1944._

Place of this marriage _530 w 10 st_

Name and title of person Performing this marriage _Rev M M Allen Minister_

His address _Indianapolis Ind. 530 w 10 st_

Witness { Name _Della Hop, Ellen Cillen_
Address _526 W 10 th St. 530 w 10th st._

## Return this Report to County Clerk with License and Certificate

# Marriage Record for Board of Health

To Be Returned by the Minister or Other Person Performing Ceremony

John W. Johnson and Marie B. Franklin

Groom's name __John W. Johnson__

His age __24__

" color __White__

" occupation __Soldier__

" Birthplace—City __Bicknell__ State __Ind.__

" Residence—Street No. __Key Field__ City __Miss.__

Single / Widower / Divorced } __Divorced__ { 1st, 2nd or 3rd marriage } __2nd__

Name of Father __John Albert Johnson__

Maiden name of Mother __Della Mae Martin__

Bride's name __Marie B. Franklin__

Her age __26__

" color __White__

" occupation __Defense Worker__

" Birthplace—City __Newberry__ State __Ind.__

" Residence—Street No. __637 E Ohio__ City __Indpls__

Single / Widow / Divorced } __Single__ { 1st, 2nd or 3rd marriage } __1st__

Name of Father __John Richard Franklin__

Maiden name of Mother __Emma Jane Sheets__

Date of this marriage __April 4-44__

Place of this marriage __Indpls Ind.__

Name and title of person Performing this marriage __Arnett T Lane Justice__

His address __157½ E 1st Court St.__

Witness { Name __Mary Jo Lane__

{ Address __3741 College Ave.__

## Return this Report to County Clerk with License and Certificate

# Marriage Record for Board of Health
### To Be Returned by the Minister or Other Person Performing Ceremony

Robert H. Larrison _____ and Helen Blair

Groom's name _Robert H. Larrison_

His age _22_

" color _white_

" occupation _soldier_

" Birthplace—City _Harrisburg_ State _Illinois_

" Residence—Street No. _Camp Border_ City _Su_

Single / Widower / Divorced } _Single_ { 1st, 2nd or 3rd marriage } _1st_

Name of Father _William Larrison_

Maiden name of Mother _Lena Almon Wright_

Bride's name _Helen Blair_

Her age _19_

" color _white_

" occupation _none_

" Birthplace—City _Bridgeport_ State _Illinois_

" Residence—Street No. _____ City _Bridgeport Ill._

Single / Widow / Divorced } _Single_ { 1st, 2nd or 3rd marriage } _1st_

Name of Father _Edward Blair_

Maiden name of Mother _Arvella Blair_

Date of this marriage _April 4-44_

Place of this marriage _Indpls Ind._

Name and title of person Performing this marriage _Everett Crane, Justice of Crane_

His address _152 East Court St._

Witness { Name _Mary Crane_ { Address _3741 College Ave._

### Return this Report to County Clerk with License and Certificate

# Marriage Record for Board of Health

### To Be Returned by the Minister or Other Person Performing Ceremony

Vernon McCune and Thelma Walters

Groom's name _Vernon McCune_

His age _24_

" color _White_

" occupation _U.S. Navy_

" Birthplace—City _French Lick_ State _Indiana_

" Residence—Street No. _224 Indiana Ave_ City _French Lick, Ind._

Single / Widower / Divorced } _Single_    1st, 2nd or 3rd marriage } _1st._

Name of Father _Jack McCune_

Maiden name of Mother _Ida Parsons_

Bride's name _Thelma Walters_

Her age _21_

" color _White_

" occupation _Machinist_

" Birthplace—City _French Lick_ State _Indiana_

" Residence—Street No. _238½ N. Wolcott_ City _Indianapolis_

Single / Widow / Divorced } _Single_    1st, 2nd or 3rd marriage } _1st._

Name of Father _Sol Walters_

Maiden name of Mother _Della Beaty_

Date of this marriage _April 4, 1944_

Place of this marriage _Indianapolis, Ind._

Name and title of person Performing this marriage _Hoyt S. Canary, Minister_

His address _1731 Ingram St._ _Indianapolis, Ind._

Witness { Name _Mrs. Hoyt S. Canary_

{ Address _1731 Ingram St. — Indpls, Ind._

## Return this Report to County Clerk with License and Certificate

# Marriage Record for Board of Health
### To Be Returned by the Minister or Other Person Performing Ceremony

John G. Sacltleben and Doris E. Weidhuner

Groom's name _John G. Sacltleben Jr._

His age _21_

" color _White_

" occupation _U. S. Army_

" Birthplace—City _Greenview_ State _Ill._

" Residence—Street No. _52nd C. T. D. Butler U._ City _Indianapolis_

Single ⎫
~~Widower~~ ⎬ ........ ⎰ 1st, ~~2nd or 3rd~~
~~Divorced~~ ⎭ ⎱ marriage

Name of Father _John G. Sacltleben_

Maiden name of Mother _Rilla Pauline Yardley_

Bride's name _Doris E. Weidhuner_

Her age _21_

" color _White_

" occupation _Stenographer_

" Birthplace—City _Greenview_ State _Ill._

" Residence—Street No. _919 S. Spring_ City _Springfield, Ill._

Single ⎫
~~Widow~~ ⎬ ........ ⎰ 1st, ~~2nd or 3rd~~
~~Divorced~~ ⎭ ⎱ marriage

Name of Father _Fred W. Weidhuner_

Maiden name of Mother _Nellie Sampson_

Date of this marriage _April 4 1944._

Place of this marriage _Indianapolis, Indiana_

Name and title of person
Performing this marriage _Rev. W. H. Ragan_

His address _129 W - 44th St._
_Indianapolis, Indiana._

Witness ⎰ Name _2/c Raymond C. School_
⎱ Address _52nd C. T. D. Butler U. Indianapolis, Indiana_

### Return this Report to County Clerk with License and Certificate

# Marriage Record for Board of Health
## To Be Returned by the Minister or Other Person Performing Ceremony

_John March_ and _Catherine P. Buchanan_

Groom's name _John March_

His age _26_

" color _White_

" occupation _U. S. Army_

" Birthplace—City _Detroit_ State _Mich._

" Residence—Street No. _52nd C.T.D. Butler U._ City _Indianapolis_

Single / ~~Widower~~ / ~~Divorced~~ — 1st, ~~2nd or 3rd~~ marriage

Name of Father _Frank March_

Maiden name of Mother _Anna Jucabowick_

Bride's name _Catherine P. Buchanan_

Her age _40_

" color _White_

" occupation _Book Keeper_

" Birthplace—City _Gasgow_ State _Scotland_

" Residence—Street No. _1130 Holcomb_ City _Detroit, Mich._

~~Single~~ / ~~Widow~~ / Divorced — ~~1st,~~ 2nd or ~~3rd~~ marriage

Name of Father _Walter M. Buchanan_

Maiden name of Mother _Mary Gillespie_

Date of this marriage _April 4 1944_

Place of this marriage _Indianapolis, Indiana_

Name and title of person Performing this marriage _Rev. V. D. Ragan_

His address _129 W - 44th St_
_Indianapolis, Indiana_

Witness — Name _Mrs. Virgil D. Ragan_
Address _129 W 44th St. Indianapolis, Ind._

## Return this Report to County Clerk with License and Certificate

# Marriage Record for Board of Health
### To Be Returned by the Minister or Other Person Performing Ceremony

_Louis A. Barth_ and _Frances W. Shayes_

Groom's name _Louis A. Barth_

His age _76_

" color _White_

" occupation _Decorator_

" Birthplace—City _Indianapolis_ State _Indiana_

" Residence—Street No. _1565 Shelby_ City _Indianapolis Ind._

~~Single~~ Widower ~~Divorced~~ } { 1st, 2nd or 3rd marriage } _Third_

Name of Father _Louis A. Barth_

Maiden name of Mother _Mary A. Burk_

Bride's name _Frances W. Shayes_

Her age _73_

" color _White_

" occupation _Housewife_

" Birthplace—City _Albany_ State _N.Y._

" Residence—Street No. _1565 Shelby St_ City _Indianapolis Ind_

~~Single~~ Widow ~~Divorced~~ } { 1st, 2nd or 3rd marriage } _Third_

Name of Father _Not known_

Maiden name of Mother _"_ _"_

Date of this marriage _April 4, 1944_

Place of this marriage _Indianapolis, Indiana_

Name and title of person Performing this marriage _Rev. J. Floyd Seelig_

His address _2956 N. Capital Ave., Indianapolis 8, Indiana_

Witness { Name _Edythe Barth_
{ Address _3439 N. Capital Ave.—Indpls Ind_

### Return this Report to County Clerk with License and Certificate

## Marriage Record for Board of Health
### To Be Returned by the Minister or Other Person Performing Ceremony

Rev. Agnes Jones _____ and 1371 S. Sheffield Ave.

Groom's name _Joseph Leonard Rybolt_

His age _20 yrs._

" color _White_

" occupation _Truck Driver & Mechanic_

" Birthplace—City _Indianapolis_ State _Indiana_

" Residence—Street No. _2557 W. Morris_ City _Indianapolis_

Single
Widower  } _Divorced_  { 1st, 2nd or 3rd  } _2 marriage_
Divorced                  marriage

Name of Father _Charles Wm Rybolt_

Maiden name of Mother _Eva Edith Spaulding._

Bride's name _Dorothy Louise Dailey_

Her age _18 yrs._

" color _White_

" occupation _None_

" Birthplace—City _Indianapolis_ State _Indiana_

" Residence—Street No. _2922 Jackson_ City _Indianapolis_

Single
Widow  } _Single_  { 1st, 2nd or 3rd  } _First_
Divorced                 marriage

Name of Father _Lawrence Harold Dailey_

Maiden name of Mother _Edith Lydia Dailey_

Date of this marriage _April 4-5-1944._

Place of this marriage _Indianapolis Indiana_

Name and title of person
Performing this marriage _Rev. Agnes Jones_

His address _1371 S. Sheffield Ave_

Witness { Name _Eva Edith Rybolt 2557 W. Morris St._
         { Address _Bob Rybolt 2557 W. Morris St. city_

### Return this Report to County Clerk with License and Certificate

# Marriage Record for Board of Health
### To Be Returned by the Minister or Other Person Performing Ceremony

Jack B. Slay and Ella E. Stein

Groom's name _Jack B. Slay_

His age _21_

" color _W._

" occupation _Soldier_

" Birthplace—City _Columbus_ State _Ohio_

" Residence—Street No. _Camp Meade_ City _Maryland_

Single Widower Divorced } _Single_ { 1st, 2nd or 3rd marriage } _1st_

Name of Father _Arthur J. Slay_

Maiden name of Mother _G. Hinkle_

Bride's name _Ella E. Stein_

Her age _22_

" color _W._

" occupation _Assist Clerk_

" Birthplace—City _Los Angeles_ State _Calif._

" Residence—Street No. _855 Sixth St_ City _San Bardina Calif._

Single Widow Divorced } _single_ { 1st, 2nd or 3rd marriage } _1st_

Name of Father _Charles Stein_

Maiden name of Mother _Ella Bell_

Date of this marriage _Apr. 4th 1944_

Place of this marriage _Indianapolis, Ind._

Name and title of person Performing this marriage _Rev. Thomas Paino_

His address _2114 Miller St,_
_Indianapolis Ind._

Witness { Name _James C. Hutchinson_
{ Address _126 So. Illinois St._

## Return this Report to County Clerk with License and Certificate

# Marriage Record for Board of Health
### To Be Returned by the Minister or Other Person Performing Ceremony

Clyde F. Jordan _and_ Mary Louise Deane

Groom's name _Clyde F. Jordan_

His age _18_

" color _White_

" occupation _Soldier_

" Birthplace—City _Indianapolis_ State _Indiana_

" Residence—Street No. _1346 De Loss_ City _Indianapolis_

Single Widower Divorced } _Single_ { 1st, 2nd or 3rd marriage } _1st_

Name of Father _Porter F. Jordan_

Maiden name of Mother _Catherine F. Mescott_

Bride's name _Mary Louise Deane_

Her age _16_

" color _White_

" occupation _Domestic Work_

" Birthplace—City _Indianapolis_ State _Indiana_

" Residence—Street No. _2354 Le Grande_ City _Indianapolis_

Single Widow Divorced } _Single_ { 1st, 2nd or 3rd marriage } _1st_

Name of Father _Herbert C. Deane_

Maiden name of Mother _Mary E Snapp_

Date of this marriage _April 5th_

Place of this marriage _2354 Le Grande_

Name and title of person Performing the _Rev. W. H. Hummerin_

His address _713 No. Belmont Ave Indianapolis_

Witness { Name _Nelson A Boruist_ { Address _2354 Le Grande_

### Return this Report to County Clerk with License and Certificate

# Marriage Record for Board of Health
### To Be Returned by the Minister or Other Person Performing Ceremony

_Charles Trammell_ and _Josephine Baumann_

Groom's name _Charles Trammell_

His age _23_

" color _White_

" occupation _U. S. N._

" Birthplace—City _Fountain had_ State _Tenn._

" Residence—Street No. _U. S. N._ City _____

Single Widower Divorced } _single_ { 1st, 2nd or 3rd marriage } _1st_

Name of Father _Noral Trammell_

Maiden name of Mother _Lesbia Hollis_

Bride's name _Josephine Baumann_

Her age _18_

" color _White_

" occupation _no._

" Birthplace—City _Indianapolis_ State _Ind._

" Residence—Street No. _1840 Ingeton_ City _Indianapolis_

Single Widow Divorced } _single_ { 1st, 2nd or 3rd marriage } _1st_

Name of Father _Albert Baumann_

Maiden name of Mother _Clara Huegele._

Date of this marriage _5 April 1944_

Place of this marriage _Indianapolis Ind._

Name and title of person Performing this marriage _Rev. A. Brady. Minister_

His address _607 Louea St_

_Indianapolis Ind._

Witness { Name _Raymond Gardner Louise Marsh_
Address _1832 Lockwood et. 1438 N. Belleview_

### Return this Report to County Clerk with License and Certificate

# Marriage Record for Board of Health
### To Be Returned by the Minister or Other Person Performing Ceremony

*Sgt. Benjamin F Harvey* and *Thelma L. Dulin*

Groom's name _Benjamin F. Harvey_

His age _37 years old_

" color _Colored_

" occupation _U. S. Army_

" Birthplace—City _Evansville_ State _Indiana_

" Residence—Street No. _Breckinridge_ City _Ky._

Single Widower Divorced } _Single_  { 1st, 2nd or 3rd marriage } _1st_

Name of Father _George W. Harvey_

Maiden name of Mother _Melissia Lytle_

Bride's name _Thelma L. Dulin_

Her age _26 years old_

" color _Colored_

" occupation _Housework_

" Birthplace—City _Crofton_ State _Ky._

" Residence—Street No. _1159 W. 27th St_ City _Indianapolis_

Single Widow Divorced } _Single_  { 1st, 2nd or 3rd marriage } _1st_

Name of Father _Ben A. Dulin_

Maiden name of Mother _Pearl H. Clemons_

Date of this marriage _April 5, 1944_

Place of this marriage _Indianapolis Ind._

Name and title of person Performing this marriage _S. S. Thomas_

His address _702 S. Illinois_
_Indianapolis Ind._

Witness { Name _Mrs. Geraldine Johnson_
{ Address _1528 Mill St._

## Return this Report to County Clerk with License and Certificate

12

# Marriage Record for Board of Health
### To Be Returned by the Minister or Other Person Performing Ceremony

*Logan X Grundy* and *Ella Thomas*

Groom's name *Logan X Grundy*

His age *60*

" color *Colored*

" occupation *Chauffer*

" Birthplace—City *Hardin County* State *Ky.*

" Residence—Street No. _____ City _____

Single / Widower / Divorced } *Divorced*   { 1st, 2nd or 3rd marriage } *3rd.*

Name of Father *Mathew X Grundy*

Maiden name of Mother *Caroline Lewis*

Bride's name *Ella Thomas*

Her age *51*

" color *colored*

" occupation *maid*

" Birthplace—City *Bufflew Ky* State *Ky*

" Residence—Street No. _____ City _____

Single / Widow / Divorced } *Divorced*   { 1st, 2nd or 3rd marriage } *3rd.*

Name of Father *Lewis Barnett*

Maiden name of Mother *Rebeca Dirt*

Date of this marriage *April 5, 1944*

Place of this marriage *801½ W. Walnut St Ludplois*

Name and title of person Performing this marriage *Rev. C. R. Gatewood – minister*

His address *801½ W. Walnut St*

Witness { Name *Mrs Wesley Lewis Mrs - Louise Graham –*
{ Address *1238 W. 26th St. — 712 W – 11th St -*

### Return this Report to County Clerk with License and Certificate

# Marriage Record for Board of Health

### To Be Returned by the Minister or Other Person Performing Ceremony

Richard A. McDowell and Loraine E. Gordon

Groom's name _Richard A. McDowell_

His age _27_

" color _White_

" occupation _Photographer_

" Birthplace—City _Dayton_ State _Ohio_

" Residence—Street No. _15 Watts_ City _Dayton, Ohio_

Single Widower Divorced } _Single_    1st, 2nd or 3rd marriage } _1st_

Name of Father _John McDowell_

Maiden name of Mother _Eugenia E. Lee_

Bride's name _Loraine E. Gordon_

Her age _29_

" color _White_

" occupation _Book Binder_

" Birthplace—City _Milltown_ State _Ohio_

" Residence—Street No. _2806 Wayne Ave._ City _Dayton_

Single Widow Divorced } _Single_    1st, 2nd or 3rd marriage } _1st_

Name of Father _William A. Gordon_

Maiden name of Mother _May B. Neugarden_

Date of this marriage _April 5, 1944_

Place of this marriage _Indianapolis, Ind._

Name and title of person Performing this marriage _Ernest L. Lane Justice of Peace_

His address _152½ Corr Court Dr_

Witness { Name _Mary Jo Lane_
{ Address _3741 College Ave_

### Return this Report to County Clerk with License and Certificate

# Marriage Record for Board of Health
### To Be Returned by the Minister or Other Person Performing Ceremony

Edward Hoelthemeyer and Fern Boucher

Groom's name _Edward Hoelthemeyer_

His age _52_

" color _white_

" occupation _Gents' Furnishing Store_

" Birthplace—City _Marion County_ State _Indiana_

" Residence—Street No. _702 N Alaba_ City _Indpl_

Single / Widower / Divorced } _Divorced_ { 1st, 2nd or 3rd marriage } _2nd_

Name of Father _Henry Hoelthemeyer (deceased)_

Maiden name of Mother _Minnie Becker_

Bride's name _Fern Boucher_

Her age _33_

" color _white_

" occupation _none_

" Birthplace—City _Coleridge_ State _Nebraska_

" Residence—Street No. _702 N Alaba_ City _Indpl_

Single / Widow / Divorced } _Single_ { 1st, 2nd or 3rd marriage } _1st_

Name of Father _Clinton Boucher_

Maiden name of Mother _Myrtle Flick_

Date of this marriage _April 5—44_

Place of this marriage _Indpl Ind_

Name and title of person Performing this marriage _Fred H Kern, Justice of Peace_

His address _152½ E Court St_

Witness { Name _Mary Jo Lane_ { Address _3741 College Ave_

### Return this Report to County Clerk with License and Certificate

# Marriage Record for Board of Health
### To Be Returned by the Minister or Other Person Performing Ceremony

Jack Vincent Tevebaugh and Gwendolyn G. Redford

Groom's name Jack Vincent Tevebaugh

His age 28

" color White

" occupation Radio Inspector RCA

" Birthplace—City Monroe City State Ind

" Residence—Street No. 301 E. North Apts City Indianapolis

Single Widower Divorced } Single

1st, 2nd or 3rd marriage } 1st

Name of Father Kent Elisha Tevebaugh

Maiden name of Mother Lydia Bartlow

Bride's name Gwendolyn G. Redford

Her age 25

" color White

" occupation Stenographer

" Birthplace—City S. Whitley Co. State Ind

" Residence—Street No. 301 E. North City Indianapolis

Single Widow Divorced } Divorced

1st, 2nd or 3rd marriage } 2nd

Name of Father Dorcey Geist

Maiden name of Mother Eva Lee Ruch

Date of this marriage April 5, 1944

Place of this marriage Indianapolis, Ind.

Name and title of person Performing this marriage Rev R. A. McCann

His address 234 N. Delaware

Indianapolis, Ind.

Witness { Name Ethel M. Hurt
Address The Ardmore, Indianapolis, Ind.

## Return this Report to County Clerk with License and Certificate

# Marriage Record for Board of Health
### To Be Returned by the Minister or Other Person Performing Ceremony

_William H. Best_ and _Juanita Gray_

Groom's name _William H. Best_

His age _26_

" color _white_

" occupation _machinist_

" Birthplace—City _Indianapolis_ State _Ind._

" Residence—Street No. _9020 E Wash St_ City _Indianapolis, Ind._

Single / Widower / Divorced } _Divorced_  { 1st, 2nd or 3rd marriage } _Second_

Name of Father _Wm Best_

Maiden name of Mother _Clara Amelia Kleinstein_

Bride's name _Juanita Gray_

Her age _20_

" color _white_

" occupation _Comp Operator_

" Birthplace—City _Indianapolis_ State _Ind._

" Residence—Street No. _218 N Summit_ City _Indianapolis_

Single / Widow / Divorced } _Never Single_ { 1st, 2nd or 3rd marriage } _First_

Name of Father _Roy Fred Gray_

Maiden name of Mother _Pauline Stockly_

Date of this marriage _April 5, 1944_

Place of this marriage _Indianapolis Ind._

Name and title of person Performing this marriage _Rev E Robert Ardry_

His address _2820 Onny Avenue_
_Indianapolis, Indiana_

Witness { Name _Iris A Voyles_
{ Address _9014 E Washington St Indianapolis Ind_

### Return this Report to County Clerk with License and Certificate

# Marriage Record for Board of Health

### To Be Returned by the Minister or Other Person Performing Ceremony

Theodore McFerran _and_ Fannie Mae Whitehead

Groom's name _Theodore McFerran_

His age _38_

" color _Negro_

" occupation _Inspector_

" Birthplace—City _Bowling Green_ State _Ky._

" Residence—Street No. _2454 Ralston_ City _Indpls_

Single
~~Widower~~ } _1st_ { 1st, 2nd or 3rd marriage } 
~~Divorced~~

Name of Father _Unknown_

Maiden name of Mother _Clyde McFerran_

Bride's name _Fannie Mae Whitehead_

Her age _26_

" color _Negro_

" occupation _Housework_

" Birthplace—City _Waco_ State _Texas_

" Residence—Street No. _2454 Ralston_ City _Indpls_

~~Single~~
~~Widow~~ } _2 and_ { 1st, 2nd or 3rd marriage }
Divorced

Name of Father _Richard Lockridge_

Maiden name of Mother _Lucile Beggers_

Date of this marriage _April 5, 1944_

Place of this marriage _Indianapolis_

Name and title of person
Performing this marriage _L. D. Hardrick  Minister_

His address _2439 Manlove Ave_
_Indpls, Ind._

Witness { Name _Audrey Hardrick_
{ Address _2439 Manlove Ave._

### Return this Report to County Clerk with License and Certificate

# Marriage Record for Board of Health
### To Be Returned by the Minister or Other Person Performing Ceremony

_Willis H. Chenault_ and _Dolores M Gulliford_

Groom's name _Willis H. Chenault_

His age _25_

" color _C._

" occupation _Radio Service_

" Birthplace—City _Indpls._ State _Ind._

" Residence—Street No. _2524 Indpls ave._ City _Indpls._

Single / Widower / Divorced _Divorced_ { 1st, 2nd or 3rd marriage _2 nd_

Name of Father _Robert H. Chenault_

Maiden name of Mother _Helen F. Collins_

Bride's name _Dolores M. Gulliford_

Her age _20_

" color _C._

" occupation _none_

" Birthplace—City _Indpls._ State _Ind._

" Residence—Street No. _2815 Shriver ave._ City _Indpls._

Single / Widow / Divorced _Divorced_ { 1st, 2nd or 3rd marriage _2 nd_

Name of Father _Herschelle H. Hayes_

Maiden name of Mother _Elizabeth M. Drake_

Date of this marriage _April 5 – 1944_

Place of this marriage _Indianapolis, Ind._

Name and title of person Performing this marriage _S A Thomas, Minister_

His address _702 So. Illinois St_
_Indianapolis, Indiana_

Witness { Name _Arlee F Brand_
{ Address _2336 Indianapolis ave_

### Return this Report to County Clerk with License and Certificate

# Marriage Record for Board of Health

### To Be Returned by the Minister or Other Person Performing Ceremony

Linus O Verhines _____ and _Ines Ruth Horton_

Groom's name _Lenis O Verhines_

His age _20_

" color _White_

" occupation _U.S. army_

" Birthplace—City _Metropolis_ State _Illinois_

" Residence—Street No. _____ City _____

Single Widower Divorced } _Single_    { 1st, 2nd or 3rd marriage } _1_

Name of Father _James Lenis Verhines_

Maiden name of Mother _Howard_

Bride's name _Ines Ruth Horton_

Her age _21_

" color _White_

" occupation _Factory Worker_

" Birthplace—City _Indianapolis_ State _Ind_

" Residence—Street No. _154 Villa_ City _Indianapolis_

Single Widow Divorced } _Single_    { 1st, 2nd or 3rd marriage } _1_

Name of Father _Wayne Leason Horton_

Maiden name of Mother _____

Date of this marriage _April 6 - 1944_

Place of this marriage _Indianapolis Ind_

Name and title of person Performing this marriage _Rev James E. Petty_

His address _1302 N Colorado_
_Indianapolis Ind_

Witness { Name _Mr and Mrs Robert H Horton_
{ Address _2009 College Ave_

## Return this Report to County Clerk with License and Certificate

# Marriage Record for Board of Health
## To Be Returned by the Minister or Other Person Performing Ceremony

Delbert Lee Williams and Martha Ellen Lewis

Groom's name _Delbert Lee Williams_

His age _21_

" color _White_

" occupation _U. S. Navy_

" Birthplace—City _Martinsville_ State _Ind._

" Residence—Street No. _Martinsville_ City

Single
Widower
Divorced } _____ { 1st, ~~2nd or 3rd~~ marriage }

Name of Father _Ora Dayton Williams_

Maiden name of Mother _Grace Helena Bales_

Bride's name ~~Grace~~ Martha Ellen Lewis

Her age _20_

" color _White_

" occupation _Stenographer_

" Birthplace—City _Cass Co._ State _Ind._

" Residence—Street No. _Monroe_ City

Single
Widow
Divorced } _Single_ { 1st, ~~2nd or 3rd~~ ~~marriage~~ }

Name of Father _Hobart E. Lewis_

Maiden name of Mother _Cora Alice Ryan_

Date of this marriage _April 6 — 1944_

Place of this marriage _Martinsville, Ind._

Name and title of person
Performing this marriage _G. W. Adams (Baptist Minister)_

His address _160 S. Jefferson St. Martinsville, Ind._

Witness { Name _Mrs. Glenn St. John_
{ Address _385 W. Morgan St Martinsville, Ind._

## Return this Report to County Clerk with License and Certificate

FILED

42  APR 10 1944

A. Jack Ilson
CLERK

## Marriage Record for Board of Health
### To Be Returned by the Minister or Other Person Performing Ceremony

Eugene McAtee _____ and Patty Barker

Groom's name _Eugene McAtee_

His age _36_

" color _white_

" occupation _Defense Worker_

" Birthplace—City _Lagota_ State _Indiana_

" Residence—Street No. _123 S Arlington_ City _Indpls._

Single Widower Divorced } _Divorced_ { 1st, 2nd or 3rd marriage } _2nd_

Name of Father _Frank McAtee_

Maiden name of Mother _Mary Conine (deceased)_

Bride's name _Patty Barker_

Her age _18_

" color _white_

" occupation _Housework_

" Birthplace—City _Russellville_ State _Ill._

" Residence—Street No. _1539 E Wash_ City _Indpls_

Single Widow Divorced } _Single_ { 1st, 2nd or 3rd marriage } _1st_

Name of Father _Tom Barker_

Maiden name of Mother _Blanche Wooden_

Date of this marriage _April 6 1944_

Place of this marriage _Indpls Ind_

Name and title of person Performing this marriage _Ernest T Sims Justice of Peace_

His address _152½ East Court_

Witness { Name _Ernest E Suizzle_
{ Address _1130 Trobridge_

### Return this Report to County Clerk with License and Certificate

# Marriage Record for Board of Health
### To Be Returned by the Minister or Other Person Performing Ceremony

*Elvin Jern Madson* and *Wanada L Fraker*

Groom's name *Elvin Jern Madson*

His age 23

" color white

" occupation Truck Driver

" Birthplace—City Mason City State Iowa

" Residence—Street No. 609 Church City Rockford

Single Widower Divorced } Single { 1st, 2nd or 3rd marriage } 1st

Name of Father Carl J. Madson

Maiden name of Mother Emma Besen

Bride's name Wanada L Fraker

Her age 16

" color white

" occupation Defense Worker

" Birthplace—City Rockford State Ill.

" Residence—Street No. 2844 N. Sheldon City Rockford

Single Widow Divorced } Single { 1st, 2nd or 3rd marriage } 1st

Name of Father Sylvester Everett Fraker

Maiden name of Mother Barnett Fay Raymond

Date of this marriage April 6 – 44

Place of this marriage Rockford Ill.

Name and title of person Performing this marriage Everett F. Kane Justice of Peace

His address 157½ E Court St.

Witness { Name Ernie Barber

{ Address 538 Marian Rockford

### Return this Report to County Clerk with License and Certificate

# Marriage Record for Board of Health
### To Be Returned by the Minister or Other Person Performing Ceremony

Bowman H. Hall _and_ Alma B. Wallman

Groom's name _Bowman H. Hall_

His age _31_

" color _White_

" occupation _Soldier_

" Birthplace—City _Richmond, Quebec, Canada_

" Residence—Street No. _Chanute Field, Ill_

Single
Widower
(Divorced)　　　　　　{ 1st, (2nd) or 3rd marriage }

Name of Father _Robert Hall_

Maiden name of Mother _Elizabeth Hall_

Bride's name _Alma B. Wallman_

Her age _33_

" color _White_

" occupation _Teacher_

" Birthplace—City _Indianapolis_ State _Indiana_

" Residence—Street No. _2333 Ransdell St._ City _Indianapolis_

(Single)
Widow
Divorced　　　　　　{ (1st) 2nd or 3rd marriage }

Name of Father _Harry E. Wallman (deceased)_

Maiden name of Mother _Marie C. Wallman_

Date of this marriage _6 April 1944_

Place of this marriage _Indianapolis, Ind._

Name and title of person
Performing this marriage _Rev. W. Franklin Lohr_

His address _2724 Napoleon St._
_Indianapolis 3. Ind._

Witness { Name _E. Raines_
{ Address _125 Pleasant Run So Dr._

### Return this Report to County Clerk with License and Certificate

# Marriage Record for Board of Health

## To Be Returned by the Minister or Other Person Performing Ceremony

*Eldrege Bowers* and *Madie Fart*

Groom's name _Eldrege Bowers._

His age _36_

" color _C_

" occupation _Feed Packer._

" Birthplace—City _Giallin_ State _Tenn_

" Residence—Street No. _16½ Blake St_ City _Indianapolis_

Single / Widower / Divorced } _Widowed_ { 1st, 2nd or 3rd marriage } _2nd._

Name of Father _January Bowers_

Maiden name of Mother _Tillie Hyde_

Bride's name ____

Her age _37_

" color _C_

" occupation _Flame Packer._

" Birthplace—City _Prusville_ State _Ky._

" Residence—Street No. _161 Blake St_ City _Indianapolis_

Single / Widow / Divorced } _Single_ { 1st, 2nd or 3rd marriage } _1st._

Name of Father _Lee Part_

Maiden name of Mother _Ella Gillens_

Date of this marriage _April 6, 1944_

Place of this marriage _Indianapolis, Ind_

Name and title of person Performing this marriage _S. S. Thomas, Minister_

His address _702 No. Illinois St_ _Indianapolis, Indiana_

Witness { Name _E. L. Johnson_ Address _152½ Court St_ }

## Return this Report to County Clerk with License and Certificate

# Marriage Record for Board of Health

### To Be Returned by the Minister or Other Person Performing Ceremony

*Raleigh Cantor Jr and Katherine M Collins*

Groom's name _RALEIGH CANTOR, JR._

His age _20 YRS._

" color _WHITE_

" occupation _CLERK_

" Birthplace—City _INDIANAPOLIS_ State _INDIANA_

" Residence—Street No. _712 BEECHER ST._ City _INDIANAPOLIS – IND_

Single ~~Widower Divorced~~ } _SINGLE_ { 1st, ~~2nd or 3rd~~ marriage } _FIRST_

Name of Father _RALEIGH CANTOR, SR._

Maiden name of Mother _ADA SIEBENTHAL_

Bride's name _KATHERINE M. COLLINS_

Her age _18_

" color _WHITE_

" occupation _SALESLADY_

" Birthplace—City _LOUISVILLE_ State _KENTUCKY_

" Residence—Street No. _717 S. 23rd ST._ City _LOUISVILLE, KY._

Single ~~Widow Divorced~~ } _SINGLE_ { 1st, ~~2nd or 3rd~~ marriage } _FIRST_

Name of Father _SAMUEL LINTON COLLINS, SR._

Maiden name of Mother _KATHERINE MARY MILLER_

Date of this marriage _April 6, 1944_

Place of this marriage _Hillcrest Baptist Church, Indianapolis Ind_

Name and title of person Performing this marriage _Rev. E. E. Ballard_

His address _1136 Churchman Ave., Indianapolis Ind_

Witness { Name _Edna McCarty_
Address _423 N. Holmes Ave_

### Return this Report to County Clerk with License and Certificate

# Marriage Record for Board of Health
## To Be Returned by the Minister or Other Person Performing Ceremony

_Metzler_ and _O'Neal_

Groom's name _Walter A. Metzler_

His age _44_

" color _White_

" occupation _Sales Supervisor_

" Birthplace—City _Indianapolis_ State _Ind._

" Residence—Street No. _2633 Napoleon_ City _Indianapolis_

Single
Widower } _Divorced_ { 1st, 2nd or 3rd } _2nd_
Divorced marriage

Name of Father _John Metzler_

Maiden name of Mother _Elizabeth C. Haag_

Bride's name _Lillian G. O'Neal_

Her age _33_

" color _white_

" occupation _Tool grinder_

" Birthplace—City _Indianapolis_ State _Ind._

" Residence—Street No. _21 S. Butler_ City _Indianapolis, Ind_

Single
Widow } _Divorced_ { 1st, 2nd or 3rd } _2nd_
Divorced marriage

Name of Father _Charles O'Neal_

Maiden name of Mother _Jessie Fox_

Date of this marriage _April 6, 1944._

Place of this marriage _Frankfort, Ind._

Name and title of person
Performing this marriage _Paschall, C.S. Rev._

His address _RR.8 Box 87_
_Indianapolis, Ind._

Witness { Name _Ethel B. _____
{ Address _1811 _____ Indianapolis, Ind._

## Return this Report to County Clerk with License and Certificate

# Marriage Record for Board of Health

### To Be Returned by the Minister or Other Person Performing Ceremony

---

_____ and _____

Groom's name _Isaiah Anderson_

His age _69_

" color _white_

" occupation _Laborer_

" Birthplace—City _Winchester Clarke_ State _Ky._

" Residence—Street No. _1026 College ave_ City _Indianapolis Ind._

Single ⎫
Widower ⎬ _____  { 1st, 2nd or 3rd marriage } _2nd Marriage_
Divorced ⎭

Name of Father _Bingham Anderson._

Maiden name of Mother _Emma Anderson._

---

Bride's name _Ella Anderson._

Her age _72 –_

" color _white_

" occupation _house Keeper_

" Birthplace—City _Hendricks co –_ State _Indiana._

" Residence—Street No. _1026 College ave_ City _Indianapolis_

Single ⎫
Widow ⎬ _____  { 1st, 2nd or 3rd marriage } _2nd Marriage_
Divorced ⎭

Name of Father _Wm H. Hughes._

Maiden name of Mother _Sally Rebecca Hughes._

---

Date of this marriage _April 6th 1944 –_

Place of this marriage _Hotell English –_

Name and title of person Performing this marriage _L. C. Leavitt, Minister_

His address _1406 E New York St, Indpls._

Witness ⎰ Name _Arthur Van Deman._
⎱ Address _Hotel Lincoln_

---

### Return this Report to County Clerk with License and Certificate

12

# Marriage Record for Board of Health

### To Be Returned by the Minister or Other Person Performing Ceremony

_Horace Sheldon Bell_ and _Iris Nadine Roth_

Groom's name _Horace Sheldon Bell_

His age _35_

" color _Wh_

" occupation _Machinist_

" Birthplace—City _Brownsburg_ State _Indiana_

" Residence—Street No. _Brownsburg, Indiana_

Single
Widower } _Widower_ { 1st, 2nd or 3rd marriage } _2nd_
Divorced

Name of Father _Charles H. Bell_

Maiden name of Mother _Iva Jane Phillips_

Bride's name _Iris Nadine Roth_

Her age _22_

" color _Wh._

" occupation _Employed Link Belt, Suffdd., Ind_

" Birthplace—City _Guthrie_ State _Ky_

" Residence—Street No. _1757 Allen Ave_ City _Indianapolis, Ind._

~~Single~~
~~Widow~~ } _Divorced_ { 1st, 2nd or 3rd marriage } _2nd_
Divorced

Name of Father _Ray Gilliam_

Maiden name of Mother _Gladys Goodman_

Date of this marriage _April 6, 1944_

Place of this marriage _Bloomington, Ind._

Name and title of person
Performing this marriage _Rev. Merrill B. McFall_

His address _414 S. College_
_Bloomington, Ind._

Witness { Name _Leslie Springer_
{ Address _Bloomington, Ind._

## Return this Report to County Clerk with License and Certificate

# Marriage Record for Board of Health

### To Be Returned by the Minister or Other Person Performing Ceremony

Harvey C. Loughmiller _____ and _____ Pauline F. Rizzi

Groom's name _Harvey C. Loughmiller_

His age _24 yrs._

" color _White_

" occupation _Carpenter_

" Birthplace—City _Indianapolis_ State _Indiana_

" Residence—Street No. _501½ Main St._ City _Beech Grove - Ind._

Single / Widower / Divorced } _Divorced_ { 1st, 2nd or 3rd marriage } _2nd_

Name of Father _Alonzo Loughmiller_

Maiden name of Mother _Marjorie Langley_

Bride's name _Pauline F. Rizzi_

Her age _18 yrs._

" color _White_

" occupation _None_

" Birthplace—City _Indianapolis_ State _Indiana_

" Residence—Street No. _218 S. 5th_ City _Beech Grove - Ind._

Single / Widow / Divorced } _Single_ { 1st, 2nd or 3rd marriage } _1st_

Name of Father _Antonio Rizzi_

Maiden name of Mother _Phyllis Susan Tucker_

Date of this marriage _April 6th 1944_

Place of this marriage _Southport - Ind._

Name and title of person Performing this marriage _Wm. K. Ellington - Justice of the Peace_

His address _Southport - Ind._

Witness { Name _C. Earl Smith_
{ Address _218 S. 5th St. Beech Grove Ind._

### Return this Report to County Clerk with License and Certificate

# Marriage Record for Board of Health
To Be Returned by the Minister or Other Person Performing Ceremony

Gordon K. Vrell _____ and _____ Donna Boyer

Groom's name _____ Gordon K. Vrell

His age _____ 30

" color _____ White

" occupation _____ Soldier

" Birthplace—City _____ Lewistown _____ State _____ Illinois

" Residence—Street No. _____ U.S. Army _____ City

Single  }
Widower }  Single        { 1st, 2nd or 3rd  }  1st
Divorced }               { marriage         }

Name of Father _____ Cleve R. Vrell

Maiden name of Mother _____ Mary Goodman

Bride's name _____ Donna Boyer

Her age _____ 28

" color _____ White

" occupation _____ Purchasing agent

" Birthplace—City _____ Sheridan _____ State _____ Indiana

" Residence—Street No. _____ 5269 Central _____ City _____ Indianapolis, Ind

Single  }
Widow  }  Divorced      { 1st, 2nd or 3rd  }  2nd
Divorced }               { marriage         }

Name of Father _____ Nola E. Boyer

Maiden name of Mother _____ Carrie Mabiath McKenzie

Date of this marriage _____ April 7th, 1944

Place of this marriage _____ Indianapolis Indiana

Name and title of person
Performing this marriage _____ Rev. Ernest F. Roesti

His address _____ 5614 Broadway
_____ Indianapolis 5, Indiana

Witness { Name _____ Edward Schoenburgn
        { Address _____ 6046 College Ave. Indianapolis, Ind.

## Return this Report to County Clerk with License and Certificate

# Marriage Record for Board of Health
## To Be Returned by the Minister or Other Person Performing Ceremony

*Claude Crider* and *Esther Jackson*

Groom's name *Claude Crider*

His age _32_

" color _White_

" occupation _Laborer_

" Birthplace—City _Bloomington_ State _Indiana_

" Residence—Street No. _1931 N. Ill_ City _Indianapolis_

Single / Widower / Divorced } _Divorced_ { 1st, 2nd or 3rd marriage } _Second_

Name of Father _James Crider_

Maiden name of Mother _Emma Fleetwood_

Bride's name _Esther Jackson_

Her age _22_

" color _White_

" occupation _Housekeeper_

" Birthplace—City _Bloomington_ State _Indiana_

" Residence—Street No. _251 S. Dearborn_ City _Indianapolis_

Single / Widow / Divorced } _Single_ { 1st, 2nd or 3rd marriage } _First_

Name of Father _Elmer Jackson_

Maiden name of Mother _Edith Gross_

Date of this marriage _April 7th 1944_

Place of this marriage _1018 Laurel St. City_

Name and title of person Performing this marriage _W. Millard Church — Minister_

His address _1018 Laurel St._
_Indianapolis, Indiana_

Witness { Name _Russell Martindale_
{ Address _2321 Prospect St_

## Return this Report to County Clerk with License and Certificate

# Marriage Record for Board of Health
### To Be Returned by the Minister or Other Person Performing Ceremony

_____ and _____

Groom's name _Samuel M. Blue_   O-660714

His age _75_

" color _white_

" occupation _Soldier_

" Birthplace—City _Belle Union_   State _Indiana_

" Residence—Street No. _710 Day St_   City _Indianapolis_

Single / ~~Widower~~ / ~~Divorced~~    { 1st, ~~2nd or 3rd~~ marriage

Name of Father _Orville Blue_

Maiden name of Mother _Zella Dobbs._

Bride's name _Martha L. Kelly_

Her age _22_

" color _white_

" occupation _Clerk_

" Birthplace—City _Athens_   State _Ohio_

" Residence—Street No. _3215 Bethincow_   _Indianapolis_

Single / ~~Widow~~ / ~~Divorced~~    { 1st, ~~2nd or 3rd~~ marriage

Name of Father _Roy G. Kelly_

Maiden name of Mother _Maude Anderson_

Date of this marriage _April 7 1944_

Place of this marriage _Fort Field, Indiana._

Name and title of person Performing this marriage _Chaplain U.S.A_

His address _Fort Field, Indiana._

Witness   { Name _Beryle B. Knox_    _Thomas C. Knox S/c_

       { Address _710 Day St Apt 7_   _710 Day St APT 7_

          _Indianapolis, Ind._   _Indianapolis, Ind._

### Return this Report to County Clerk with License and Certificate

# Marriage Record for Board of Health

## To Be Returned by the Minister or Other Person Performing Ceremony

*Melvin Carpenter* and *Marjorie Douglas*

Groom's name _Melvin Carpenter_

His age _23_

" color _White_

" occupation _Lathe Operator_

" Birthplace—City _Champaign_ State _Illinois_

" Residence—Street No. _462 N. State_ City _Indianapolis_

Single / Widower / Divorced } _Single_ { 1st, 2nd or 3rd marriage } _1st_

Name of Father _Thomas Carpenter_

Maiden name of Mother _Marie Carpenter_

Bride's name _Marjorie Douglas_

Her age _23_

" color _White_

" occupation _None_

" Birthplace—City _Roachdale_ State _Indiana_

" Residence—Street No. _462 N. State_ City _Indpls_

Single / Widow / Divorced } _Divorced_ { 1st, 2nd or 3rd marriage } _2nd_

Name of Father _Ira Holland_

Maiden name of Mother _Lester Young_

Date of this marriage _April 7, 1944_

Place of this marriage _Indianapolis Indiana_

Name and title of person Performing this marriage _Ernest Lane Justice of the Peace_

His address _152½ East Court St._

Witness { Name _Mary Jo Lane_
{ Address _374 College Ave_

## Return this Report to County Clerk with License and Certificate

# Marriage Record for Board of Health

## To Be Returned by the Minister or Other Person Performing Ceremony

_____ and _____

Groom's name _Garnett W. Kiplinger_

His age _23_

" color _White_

" occupation _U. S. Army_

" Birthplace—City _Maysville_ State _K. ??_

" Residence—Street No. _Ft. Harrison_ City _Indiana_

Single / Widower / Divorced } _Single_ { 1st, 2nd or 3rd marriage } _1st_

Name of Father _C. Herman Kiplinger_

Maiden name of Mother _Clark_

Bride's name _Harriet A. DeVault_

Her age _22_

" color _White_

" occupation _office girl_

" Birthplace—City _Holden, Mo._ State _Okla_

" Residence—Street No. _501 W. 30_ City _Indianapolis_

Single / Widow / Divorced } _Single_ { 1st, 2nd or 3rd marriage } _1st_

Name of Father _William Walker DeVault_

Maiden name of Mother _Stella Mae Teads_

Date of this marriage _April ? 191?_

Place of this marriage _501 W. 30th Indianapolis_

Name and title of person Performing this marriage _????_

His address _1029 W. 2? St._
_Indianapolis, Ind._

Witness { Name _Richard T. ????_
{ Address _618 W. 4 ??_

## Return this Report to County Clerk with License and Certificate

# Marriage Record for Board of Health

To Be Returned by the Minister or Other Person Performing Ceremony

_Clarence Means Jr_ and _Doris Marie Archer_

Groom's name _Clarence Means Jr_

His age _18_

" color _White_

" occupation _Switchman_

" Birthplace—City _Indianapolis_ State _Ind_

" Residence—Street No. _646 Wash St_ City _Indianapolis_

Single
Widower
Divorced } ~~Widow~~ _Single_ { 1st, 2nd or 3rd marriage } _1st._

Name of Father _Clarence M. Means._

Maiden name of Mother _Florence Edna Richardson_

Bride's name _Doris Marie Archer_

Her age _15_

" color _White_

" occupation _House keeping._

" Birthplace—City _Picksburg_ State _Ind_

" Residence—Street No. _283½ East St_ City _Plainfield._

Single
Widow
Divorced } _Single_ { 1st, 2nd or 3rd marriage } _1st._

Name of Father _Edward Alton Archer_

Maiden name of Mother _Iva Crow_

Date of this marriage _April 7 1944_

Place of this marriage _Mt Olive Methodist Parsonage_

Name and title of person Performing this marriage _Rev. C. H. Loveland_

His address _1447 S. High School Rd_

_Indianapolis_

Witness { Name _Iva Archer_
{ Address _283 north s plainfield_

**Return this Report to County Clerk with License and Certificate**

# Marriage Record for Board of Health
## To Be Returned by the Minister or Other Person Performing Ceremony

*Willis P Howe* and *Betty Lou Campbell*

Groom's name _Willis P. Howe_

His age _2 2_

" color _White_

" occupation, _Eng._

" Birthplace—City _Indianapolis_ State _Ind_

" Residence—Street No. _3356 Carrollton_ City _Indianapolis Ind_

Single / Widower / Divorced } _Single_  { 1st, 2nd or 3rd marriage } _1st_

Name of Father _Willis P Howe_

Maiden name of Mother _Luella Hull_

Bride's name _Betty Lou Campbell_

Her age _1 8_

" color _White_

" occupation _Sec._

" Birthplace—City _Indianapolis_ State _Ind_

" Residence—Street No. _1412 Park_ City _Indpls Ind_

Single / Widow / Divorced } _Single_  { 1st, 2nd or 3rd marriage } _1st_

Name of Father _Orville L. Campbell_

Maiden name of Mother _Mary R Dickson_

Date of this marriage _April 7, 1944_

Place of this marriage _Indianapolis Ind_

Name and title of person Performing this marriage _Minister Sammy G. Martin_

His address _6234 Haverford ave_
_Indianapolis Ind._

Witness { Name _Bronaugh G. Chamber_
{ Address _____

## Return this Report to County Clerk with License and Certificate

# Marriage Record for Board of Health

### To Be Returned by the Minister or Other Person Performing Ceremony

_Bayard_ and _Westfall_

Groom's name _Paul E. Bayard_

His age _34_

" color _White_

" occupation _Assistant Water Engineer_

" Birthplace—City _Washington_ State _Indiana_

" Residence—Street No. _5137 E. ___ St._ City _Indianapolis_

Single / Widower / Divorced } _Single_ { 1st, 2nd or 3rd marriage } _First_

Name of Father _Noel E. Bayard_

Maiden name of Mother _Deborah Cline_

Bride's name _Bertha Pearl Westfall_

Her age _18_

" color _White_

" occupation ___

" Birthplace—City _Indianapolis_ State _Indiana_

" Residence—Street No. _37 Johnson Ave_ City _Indianapolis_

Single / Widow / Divorced } _Single_ { 1st, 2nd or 3rd marriage } _First_

Name of Father _George H. Westfall_

Maiden name of Mother _Clara Bell Curry_

Date of this marriage _April 7, 1922_

Place of this marriage _Third Christian Church, Indianapolis_

Name and title of person Performing this marriage ___

His address _3253 Washington ___, Indianapolis_

Witness { Name ___ { Address _5137 ___

## Return this Report to County Clerk with License and Certificate

12

# Marriage Record for Board of Health

### To Be Returned by the Minister or Other Person Performing Ceremony

Robert G. Stevens _and_ Beulah Clifton

Groom's name _Robert G. Stevens_

His age _24_

" color _White_

" occupation _Wireman_ RCH.

" Birthplace—City _Indianapolis_ State _Ind._

" Residence—Street No. _2221 Kenwood_ City _Indpls._

Single / ~~Widower~~ / ~~Divorced~~ } _Single_ { 1st, ~~2nd or 3rd~~ ~~marriage~~ } _First_

Name of Father _Gale Stephens_

Maiden name of Mother _Vera Elaine Shannon_

Bride's name _Beulah Clifton_

Her age _20_

" color _White_

" occupation _Elec. Assembly_ RCH.

" Birthplace—City _Lawton_ State _Kentucky_

" Residence—Street No. _121 N. Grant Ave._ City _Indpls._

Single / ~~Widow~~ / ~~Divorced~~ } _Single_ { 1st, ~~2nd or 3rd~~ ~~marriage~~ } _First_

Name of Father _Tracy Clifton_

Maiden name of Mother _Bessie Collins_

Date of this marriage _April 7th 1944_

Place of this marriage _East Park Methodist Parsonage_

Name and title of person Performing this marriage _Rev Golden G. Smith_

His address _2609 East New York St. Indianapolis 1, Ind._

Witness { Name _Mr & Mrs. Gene Waggoner_ { Address _59 S. Oxford — Indpls Ind_

### Return this Report to County Clerk with License and Certificate

12

# Marriage Record for Board of Health

### To Be Returned by the Minister or Other Person Performing Ceremony

*Clarence Forman* and *Mary E. Sherman*

Groom's name *Clarence Forman*

His age *(45) fourty-five*

" color *white*

" occupation *master carpenter*

" Birthplace—City *Terre Haute* State *Indiana*

" Residence—Street No. *1808 N. New Jersey* City *Indianapolis*

Single
Widower } *widower*
Divorced

{ 1st, 2nd or 3rd marriage } *second*

Name of Father *Chas. L. Forman*

Maiden name of Mother *Tena Smith*

Bride's name *Mary E. Sherman*

Her age *(36) thirty six*

" color *white*

" occupation *housewife — Defense worker*

" Birthplace—City *Bell City* State *Mo.*

" Residence—Street No. *Rt. 20, box 313* City *Indianapolis, 44*

Single
Widow } *widow*
Divorced

{ 1st, 2nd or 3rd marriage } *second*

Name of Father *Henry Day*

Maiden name of Mother *Mandy Kent*

Date of this marriage *April 7, 1944*

Place of this marriage *Rt. 20, box 313, Indianapolis, Ind.*

Name and title of person
Performing this marriage *George O. Tietze, minister,*
*Drexel Gardens Church of Christ.*

His address
*4324 E. Wash. St. Indianapolis, Ind.*

Witness { Name *Mrs. Helen Strubbe*
{ Address *908 Buchanan St., Indianapolis*

## Return this Report to County Clerk with License and Certificate

# Marriage Record for Board of Health

To Be Returned by the Minister or Other Person Performing Ceremony

*John B. Kennelly* and *Anna Marie Ladwig*

Groom's name _John B Kennelly_ 37437037

His age _29_

" color _White_

" occupation _Soldier_

" Birthplace—City _Albert Lea_ State _Minn._

" Residence—Street No. _318 Court St_ City

Single / ~~Widower~~ / ~~Divorced~~    { 1st, ~~2nd or 3rd~~ marriage }

Name of Father _John Francis Kennelly_

Maiden name of Mother _Inez Hansen_

Bride's name _Anna Marie Ladwig_

Her age _26_

" color _White_

" occupation _Inspector_

" Birthplace—City _Denison_ State _Iowa_

" Residence—Street No _125 E St Joseph_ City _Indianapolis_

Single / ~~Widow~~ / ~~Divorced~~    { 1st, ~~2nd or 3rd~~ marriage }

Name of Father _Herman_

Maiden name of Mother _Ingeberg Andriesson_

Date of this marriage _April 7 1944_

Place of this marriage _Stout Field chapel_

Name and title of person Performing this marriage _Chaplain Wallis Lartsch Capt,_

His address _Stout Field, Indiana._

Witness { Name _Allen Curtis_    _Mrs Nina Pindley_
Address _125 E St Joseph_    _3012 Meredith Ave._

_311 23862_

**Return this Report to County Clerk with License and Certificate**

# Marriage Record for Board of Health

## To Be Returned by the Minister or Other Person Performing Ceremony

_____ and _____

Groom's name _Cecil Harold Boardman_

His age _26_

" color _White_

" occupation _Guard Officer_

" Birthplace—City _Jefferson County_ State _Indiana_

" Residence—Street No. _2nd Reformatory_ City _Pendleton_

Single / Widower / Divorced } _Single_ { 1st, 2nd or 3rd marriage } _First_

Name of Father _Harry Robert Boardman_

Maiden name of Mother _Tura Merle Carr_

Bride's name _Ruth Irene Knox_

Her age _20_

" color _White_

" occupation _____

" Birthplace—City _Washington County_ State _Indiana_

" Residence—Street No. _3711 E. Michigan_ City _Indianapolis_

Single / Widow / Divorced } _Single_ { 1st, 2nd or 3rd marriage } _First_

Name of Father _Harry Wallace Knox_

Maiden name of Mother _Emma Lucile Rink_

Date of this marriage _April 7 - 1944_

Place of this marriage _Indianapolis, Indiana_

Name and title of person Performing this marriage _Rev. J. N. Greene_

His address _1841 Cross Drive Woodruff Place_
_Indianapolis Indiana_

Witness { Name _Mrs. J. N. Greene_
{ Address _1841 Cross Drive, Woodruff Place_

## Return this Report to County Clerk with License and Certificate

# Marriage Record for Board of Health
### To Be Returned by the Minister or Other Person Performing Ceremony

*Charles Skaggs* and *Anna B. Eades*

Groom's name _____ Charles Skaggs

His age _____ 60

" color _____ White

" occupation _____ Carpenter

" Birthplace—City _____ Green County _____ State _____ Kentucky

" Residence—Street No. 399 E. King St. City _____ Franklin

Single / Widower / Divorced } Widower { 1st, 2nd or 3rd marriage } 2nd

Name of Father _____ Hiram Skaggs

Maiden name of Mother _____ Martha Shumaker

Bride's name _____ Anna B. Eades

Her age _____ 55

" color _____ white

" occupation _____ housewife

" Birthplace—City _____ Clay Co. _____ State _____ Illinois

" Residence—Street No. 399 E. King St. City _____ Franklin, Ind.

Single / Widow / Divorced } Widow { 1st, 2nd or 3rd marriage } 2nd

Name of Father _____ J. A. Brown

Maiden name of Mother _____ Mary Crouch

Date of this marriage _____ April 7, 1944

Place of this marriage _____ Indianapolis, Ind.

Name and title of person Performing this marriage _____ Aaron J. Coble

His address _____ 8 S. Warman Ave Indianapolis, Ind.

Witness { Name _____ Beatrice S. Coble
{ Address _____ 8 S. Warman Ave.

### Return this Report to County Clerk with License and Certificate

12

# Marriage Record for Board of Health
## To Be Returned by the Minister or Other Person Performing Ceremony

Mr. Jessie Moore _____ and _Lavonia Magby_

Groom's name _Mr. Jessie Moore_

His age _37_

" color _colored_

" occupation _Laborer_

" Birthplace—City _Galena_ State _Kansas_

" Residence—Street No. _R.R.2# Box 396_ City _Galena_

Single
Widower } _Divorced_ { 1st, 2nd or 3rd } _2nd._
Divorced      marriage

Name of Father _William Moore_

Maiden name of Mother _Fannie Boston_

Bride's name _Lavonia Magby_

Her age _21_

" color _colored_

" occupation _____

" Birthplace—City _Bill County_ State _Georgia_

" Residence—Street No. _____ City _____

Single
Widow } _Single_ { 1st, 2nd or 3rd } _1st_
Divorced      marriage

Name of Father _(dead) Luke Magby_

Maiden name of Mother _Fannie Strong (dead)_

Date of this marriage _April 7th, 1924_

Place of this marriage _1664 Columbia Ave. Indianapolis, Ind._

Name and title of person
Performing this marriage _Elder John Higginson (minister)_

His address _921 Paca Street, Indianapolis, Ind._

_Eld Eld John Higginson_

Witness { Name _Bettie Smith 1441 E. 16 St._
         { Address _Georgia Hopkins 1664 columbia ave_

## Return this Report to County Clerk with License and Certificate

# Marriage Record for Board of Health
## To Be Returned by the Minister or Other Person Performing Ceremony

_____ and _____

Groom's name _Robert C. Jordan III_

His age _23_

" color _white_

" occupation _Air Corp_

" Birthplace—City _Shreveport_ State _La_

" Residence—Street No. _Seymour_ City _Ind_

Single Widower Divorced } _single_ { 1st, 2nd or 3rd marriage } _1_

Name of Father _Colonel B C Jordan_

Maiden name of Mother _Jennie Mae McClure_

Bride's name _Sue Ann Stewart_

Her age _19_

" color _white_

" occupation _Clerk_

" Birthplace—City _Seymour_ State _Ind_

" Residence—Street No. _314 W 7th_ City _Seymour_

Single Widow Divorced } _single_ { 1st, 2nd or 3rd marriage } _1_

Name of Father _Harold C. Stewart_

Maiden name of Mother _Iora Reynolds_

Date of this marriage _April 7-44_

Place of this marriage _Seymour Indiana_

Name and title of person Performing this marriage _John T Prentice, minister_

His address _621 N. Chestnut St_ _Seymour Ind_

Witness { Name _Roy C Glynn_
{ Address _Freeman Field, Seymour, Ind._

## Return this Report to County Clerk with License and Certificate

# Marriage Record for Board of Health
## To Be Returned by the Minister or Other Person Performing Ceremony

*Louie M. Shull* and *Beulah N. Boyd*

Groom's name _Louie M. Shull_

His age _40, Forty_

" color _White_

" occupation _Machinist_

" Birthplace—City _Dortville_ State _Indiana_

" Residence—Street No. _1830 Ludlow_ City _Indianapolis_

Single / Widower / Divorced } _Divorced_ { 1st, 2nd or 3rd marriage } _2nd_

Name of Father _Edward N. Shull_

Maiden name of Mother _Laura V. Mc. Adams_

Bride's name _Beulah N. Boyd_

Her age _29, Twenty-nine_

" color _White_

" occupation _Housework_

" Birthplace—City _Clifford_ State _Indiana_

" Residence—Street No. _1429 Shelby_ City _Indianapolis_

Single / Widow / Divorced } _Single_ { 1st, 2nd or 3rd marriage } _1st_

Name of Father _Charles B. Boyd_

Maiden name of Mother _Nellie Kendall_

Date of this marriage _April 8, 1944_

Place of this marriage _Indianapolis, Indiana_

Name and title of person Performing this marriage _Rev. Carroll Heatley, Pastor_

His address _611 E Southern, Indianapolis, Ind._

Witness { Name _Woodrow W. Craig_ _Hazel M. Craig, Indianapolis, Indiana_
Address _1429 Shelby St. Indianapolis Indiana_

## Return this Report to County Clerk with License and Certificate

# Marriage Record for Board of Health
## To Be Returned by the Minister or Other Person Performing Ceremony

*Frank Burford* and *Mary Jones*

Groom's name _Frank Burford_

His age _47_

" color _C_

" occupation _Labor_

" Birthplace—City _Galton_ State _Tenn_

" Residence—Street No. _2863_ City _N. Lasalle, Indianapolis_

Single Widower Divorced } _widower_ { 1st, 2nd or 3rd marriage } _2nd_

Name of Father _Lou Burford_

Maiden name of Mother _Julia Clay_

Bride's name _Mary Jones_

Her age _18_

" color _C_

" occupation _Coach cleaner_

" Birthplace—City _Indianapolis_ State _Indiana_

" Residence—Street No. _212 N_ City _N. 13_

Single Widow Divorced } _912 widow_ { 1st, 2nd or 3rd marriage } _2st nd_

Name of Father _Sollie Allen_

Maiden name of Mother _Addie Douglas_

Date of this marriage _April 8th, 1944_

Place of this marriage _Indianapolis Ind._

Name and title of person Performing this marriage _SS Thomas, Minister_

His address _702 S Illinois St_

Witness { Name _Mary Hall_ Address _2332 Indianapolis Avenue_

## Return this Report to County Clerk with License and Certificate

12

# Marriage Record for Board of Health

### To Be Returned by the Minister or Other Person Performing Ceremony

Robert Lee Sink and Mary Janet Ferguson

Groom's name _Robert Lee Sink_

His age _27_

" color _white_

" occupation _Manufacturing methods engineer_

" Birthplace—City _Indianapolis_ State _Indiana_

" Residence—Street No. _817 N. Oakland Ave_ City _Indianapolis, Ind._

Single Widower Divorced } _Single_ { 1st, 2nd or 3rd marriage } _First_

Name of Father _Charles E. Sink_

Maiden name of Mother _Geraldine King_

Bride's name _Mary Janet Ferguson_

Her age _24_

" color _white_

" occupation _Stenographer_

" Birthplace—City _Indianapolis_ State _Indiana_

" Residence—Street No. _1123 N. Oakland_ City _Indianapolis, Ind._

Single Widow Divorced } _Single_ { 1st, 2nd or 3rd marriage } _First_

Name of Father _Floyd T. Ferguson (deceased)_

Maiden name of Mother _Mary E. Mabitt_

Date of this marriage _April 8, 1944_

Place of this marriage _Indianapolis, Indiana_

Name and title of person Performing this marriage _Ralph E. Neisser, Pastor First Evang. & Ref. Church_

His address _1007 N. Oakland Ave., Indianapolis, Ind._

Witness { Name _R. W. McKittRick, Indianapolis_ { Address _Mrs. Louis Pries, Indianapolis_

## Return this Report to County Clerk with License and Certificate

# Marriage Record for Board of Health
## To Be Returned by the Minister or Other Person Performing Ceremony

James Randolph Macredy and Alice Chatfield

Groom's name _James Randolph Macredy._

His age _25_

" color _white_

" occupation _Engineer_

" Birthplace—City _Roanoke_ State _Va_

" Residence—Street No. _1702 W_ City _Bedford Ind._

Single / Widower / Divorced } _Single_ { 1st, 2nd or 3rd marriage }

Name of Father _James Roderick Macredy_

Maiden name of Mother _Rosalie Digges Miller_

Bride's name _Alice Chatfield_

Her age _22_

" color _white_

" occupation _job analyst._

" Birthplace—City _Tulsa_ State _Okla_

" Residence—Street No. _48 N. Audubon_ City _Indianapolis_

Single / Widow / Divorced } _Single_ { 1st, 2nd or 3rd marriage }

Name of Father _Josiah Clark Chatfield_

Maiden name of Mother _Vanetta Jones_

Date of this marriage _April 8th 1944_

Place of this marriage _Indianapolis Ind_

Name and title of person Performing this marriage _Rev. John B Ferguson_

His address _312 N. Ritter avenue_

_Indianapolis Indiana_

Witness { Name _James Roderick Macredy_
Address _510 Wappa Road Towson Md._

## Return this Report to County Clerk with License and Certificate

12

# Marriage Record for Board of Health

### To Be Returned by the Minister or Other Person Performing Ceremony

_Carl Owen Windisch_ and _Anita Dale Hall_

Groom's name _Carl Owen Windisch_

His age _Twenty five_

" color _White_

" occupation _Batman_

" Birthplace—City _Indianapolis_ State _Indiana_

" Residence—Street No. _2506 N. Capitol_ City _Indianapolis_

Single / Widower / Divorced } _Widower_   { 1st, 2nd or 3rd marriage } _2nd_

Name of Father _Carl John Windisch_

Maiden name of Mother _Marilyn Borah_

Bride's name _Anita Dale Hall_

Her age _Twenty two_

" color _White_

" occupation _Machinist_

" Birthplace—City _Clark Township Johnson_ State _Indiana_

" Residence—Street No. _2506 N. Capitol_ City _Indianapolis_

Single / Widow / Divorced } _Divorced_   { 1st, 2nd or 3rd marriage } _2nd_

Name of Father _Loren E. Bille_

Maiden name of Mother _Sylvia Ewing_

Date of this marriage _April 8 1944_

Place of this marriage _1941 Bancroft, Indianapolis, Indiana_

Name and title of person Performing this marriage _David W. Morris, minister_

His address _550 West 46th St._
_Indianapolis, Indiana._

Witness { Name _Thomas J. Kelso_
{ Address _1941 Bancroft St. Indpls. Ind._

## Return this Report to County Clerk with License and Certificate

# Marriage Record for Board of Health

## To Be Returned by the Minister or Other Person Performing Ceremony

_Leach_ and _Pitree_

Groom's name _Donald W. Leach_

His age _24_

" color _white_

" occupation _Army Lieutenant_

" Birthplace—City _Indianapolis_ State _Indiana_

" Residence—Street No. _1547 Finley_ City _Indianapolis_

Single / Widower / Divorced } _Single_ { 1st, 2nd or 3rd marriage } _1st_

Name of Father _Leo Leach_

Maiden name of Mother _Dora Hair_

Bride's name _Anna Ruth Pitree_

Her age _20_

" color _white_

" occupation _Comptometer Operator_

" Birthplace—City _Connersville_ State _Indiana_

" Residence—Street No. _5105 College_ City _Indianapolis_

Single / Widow / Divorced } _Single_ { 1st, 2nd or 3rd marriage } _First_

Name of Father _John H. Pitree_

Maiden name of Mother _Ruth Kirkoff_

Date of this marriage _April 8, 1944_

Place of this marriage _Indianapolis, Ind._

Name and title of person Performing this marriage _C. S. Paschall Rev._

His address _RR8, Box 81_
_Indianapolis, Ind._

Witness { Name _Miss Thelma Cushing_
Address _1105 N___ St. ___ Ind._

## Return this Report to County Clerk with License and Certificate

# Marriage Record for Board of Health
### To Be Returned by the Minister or Other Person Performing Ceremony

_____ Henry I. Lammert _____ and _____ Alma E. Wischmeier _____

Groom's name _____ Henry I. Lammert _____

His age _____ 61

" color _____ White

" occupation _____ Electrician

" Birthplace—City _____ Germany _____ State _____

" Residence—Street No. 3224 N. Brookside City _____ Indianapolis, Ind.
Parkway

Single ⎫
Widower ⎬ _____ Widower _____ ⎰ 1st, 2nd or 3rd ⎱ _____ 2nd
Divorced ⎭                                    ⎱ marriage ⎰

Name of Father _____ Henry Lammert _____

Maiden name of Mother _____ Louisa Coleman _____

---

Bride's name _____ Alma E. Wischmeier _____

Her age _____ 50

" color _____ White

" occupation _____ Stenographer

" Birthplace—City _____ Indianapolis _____ State _____ Indiana

" Residence—Street No. 2836 E. New York City _____ Indpls., Ind.
Street

Single ⎫
Widow ⎬ _____ Widow _____ ⎰ 1st, 2nd or 3rd ⎱ _____ 2nd
Divorced ⎭                                  ⎱ marriage ⎰

Name of Father _____ Henry F. W. Ossenforth _____

Maiden name of Mother _____ Sophia Mehrling _____

---

Date of this marriage _____ April 8, 1944

Place of this marriage _____ Trinity Ev. Lutheran Church, Ohio at East St.
Indianapolis
Name and title of person
Performing this marriage _____ Walter C. Maas, Pastor

His address _____ 5444 Carrollton Ave., Indpls., Ind.

Witness ⎰ Name _____ Mr. & Mrs. Harold Weimer _____ Charles Lammert
⎱ Address _____ 442 Ruddell Drive, Kokomo, Ind. _____ U. S. Army

## Return this Report to County Clerk with License and Certificate

# Marriage Record for Board of Health

### To Be Returned by the Minister or Other Person Performing Ceremony

*John J. Elliott* and *Hill Joyce*

Groom's name _John J. Elliott_

His age _22_

" color _White_

" occupation _Salesman_

" Birthplace—City _St. Louis_ State _Missouri_

" Residence—Street No. _433 N Illinois_ City _Indianapolis_

Single / Widower / Divorced } _Single_   { 1st, 2nd or 3rd marriage } _1st_

Name of Father _George Elliott_

Maiden name of Mother _Dorrance Dickup_

Bride's name _Joyce Hilt_

Her age _20_

" color _White_

" occupation _Mail Clerk_

" Birthplace—City _Greensburg_ State _Indiana_

" Residence—Street No. _2224 Broadway_ City _Indianapolis, Ind_

Single / Widow / Divorced } _Single_   { 1st, 2nd or 3rd marriage } _1st_

Name of Father _Noel Hilt_

Maiden name of Mother _Mary Ellen Trefut_

Date of this marriage _April 8 – 1944_

Place of this marriage _2209 Park Av. Indianapolis, Ind_

Name and title of person Performing this marriage _Norwood Calhoun_

His address _2209 Park Av. Indianapolis, Ind_

Witness { Name _M Calhoun_
{ Address _2209 Park Av. Indianapolis, Ind_

### Return this Report to County Clerk with License and Certificate

12

# Marriage Record for Board of Health
## To Be Returned by the Minister or Other Person Performing Ceremony

*Damon L. Kromer* and *Sarah Ann Hull*

Groom's name _Damon L. Kromer_

His age _27 years_

" color _White_

" occupation _Army Air Corps_

" Birthplace—City _Newburg_ State _Penna_

" Residence—Street No. _1213 Market_ City _Newbury_

Single } _Single_ 1st, 2nd or 3rd } _First_
Widower } marriage }
Divorced }

Name of Father _____

Maiden name of Mother _____

Bride's name _Sarah Ann Hull_

Her age _21_

" color _white_

" occupation _none_

" Birthplace—City _Connersville_ State _Indiana_

" Residence—Street No. _114 East 12th St._ City _Connersville, Indiana_

Single } _Single_ 1st, 2nd or 3rd } _First_
Widow } marriage }
Divorced }

Name of Father _____ Hull

Maiden name of Mother _Mildred Camp_

Date of this marriage _April 8, 1944_

Place of this marriage _114 East 12th St. Connersville, Indiana_

Name and title of person
Performing this marriage _Joseph S. Moore, Minister_

His address _118 W. 11th Street_
_Connersville, Ind._

Witness { Name _M. Lair Hull_
{ Address _114 E 12th St. Connersville, Ind._

## Return this Report to County Clerk with License and Certificate

12

# Marriage Record for Board of Health

### To Be Returned by the Minister or Other Person Performing Ceremony

*George McKinney* and *Myrtle Martin*

Groom's name *George McKinney*

His age *48*

" color *W.*

" occupation *Polisher*

" Birthplace—City *Paris* State *Ill*

" Residence—Street No. *118 W. Walnut* City *Indianapolis*

Single
Widower *Widower*   1st, 2nd or 3rd marriage *2nd.*
Divorced

Name of Father *Jack McKinney*

Maiden name of Mother *Mahala Sanders*

Bride's name *Myrtle Martin*

Her age *44*

" color *W*

" occupation *Polisher*

" Birthplace—City *Williamsburg* State *Ind.*

" Residence—Street No. *2542 Foltz St.* City *Indianapolis*

Single
Widow *Single*   1st, 2nd or 3rd marriage *1st.*
Divorced

Name of Father *Louis Martin*

Maiden name of Mother *Martha Wilder*

Date of this marriage *Apr. 8, 1944*

Place of this marriage *Indianapolis, Ind.*

Name and title of person
Performing this marriage *Rev. Thomas Paino ordained*

His address *2114 Miller St., Indianapolis Ind.*

Witness { Name *Lyda Paino*
{ Address *2114 Miller St*

## Return this Report to County Clerk with License and Certificate

# Marriage Record for Board of Health

### To Be Returned by the Minister or Other Person Performing Ceremony

MILLARD F. HORTON, JR.     FILMORE     and    MARY ALICE SPARKS

Groom's name _____ MILLARD F. HORTON

His age _____ 23

" color _____ White

" occupation _____ Representative Carnation Milk Co.

" Birthplace—City Lexington _____ State __ Ky.

" Residence—Street No. 2848 W Penn St. _____ City _____ Evansville, Ind.

Single / Widower / Divorced } Single     { 1st, 2nd or 3rd marriage } 1st

Name of Father _____ MILLARD FILMORE HORTON, SR.

Maiden name of Mother _____ ADDIE _____ NORMAN

---

Bride's name _____ ~~MILLARD FILMORE HORTON, JR.~~     MARY ALICE SPARKS

Her age _____ 20

" color _____ White

" occupation _____ None

" Birthplace—City Indianapolis _____ State _____ Ind.

" Residence—Street No. 114 Kansas St. _____ City _____ Indianapolis, Ind.

Single / Widow / Divorced } Single     { 1st, 2nd or 3rd marriage } 1st

Name of Father _____ JOHN SPARKS

Maiden name of Mother _____ MARGARET PALM

---

Date of this marriage _____ April 8, 1944

Place of this marriage _____ Christ Episcopal Church, Monument Circle, Indianapolis, Ind.

Name and title of person Performing this marriage _____ *George Lowen* _____ Rector, Christ Episcopal Church, Indianapolis, Ind.

His address _____ 126 E. 43rd St.

_____ Indianapolis, Ind.

Witness { Name _____ Leona Hodge

{ Address _____ 2214 W Market St., Indianapolis, Ind.

## Return this Report to County Clerk with License and Certificate

13

# Marriage Record for Board of Health

### To Be Returned by the Minister or Other Person Performing Ceremony

Groom's name _Benjamin Crossley_ and _Lois Collier_

His age _24 yrs._

" color _White_

" occupation _Laborer_

" Birthplace—City _City_ State _____

" Residence—Street No. _1207 S. Dryer_ City _City_

Single Widower Divorced } _Single_ { 1st, 2nd or 3rd marriage } _____

Name of Father _Theo. J. Crossley_

Maiden name of Mother _Martha May Lipscomb_

Bride's name _____

Her age _20 yrs._

" color _White_

" occupation _R.C.A. Employee_

" Birthplace—City _City_ State _____

" Residence—Street No. _359 Sanders_ City _____

Single Widow Divorced } _Single_ { 1st, 2nd or 3rd marriage } _____

Name of Father _Clint Albert Collier_

Maiden name of Mother _Mary M. Ancell_

Date of this marriage _April 8, 1944_

Place of this marriage _Indianapolis, Ind._

Name and title of person Performing this marriage _Rev. John J. Williams_

His address _284 N. Elder_
_Indianapolis, Ind._

Witness { Name _Vera Ingram_
{ Address _814 N. Linwood_

## Return this Report to County Clerk with License and Certificate

# Marriage Record for Board of Health
### To Be Returned by the Minister or Other Person Performing Ceremony

Oren C Bridges _____ and _____ Clara Reily

Groom's name _____ Oren C Bridges

His age _____ 36

" color _____ White

" occupation _____ Farmer

" Birthplace—City _____ Greenfield _____ State _____ Indiana

" Residence—Street No. _____ RR #6 _____ City _____ Greenfield

Single / Widower / Divorced } _____ Single _____ { 1st, 2nd or 3rd marriage } _____ first

Name of Father _____ James E Bridges

Maiden name of Mother _____ Nova Belle Curry

---

Bride's name _____ Clara Reily

Her age _____ 40

" color _____ White

" occupation _____ office work

" Birthplace—City _____ Blakesburg _____ State _____ Iowa

" Residence—Street No. _____ 1315 N Hale _____ City _____ Indianapolis

Single / Widow / Divorced } _____ divorced _____ { 1st, 2nd or 3rd marriage } _____ second

Name of Father _____ Ernest Thompson

Maiden name of Mother _____ Clara Maude Anderson

---

Date of this marriage _____ April 8 1944

Place of this marriage _____ 547 N Beville Indianapolis Ind.

Name and title of person Performing this marriage _____ Rev Charles L Haney

His address _____ 523 N Beville Indianapolis Indiana

Witness { Name _____ Lulu E. Clark

{ Address _____ 1315 N. Oak St. Indianapolis, Indiana.

### Return this Report to County Clerk with License and Certificate

# Marriage Record for Board of Health

To Be Returned by the Minister or Other Person Performing Ceremony

*Andrew Murrain* and *Jessie E. Kennedy*

Groom's name _Andrew Murrain_

His age _48_

" color _white_

" occupation _Carpenter_

" Birthplace—City _Lynn County_ State _Mo_

" Residence—Street No. _1516 A Grant_ City _Joplin_

Single / Widower / Divorced } _Widower_ { 1st, 2nd or 3rd marriage } _2nd_

Name of Father _William Henry Murrain_

Maiden name of Mother _Rose Barnes_

Bride's name _Jessie E. Kennedy_

Her age _47_

" color _white_

" occupation _Factory Worker_

" Birthplace—City _Clay County_ State _Kentucky_

" Residence—Street No. _Clinton_ City _Oklahoma_

Single / Widow / Divorced } _Divorced_ { 1st, 2nd or 3rd marriage } _3rd_

Name of Father _Alonzo D. Kennedy_

Maiden name of Mother _Elizabeth Delph_

Date of this marriage _April 8 - 44_

Place of this marriage _Joplin, Mo._

Name and title of person Performing this marriage _Ernest T Lane, J.P._

His address _152½ E Court_

Witness { Name _Mary J Lane_ { Address _2741 Oliege Ave_

## Return this Report to County Clerk with License and Certificate

# Marriage Record for Board of Health
### To Be Returned by the Minister or Other Person Performing Ceremony

*William E. Ellis* and *Julia L. Ridenour*

Groom's name *William E. Ellis*

His age 23

" color White

" occupation Painter

" Birthplace—City _____ State Ind.

" Residence—Street No. 40 N. _____ City _____

Single / Widower / Divorced } Divorced { 1st, 2nd or 3rd marriage } 2nd

Name of Father Everett L. Ellis

Maiden name of Mother Ruby Mae Brown

Bride's name Julia L. Ridenour

Her age 22

" color White

" occupation Housekeeper

" Birthplace—City La Follette State Tenn.

" Residence—Street No. 41 N. Bentley City _____

Single / Widow / Divorced } Single { 1st, 2nd or 3rd marriage } 1st

Name of Father Jordan Herman Ridenour

Maiden name of Mother Elizabeth Mae Landman

Date of this marriage April 8-44

Place of this marriage _____ Ind.

Name and title of person Performing this marriage _____ J P

His address 158½ E Court

Witness { Name Paul Ellis
{ Address 41 N. Bentley

### Return this Report to County Clerk with License and Certificate

## Marriage Record for Board of Health

To Be Returned by the Minister or Other Person Performing Ceremony

_Harry H Pierce_ and _Vera H Trissal_

Groom's name _Harry H Pierce_

His age _52_

" color _white_

" occupation _Roofing_

" Birthplace—City _Adam/ Co_ State _Iowa_

" Residence—Street No. _5730 Northwestern_ City _Indianapolis_

Single / Widower / Divorced } _Divorced_ { 1st, 2nd or 3rd marriage } _2 nd_

Name of Father _Bert E. Pierce_

Maiden name of Mother _Carrie Morrison_

Bride's name _Vera H Trissal_

Her age _28_

" color _white_

" occupation _Inspector_

" Birthplace—City _Indianapolis_ State _Indiana_

" Residence—Street No. _2151 N. Delaware_ City _Indianapolis_

Single / Widow / Divorced } _Single_ { 1st, 2nd or 3rd marriage } _1st_

Name of Father _Roland Trissal_

Maiden name of Mother _Mae Ingram_

Date of this marriage _April 8, 1944_

Place of this marriage _Indianapolis Ind_

Name and title of person Performing this marriage _Ernest Law Justice of Peace_

His address _152½ East County Bld_

Witness { Name _Mary Jo Lane_ { Address _3741 College Ave_

## Return this Report to County Clerk with License and Certificate

# Marriage Record for Board of Health

### To Be Returned by the Minister or Other Person Performing Ceremony

Henry A. Rager and Eleanor J. Easter

Groom's name _Henry A. Rager_

His age _21_

" color _white_

" occupation _Clerk_

" Birthplace—City _Pitcairn_ State _Pennsylvania_

" Residence—Street No. _2206 Sloan Ave_ City _Norwood, Ohio_

Single / Widower / Divorced } _Single_ { 1st, 2nd or 3rd marriage } _1st_

Name of Father _George W. Rager_

Maiden name of Mother _Rose M. Sang_

Bride's name _Eleanor J. Easter_

Her age _19_

" color _white_

" occupation _Typist Clerk_

" Birthplace—City _Cincinnati_ State _Ohio_

" Residence—Street No. _2206 Sloan Ave_ City _Norwood, Ohio_

Single / Widow / Divorced } _Single_ { 1st, 2nd or 3rd marriage } _1st_

Name of Father _Paul Wesley Easter_

Maiden name of Mother _Florence Maria Ferguson_

Date of this marriage _April 8 - 44_

Place of this marriage _Norwood, Ohio_

Name and title of person Performing this marriage _Ernest H. Lane, Justice of Peace_

His address _1542 E Court_

Witness { Name _Mary Jo Lane_

{ Address

### Return this Report to County Clerk with License and Certificate

# Marriage Record for Board of Health

## To Be Returned by the Minister or Other Person Performing Ceremony

Joseph R. Mendenhall and Lila Faulkner

Groom's name _Joseph R. Mendenhall_

His age _60_

" color _white_

" occupation _Carpenter_

" Birthplace—City _Randolph County Indiana_

" Residence—Street No. _Muncie_ City _Ind. R R # 1_

Single }
Widower } _Divorced_ { 1st, 2nd or 3rd marriage } _4th_
Divorced }

Name of Father _John M. Mendenhall_

Maiden name of Mother _Mary A. McGuire_

Bride's name _Lila Faulkner_

Her age _66_

" color _white_

" occupation _none_

" Birthplace—City _Lawrence County_ State _Illinois_

" Residence—Street No. _17 N. Gray_ City _Indpls_

Single }
Widow } _Widow_ { 1st, 2nd or 3rd marriage } _3rd_
Divorced }

Name of Father _Henry Meadows_

Maiden name of Mother _Amanda Todd_

Date of this marriage _April 8 - 44_

Place of this marriage _Indpls Ind_

Name and title of person Performing this marriage _Robert T. Paine Justice of Peace_

His address _153½ E Court St_

Witness { Name _Vernice Turner_
{ Address _17 N. Gray_

## Return this Report to County Clerk with License and Certificate

12

# Marriage Record for Board of Health

### To Be Returned by the Minister or Other Person Performing Ceremony

*Robert G. Wilder* and *Alma Darleen Douglass*

Groom's name _____ *Robert G. Wilder* _____

His age _____ 19 _____

" color _____ *white* _____

" occupation _____ *U. S. Army* _____

" Birthplace—City _____ *Wadsworth* _____ State _____ *___* _____

" Residence—Street No. _____ *Ft. Harrison* _____ City _____ *___* _____

Single
Widower
Divorced } _____ { 1st, 2nd or 3rd marriage } _____

Name of Father _____ *Paul D. Wilder* _____

Maiden name of Mother _____ *Rhea Ryan* _____

Bride's name _____ *Alma Darleen Douglass* _____

Her age _____ 19 _____

" color _____ *white* _____

" occupation _____ *Secretary* _____

" Birthplace—City _____ *St. Louis* _____ State _____ *Mo.* _____

" Residence—Street No. _____ *32 Constance Ave,* _____ City _____ *Dayton, O.* _____

Single
Widow
Divorced } _____ { 1st, 2nd or 3rd marriage } _____

Name of Father _____ *Leonard Belmont Douglass* _____

Maiden name of Mother _____ *Alma Favrite Davis* _____

Date of this marriage _____ *___* _____

Place of this marriage _____ *___* _____

Name and title of person
Performing this marriage _____ *___* _____

His address _____ *3652 W. Delaware St.* _____
_____ *___* _____

Witness { Name _____ *Leonard B Douglass* _____
{ Address _____ *32 Constance Ave Dayton ohio* _____

### Return this Report to County Clerk with License and Certificate

# Marriage Record for Board of Health
## To Be Returned by the Minister or Other Person Performing Ceremony

_____ Dowell _____ and _____ Kingrey _____

Groom's name __ DOWELL — Johnie WaLTER __

His age __38__ (oct. 6)

" color __white__

" occupation __Van Camp Packing Co.__

" Birthplace—City __Metcalf__ State __Ky__

" Residence—Street No. __331 E. 10th__ City _____

Single / Widower / Divorced } __Single__   { 1st, 2nd or 3rd marriage } __1st__

Name of Father __Charlie Dowell__

Maiden name of Mother __Susan Kinser__

Bride's name __Kingrey — Myrtle__

Her age __23__ (mch. 2)

" color __white__

" occupation __Van Camp Packing Co.__

" Birthplace—City __Tallcottville__ State __Ky__

" Residence—Street No. __646 S. meridian__ City _____

Single / Widow / Divorced } __Single__   { 1st, 2nd or 3rd marriage } __1st__

Name of Father __Lee Kingrey__

Maiden name of Mother __Lovell Parsley__

Date of this marriage __April 8, 1944__

Place of this marriage __Indianapolis__

Name and title of person Performing this marriage __Sappleton W. Atwater__

His address __First Baptist Church__

Witness { Name __mr. and mrs. arthur Ewing__

{ Address __3706 English av__

## Return this Report to County Clerk with License and Certificate

# Marriage Record for Board of Health
### To Be Returned by the Minister or Other Person Performing Ceremony

Donald M. Weathers and Mary Jane Cass

Groom's name _Donald M. Weathers_

His age _20_

" color _White_

" occupation _U.S.N - Pilot_

" Birthplace—City _Salem_ State _Indiana_

" Residence—Street No. _USNTS - Great Lakes_ City _Illinois_

Single / Widower / Divorced } _Single_ { 1st, 2nd or 3rd marriage } _First_

Name of Father _Roland C. Weathers_

Maiden name of Mother _Geneva Madge Slagley_

Bride's name _Mary Jane Cass_

Her age _19_

" color _White_

" occupation _House Keeping_

" Birthplace—City _Indianapolis_ State _Indiana_

" Residence—Street No. _26 So. Arlington_ City _Indianapolis, Ind_

Single / Widow / Divorced } _Single_ { 1st, 2nd or 3rd marriage } _First_

Name of Father _Geo. N. Cass_

Maiden name of Mother _Betsy Jane McCray_

Date of this marriage _April 8, 1944_

Place of this marriage _Emmerson Avenue Baptist Church, Indianapolis_

Name and title of person Performing this marriage _Rev Earl W. Johnston_

His address _911 High St._
_Logansport, Indiana_

Witness { Name _George N Cass_ | _Roland C Weathers_
{ Address _26 So Arlington_ | _Salem Ind_
_Indianapolis, Ind_

## Return this Report to County Clerk with License and Certificate

# Marriage Record for Board of Health

### To Be Returned by the Minister or Other Person Performing Ceremony

_George Garrison_ and _Lula Schneider_

Groom's Name _George Garrison_

His age _64_

" color _White_

" occupation _Janitor_

" Birthplace—City _Shelby County_ State _Indiana_

" Residence—Street No. _1127 Jackson_ City _Columbus, Ind._

Single
Widower } _Widower_ { 1st, 2nd or 3rd marriage } _2nd_
Divorced

Name of Father _Oliver Garrison_

Maiden name of Mother _Cassie Fleming_

Bride's name _Lula Schneider_

Her age _38_

" color _White_

" occupation _Defense Worker_

" Birthplace—City _Columbus_ State _Indiana_

" Residence—Street No. _1127 Jackson_ City _Columbus, Ind._

Single
Widow } _Single_ { 1st, 2nd or 3rd marriage } _1st_
Divorced

Name of Father _Louis Schneider_

Maiden name of Mother _Maggie Meckley_

Date of this marriage _April 3-44_

Place of this marriage _Gnpls, Ind._

Name and title of person
Performing this marriage _Ora H. Kern, Justice of Peace_

His address _152½ E Court Av._

Witness { Name _Mary Jo Lane_
{ Address _3741 College Ave_

### Return this Report to County Clerk with License and Certificate

# Marriage Record for Board of Health

To Be Returned by the Minister or Other Person Performing Ceremony

*Chester K. Olszewski* and *Ruth Bolton*

Groom's name _Chester K Olszewski_

His age _21_

" color _white_

" occupation _Soldier_

" Birthplace—City _Chelsie_ State _Mass_

" Residence—Street No. _Atterbury_ City _Indpls_

Single Widower Divorced _Single_ — 1st, 2nd or 3rd marriage _1st_

Name of Father _Henry Olszewski_

Maiden name of Mother _____

Bride's name _Ruth Bolton_

Her age _19_

" color _white_

" occupation _Defense worker_

" Birthplace—City _Laurel Co_ State _Kentucky_

" Residence—Street No. _320 E North_ City _Indianapolis_

Single Widow Divorced _Single_ — 1st, 2nd or 3rd marriage _1st_

Name of Father _Noah Bolton_

Maiden name of Mother _Ethel Jones_

Date of this marriage _April 8, 1944_

Place of this marriage _Indianapolis, Ind_

Name and title of person Performing this marriage _Ernest Lane Justice of Peace_

His address _152½ East Church_

Witness { Name _Mary Jo Lane_
{ Address _3744 College Ave_

Return this Report to County Clerk with License and Certificate

# Marriage Record for Board of Health

## To Be Returned by the Minister or Other Person Performing Ceremony

*Arthur Dexter Garriott* and *Christine Smith*

Groom's name _Arthur D. Garriott_

His age _30_

" color _white_

" occupation _~~Chauffeur~~ prospector_

" Birthplace—City _Little York_ State _Indiana_

" Residence—Street No. _1235 State_ City _Indianapolis_

~~Single~~
~~Widower~~
Divorced } ————— { 1st, 2nd or 3rd marriage } _second_

Name of Father _Dexter Garriott_

Maiden name of Mother _Christa Rosezella Young_

Bride's name _Christine Smith_

Her age _20_

" color _White_

" occupation _____

" Birthplace—City _Liberty_ State _Kentucky_

" Residence—Street No. _2317 Kentucky_ City _Indianapolis_

Single
~~Widow~~
~~Divorced~~ } { 1st, ~~2nd or 3rd~~ marriage }

Name of Father _Elmer Smith_

Maiden name of Mother _Ruby Myrtle Wilkinson_

Date of this marriage _April 8 1944_

Place of this marriage _Greenwood_

Name and title of person
Performing this marriage _D D Dorrell Justice of the Peace_

His address _Greenwood Indiana_

Witness { Name _Orville Carter 111 East Walnut St._
{ Address _Ruth Ashmore 3312 S Tacoma._

## Return this Report to County Clerk with License and Certificate

12

# Marriage Record for Board of Health

To Be Returned by the Minister or Other Person Performing Ceremony

Omer Huel Bennett _and_ Roberta Isabell Thomas

Groom's name __Omer Huel Bennett__

His age __28__

" color __White__

" occupation __Soldier__

" Birthplace—City __Russell Springs__ State __Kentucky__

" Residence—Street No. __Camp Robinson__ City __Arkansas__

Single } __Single__ { 1st, 2nd or 3rd } __1st__
Widower
Divorced marriage

Name of Father __William Thomas Bennett__

Maiden name of Mother __Lizzie Pearl Farter__

Bride's name __Roberta Isabell Thomas__

Her age __28__

" color __White__

" occupation __Clerk__

" Birthplace—City __Waverly__ State __Kentucky__

" Residence—Street No. __928 Woodlawn__ City __Indianapolis, Ind.__

Single } __Single__ { 1st, 2nd or 3rd } __1st__
Widow
Divorced marriage

Name of Father __Otto Fredick Martin Thomas__

Maiden name of Mother __Mary Geneive Clark__

Date of this marriage __April 8 — 1944__

Place of this marriage __928 Woodlawn Ave. Indianapolis, Ind.__

Name and title of person
Performing this marriage __Rev. Russell L. Menges (Minister)__

His address __1040 Wright St. Indianapolis Indiana__

Witness { Name __Mrs Florence Webb — David R. Webb__
{ Address __928 Woodlawn ave.__

## Return this Report to County Clerk with License and Certificate

12

# Marriage Record for Board of Health

### To Be Returned by the Minister or Other Person Performing Ceremony

_Gomer Justice_ and _Christine Huffaker_

Groom's name _Gomer Justice_

His age _26_

" color _White_

" occupation _Defense work_

" Birthplace—City _Edo Ky._ State _Ky_

" Residence—Street No. _20 W 22nd_ City _Indianapolis_

Single Widower Divorced } _Single_    { 1st, 2nd or 3rd, marriage } _yes_

Name of Father _John Justice_

Maiden name of Mother _Annie Hunt_

Bride's name _Christine Huffaker_

Her age _18 yrs_

" color _White_

" occupation _Defense work_

" Birthplace—City _Monticello_ State _Ky_

" Residence—Street No. _630 No Park_ City _Indianapolis_

Single Widow Divorced } _Single_    { 1st, 2nd or 3rd marriage } _yes_

Name of Father _Elder ezer Huffaker_

Maiden name of Mother _Ruth Adair_

Date of this marriage _April 8th 1944_

Place of this marriage _Indianapolis Ind_

Name and title of person Performing this marriage _Wm R Ellington Justice the Peace_

His address _Southport Ind_

Witness { Name _Lola Justice_    { Address _20 W 22 St_

### Return this Report to County Clerk with License and Certificate

# Marriage Record for Board of Health

### To Be Returned by the Minister or Other Person Performing Ceremony

_____ and _____

Groom's name _William A Simcox Jr._

His age _22_

" color _White_

" occupation _Aviation Cadet_

" Birthplace—City _Portland_ State _Oregon_

" Residence—Street No. _Butler Univ_ City _Indianapolis_

Single Widower Divorced } _Single_ { 1st, 2nd or 3rd marriage } _First_

Name of Father _Wm. A Simcox_

Maiden name of Mother _Madge Duella Tuttle_

Bride's name _Mary Rose Heizinger_

Her age _21_

" color _White_

" occupation _Key Punch Operator_

" Birthplace—City _Indianapolis_ State _Indiana_

" Residence—Street No. _2441 Pierson_ Apartment City _Indianapolis_

Single Widow Divorced } _Single_ { 1st, 2nd or 3rd marriage } _First_

Name of Father _Harry John Heizinger_

Maiden name of Mother _Mary Rose Parker_

Date of this marriage _April 8 - 1944_

Place of this marriage _Indianapolis, Indiana_

Name and title of person Performing this marriage _Rev J. N. Greene_

His address _1841 Cross Drive Woodruff Place Indianapolis, Indiana_

Witness { Name _William Bry T_ Address _3303 - 9th Des Moines, Iowa_

## Return this Report to County Clerk with License and Certificate

12

# Marriage Record for Board of Health
### To Be Returned by the Minister or Other Person Performing Ceremony

_William H. Hardin_ and _Miss Audria Suggs_

Groom's name _William H. Hardin_

His age _28 years_

" color _Brown_

" occupation _Soldier_

" Birthplace—City _Nashville_ State _Tenn._

" Residence—Street No. _1725 Martindale_ City _Indianapolis_

~~Single~~ ~~Widower~~ ~~Divorced~~ } _Single_ { 1st, ~~2nd or 3rd~~ marriage } _First_

Name of Father _Alfred Dews Hardin_

Maiden name of Mother _Jennie Oakley_

Bride's name _Miss Audria Suggs_

Her age _28 years_

" color _Brown_

" occupation _Substitute Teacher_

" Birthplace—City _Dixon_ State _Tenn._

" Residence—Street No. _1725 Martindale_ City _Indianapolis, Ind._

~~Single~~ ~~Widow~~ ~~Divorced~~ } _Single_ { 1st, ~~2nd or 3rd~~ marriage } _First_

Name of Father _John Suggs_

Maiden name of Mother _Miss Eua Cunningham_

Date of this marriage _April 8th 1944_

Place of this marriage _Indianapolis, Indiana_

Name and title of person Performing this marriage _Rev. S. R. Jenkins_

His address _2026 Bluff Pl. Indianapolis_

Witness { Name _Charles L. Goodman_ Address _729 Roache Street_

### Return this Report to County Clerk with License and Certificate

# Marriage Record for Board of Health

### To Be Returned by the Minister or Other Person Performing Ceremony

_Dwight G Campbell_ and _Ruby M Past_

Groom's name _Dwight G Campbell_

His age _22_

" color _white_

" occupation _Student_

" Birthplace—City _Buckingham_ State _Ohio_

" Residence—Street No. _Columbus_ City _Ohio_
_332 no warren_

Single / Widower / Divorced } _Single_ { 1st, 2nd or 3rd marriage } _1st_

Name of Father _Dwight T Campbell_

Maiden name of Mother _Emma Goodman_

Bride's name _Ruby M Past_

Her age _24_

" color _white_

" occupation _Stena_

" Birthplace—City _Belfountain_ State _Ohio_

" Residence—Street No. _Columbus_ City _Ohio_
_34 no warren_

Single / Widow / Divorced } _Single_ { 1st, 2nd or 3rd marriage } _1st_

Name of Father _Geo Past_

Maiden name of Mother _Mary Swarty_

Date of this marriage _April 8 1940_

Place of this marriage _Minister L Indianapolis_

Name and title of person Performing this marriage _Minister Sumner L Martin_

His address _6234 Haverford ave._
_Indianapolis Ind_

Witness { Name _Mrs S L Martin_
{ Address _6234 Haverford ave Indianapolis, Ind_

## Return this Report to County Clerk with License and Certificate

# Marriage Record for Board of Health
### To Be Returned by the Minister or Other Person Performing Ceremony

_____ Scott _____ and _____ Harrell _____

Groom's name _____ Albert C. Scott _____

His age _____ 25 _____

" color _____ White _____

" occupation _____ Allison Employee _____

" Birthplace—City _____ Indianapolis _____ State _____ Indiana _____

" Residence—Street No. 3427½ Col. City _____ Indianapolis _____

Single
Widower } _____ Divorced _____  { 1st, 2nd or 3rd marriage } _____ Second _____
Divorced

Name of Father _____ Albert E. Scott _____

Maiden name of Mother _____ Florence E. Hood _____

Bride's name _____ Pauline M. Harrell _____

Her age _____ 21 _____

" color _____ White _____

" occupation _____ Allison Employee _____

" Birthplace—City _____ Shelby County _____ State _____ Indiana _____

" Residence—Street No. 3442 N. Rural City _____ Indianapolis _____

Single
Widow } _____ Single _____  { 1st, 2nd or 3rd marriage } _____ First _____
Divorced

Name of Father _____ Herbert Harrell _____

Maiden name of Mother _____ Ruth Ann Scott _____

Date of this marriage _____ April 2, 1938 _____

Place of this marriage _____ Third Christian Church, Indianapolis _____

Name and title of person
Performing this marriage _____ C. C. Connolly, Minister _____

His address _____ 3853 Washington Blvd. _____
_____ Indianapolis, Indiana _____

Witness { Name _____
{ Address _____

## Return this Report to County Clerk with License and Certificate

# Marriage Record for Board of Health

### To Be Returned by the Minister or Other Person Performing Ceremony

Paul R. Mason _and_ Helen Johnson

Groom's name _Paul R. Mason_

His age _23_

" color _Negro_

" occupation _Soldier_

" Birthplace—City _Indianapolis_ State _Indiana_

" Residence—Street No. _Camp Plasbue_ City _La_

Single
Widower } _Single_  { 1st, 2nd or 3rd } _First._
Divorced      { marriage

Name of Father _John Mason_

Maiden name of Mother _Evangeline Milton_

Bride's name _Helen Johnson_

Her age _18_

" color _Negro_

" occupation _Housewife_

" Birthplace—City _Indianapolis_ State _Indiana_

" Residence—Street No. _924½ N 11th_ City _Indianapolis_

Single
Widow } _Single_  { 1st, 2nd or 3rd } _First_
Divorced      { marriage

Name of Father _Ausberry Johnson_

Maiden name of Mother _Anna Belle Alexander_

Date of this marriage _April 8, 1944_

Place of this marriage _Indianapolis Ind._

Name and title of person
Performing this marriage _S.S. Thomas, Minister_

His address _702 S. Illinois_

Witness { Name _Arlee F Brand_
        { Address _2336 Indianapolis Ind._

## Return this Report to County Clerk with License and Certificate

12

# Marriage Record for Board of Health
## To Be Returned by the Minister or Other Person Performing Ceremony

Joseph Waltham and Edna M Maypreather

Groom's name ___ Joseph Waltham

His age ___ 29

" color ___ Colored.

" occupation ___ Soldier.

" Birthplace—City ___ State ___ Georgia

" Residence—Street No. ___ Army ___ City ___

Single / Widower / Divorced } ___ First time ___ 1st, 2nd or 3rd marriage ___ First

Name of Father ___ Walter Waltham

Maiden name of Mother ___ Susan Easeling

Bride's name ___ Edna M Maypreather

Her age ___ 32

" color ___ Colored.

" occupation ___

" Birthplace—City ___ State ___ Tennessee

" Residence—Street No. ___ 640 W North St ___ City ___ Indianapolis

Single / Widow / Divorced } ___ Divorced ___ 1st, 2nd or 3rd marriage } ___ Second

Name of Father ___ Charles Moore

Maiden name of Mother ___ Susie Munns

Date of this marriage ___ April 8 1944

Place of this marriage ___ Indianapolis Ind,

Name and title of person Performing this marriage ___ Rev J L Highness

His address ___ 433 N California St Indianapolis Ind

Witness { Name ___ Susie Anderson { Address ___ 111 Douglas St

## Return this Report to County Clerk with License and Certificate

12

# Marriage Record for Board of Health

### To Be Returned by the Minister or Other Person Performing Ceremony

*Harold B James* and *K. Jean Newby*

Groom's name _Harold B James_

His age _28_

" color _white_

" occupation _Clerk_

" Birthplace—City _Indianapolis_ State _Indiana_

" Residence—Street No. _1408 N. Keal_ City _Indianapolis_

Single / Widower / Divorced } _Single_   { 1st, 2nd or 3rd marriage } _First_

Name of Father _Orville P. James_

Maiden name of Mother _Marie L. Thurneman_

Bride's name _K Jean Newby_

Her age _21_

" color _white_

" occupation _housewife_

" Birthplace—City _Hamilton_ State _Indiana_

" Residence—Street No. _205 E 34th_ City _Indianapolis_

Single / Widow / Divorced } _Single_   { 1st, 2nd or 3rd marriage } _First_

Name of Father _Burton J Newby_

Maiden name of Mother _Nina Gladys Cox_

Date of this marriage _April — 8 — 1944_

Place of this marriage _11th & 2nd St. Indianapolis_

Name and title of person Performing this marriage _Rev David S McNelly_

His address _3105 E. 11th St_
_Indianapolis —_

Witness { Name _Jane H Pinkney_
{ Address _956 N. Hawthorne Lane_

## Return this Report to County Clerk with License and Certificate

# Marriage Record for Board of Health
## To Be Returned by the Minister or Other Person Performing Ceremony

Henry H. Lynch and Esther E. Hubbard

Groom's name _Henry H. Lynch_

His age _58_

" color _Colored_

" occupation _Blacksmith_

" Birthplace—City _Ashville_ State _N.C._

" Residence—Street No. _Danville_ City _Ind_

Single Widower Divorced } _widower_ { 1st, 2nd or 3rd marriage } _2_

Name of Father _William Lynch_

Maiden name of Mother _Callie Burgett_

Bride's name _Esther E. Hubbard_

Her age _25_

" color _Colored_

" occupation _Housewife_

" Birthplace—City _Guthrie_ State _Ky_

" Residence—Street No. _2060 Martindale_ City _Ind_

Single Widow Divorced } _widow_ { 1st, 2nd or 3rd marriage } _2_

Name of Father _Erwin Hatcher_

Maiden name of Mother _Mary Burse_

Date of this marriage _April 8 – 1944_

Place of this marriage _Indianapolis_

Name and title of person Performing this marriage _George Baltimore, minister._

His address _3053 Station St, Indpls, Ind_

Witness { Name _Mary Hatcher_
         { Address _2047 Columbia ave_

## Return this Report to County Clerk with License and Certificate

# Marriage Record for Board of Health

### To Be Returned by the Minister or Other Person Performing Ceremony

Donald Evans Spangler _and_ Ethel Audrey Smith

Groom's name _Donald Evans Spangler_

His age _23_

" color _white_

" occupation _U S Marine Corps_

" Birthplace—City _Cataract_ State _Indiana_

" Residence—Street No. _U.S. Marines_ City

Single
Widower
Divorced } _Single_ { 1st, 2nd or 3rd marriage } _First_

Name of Father _Forrest Alden Spangler_

Maiden name of Mother _Jewel McKinley Evans_

Bride's name _Ethel Audrey Smith_

Her age _23_

" color _white_

" occupation _Teacher_

" Birthplace—City _McLeansboro_ State _Ill._

" Residence—Street No. _Dublin Ind._

Single
Widow
Divorced } _Single_ { 1st, 2nd or 3rd marriage } _First_

Name of Father _Lawrence Smith_

Maiden name of Mother _Maggie Elizabeth Hardin_

Date of this marriage _April 8th 1944_

Place of this marriage _East Park Methodist Parsonage_

Name and title of person Performing this marriage _Rev Golden G. Smith_

His address _7609 East New York St._
_Indianapolis 1, Ind._

Witness { Name _John M. Johnson_
{ Address _Indianapolis Ind._

## Return this Report to County Clerk with License and Certificate

12

# Marriage Record for Board of Health
### To Be Returned by the Minister or Other Person Performing Ceremony

_Donald Mattingly_ and _Loraine Hott_

Groom's name _Donald_

His age _20_

" color _White_

" occupation _Machinist_

" Birthplace—City _Indianapolis_ State _Ind_

" Residence—Street No. _314 Easton_ City _Indianapolis_

Single ~~Widower~~ Divorced } _Single_ { 1st, ~~2nd or 3rd~~ marriage } _1st_

Name of Father _Nicholas Chas_

Maiden name of Mother _Josphine Patterson_

Bride's name _Loraine Hott_

Her age _19_

" color _White_

" occupation _Sales-girl_

" Birthplace—City _Indianapolis_ State _Ind_

" Residence—Street No. _320 Easton_ City _Indianapolis_

Single ~~Widow Divorced~~ } _Single_ { 1st, 2nd or 3rd marriage } _1st_

Name of Father _Carmen Hott_

Maiden name of Mother _Rose La Mar_

Date of this marriage _April 8, 1944_

Place of this marriage _550 N Rural St Indianapolis Ind_

Name and title of person Performing this marriage _Wiley Mercy - Cath Priest_

His address _550 N Rural St_
_Indianapolis Ind_

Witness { Name _Ralph Mattingly - 1214 S. Ohio_
Address _Helen Mattingly - 314 Easton Ave_

### Return this Report to County Clerk with License and Certificate

# Marriage Record for Board of Health
## To Be Returned by the Minister or Other Person Performing Ceremony

_George R Soder_ and _Velma Stewart_

Groom's name _George R Soder_

His age _28_

" color _White_

" occupation _U. S. Army_

" Birthplace—City _Lock Haven_ State _Pennsylvania_

" Residence—Street No. _Fort Henison_ City _Ft. Henison_

Single / Widower / Divorced } _Divorced_    { 1st, 2nd or 3rd marriage } _2nd_

Name of Father _Roy A Soder_

Maiden name of Mother _Charlotta C. Wolfe Solfe_

Bride's name _Velma Stewart_

Her age _25_

" color _White_

" occupation _Steno_

" Birthplace—City _Cynthiana_ State _Ind._

" Residence—Street No. _57 N 9th_ City _Beech Grove_

Single / Widow / Divorced } _Single_    { 1st, 2nd or 3rd marriage } _1st_

Name of Father _Roland L. Stewart_

Maiden name of Mother _Faye McElroy_

Date of this marriage _April 8, 1944_

Place of this marriage _Beech Grove, Indiana_

Name and title of person Performing this marriage _Rev. Kenneth D. Vanderenter_

His address _91 South 9th Ave._
_Beech Grove Ind_

Witness { Name _Mr. + Mrs. Roland Stewart_
{ Address _57 N 9th Ave, Beech Grove, Ind._

## Return this Report to County Clerk with License and Certificate

# Marriage Record for Board of Health

### To Be Returned by the Minister or Other Person Performing Ceremony

Charles C. Hobby                    and    Vivian E. Wade

Groom's name _____ Charles C. Hobby _____

His age _____ 21 _____

" color _____ White _____

" occupation _____ Rock Wool Paper Pully _____

" Birthplace—City _____ Portland _____ State _____ Tennessee _____

" Residence—Street No. _____ 143 N. Highland _____ City _____ Indianapolis, Ind _____

Single
Widower    } _____ Single _____    { 1st, 2nd or 3rd    } _____ First _____
Divorced                                  marriage

Name of Father _____ Charles F. Hobby _____

Maiden name of Mother _____ Dosa B. Drumm _____

Bride's name _____ Vivian E. Wade _____

Her age _____ 19 _____

" color _____ White _____

" occupation _____ Central States _____

" Birthplace—City _____ Turnersville _____ State _____ Kentucky _____

" Residence—Street No. _____ 20½ Main St _____ City _____ Beech Grove, Ind _____

Single
Widow    } _____ Single _____    { 1st, 2nd or 3rd    } _____ First _____
Divorced                                marriage

Name of Father _____ Clifton Wade _____

Maiden name of Mother _____ Ina B. Douglas _____

Date of this marriage _____ April 8, 1944 _____

Place of this marriage _____ City Hall Beech Grove Ind _____

Name and title of person
Performing this marriage _____ E. Allen Kunter Mayor _____

His address _____ City Hall Beech Grove Ind _____

Witness { Name _____ Frossia McLuiston 143 N. Highland Indpls Ind
         { Address _____ Owen Hazlette 143 N. Highland Indpls Ind

### Return this Report to County Clerk with License and Certificate

12

# Marriage Record for Board of Health

### To Be Returned by the Minister or Other Person Performing Ceremony

Ralph Hall and Georgia Sawyer

Groom's name Ralph Hall

His age 21

" color white

" occupation U. S. N.

" Birthplace—City Indianapolis State Indiana

" Residence—Street No. R R 1 Box 417A City Bridgeport

Single Widower Divorced } Single { 1st, 2nd or 3rd marriage }

Name of Father Herbert Hall

Maiden name of Mother Lottie I Fidler

Bride's name Georgia Sawyer

Her age 17

" color white

" occupation Waitress

" Birthplace—City Brazil State Indiana

" Residence—Street No. 403 W. Knight St City Brazil

Single Widow Divorced } Single { 1st, 2nd or 3rd marriage }

Name of Father Bernice Sawyer

Maiden name of Mother Louise Brockmeier

Date of this marriage April 8th 1944

Place of this marriage 62 Berwick ave

Name and title of person Performing this marriage Rev. Charles Buckrof

His address 43 S Harris ave

Witness { Name Mrs Lottie I Hall.
{ Address R.R.1.Box.417a. Bridgeport Ind.

## Return this Report to County Clerk with License and Certificate

12

# Marriage Record for Board of Health
### To Be Returned by the Minister or Other Person Performing Ceremony

James E. Martin and Georgia Lee Osthof

Groom's name _James E. Martin_

His age _20_

" color _White_

" occupation _U.S. Army_

" Birthplace—City _Covington_ State _Ind._

" Residence—Street No _411 Pleasant Run_ city _Indianapolis_

Single / Widower / Divorced } _Single_ { 1st, 2nd or 3rd marriage } _First_

Name of Father _James P. Martin_

Maiden name of Mother _Maude M. Lockhart_

Bride's name _Georgia Lee Osthof_

Her age _18_

" color _White_

" occupation _Secretary_

" Birthplace—City _St. Louis_ State _Mo._

" Residence—Street No _735 N. Emerson_ city _Indiana pls._

Single / Widow / Divorced } _Single_ { 1st, 2nd or 3rd marriage } _First_

Name of Father _Ambros L. Osthof_

Maiden name of Mother _Marjory L. Devore_

Date of this marriage _April 8, 1944_

Place of this marriage _Indianapolis Ind._ (_Taylor Hotel_)

Name and title of person Performing this marriage _B. R. Hamilton_ (_Minister_)

His address _73 N. Tenth Ave._

_Beech Grove Ind._

Witness { Name _Mrs. J. Edward Andrews_
{ Address _5740 E. Michigan St._

### Return this Report to County Clerk with License and Certificate

# Marriage Record for Board of Health

### To Be Returned by the Minister or Other Person Performing Ceremony

*Charles Bressler* and *Elizabeth P. Woolridge*

Groom's name _Charles Bressler_

His age _21_

" color _White_

" occupation _U. S. Army_

" Birthplace—City _Muir_, State _Penn._

" Residence—Street No. _908 Green St._ City _Harrisburg, Pa._

Single ~~Widower~~ ~~Divorced~~ } _Single_ { 1st, ~~2nd or 3rd~~ marriage } _1st._

Name of Father _Charles E. Bressler_

Maiden name of Mother _Katie Troutman_

Bride's name _Elizabeth P. Woolridge_

Her age _20_

" color _White_

" occupation _Secretary_

" Birthplace—City _Needham_ State _Ind._

" Residence—Street No. _516 E 31._ City _Indpls, Ind._

Single ~~Widow~~ ~~Divorced~~ } _Single_ { 1st, ~~2nd or 3rd~~ marriage } _1st_

Name of Father _Seymour Woolridge_

Maiden name of Mother _Flora Duncan_

Date of this marriage _April 8, 1944_

Place of this marriage _Lafayette, Ind._

Name and title of person Performing this marriage _Doyle Mullen, Minister_

His address _1130 State, Lafayette, Ind._

Witness { Name _Nona Horton_ Address _Mag Horton_ } _1105 South_ _Lafayette, Ind._

## Return this Report to County Clerk with License and Certificate

12

# Marriage Record for Board of Health
## To Be Returned by the Minister or Other Person Performing Ceremony

Reuben C. Ogden and Beverly Ann Taylor

Groom's name _Reuben C. Ogden_

His age _29_

" color _White_

" occupation _Record Clerk_

" Birthplace—City _Owenton_ State _Ky_

" Residence—Street No. _1262 S. High School Rd._, City _Indianapolis, Ind._

Single
Widower
Divorced

1st, 2nd or 3rd marriage

Name of Father _Guy Ogden_

Maiden name of Mother _Lela Lyon_

Bride's name _Beverly Ann Taylor_

Her age _19_

" color _White_

" occupation _Mail Clerk_

" Birthplace—City _Frankfort_ State _Ind._

" Residence—Street No. _914 W. Noble_ City _Lebanon, Ind._

Single
Widow
Divorced

1st, 2nd or 3rd marriage

Name of Father _Adron J. Taylor_

Maiden name of Mother _Maurine A. Foster_

Date of this marriage _Sat., April 8 - 44_

Place of this marriage _Indianapolis, Ind._

Name and title of person Performing this marriage _Rev. C. N. Schenck_

His address _5126 Chelsea Rd._
_Indianapolis, Ind._

Witness { Name _Karl Kent_
Address _2220 N. Meridian, Indpls., Ind._

## Return this Report to County Clerk with License and Certificate

12

# Marriage Record for Board of Health
### To Be Returned by the Minister or Other Person Performing Ceremony

_____Scott_____ and _____Pierce_____

Groom's name ___Sgt. Robert Scott___

His age ___30___

" color___White___

" occupation___United States Army___

" Birthplace—City___Philadelphia___ State ___Pennsylvania___

" Residence—Street No.___Stout Field___ City ___Indianapolis___

Single / Widower / Divorced } ___Single___ { 1st, 2nd or 3rd marriage } ___First___

Name of Father___Samuel Alvin Scott___

Maiden name of Mother___Bessie Mae Wilcutts___

Bride's name ___Elizabeth Jane Pierce___

Her age ___29___

" color___White___

" occupation___Bookkeeper___

" Birthplace—City___Indianapolis___ State ___Indiana___

" Residence—Street No.___1555 Carrollton___ City ___Indianapolis___

Single / Widow / Divorced } ___Single___ { 1st, 2nd or 3rd marriage } ___2nd (free)___

Name of Father___Robert Roy Wolfe___

Maiden name of Mother___Nellie Varin___

Date of this marriage___April 8, 1944    (11:30 A.M.)___

Place of this marriage___Parlor, Memorial Presbyterian Church___

Name and title of person Performing this marriage___Ralph L. O'Dell, Minister___

His address___4319 Carrollton Av., Indianapolis___

Witness { Name _Susan Hill_
{ Address _1507 E. Raymond St_

## Return this Report to County Clerk with License and Certificate

12

# Marriage Record for Board of Health

### To Be Returned by the Minister or Other Person Performing Ceremony

_____ and _____

Groom's name _George L. Swayze_

His age _19 years_

" color _White_

" occupation _Vibrator Adjuster P.R Mallory_

" Birthplace—City _Martin County_ State _Indiana_

" Residence—Street No. _927 N. Oakland_ City _Indianapolis_

Single
Widower } _Single_ {1st, 2nd or 3rd marriage} _First_
Divorced

Name of Father _Mr. Earl Walter Swayze_

Maiden name of Mother _Ruby Sheetze_

Bride's name _Mary Joan Stanley_

Her age _19 years_

" color _white_

" occupation _P.R. Mallory_

" Birthplace—City _Jamestown_ State _Indiana_

" Residence—Street No. _346 N. Jefferson_ City _Indianapolis_

Single
Widow } _Single_ {1st, 2nd or 3rd marriage} _First_
Divorced

Name of Father _Charles Alfred Stanley_

Maiden name of Mother _Hester Hermaine Ayers_

Date of this marriage _April 8, 1944_

Place of this marriage _First Trinity Lutheran Parsonage_

Name and title of person
Performing this marriage _A. Steensen, Lutheran Pastor_

His address _917 E. Orange Street,_
_Indianapolis, Indiana_

Witness { Name _Carl Swayze Ruby M. Swayze_
{ Address _927 N. Oakland_

### Return this Report to County Clerk with License and Certificate

# Marriage Record for Board of Health

### To Be Returned by the Minister or Other Person Performing Ceremony

*Earl Eugene Rutledge* and *Juanita B. Worthy*

Groom's name _Earl Eugene Rutledge_

His age _26_

" color _White_

" occupation _X ray Technician_

" Birthplace—City _Indianapolis_ State _Indiana_

" Residence—Street No. _425 Hill Road_ City _Indianapolis_

Single
Widower
Divorced } _Single_ {1st, 2nd or 3rd marriage} _1st_

Name of Father _Homer Rutledge_

Maiden name of Mother _Agnes Orissa Johnson_

Bride's name _Juanita L. Worthington_

Her age _20_

" color _White_

" occupation _Housewife_

" Birthplace—City _Indianapolis_ State _Indiana_

" Residence—Street No. _1344 Carlos_ City _Indianapolis_

Single
Widow
Divorced } _Single_ {1st, 2nd or 3rd marriage} _1st_

Name of Father _Myron William Worthington_

Maiden name of Mother _Nellie Ellsworth_

Date of this marriage _April 2, 1944_

Place of this marriage _Indianapolis, Ind._

Name and title of person
Performing this marriage _Rev. Edward L. Irwin_

His address _1926 S Talbott Ave_

_Indianapolis, Ind._

Witness { Name _Donald C. Gray 425 Hill Co._
         { Address

## Return this Report to County Clerk with License and Certificate

# Marriage Record for Board of Health

## To Be Returned by the Minister or Other Person Performing Ceremony

×  *Eddie Lee Allison*  and  ×  *Georgia E Rickman*

Groom's name _Eddie Lee Allison_

His age _19_

" color _White_

" occupation _U. S. Navy_

" Birthplace—City _Galeton_ State _Colorado_

" Residence—Street No _Naval Armory_ City _Indianapolis, Ind_

Single
Widower  } _Single_  { 1st, 2nd or 3rd marriage } _1st._
Divorced

Name of Father _Edgar C. Allison_

Maiden name of Mother _Lydia Jewell Nazarenus_

Bride's name _Georgia E Rickman_

Her age _18_

" color _white_

" occupation _Waitress_

" Birthplace—City _Ault_ State _Colorado_

" Residence—Street No. _641 Fort Wayne Ave_ City _Indianapolis, Ind._

Single
Widow  } _Single_  { 1st, 2nd or 3rd marriage } _1st._
Divorced

Name of Father _Jesse B. Rickman_

Maiden name of Mother _Anna Pearl Janey_

Date of this marriage _April 8 1944_

Place of this marriage _31st St. Baptist Church, Indianapolis_

Name and title of person
Performing this marriage _Rev. Robert D. McCarthy - Minister_

His address _711 W. 31st. Indianapolis 8_
_Indiana_

Witness { Name _Margaret Tucker_  _Edgar C Allison_
{ Address _718 W. 31st Indianapolis, Ind._  _Galeton Colo_

## Return this Report to County Clerk with License and Certificate

12

# Marriage Record for Board of Health
### To Be Returned by the Minister or Other Person Performing Ceremony

*Rose Holt* and *Anna Mary Jackson*

Groom's name _Rose Holt_

His age _29_

" color _Negro_

" occupation _Soldier_

" Birthplace—City _Nashville_ State _Tenn._

" Residence—Street No. _Houston_ City _Texas_

Single / Widower / Divorced } _X Divorced_ { 1st, 2nd or 3rd marriage } _Second_

Name of Father _Walter Holt_

Maiden name of Mother _Elizabeth Bostick_

Bride's name _Anna Mary Jackson_

Her age _27_

" color _Negro_

" occupation _Domestic Servant._

" Birthplace—City _Cedartown_ State _Georgia_

" Residence—Street No. _2134 Arsenal_ City _Indianapolis_

Single / Widow / Divorced } _Single_ { 1st, 2nd or 3rd marriage } _First_

Name of Father _Robert Jackson_

Maiden name of Mother _Mattie English_

Date of this marriage _April 8, 1944_

Place of this marriage _Indianapolis Ind._

Name and title of person Performing this marriage _S S Thomas, minister_

His address _702 S Illinois St._
_Indpls Ind._

Witness { Name _Alec Brand_
{ Address _2336 Indpls Ave._

### Return this Report to County Clerk with License and Certificate

# Marriage Record for Board of Health
## To Be Returned by the Minister or Other Person Performing Ceremony

_Sullivan_ and _Loeper_

Groom's name _Victor J. Sullivan_

His age _18_

" color _White_

" occupation _Sailor – Radio 3d Cl._

" Birthplace—City _Scranton_ State _Pennsylvania_

" Residence—Street No. _Naval Armory_ City _Indianapolis_

Single / Widower / Divorced } _Single_  { 1st, 2nd or 3rd marriage } _First_

Name of Father _Daniel Sullivan_

Maiden name of Mother _Mary Dorothy Fischer_

Bride's name _Lillian Loeper_

Her age _22_

" color _White_

" occupation _Sales Clerk_

" Birthplace—City _Indianapolis_ State _Indiana_

" Residence—Street No. _2620 Stanley_ City _Indianapolis_

Single / Widow / Divorced } _Single_  { 1st, 2nd or 3rd marriage } _First_

Name of Father _William Loeper_

Maiden name of Mother _Ruth Hensley_

Date of this marriage _April 8th, 1944._

Place of this marriage _1121 Linden St. Indianapolis_

Name and title of person Performing this marriage _R. H. Benting_

His address _1121 Linden Street Indianapolis Indiana_

Witness { Name _Virgil V. Taylor, Cuba,_
{ Address _Sue Thompson, 1305 W. 19th St. Indianapolis Ind._

## Return this Report to County Clerk with License and Certificate

# Marriage Record for Board of Health
## To Be Returned by the Minister or Other Person Performing Ceremony

*Mr Jerry Massy* and *Mrs A Marie Ray*

Groom's name _Jerry Massy_

His age _57_

" color _Brown_

" occupation _Labor_

" Birthplace—City _Bowlingreen_ State _Ky_

" Residence—Street No. _Parish 2631_ City _Indianapolis_

Single / Widower / Divorced } _Widow_ { 1st, 2nd or 3rd marriage } _Second_

Name of Father _Joel Massey_

Maiden name of Mother _America Akin_

Bride's name _Alis Marie Ray_

Her age _47_

" color _Colored_

" occupation _House Wife_

" Birthplace—City _Springfield_ State _Ohio_

" Residence—Street No. _2039 Bamberd_ City _Indianapolis_

Single / Widow / Divorced } _Widow_ { 1st, 2nd or 3rd marriage } _Third_

Name of Father _Henry Carter_

Maiden name of Mother _Jualia Brown_

Date of this marriage _8 day of April_

Place of this marriage _2631 Parish ave_

Name and title of person Performing this marriage _Rev J L Barnett_

His address _4130 Highland Place_

Witness { Name _Susie Willson  Robert Jones_ / Address _546 Paterson St  1728 Belfountain Sf_

## Return this Report to County Clerk with License and Certificate

# Marriage Record for Board of Health
### To Be Returned by the Minister or Other Person Performing Ceremony

_____ John Frederick _____ and _____ Mariatta Moore _____

Groom's name _____ John Frederick _____

His age _____ 27 _____

" color _____ white _____

" occupation _____ soldier _____

" Birthplace—City _____ Terre Haute _____ State _____ Ind. _____

" Residence—Street No. _____ Ft. Harrison _____ City _____ Indiana _____

Single / Widower / Divorced } _____ Divorced _____ { 1st, 2nd or 3rd marriage } _____ Second _____

Name of Father _____ Leslie Frederick _____

Maiden name of Mother _____ Ella McCosky _____

Bride's name _____ Mariatta Moore _____

Her age _____ 20 _____

" color _____ white _____

" occupation _____ Restaurant _____

" Birthplace—City _____ Princeton _____ State _____ Indiana _____

" Residence—Street No. _____ 1919 ½ Delaware City _____ Indianapolis _____

Single / Widow / Divorced } _____ Divorced _____ { 1st, 2nd or 3rd marriage } _____ Second _____

Name of Father _____ Irvin Tooley _____

Maiden name of Mother _____ Beatrice King _____

Date of this marriage _____ April 8th _____

Place of this marriage _____ 1914 Park Ave., Indianapolis, Ind. _____

Name and title of person Performing this marriage _____ Rev. Klaer Leo Peters minister _____

His address _____ 1914 Park Ave. _____
_____ Indianapolis, Ind. _____

Witness { Name _____ Virginia L. Tryon _____
{ Address _____ 1902 Park Ave. Indianapolis, Indiana _____

## Return this Report to County Clerk with License and Certificate

# Marriage Record for Board of Health
### To Be Returned by the Minister or Other Person Performing Ceremony

Elem Clark _and_ Fannie E Booker

Groom's name _Elem Clark_

His age _44_

" color _Negro_

" occupation _Laborer_

" Birthplace—City _Edmonton_ State _Ky_

" Residence—Street No. _2133 Valley_ City _Indianapolis_

Single / Widower / Divorced } _Single_   { 1st, 2nd or 3rd marriage } _1st Marriage_

Name of Father _Samuel Clark_

Maiden name of Mother _Alice Hatchet_

Bride's name _Fannie E. Booker_

Her age _56_

" color _Negro_

" occupation _House keeper_

" Birthplace—City _Pontac, Miss_ State _Miss._

" Residence—Street No. _2133 Valley_ City _Indianapolis_

Single / Widow / Divorced } _Widow_   { 1st 2nd or 3rd marriage } _2nd Marriage_

Name of Father _Carl Baxter_

Maiden name of Mother _Sophie Bramlet_

Date of this marriage _April 8, 1944_

Place of this marriage _Indianapolis Ind._

Name and title of person Performing this marriage _James La Mitcham, Minister_

His address _1445 Columbia Ave_

Witness { Name _Eva M. Cain_
{ Address _2133 Valley ave Indianapolis Ind._

### Return this Report to County Clerk with License and Certificate

# Marriage Record for Board of Health

To Be Returned by the Minister or Other Person Performing Ceremony

*Wallace W. Whiffing* and *Mary Josephine Bunch*

Groom's name _Wallace W. Whiffing_

His age _38_

" color _White_

" occupation _Personnel director_

" Birthplace—City _Indpls_ State _Ind_

" Residence—Street No. _16 S. Harris_ City _Indpls_

Single }
Widower } _single_
Divorced }

1st, 2nd or 3rd }
marriage } _first_

Name of Father _Wm Whiffle_

Maiden name of Mother _Anna Mosman_

Bride's name _Mary Josephine Bunch_

Her age _21_

" color _White_

" occupation _stenographer_

" Birthplace—City _Indpls_ State _Ind_

" Residence—Street No. _834 Highland_ City _Indpls_

Single }
Widow } _single_
Divorced }

1st, 2nd or 3rd }
marriage } _first_

Name of Father _Lester J Bunch_

Maiden name of Mother _Violet J Browning_

Date of this marriage _April 8, 1944_

Place of this marriage _Colony Tabernacle_

Name and title of person
Performing this marriage _Rev Raymond L Hacketer_

His address _902 Fletcher Ave_
_Indianapolis Ind_

Witness {
Name _Bernard Irwin_
Address _465 N. State St_

**Return this Report to County Clerk with License and Certificate**

12

# Marriage Record for Board of Health

### To Be Returned by the Minister or Other Person Performing Ceremony

_Jesse C. Huser_ ___ and ___ _Lenore E. Danberg_

Groom's name _Jesse C. Huser_

His age _32_

" color _white_

" occupation _Mechanic_

" Birthplace—City _Harrisburg_ State _Kentucky_

" Residence—Street No. _2155 College_ City _Indianapolis_

Single / Widower / Divorced } _Single_ { 1st, 2nd or 3rd marriage } _1st_

Name of Father _Tony Huser_

Maiden name of Mother _Anna Swear_

Bride's name _Lenore E. Danberg_

Her age _24_

" color _white_

" occupation _Auto Lady_

" Birthplace—City _Minneapolis_ State _Minn_

" Residence—Street No. _1422 N 27_ City _Indianapolis_

Single / Widow / Divorced } _Single_ { 1st, 2nd or 3rd marriage } _1st_

Name of Father _Theodore Danberg_

Maiden name of Mother _Ruth Larsen_

Date of this marriage _April 8, 1944_

Place of this marriage _Indianapolis Ind_

Name and title of person Performing this marriage _Carey C. Dobson Minister_

His address _101 Belmar._
_Indianapolis_

Witness { Name _Hershel Alford_
{ Address _807 7th ave. Beech Grove Ind_

### Return this Report to County Clerk with License and Certificate

# Marriage Record for Board of Health
### To Be Returned by the Minister or Other Person Performing Ceremony

*James H Sartain* and *Gladys I Norman*

Groom's name _James H Sartain_

His age _40_

" color _white_

" occupation _Policeman_

" Birthplace—City _Tracy City_ State _Tenn_

" Residence—Street No. _1545 E Kelly_ City _Indianapolis_

Single ~~Widower~~ ~~Divorced~~ } { 1st, ~~2nd, 3rd~~ marriage

Name of Father _Samuel F B Sartain_

Maiden name of Mother _Betty Lee Meeks_

Bride's name _Gladys I Norman_

Her age _36_

" color _white_

" occupation _Credit Mgr_

" Birthplace—City _Indianapolis_ State _Indiana_

" Residence—Street No. _1545 Kelly St_ City _Indianapolis_

~~Single~~ ~~Widow~~ Divorced } { ~~1st, 2nd, 3rd~~ 4th marriage

Name of Father _Ralph E Norman_

Maiden name of Mother _Daisy Zike_

Date of this marriage _April 8, 1944_

Place of this marriage _Indianapolis, Indiana_

Name and title of person Performing this marriage _Rev Robert R Rowland — Clergyman_

His address _1405 Dudley Avenue_
_Indianapolis Indiana_

Witness { Name _Griffin Stradham_
{ Address _1410 La Grande St._

## Return this Report to County Clerk with License and Certificate

12

# Marriage Record for Board of Health
### To Be Returned by the Minister or Other Person Performing Ceremony

_Creamer_ and _Crisp_

Groom's name _Earnest Creamer Jr_

His age _21_

" color _White_

" occupation _Carpenter_

" Birthplace—City _Sellersburg_ State _Indiana_

" Residence—Street No. _1850 E. Van Buren_ City _Indpls Ind._

Single } _Single_  {1st, 2nd or 3rd marriage } _First_
~~Widower~~
~~Divorced~~

Name of Father _Earnest Creamer Sr._

Maiden name of Mother _Bertrude Whitson_

Bride's name _Martha Crisp_

Her age _19_

" color _White_

" occupation _Stenographer_

" Birthplace—City _Indianapolis_ State _Indiana_

" Residence—Street No. _3144 Mars Hill Rd_ City _Indpls. Ind._

Single } _Single_  {1st, 2nd or 3rd marriage } _First_
~~Widow~~
~~Divorced~~

Name of Father _Rotha Crisp_

Maiden name of Mother _Daisy Strother_

Date of this marriage _Apr 8th 1944_

Place of this marriage _2735 N. Meridian Apt 1 Indpls Ind._

Name and title of person Performing this marriage _William E. Bell, Minister_

His address _2735 N. Meridian Apt 1 Indpls Ind._

Witness { Name _Rotha F. Crisp  Mrs Daisy Crisp_
{ Address _3144 Mars Hill Road  3144 Mars Hill Rd_

### Return this Report to County Clerk with License and Certificate

# Marriage Record for Board of Health

### To Be Returned by the Minister or Other Person Performing Ceremony

*Maynard D. Upper* and *Delores M. Foor*

Groom's name _Maynard D. Upper_

His age _25_

" color _white_

" occupation _U.S. Army_

" Birthplace—City _Goodrich_ State _Mich._

" Residence—Street No _Butler, U._ City _Indianapolis_

~~Single~~ ~~Widower~~ Divorced } ~~1st, 2nd~~ or 3rd marriage }

Name of Father _Eldon D. Upper_

Maiden name of Mother _Grace McCandlish_

Bride's name _Delores M. Foor_

Her age _23_

" color _white_

" occupation

" Birthplace—City _Cloverdale_ State _Ohio_

" Residence—Street No _4937 Blvd Place_ City _Indianapolis_

~~Single~~ ~~Widow~~ Divorced } ~~1st~~, 2nd or ~~3rd~~ marriage }

Name of Father _Glover Cleveland Fought_

Maiden name of Mother _Arvesta Richardson_

Date of this marriage _April 8 1944_

Place of this marriage _Indianapolis, Indiana_

Name and title of person Performing this marriage _Rev. M. H. Ragan_

His address _129 W - 44d St Indianapolis, Indiana_

Witness { Name _Mr & Mrs Milton Warren_ Address _4937 Blvd Place_

### Return this Report to County Clerk with License and Certificate

# Marriage Record for Board of Health
### To Be Returned by the Minister or Other Person Performing Ceremony

_Brady E. Parham_ and _Mary Elizabeth Grindle_

Groom's name _Brady E. Parham_

His age _20_

" color _White_

" occupation _U. S. Army_

" Birthplace—City _Corsor_ State _N. Y._

" Residence—Street No. _Army Dist._ City _Va._

Single Widower Divorced } _Single_ { 1st, 2nd or 3rd marriage } _1st_

Name of Father _Arthur C. Parham_

Maiden name of Mother _Elena Ettel Britton_

Bride's name _Mary Elizabeth Grindle_

Her age _20_

" color _White_

" occupation _Telephone Operator_

" Birthplace—City _Farmington_ State _Indiana_

" Residence—Street No. _5405 Madison_ City _Indianapolis_

Single Widow Divorced } _Single_ { 1st, 2nd or 3rd marriage } _1st_

Name of Father _Kenneth Grindle_

Maiden name of Mother _Lottie Josephine Hershelet_

Date of this marriage _April 9th 1944_

Place of this marriage _Indianapolis Ind._

Name and title of person Performing this marriage _Rev. Roy E. Carter_

His address _136 Case St._

Witness { Name _Bonnie Stepilik_
{ Address _Camp Atterbury Ind._

## Return this Report to County Clerk with License and Certificate

## Marriage Record for Board of Health
### To Be Returned by the Minister or Other Person Performing Ceremony

*Paul E. Slinp* and *Virginia A. Speer*

Groom's name _Paul E. Slinp._

His age _24_

" color _White_

" occupation _In army - 29th Field Hospital Secretary_

" Birthplace—City _Rupert_ State _Idaho._

" Residence—Street No. _Camp Bowie_ City _Texas._

Single / Widower / Divorced } _Single_ { 1st, 2nd or 3rd marriage } _First_

Name of Father _Rev. J. E. Slinp._

Maiden name of Mother _Grace E. Benham._

Bride's name _Virginia A. Speer._

Her age _19_

" color _White (Employed in Lukas Harvey)_

" occupation _"Riveter" in War Plant_

" Birthplace—City _Orangeld._ State _Indiana_

" Residence—Street No. _2044 College A_ City _Indianapolis_

Single / Widow / Divorced } _Single_ { 1st, 2nd or 3rd marriage } _First._

Name of Father _George W. Speer_

Maiden name of Mother _Anna B Clements_

Date of this marriage _April 9th. - 44_

Place of this marriage _Boone Grove, Ind._

Name and title of person Performing this marriage _Rev. J. E. Slinp._

His address _Boone Grove, Ind. Box 112_

Witness { Name _Mrs. Margaret Colglazier_ { Address _2044 College Ave, Indp, Indiana_

### Return this Report to County Clerk with License and Certificate

# Marriage Record for Board of Health

## To Be Returned by the Minister or Other Person Performing Ceremony

*Stanley W. Goloski* and *Ruby B. Corne*

Groom's name *Stanley William Goloski*

His age *25*

" color *White*

" occupation *Soldier United States Army*

" Birthplace—City *Calverton* State *New York*

" Residence—Street No. *312 East North St* City *Indianapolis Ind.*

Single Widower Divorced } *Single*   { 1st, 2nd or 3rd marriage } *First*

Name of Father *Joseph Goloski*

Maiden name of Mother *Mary Gryder*

Bride's name *Ruby B. Corne*

Her age *21*

" color *White*

" occupation *Typist*

" Birthplace—City *Hendersonville* State *North Carolina*

" Residence—Street No. *312 East North St* City *Indianapolis Ind.*

Single Widow Divorced } *Single*   { 1st, 2nd or 3rd marriage } *First*

Name of Father *George Ferr Corne*

Maiden name of Mother *Lula B. Heaton*

Date of this marriage *April 9th*

Place of this marriage *Indianapolis*

Name and title of person Performing this marriage *Rev. Reb. Green*

His address *1317 S. Belmont St Indianapolis Ind.*

Witness { Name *Louise Evans*  Address *Arthur Evans*

## Return this Report to County Clerk with License and Certificate

# Marriage Record for Board of Health

### To Be Returned by the Minister or Other Person Performing Ceremony

_____ and _____

Groom's name _____ Morris Prosen

His age _____ 33

" color _____ White

" occupation _____ Contractor — Farmer

" Birthplace—City _____ Johnson County State _____ Indiana

" Residence—Street No. _____ City _____ Hartsville Ind.

Single } Widower } _____ Divorced { 1st, 2nd or 3rd } _____ 2nd
Divorced } { marriage }

Name of Father _____ R. T. Prosen

Maiden name of Mother _____ Myrl Keaton

Bride's name _____ Martha Louise Casey

Her age _____ 25

" color _____ white

" occupation _____ Bottler, Pitman-Moore Co.

" Birthplace—City _____ Louisville State _____ Ky.

" Residence—Street No. _____ 376 Parkway Ave City _____ Indianapolis, Ind.

Single } Widow } _____ Divorced { 1st, 2nd or 3rd } _____ 2nd,
Divorced } { marriage }

Name of Father _____ Paul M. Ibauet Sr.

Maiden name of Mother _____ Gertrude Allen

Date of this marriage _____ April 9th 1944

Place of this marriage _____ Wesley Chapel Church New Albany, Ind.

Name and title of person Performing this marriage _____ Rev. Carl Allinger

His address _____ New Albany, Indiana
_____ 202 W. Market

Witness { Name _____ Mr. & Mrs. Carl Bennett
{ Address _____ 226 W. 4th St. New Albany, Ind.

## Return this Report to County Clerk with License and Certificate

12

# Marriage Record for Board of Health

### To Be Returned by the Minister or Other Person Performing Ceremony

*Floyd W. Hassler* and *Feril Van Valer*

Groom's name _Floyd W. Hassler_

His age _59_

" color _white_

" occupation _Sporting Goods Business_

" Birthplace—City _Ft Wayne_ State _Indiana_

" Residence—Street No. _121 Burlington Dr_ City _Kokomo_

Single / Widower / Divorced _____  1st, 2nd or 3rd marriage _____

Name of Father _Anson L. Hassler_ (deceased)

Maiden name of Mother _Hattie E Mowen_ (deceased)

Bride's name _Feril Van Valer_

Her age _47_

" color _white_

" occupation _Office_

" Birthplace—City _Tipton_ State _Indiana_

" Residence—Street No. _221 E Mich_ City _Kokomo_

Single / Widow / Divorced _____  1st, 2nd or 3rd marriage _____

Name of Father _Eugene Van Ness_ (deceased)

Maiden name of Mother _Emily Garrison_

Date of this marriage _Apr 9 - 44_

Place of this marriage _Kokomo Ind_

Name and title of person Performing this marriage _E Amos Clegg Minister_

His address _Kokomo Ind_

Witness { Name _____
{ Address _____

## Return this Report to County Clerk with License and Certificate

# Marriage Record for Board of Health

## To Be Returned by the Minister or Other Person Performing Ceremony

Carl H. Smith and Helen M. Fender

Groom's name _Carl H. Smith_

His age _23_

" color _white_

" occupation _Soldier_

" Birthplace—City _Weston,_ State _W. Virginia_

" Residence—Street No. _Camp Carson_ City _Colo._

Single
Widower
Divorced } _Single_ 1st, 2nd or 3rd marriage } _1st._

Name of Father _Carl Luther Smith_

Maiden name of Mother _Mona Lee Garrett_

Bride's name _Helen M. Fender_

Her age _21_

" color _white_

" occupation _Clerk — Ind. Bell Telephone_

" Birthplace—City _Indianapolis_ State _Ind._

" Residence—Street No. _2109 New St._ City _Indianapolis, Ind._

Single
Widow
Divorced } _Single_ 1st, 2nd or 3rd marriage } _1st._

Name of Father _Charles Everett Fender_

Maiden name of Mother _Maude K Catherine Carson_

Date of this marriage _April 9, 1944_

Place of this marriage _Indianapolis, Indiana_

Name and title of person Performing this marriage _Ordained Minister - Norman H. Schultz_

His address _2117 Napolean St._
_Indianapolis, Ind._

Witness { Name _Millard J Carson_
{ Address _2164 S Delaware, Indpls, Ind._

## Return this Report to County Clerk with License and Certificate

# Marriage Record for Board of Health
## To Be Returned by the Minister or Other Person Performing Ceremony

Russell E. Therien _____ and _____ Mary C. King

Groom's name _____ Russell Edward Therien

His age _____ 30

" color _____ White

" occupation _____ Jig-saw operator

" Birthplace—City _____ Chicago _____ State _____ Illinois

" Residence—Street No. _____ 619 N. Miles Ave City _____ South Bend, Ind

Single Widower Divorced } _____ Divorced _____ 1st, 2nd or 3rd marriage } _____ Second

Name of Father _____ Edward Therien

Maiden name of Mother _____ Lillian Piffer

Bride's name _____ Mary Catherine King

Her age _____ 18

" color _____ White

" occupation _____ Domestic

" Birthplace—City _____ Indianapolis _____ State _____ Ind.

" Residence—Street No. _____ 1437 N. Fulton St City _____ Indianapolis

Single Widow Divorced } _____ Single _____ 1st, 2nd or 3rd marriage } _____ First

Name of Father _____ Elmer King Virgil King

Maiden name of Mother _____ Ruth Summers

Date of this marriage _____ April 9, 1944

Place of this marriage _____ 1744 N. Penna St., Indianapolis

Name and title of person Performing this marriage _____ Arthur H. Norris, Minister

His address _____ 1744 N. Penna St., Indianapolis, Ind

Witness { Name _____ Preston Lone

{ Address _____ 2403 Kenwood Ave., Indianapolis, 8, Ind

## Return this Report to County Clerk with License and Certificate

12

# Marriage Record for Board of Health

### To Be Returned by the Minister or Other Person Performing Ceremony

Roy William Gillespie and Sally Lou Campbell

Groom's name _Roy William Gillespie_

His age _26_

" color _White_

" occupation _Accountant_

" Birthplace—City _St. Louis_ State _Missouri_

" Residence—Street No. _4707 E. Washington St._ City _Indianapolis_

Single / Widower / Divorced } _Single_   { 1st, 2nd or 3rd marriage } _1st_

Name of Father _John Gillespie_

Maiden name of Mother _Dora Junkerman_

Bride's name _Sally Lou Campbell_

Her age _26_

" color _white_

" occupation _clerk_

" Birthplace—City _Republic_ State _Penna_

" Residence—Street No. _4830 E. Washington St._ City _Indianapolis_

Single / Widow / Divorced } _Single_   { 1st, 2nd or 3rd marriage } _1st_

Name of Father _Benjamin Campbell_

Maiden name of Mother _Tessie Dotchin_

Date of this marriage _April 9, 1944_

Place of this marriage _5530 N. Delaware St. Indianapolis_

Name and title of person Performing this marriage _Dallas L. Browning, Minister_

His address _5530 N. Delaware St._
_Indianapolis, Ind_

Witness { Name _Mrs. D. R. Browning_
{ Address _5530 N. Delaware St. Indianapolis, Ind._

### Return this Report to County Clerk with License and Certificate

12

# Marriage Record for Board of Health
### To Be Returned by the Minister or Other Person Performing Ceremony

Mahlon A. Lowry _____ and Willard L. Ransdell

Groom's name _Mahlon A. Lowry_

His age _42_

" color _white_

" occupation _Cafeteria Manager_

" Birthplace—City _Pulaski_ State _Kentucky_

" Residence—Street No. _1212 Garvin Pl._ City _Louisville, Ky._

Single } _Single_    { 1st, 2nd or 3rd } _First_
Widower             { marriage
Divorced

Name of Father _William Mahlon Lowry_

Maiden name of Mother _Jennie Meese_

Bride's name _Willard L. Ransdell_

Her age _33_

" color _white_

" occupation _saleslady_

" Birthplace—City _Crestwood_ State _Kentucky_

" Residence—Street No. _1212 Garvin Pl._ City _Louisville, Ky._

Single } _Single_    { 1st, 2nd or 3rd } _1st._
Widow             { marriage
Divorced

Name of Father _William L. Ransdell_

Maiden name of Mother _Frances Willard Mayes_

Date of this marriage _April 9, 1944_

Place of this marriage _North Methodist Church Indianapolis_

Name and title of person
Performing this marriage _Dallas L. Browning, Minister_

His address _5530 N. Delaware St_
_Indianapolis_

Witness { Name _William L. Ransdell_
{ Address _3551 N. Illinois St., Indianapolis_

## Return this Report to County Clerk with License and Certificate

# Marriage Record for Board of Health
## To Be Returned by the Minister or Other Person Performing Ceremony

_Robert C Earlywine_ and _Betty Jean Harper_

Groom's name _Robert C Earlywine_

His age _21_

" color _white_

" occupation _Railroad break man_

" Birthplace—City _Peleston_ State _Ill._

" Residence—Street No. _1424 C 65 ½._ City _Chicago Ill._

Single Widower Divorced } _Single_    1st, 2nd or 3rd marriage } _1st_

Name of Father _Clem Earl Earlywine_

Maiden name of Mother _Hallie Frances McDade_

Bride's name _Betty Jean Harper_

Her age _19_

" color _white_

" occupation _—_

" Birthplace—City _Indianapolis_ State _Ind._

" Residence—Street No. _1032 S New Jersey_ City _Indianapolis Ind._

Single Widow Divorced } _Single_    1st, 2nd or 3rd marriage } _1st_

Name of Father _Lawrence Edward Harper_

Maiden name of Mother _Alice Rebecca Monts_

Date of this marriage _April 9 1944_

Place of this marriage _Indianapolis Ind._

Name and title of person Performing this marriage _Rev Basil M. Stultz_

His address _28 N Addison St Indianapolis Ind._

Witness { Name _Wesley C Iverside_
          { Address _1030 S New Jersey St Indpls Ind_

## Return this Report to County Clerk with License and Certificate

12

# Marriage Record for Board of Health

### To Be Returned by the Minister or Other Person Performing Ceremony

_Richard G. Wells_ and _Kathryn M. Olory_

Groom's name _Richard G. Wells_

His age _27_

" color _White_

" occupation _Army_

" Birthplace—City _So Bend_ State _Ind_

" Residence—Street No. _514 E. Ind_ City _So Bend Ind_

Single / Widower / Divorced } _Single_    { 1st, 2nd or 3rd marriage } _First_

Name of Father _Elmer Ghamane Wells_

Maiden name of Mother _Hazel Fern Andrews_

Bride's name _Kathryn M. Olory_

Her age _24_

" color _White_

" occupation _____

" Birthplace—City _Indianapolis_ State _Indiana_

" Residence—Street No. _6196 Central_ City _Indianapolis Ind_

Single / Widow / Divorced } _Single_    { 1st, 2nd or 3rd marriage } _Second_

Name of Father _Basil Aheb Hamilton_

Maiden name of Mother _Mabel King_

Date of this marriage _April 9_

Place of this marriage _So. Bend Ind_

Name and title of person Performing this marriage _George W. Ross minister_

His address _1902 Marine So Bend Ind._

Witness { Name _LaVina K. Fontaine_
Address _1125 N. Beville, Indianapolis, Indiana_

## Return this Report to County Clerk with License and Certificate

12

## Marriage Record for Board of Health
### To Be Returned by the Minister or Other Person Performing Ceremony

*Russell Eugean Fisher and + Betty J Taylor*

Groom's name *Ruskell Eugean Fisher*

His age *20*

" color *White*

" occupation *Drill Press opperator*

" Birthplace—City *Seircleville* State *Ind*

" Residence—Street No. *16 S Richwine* City *Indpls*

Single Widower Divorced } *Single*   { 1st, 2nd or 3rd marriage } *1st marriage*

Name of Father *Theodore Fisher*

Maiden name of Mother *Edna M. Timmons*

Bride's name *Betty J. Taylor*

Her age *18*

" color *White*

" occupation *Housewife*

" Birthplace—City *Indianapolis* State *Ind*

" Residence—Street No. *934 S. Missouri* City *Ind*

Single Widow Divorced } *Single*   { 1st, 2nd or 3rd marriage } *1st marriage*

Name of Father *Herbert Taylor*

Maiden name of Mother *Emma Lorell*

Date of this marriage *April 9, 1944*

Place of this marriage *Berean Tabernacle*

Name and title of person Performing this marriage *Rev. William Hafer Pastor*

His address *R.3 Box 61-H Indianapolis Ind.*

Witness { Name *Mrs. Emma J. Taylor*
{ Address *934 S. Missouri*

### Return this Report to County Clerk with License and Certificate

# Marriage Record for Board of Health

## To Be Returned by the Minister or Other Person Performing Ceremony

Victor W. Baker _____ and _Estella Thomas_

Groom's name _Victor W. Baker_

His age _69_

" color _White_

" occupation _Retired R. R. man_

" Birthplace—City _Terre Haute_ State _Ind._

" Residence—Street No. _858 College_ City _Indianapolis_

~~Single~~
~~Widower~~ } ———————— { ~~1st,~~ 2nd ~~or 3rd~~
~~Divorced~~ marriage

Name of Father _George C_

Maiden name of Mother _Hannah Osborn_

Bride's name _Bertha Estella Thomas_

Her age _60_

" color _White_

" occupation _____

" Birthplace—City _Rochester_ State _Pa_

" Residence—Street No. _432 E. Michigan_ City _Indianapolis_

~~Single~~
Widow } ———————— { ~~1st,~~ 2nd ~~or 3rd~~
Divorced marriage

Name of Father _Patrick O'Keane_

Maiden name of Mother _Elizabeth Saraht_

Date of this marriage _April 9, 1944_

Place of this marriage _Indianapolis, Ind._

Name and title of person
Performing this marriage _Rev. F. R. Davies_

His address _3610 Guilford_
_Indianapolis, Ind._

Witness { Name _Mr. and Mrs. Bernice Lennon_
{ Address _____

## Return this Report to County Clerk with License and Certificate

# Marriage Record for Board of Health
## To Be Returned by the Minister or Other Person Performing Ceremony

Wilbur F. Baughman and Margaret Ely

Groom's name _Wilber F. Baughman_

His age _46_

" color _White_

" occupation _Decorator_

" Birthplace—City _Charlotte_ State _North_

" Residence—Street No. _1105 N. capitol_ City _Indianapolis, Ind._

Single
Widower
Divorced } — { 1st, 2nd or 3rd marriage } —

Name of Father _W. F._

Maiden name of Mother _Mary Polley_

Bride's name _Margaret Ely_

Her age _38_

" color _White_

" occupation _Bookkeeper_

" Birthplace—City _Indianapolis_ State _Ind._

" Residence—Street No. _122 W. 12th_ City _Indianapolis, Ind_

Single
Widow
Divorced } — { 1st, 2nd or 3rd marriage } —

Name of Father _Henry Hoffman_

Maiden name of Mother _Lena Hornberger_

Date of this marriage _April 9, 1944_

Place of this marriage _Indianapolis, Ind._

Name and title of person Performing this marriage _Rev. F. R. Bares_

His address _3610 Guilford_
_Indianapolis, Ind._

Witness { Name _Geo. W. Lingenfelter_ _Bertha Hofman_
Address _515 N. East_ _122 W. 12th._

## Return this Report to County Clerk with License and Certificate

# Marriage Record for Board of Health

### To Be Returned by the Minister or Other Person Performing Ceremony

_____ and _____

Groom's name _Syle albert Arthur_

His age _20_

" color _White_

" occupation _Labor_

" Birthplace—City _Earlville_ State _Ky_

" Residence—Street No. _____ City _____

Single / Widower / Divorced } _Single_   {1st} 2nd or 3rd marriage } _._

Name of Father _Harry Arthur_

Maiden name of Mother _Nellie Burris_

Bride's name _Mildred Elaine Barrick_

Her age _15 yr_

" color _White_

" occupation _House Keeper_

" Birthplace—City _City Hospital_ State _Ind_

" Residence—Street No. _____ City _____

Single / Widow / Divorced } _____   {1st} 2nd or 3rd marriage } _____

Name of Father _Dennis Barrick_

Maiden name of Mother _Florence Beck_

Date of this marriage _Apr 9 1934_

Place of this marriage _Glad Tidings Mission_

Name and title of person Performing this marriage _Verdi Allen_

His address _111 E Market St Indpls_

Witness { Name _Dennis Barrick_   Address _36 N East St_

## Return this Report to County Clerk with License and Certificate

12

# Marriage Record for Board of Health

To Be Returned by the Minister or Other Person Performing Ceremony

_____Robert C. McCafferty_____ and ___Clara M. Young_____

Groom's name _____Robert C. McCafferty_____

His age _____20_____

" color_____White_____

" occupation_____U. S. Coast Guard_____

" Birthplace—City____Washington_____State _____Indiana_____

" Residence—Street No. __3231 W. Michigan__City __Indpls. Ind.__
St.

Single }
Widower } _____Single_____ { 1st, 2nd or 3rd marriage } _____1st_____
Divorced }

Name of Father____Homer L. McCafferty_____

Maiden name of Mother____Ruby Browning_____

Bride's name _____Clara M. Young_____

Her age _____21_____

" color_____white_____

" occupation_____Secretary_____

" Birthplace—City____Laurel_____State ___Indiana_____

" Residence—Street No. __101 N. Riley_____City _____Indpls. Ind.__

Single }
Widow } _____Single_____ { 1st, 2nd or 3rd marriage } ___1st_____
Divorced }

Name of Father_____Clarence Young_____

Maiden name of Mother____Myrtle Giffent_____

Date of this marriage_____April 9, 1944_____

Place of this marriage__Trinity Ev. Lutheran Church, Ohio at East St.__
Indpls.
Name and title of person
Performing this marriage__Walter C. Maas, Pastor_____

His address__5444 Carrollton Ave., Indpls. Ind._____

Witness { Name ___Mr. & Mrs. Roland Bohn_____
{ Address _4151 College Ave., xxx. Indianapolis, Ind.__

## Return this Report to County Clerk with License and Certificate

12

# Marriage Record for Board of Health

### To Be Returned by the Minister or Other Person Performing Ceremony

*Wilbur K. Dossee* and *Martha Hopping*

Groom's name _Wilbur K. Dossee_

His age _22_

" color _White_

" occupation _U.S. Navy_

" Birthplace—City _Monticello_ State _Iowa_

" Residence—Street No. _U.S.N.H._ City _Norman, Okla_

Single Widower Divorced } _Single_    {1st, 2nd or 3rd marriage} _1st_

Name of Father _Charles A. Dossee_

Maiden name of Mother _Alma Korslund_

Bride's name _Martha E. Hopping_

Her age _18_

" color _White_

" occupation _Secretary_

" Birthplace—City _Indianapolis_ State _Ind._

" Residence—Street No. _1424 W. Pruitt_ City _Indianapolis, Ind._

Single Widow Divorced } _Single_    {1st, 2nd or 3rd marriage} _1st_

Name of Father _John S. Hopping Sr._

Maiden name of Mother _Minnie Weaver_

Date of this marriage _April 7, 1944_

Place of this marriage _Indianapolis, Indiana_

Name and title of person Performing this marriage _Blaine E Kirkpatrick, Minister_

His address _2448 N. Harding St._ _Indianapolis, Indiana_

Witness { Name _Donald G. Emery_
         { Address _4604 E. Washington, Indpls., Ind._

### Return this Report to County Clerk with License and Certificate

# Marriage Record for Board of Health

### To Be Returned by the Minister or Other Person Performing Ceremony

*Stinson* and *Holzbog*

Groom's name *Arthur Stinson*

His age *21*

" color *white*

" occupation *laborer*

" Birthplace—City *Johnson Co.* State *Ky.*

" Residence—Street No. *Union St.* City *Southport Ind*

Single / Widower / Divorced } *Single*    { 1st, 2nd or 3rd marriage } *1st*

Name of Father *Austin Stinson*

Maiden name of Mother *Rosie Cox*

Bride's name *Lillian Holzbog*

Her age *21*

" color *white*

" occupation *Housewife*

" Birthplace—City *Birdseye* State *Ind.*

" Residence—Street No. *1534 E Castle* City *Indianapolis*

Single / Widow / Divorced } *Single*    { 1st, 2nd or 3rd marriage } *1st*

Name of Father *Clos. Holzbog*

Maiden name of Mother *Edith Bobbitt*

Date of this marriage *April 9, 1944*

Place of this marriage *Southport, Ind.*

Name and title of person Performing this marriage *Rev. W. M. Taylor*

His address *Southport Ind*

Witness { Name *Doris Stinson* / Address *4026 S. Madison Ave, Indpls, Ind.*

## Return this Report to County Clerk with License and Certificate

12

# Marriage Record for Board of Health
### To Be Returned by the Minister or Other Person Performing Ceremony

*Charles Jones* and *Cloteal Doris Brackin*

Groom's name _Charles Jones_

His age _36_

" color _Colored_

" occupation _City employe_

" Birthplace—City _Louisville_ State _Ky._

" Residence—Street No. _954 Camp St._ City _Indpls._

Single Widower Divorced } _Single_   1st, 2nd or 3rd marriage } _1st_

Name of Father _Marcus Jones_

Maiden name of Mother _Hallie Hodges_

Bride's name _Cloteal Doris Brackin_

Her age _28_

" color _Colored_

" occupation _Maid_

" Birthplace—City _Forrest_ State _Miss._

" Residence—Street No. _954 Camp St._ City _Indpls._

Single Widow Divorced } _Divorced_   1st, 2nd or 3rd marriage } _2nd_

Name of Father _Walter Lyles_

Maiden name of Mother _Sammie Smith_

Date of this marriage _April 9th 1944_

Place of this marriage _Indianapolis Indiana_

Name and title of person Performing this marriage _H. T. Toliver minister_

His address _823 W. 27th St. Indianapolis Ind._

Witness { Name _Christina Pierson_
         { Address _512 W 10th St_

## Return this Report to County Clerk with License and Certificate

# Marriage Record for Board of Health
### To Be Returned by the Minister or Other Person Performing Ceremony

_Glen E. Newby_ and _Evelyn M. Moss_

Groom's name _Glen E. Newby_

His age _19_

" color _white_

" occupation _Farming_

" Birthplace—City _Marion Co._ State _Indiana_

" Residence—Street No. _Marion Co._ City

Single Widower Divorced } _Single_ { 1st, 2nd or 3rd marriage } _First_

Name of Father _Lee Newby_

Maiden name of Mother _Edith Weiss_

Bride's name _Evelyn M. Moss_

Her age _17_

" color _white_

" occupation _Stenographer_

" Birthplace—City _Indpls_ State _Ind_

" Residence—Street No. _1353 Lindley_ City _Indpls_

Single Widow Divorced } _Single_ { 1st, 2nd or 3rd marriage } _First_

Name of Father _Chas Arthur Moss_

Maiden name of Mother _Betty Mildred King_

Date of this marriage _April 9, 19__

Place of this marriage _426 W. 30th, Indpls._

Name and title of person Performing this marriage _Vaughn T. Crews, Minister_

His address _426 W. 30th, Indpls._

Witness { Name _Lee Newby_
{ Address _Mrs. Betty Moss_

### Return this Report to County Clerk with License and Certificate

 12

# Marriage Record for Board of Health

To Be Returned by the Minister or Other Person Performing Ceremony

_William Owens_ and _Kathleen Runyon_

Groom's name _William Owens_

His age _20 Years. Sept. 8 - 1923_

" color _White_

" occupation _Machine Operator_

" Birthplace—City _Sullivan_ State _Indiana_

" Residence—Street No. _283 Addison_ City _Indianapolis Ind_

Single / Widower / Divorced } _Single_   1st, 2nd or 3rd marriage } _First_

Name of Father _Harold Owens_

Maiden name of Mother _Dorothy Brown_

Bride's name _Kathleen Runyon_

Her age _20 years Oct 4 - 1923_

" color _White_

" occupation _House Wife_

" Birthplace—City _Orange County_ State _Indiana_

" Residence—Street No. _702 N. Sherman Dr._ City _Indianapolis Ind._

Single / Widow / Divorced } _Divorced_   1st, 2nd or 3rd marriage } _Second_

Name of Father _Glenn Lane_

Maiden name of Mother _Josephine Lamb_

Date of this marriage _April 9 - 1944_

Place of this marriage _Mooresville Indiana_

Name and title of person Performing this marriage _Rev. E. C. Freeman_

His address _27 E Main St. Mooresville Indiana_

Witness { Name _Dorothy Emory & William Emory_

{ Address _28 South Addison, Indianapolis, Ind_

## Return this Report to County Clerk with License and Certificate

12

# Marriage Record for Board of Health

### To Be Returned by the Minister or Other Person Performing Ceremony

*Glen Michener* and *Wilma Pendergast*

Groom's name *Glen Michener*

His age *22*

" color *White*

" occupation *Soldier*

" Birthplace—City *Indianapolis* State *Indiana*

" Residence—Street No. *1341 W. 27th* City *Indianapolis, Ind*

Single Widower Divorced *Single* — 1st, 2nd or 3rd marriage *First*

Name of Father *Glen E. Michener*

Maiden name of Mother *Bessie Clark.*

Bride's name *Wilma Pendergast*

Her age *22*

" color *White*

" occupation *Stenographer*

" Birthplace—City *Indianapolis* State *Indiana*

" Residence—Street No. *2849 N. Alabama* City *Indianapolis, Ind.*

Single Widow Divorced *Single* — 1st, 2nd or 3rd marriage *First*

Name of Father *Harley Pendergast*

Maiden name of Mother *Ida Pickett*

Date of this marriage *April 9, 1944*

Place of this marriage *Indianapolis, Ind.*

Name and title of person Performing this marriage *Rev. J. Ray Stanton*

His address *Indianapolis, Ind.*

Witness { Name *Lola Pendergast* { Address *Indianapolis, Indiana.*

### Return this Report to County Clerk with License and Certificate

 12

# Marriage Record for Board of Health

To Be Returned by the Minister or Other Person Performing Ceremony

_James O. Wray_ and _Doris E. McKinney_

Groom's name _James O. Wray_

His age _24_

" color _white_

" occupation _Machinist_

" Birthplace—City _Indianapolis_ State _Ind._

" Residence—Street No. _1629 Cottage_ City _Indianapolis_

Single / Widower / Divorced } _divorced_ { 1st, 2nd or 3rd marriage } _Second_

Name of Father _James L. Wray   deceased_

Maiden name of Mother _Florence W. Hubbell_

Bride's name _Doris E. McKinney_

Her age _20_

" color _white_

" occupation _house wife_

" Birthplace—City _Indianapolis_ State _Ind._

" Residence—Street No. _3230 Moral Hill_ City _Indianapolis_

Single / Widow / Divorced } _divorced_ { 1st, 2nd or 3rd marriage } _Second_

Name of Father _Orville Brison_

Maiden name of Mother _Emma Anderson_

Date of this marriage _April 9th 1944_

Place of this marriage _Indianapolis, Ind._

Name and title of person Performing this marriage _William J. Brown Minister_

His address _649 W. 43rd St._

_Indianapolis, Ind._

Witness { Name _Gene Wilkinson_
{ Address _Westfield, Indiana_

**Return this Report to County Clerk with License and Certificate**

# Marriage Record for Board of Health
## To Be Returned by the Minister or Other Person Performing Ceremony

Forrest Lee Duff _and_ Thelma Lyons

Groom's name _Forrest Lee Duff_

His age _39_

" color _White_

" occupation _Truck Driver_

" Birthplace—City _Mendon_ State _Ohio_

" Residence—Street No. _____ City _Ft. Wayne, Ind_

Single
Widower } _Divorced_ { 1st, 2nd or 3rd } _Second_
Divorced      marriage

Name of Father _William J. Duff_

Maiden name of Mother _LuBertie Everett_

Bride's name _Thelma Lyons_

Her age _39_

" color _White_

" occupation _Governess_

" Birthplace—City _Greensburg_ State _Indiana_

" Residence—Street No._3025 N. Meridian_ City _Indianapolis, Ind_

Single
Widow } _Widow_ { 1st, 2nd or 3rd } _Second_
Divorced      marriage

Name of Father _Bert Lyons_

Maiden name of Mother _Victoria Worland_

Date of this marriage _April 9, 1944_

Place of this marriage _Richmond, Indiana_

Name and title of person
Performing this marriage _Rev. Frank C. Hunt, Minister_

His address _208 S. 18th St,_
_Richmond, Indiana._

Witness { Name _Mr. & Mrs. Harry Smithmeyer_
        { Address _26 N. W. 18th St. Richmond, Ind._

## Return this Report to County Clerk with License and Certificate

# Marriage Record for Board of Health

### To Be Returned by the Minister or Other Person Performing Ceremony

George E Dirr Jr _and_ Mary Catherine Day

Groom's name _George E Dirr, Jr_

His age _27_

" color _White_

" occupation _Soldier_

" Birthplace—City _Indianapolis_ State _Ind_

" Residence—Street No. _1445 N. Wallace_ City _Indianapolis, Ind_

Single / Widower / Divorced } _Single_ {1st, 2nd or 3rd marriage} _1st_

Name of Father _Geo. E Dirr, Sr_

Maiden name of Mother _Jesse Brayles_

Bride's name _Mary Catherine Day_

Her age _22_

" color _White_

" occupation _Clerk - Stenographer_

" Birthplace—City _Indianapolis_ State _Ind_

" Residence—Street No. _3616 E 11th_ City _Indianapolis, Ind_

Single / Widow / Divorced } _Single_ {1st, 2nd or 3rd marriage} _1st_

Name of Father _Albert Day_

Maiden name of Mother _Katherine Christine Hauss_

Date of this marriage _April 9, 1944_

Place of this marriage _Indianapolis, Ind_

Name and title of person Performing this marriage _W. Nordsieck, Luth. Minister_

His address _1078 N. Temple_
_Indianapolis, Ind._

Witness { Name _LaVerne Day_
{ Address _2200 Madison Road, Cincinnati, Ohio_

### Return this Report to County Clerk with License and Certificate

12

## Marriage Record for Board of Health
### To Be Returned by the Minister or Other Person Performing Ceremony

Richard O. Duncan — and Betty Lee McKinney

Groom's name _Richard O. Duncan_

His age _21_

" color _White_

" occupation _U.S. Army_

" Birthplace—City _Indianapolis_ State _Ind_

" Residence—Street No. _U.S. Army_ City

Single Widower Divorced } _1st_ { 1st, 2nd or 3rd marriage }

Name of Father _Gordon_

Maiden name of Mother _Alice Jones_

Bride's name _Betty Lee McKinney_

Her age _19_

" color _White_

" occupation _Army Map Service_

" Birthplace—City _Indpls_ State _Ind_

" Residence—Street No. _1221 Gale_ City _Indpls_

Single Widow Divorced } _Single_ { 1st, 2nd or 3rd marriage } _1st_

Name of Father _Charles McKinney_

Maiden name of Mother _Ruth Burnside_

Date of this marriage _April 9, 1944_

Place of this marriage _Indianapolis Ind_

Name and title of person Performing this marriage _Rev. W. R. Montgomery_

His address _1576 N. Olney St._ _Indpls Ind._

Witness { Name _Virginia McKinney_ _Richard J. Vickey_ { Address _1221 Gale St_ _1510 Olney St_

### Return this Report to County Clerk with License and Certificate

# Marriage Record for Board of Health
### To Be Returned by the Minister or Other Person Performing Ceremony

Billie Louise Howlett and Chas H. Redd

Groom's name _Chas H. Redd_

His age _25_

" color _colored_

" occupation _Blacksmith_

" Birthplace—City _Cadiz_ State _Ky_

" Residence—Street No. _241 Shrewes_ City

Single / Widower / Divorced _Single_    1st, 2nd or 3rd marriage _1_    Father's Name _Lucien Redd_

Name of Father _____

Maiden name of Mother _Anna Roberts_

Bride's name _Billie Loise Howlett_

Her age _16_

" color _Colored_

" occupation _Housewife_

" Birthplace—City _Brazil_ State _Ind_

" Residence—Street No. _____ City

Single / Widow / Divorced _Single_    1st, 2nd or 3rd marriage _1_

Name of Father _William Howlett_

Maiden name of Mother _Cora Gray._

Date of this marriage _april 9—1944_

Place of this marriage _Indpls. Ind._

Name and title of person Performing this marriage _George Baltimore, minister_

His address _3053 Station at Indpls, Ind._

Witness { Name _Anna Howlett_    Address _____

### Return this Report to County Clerk with License and Certificate

# Marriage Record for Board of Health

### To Be Returned by the Minister or Other Person Performing Ceremony

_____ and _____

Groom's name _John Martin Carroll_

His age _25_

" color _White_

" occupation _U. S. Army_

" Birthplace—City _Indianapolis_ State _Indiana_

" Residence—Street No. _540 No Oriental_ City _Indianapolis_

Single Widower Divorced } _Single_  { 1st, 2nd or 3rd marriage } _____

Name of Father _John Carroll_

Maiden name of Mother _Ellen Dugan_

Bride's name _Mary Ellen Clark_

Her age _20_

" color _White_

" occupation _Statistician_

" Birthplace—City _Indianapolis_ State _Indiana_

" Residence—Street No. _639 No. Gray_ City _Indianapolis_

Single Widow Divorced } _Single_  { 1st, 2nd or 3rd marriage } _____

Name of Father _Virgil Clark_

Maiden name of Mother _Elizabeth Maratta_

Date of this marriage _April 9, 1944_

Place of this marriage _Indianapolis, Ind._

Name and title of person Performing this marriage _Rev. Victor L. Goossens_

His address _125 No. Oriental St._

Witness { Name _Cecil Maddalena_
          { Address _Carolyn Langsford_

### Return this Report to County Clerk with License and Certificate

# Marriage Record for Board of Health

### To Be Returned by the Minister or Other Person Performing Ceremony

Louise Dwight Barkley _____ and ____ Helen Eva McBride _____

Groom's name _Louie D Wight Barkley_

His age _34_

" color _white_

" occupation _Farmer_

" Birthplace—City _French Lick_ State _Ind_

" Residence—Street No. _Sheridan_ City _Ind_

Single / Widower / Divorced } _Single_ { 1st, 2nd or 3rd marriage } _First_

Name of Father _Albert S Barkley_

Maiden name of Mother _Lucy Wininger_

Bride's name _Helen Eva McBride_

Her age _35_

" color _White_

" occupation _Inspector_

" Birthplace—City _Jasonville_ State _Ind._

" Residence—Street No. _623 N. Rural_ City _Indianapolis, Ind._

Single / Widow / Divorced } _Single_ { 1st, 2nd or 3rd marriage } _First_

Name of Father _Homer McBride_

Maiden name of Mother _Lola E. Cunningham_

Date of this marriage _April 9 1944_

Place of this marriage _East Tenth St Methodist Church, Indianapolis, Ind_

Name and title of person Performing this marriage _Reverend Archiless M Brown_

His address _937 W. Dr. woodruff Pl. Indianapolis, Ind._

Witness { Name _Walter R. Latshaw_
{ Address _2127 N. Meridian St._

## Return this Report to County Clerk with License and Certificate

12

# Marriage Record for Board of Health
### To Be Returned by the Minister or Other Person Performing Ceremony

---

Edward Franklin Garber and Christine Marie Miller

Groom's name Edward Franklin Garber

His age 46

" color White

" occupation Assistant Branch Manager-Allis Chalmers Manufacturing
Co.,Atlanta, Ga.

" Birthplace—City Harrisonburg State Virginia

" Residence—Street No. 1044 Eultala Road City Atlanta, Georgia

Single
Widower } Single { 1st, 2nd or 3rd } First
Divorced marriage

Name of Father E.T. Garber (Deceased)

Maiden name of Mother Anna Rebecca Burnshire

---

Bride's name Christine Marie Miller

Her age 30

" color White

" occupation Clerk-Standard Oil Company-Indianapolis, Indiana

" Birthplace—City Bowling Green State Kentucky

" Residence—Street No. 3310 N. Meridian City Indianapolis

Single
Widow } Divorced { 1st, 2nd or 3rd } Second
Divorced marriage

Name of Father Geroge Henry Miller

Maiden name of Mother Minnie Wright

---

Date of this marriage April 9, 1944

Place of this marriage McKee Chapel-Tabernacel Presbyterian Church-
Name and title of person Indianapolis, Ind.
Performing this marriage *Cow hewing Vale* Minister of above Church

His address 418 E. 34th Street

Indianapolis, Indiana

Witness { Name *Virginia Miller Barton (mrs Carl)*
{ Address *613 N Lafayette S. Bend, Ind*

---

## Return this Report to County Clerk with License and Certificate

12

FILED
42 APR 12 1944
CLERK

# Marriage Record for Board of Health
## To Be Returned by the Minister or Other Person Performing Ceremony

_Joseph J. McCown_ and _Helen Mae Phillips_

Groom's name _Joseph J. McCown_

His age _30_

" color _White_

" occupation _Telegraph Operator_

" Birthplace—City _Martinsville_ State _Indiana_

" Residence—Street No. _1850 Applegate_ City _Indpls. Ind._

Single Widower Divorced _Single_   1st, 2nd or 3rd marriage _First_

Name of Father _Joseph J. McCown_

Maiden name of Mother _Laura Sophene Kaufman_

Bride's name _Helen Mae Phillips_

Her age _25_

" color _White_

" occupation _Defense Worker_

" Birthplace—City _Bedford_ State _Indiana_

" Residence—Street No. _R R No 2 51 61_ City _Indpls_

Single Widow Divorced _Single_   1st, 2nd or 3rd marriage _First_

Name of Father _Alfred W. Phillips_

Maiden name of Mother _Tilly H. Tesh_

Date of this marriage _April 4, 1942_

Place of this marriage _Indpls Ind_

Name and title of person Performing this marriage _Minister_

His address _420 N. 30th St._

_Indianapolis_

Witness { Name _Joseph A. Elliott_

Address _Indpls In._

## Return this Report to County Clerk with License and Certificate

# Marriage Record for Board of Health
### To Be Returned by the Minister or Other Person Performing Ceremony

Paul F. Locke _____ and _____ Audrey Hanner

Groom's name _____ Paul F. Locke

His age _____ 20

" color _____ white

" occupation _____ Drill press operator

" Birthplace—City _____ Indianapolis _____ State _____ Indiana

" Residence—Street No. _____ 229 S. Summit _____ City _____ Indianapolis

Single
Widower } _____ Single _____ { 1st, 2nd or 3rd marriage
Divorced

Name of Father _____ John H. Locke

Maiden name of Mother _____ Elizabeth Locke

Bride's name _____ Audrey Mae Hanner

Her age _____ 18

" color _____ white

" occupation _____ Domestic

" Birthplace—City _____ Clay County _____ State _____ Indiana

" Residence—Street No. _____ 906 Woodlawn _____ City _____ Indianapolis

Single
Widow } _____ Single _____ { 1st, 2nd or 3rd marriage
Divorced

Name of Father _____ John W. Hanner

Maiden name of Mother _____ Zettie Barker

Date of this marriage _____ April 9, 1944

Place of this marriage _____ Beech Grove, Ind.

Name and title of person Performing this marriage _____ Rev. Leonard Fletcher

His address _____ 138 So. 4th Ave.
_____ Beech Grove, Indiana

Witness { Name _____ Margie L. Bundy
{ Address _____ 1407 Southeastern Ave.

### Return this Report to County Clerk with License and Certificate

# Marriage Record for Board of Health

### To Be Returned by the Minister or Other Person Performing Ceremony

*Tom R Caldwell* and *Norma Jeanne Huske*

Groom's name _____ *Tom R Caldwell*

His age _____ *22*

" color _____ *white*

" occupation _____ *U. S. N.*

" Birthplace—City _____ *Cleveland* State _____ *Ohio*

" Residence—Street No. *725 N Emerson Ave* City _____ *Indianapolis*

Single / Widower / Divorced ———— { 1st, 2nd or 3rd marriage }

Name of Father _____ *Tom Caldwell*

Maiden name of Mother _____ *Mary Isabella Kerr Kirk*

Bride's name _____ *Norma Jeanne Huske*

Her age _____ *19*

" color _____ *white*

" occupation _____ *Inspector*

" Birthplace—City _____ *Chicago* State _____ *Ill*

" Residence—Street No. *5237 E 9th* City _____ *Indianapolis*

Single / Widow / Divorced ———— { 1st, 2nd or 3rd marriage }

Name of Father _____ *George Huske*

Maiden name of Mother _____ *Norma Miller*

Date of this marriage _____ *April 9, 1944*

Place of this marriage _____ *Wallace H Purdy St. Indianapolis Ind.*

Name and title of person Performing this marriage _____ *Rev Roy E Mueller*

His address _____ *4805 E 10th St.*

_____ *Indianapolis*

Witness { Name _____ *Tom Caldwell*
{ Address _____ *725 N Emerson Ave, Indianapolis, Ind*

### Return this Report to County Clerk with License and Certificate

FILED
42 APR 11 1944

CLERK

# Marriage Record for Board of Health
## To Be Returned by the Minister or Other Person Performing Ceremony

_Gerald P. Miller_ and _Winifred Overman_

Groom's name _Gerald P. Miller_

His age _28 yrs_

" color _white_

" occupation _Jeweler_

" Birthplace—City _Shelby County_ State _Indiana_

" Residence—Street No. _2307 Stewart_ City _Indianapolis_

Single
Widower  } _Single_    { 1st, 2nd or 3rd
Divorced            marriage  } _1st_

Name of Father _Howard Cecil Miller_

Maiden name of Mother _Mary Ethel Sedgwick_

Bride's name _Winifred Overman_

Her age _32 yrs_

" color _white_

" occupation _____

" Birthplace—City _Homer_ State _Illinois_

" Residence—Street No. _1321 College Ave_ City _Indianapolis_

Single
Widow  } _single_    { 1st, 2nd or 3rd
Divorced          marriage  } _1st_

Name of Father _Dayton R. Overman_

Maiden name of Mother _Alice McGinty_

Date of this marriage _April 9, 1944_

Place of this marriage _Carmel, Indiana_

Name and title of person
Performing this marriage _Rev. Glen Rinard_

His address _330 N. Range Line Road_
_Carmel, Indiana_

Witness { Name _Kenneth D. Sever, Cpl._
         { Address _Madison, Indiana_

## Return this Report to County Clerk with License and Certificate

# Marriage Record for Board of Health

### To Be Returned by the Minister or Other Person Performing Ceremony

_____ and _____

Groom's name _William E Monier_

His age _26_

" color _White_

" occupation _Navy_

" Birthplace—City _Stanley_ State _Wisconsin_

" Residence—Street No. _____ City _____

Single / Widower / Divorced } _____ { 1st, 2nd or 3rd marriage } _First_

Name of Father _Clifford Monier_

Maiden name of Mother _Bessie Ulry_

Bride's name _Phyllis Josephine Reddick_

Her age _19_

" color _White_

" occupation _Defense work_

" Birthplace—City _Lebanon_ State _Indiana_

" Residence—Street No. _____ City _____

Single / Widow / Divorced } _____ { 1st, 2nd or 3rd marriage } _First_

Name of Father _Clarence Reddick_

Maiden name of Mother _Edna Mae Wills Reddick_

Date of this marriage _April 9 — 1944_

Place of this marriage _Residence of Emma Hedderich Lafayette 4, Ind_

Name and title of person Performing this marriage _Rev. Wilson W. Root_

His address _Lafayette Indiana R.R. 3_

Witness { Name _Emile P Monier 5307 N. Latrobe Chi_
{ Address _Jane Ulrey — 2052 N. Delaware, Indpls, Ind_

## Return this Report to County Clerk with License and Certificate

# Marriage Record for Board of Health
### To Be Returned by the Minister or Other Person Performing Ceremony

Kenneth Blunk _____ and Elnora Grebaugh

Groom's name _Kenneth W. Blunk_

His age _17_

" color _Wh._

" occupation _Trucking_

" Birthplace—City _Owen County_ State _Indiana_

" Residence—Street No. _RR, Box 352_ City _Bridgeport, Ind._

Single Widower Divorced } _Single_ { 1st, 2nd or 3rd marriage } _1st_

Name of Father _Elmer W. Blunk_

Maiden name of Mother _Hazel Pettit_

Bride's name _Elnora Grebaugh_

Her age _17_

" color _Wh._

" occupation _Housekeeper_

" Birthplace—City _Indianapolis_ State _Indiana_

" Residence—Street No. _RR,_ City _Plainfield, Ind._

Single Widow Divorced } _Single_ { 1st, 2nd or 3rd marriage } _1st_

Name of Father _Raymond D. Grebaugh_

Maiden name of Mother _Maggie Gadient_

Date of this marriage _April 9, 1944_

Place of this marriage _Friendswood Baptist Church, Friendswood, In._

Name and title of person Performing this marriage _Ralph P. Wade — Minister_

His address _RR, Box 351 B_

_Bridgeport, Indiana_

Witness { Name _Elmer Blunk_
{ Address _Bridgeport Ind R # 1_

### Return this Report to County Clerk with License and Certificate

## Marriage Record for Board of Health
### To Be Returned by the Minister or Other Person Performing Ceremony

*Bruce O Broadstreet* and *Eleanor June King*

Groom's name *Bruce O. Broadstreet*

His age 28

" color White

" occupation Farmer

" Birthplace—City Cloverdale State Ind

" Residence—Street No. RR6 City Crawfordsville Ind

Single / Widower / Divorced } Single

1st, 2nd or 3rd marriage } First.

Name of Father Henry Broadstreet

Maiden name of Mother Hazel Withers

Bride's name Eleanor June King

Her age 20

" color White

" occupation At Home

" Birthplace—City Bomont State W. Va

" Residence—Street No. 3548 Salem City Indianapolis Ind.

Single / Widow / Divorced } Single

1st, 2nd or 3rd marriage } First.

Name of Father C. F. King

Maiden name of Mother Lillian Anderson

Date of this marriage April 9 1944

Place of this marriage Indianapolis

Name and title of person Performing this marriage Rev. R. G. Skidmore

His address 1822 E. Efler ave Indianapolis, Ind.

Witness { Name Winston Coffman

{ Address Brownsburg Ind

### Return this Report to County Clerk with License and Certificate

FILED
42 APR 1 2 1944
CLERK

# Marriage Record for Board of Health
## To Be Returned by the Minister or Other Person Performing Ceremony

_Thomas Henderson_ and _Adelaide Woods_

Groom's name _Thomas Henderson_

His age _Thirty eight_

" color _Brown_

" occupation _Moulder_

" Birthplace—City _Knoxville_ State _Tenn._

" Residence—Street No. _2458 Blvd Pl._ City _Indianapolis_

Single / Widower / Divorced } _Divorced_ { 1st, 2nd or 3rd marriage } _Second_

Name of Father _Gore Henderson_

Maiden name of Mother _Georgia Ludie_

Bride's name _Adelaide Woods_

Her age _Forty-five_

" color _Brown_

" occupation _Housewife_

" Birthplace—City _Seymour_ State _Ind._

" Residence—Street No. _329 W. 25th_ City _Indianapolis_

Single / Widow / Divorced } _Divorced_ { 1st, 2nd or 3rd marriage } _Second_

Name of Father _Finch Sharpe_

Maiden name of Mother _Mintie Phillip._

Date of this marriage _9th of April 1944_

Place of this marriage _Indianapolis Ind._

Name and title of person Performing this marriage _R J Andrews Minister_

His address _1235 W. 25th St. Indianapolis Ind_

Witness { Name _Hope Handa Phillips_
{ Address _633 Locke #368,_

## Return this Report to County Clerk with License and Certificate

## Marriage Record for Board of Health
### To Be Returned by the Minister or Other Person Performing Ceremony

*James F. Shirley* and *Helen L. Peters*

Groom's name _James F. Shirley_

His age _23_

" color _Negro_

" occupation _Ind. Gear Co._

" Birthplace—City _South Bend_ State ____

" Residence—Street No. _531 W 14._ City ____

Single Widower Divorced } _Single_  { 1st, 2nd or 3rd marriage } _First_

Name of Father _Frank Shirley_

Maiden name of Mother _Mary Esters_

Bride's name _Helen L. Peters_

Her age _21_

" color _Negro_

" occupation _Housewife_

" Birthplace—City _Indianapolis_ State ____

" Residence—Street No. _145 E 16._ City ____

Single Widow Divorced } _Single_  { 1st, 2nd or 3rd marriage } _First_

Name of Father _Miles Peters_

Maiden name of Mother _Anna Esters_

Date of this marriage _April 10, 1944_

Place of this marriage _Indianapolis, Ind_

Name and title of person Performing this marriage _H. Thomas, Minister_

His address _702 S. Illinois St. Indianapolis_

Witness { Name _Arlee F. Brand_ { Address _2336 Indianapolis_

## Return this Report to County Clerk with License and Certificate

12

# Marriage Record for Board of Health
### To Be Returned by the Minister or Other Person Performing Ceremony

*Bert Troutman* and *Kathleen Neiderer*

Groom's name _Bert Troutman_

His age _45_

" color _white_

" occupation _Factory superintendent_

" Birthplace—City _Kewanna_ State _Ind._

" Residence—Street No. _1133 Huey St._ City _South Bend._

~~Single~~
~~Widower~~
Divorced } _Divorced_ {1st, 2nd or 3rd marriage} _Second._

Name of Father _Alonzo Troutman_

Maiden name of Mother _Sally Calvin,_

═══════════════════════════════

Bride's name _Kathleen Marie Neiderer_

Her age _37_

" color _white_

" occupation _Beautician_

" Birthplace—City _Hanover_ State _Pa._

" Residence—Street No. _1218 W. Washington_ City _South Bend, Ind._

Single
Widow
Divorced } _Divorced_ {1st, 2nd or 3rd marriage} _2nd._

Name of Father _Peter Neiderer_

Maiden name of Mother _Mary Agnes Wagaman_

═══════════════════════════════

Date of this marriage _April 10, 1944_

Place of this marriage _Indianapolis, Indiana_

Name and title of person Performing this marriage _Sidney Blair Harry Minister_

His address _Meridian Heights Pres. Ch._
_Indianapolis, Ind._

Witness { Name _Mm. S. B. Harry_
{ Address _4720 Park Ave. Indianapolis Indiana_

### Return this Report to County Clerk with License and Certificate

# Marriage Record for Board of Health
### To Be Returned by the Minister or Other Person Performing Ceremony

*Charles C. Bruens* and *Blanche Finley*

Groom's name _Charles C. Bruens_

His age _58_

" color _Colored_

" occupation _Pharmacist_

" Birthplace—City _Mayesleck_ State _Kentucky_

" Residence—Street No. _1022 N West_ City _Indianapolis_

Single / Widower / Divorced } _Single_     { 1st, 2nd or 3rd marriage } _First Ind_

Name of Father _William Bruens_

Maiden name of Mother _Lula Gulley_

Bride's name _Blanch Finley_

Her age _49_

" color _Colored_

" occupation _Beautician_

" Birthplace—City _Granville_ State _Ohio, Kentucky_

" Residence—Street No. _Granville_ City _Ohio_

Single / Widow / Divorced } _Widowed_     { 1st, 2nd or 3rd marriage } _Second_

Name of Father _John Henry Sedford_

Maiden name of Mother _Carolyn Nichols_

Date of this marriage _Apr. 10 1944_

Place of this marriage _Indianapolis Ind_

Name and title of person Performing this marriage _John___

His address _433 N Chapring St._ _Indianapolis Ind._

Witness { Name _Leo H Ferguson_
        { Address _2920 N ___

### Return this Report to County Clerk with License and Certificate

12

# Marriage Record for Board of Health

### To Be Returned by the Minister or Other Person Performing Ceremony

Russell B. Meador and Myrtle K. Bennett

Groom's name _Russell B. Meador_

His age _23 yrs._

" color _white_

" occupation _Laundry Rout Man_

" Birthplace—City _Bowling Green_ State _Kentucky_

" Residence—Street No. _64 High St_ City _Indianapolis_

Single
~~Widower~~
~~Divorced~~
} 1st, ~~2nd or 3rd~~ marriage

Name of Father _Lonnie May ~~Delk~~ Meador_

Maiden name of Mother _Allie May Delk_

Bride's name _Myrtle Katherine Bennett_

Her age _17 yrs._

" color _white_

" occupation _Clerk, R. C. A._

" Birthplace—City _Indianapolis_ State _Indiana_

" Residence—Street No. _1236 Beecher_ City _Indianapolis_

Single
~~Widow~~
~~Divorced~~
} 1st, ~~2nd or 3rd~~ marriage

Name of Father _Ralph Bennett_

Maiden name of Mother _Lillian Robinson_

Date of this marriage _April 10, 1944,_

Place of this marriage _St. Catherines R.C. Church,_

Name and title of person Performing this marriage _Rev. J. M. Downey_

His address _1109 E Tabor St. Indianapolis, Indiana_

Witness { Name _George Werntz_
{ Address _Mary Alice Munsch_

### Return this Report to County Clerk with License and Certificate

# Marriage Record for Board of Health

To Be Returned by the Minister or Other Person Performing Ceremony

Orville D. Worrell and Dorothy Sherlin

Groom's name _Orville D. Worrell_

His age _24_

" color _White_

" occupation _Soldier_

" Birthplace—City _Wisner_ State _Nebr_

" Residence—Street No. _Stout Field_ City _Indianapolis - Ind_

Single / Widower / Divorced } _Single_ { 1st, 2nd or 3rd marriage } _1st_

Name of Father _Emery Worrell_

Maiden name of Mother _Marie Rienholt_

Bride's name _Dorothy Sherlin_

Her age _23_

" color _white_

" occupation _____

" Birthplace—City _Chicago_ State _Ill_

" Residence—Street No. _St. James_ City _Minnesota_

Single / Widow / Divorced } _Single_ { 1st, 2nd or 3rd marriage } _1st_

Name of Father _George Sherlin_

Maiden name of Mother _Susanne Kling_

Date of this marriage _April 10. 1944_

Place of this marriage _Indianapolis_

Name and title of person Performing this marriage _Rev. Raymond R. Noll_

His address _1347 N. Meridian St_ _Indianapolis_

Witness { Name _John J. O'Malley_ (Marian C'/n) { Address _Stout Field - Indianapolis_

**Return this Report to County Clerk with License and Certificate**

12

Oct 26, 1939

# Marriage Record for Board of Health
### To Be Returned by the Minister or Other Person Performing Ceremony

_Caroselli_ and _Hosier_

Groom's name _Clarence J. Caroselli_

His age _33_

" color _White_

" occupation _Tailor_

" Birthplace—City _Indianapolis_ State _Indiana_

" Residence—Street No. _709 W 30th_ City _Indianapolis, Ind._

Single Widower Divorced } _Single_ { 1st, 2nd or 3rd marriage } _1st._

Name of Father _Vincent Caroselli_

Maiden name of Mother _Josephine Marsella_

Bride's name _Beatrice Hosier_

Her age _38_

" color _White_

" occupation _Hair-Stylist_

" Birthplace—City _West Terre Haute_ State _Indiana_

" Residence—Street No. _1020 W. 32nd_ City _Indianapolis, Ind._

Single Widow Divorced } _Divorced_ { 1st, 2nd or 3rd marriage } _4th_

Name of Father _William Alfred Garrison_

Maiden name of Mother _Mary Gaffey_

Date of this marriage _April 10, 1944_

Place of this marriage _Holy Angels Church_

Name and title of person Performing this marriage _Rev. Henry A. Crapp_

His address _2826 Northwestern Ave._
_Indianapolis, Indiana_

Witness { Name _William A. Garrison, Jr._
{ Address _Mary A. Schultz_

### Return this Report to County Clerk with License and Certificate

# Marriage Record for Board of Health

To Be Returned by the Minister or Other Person Performing Ceremony

_Ray Allen_ and _Ruby Cox_

Groom's name _Ray Allen_

His age _49_

" color _white_

" occupation _Bus Driver_

" Birthplace—City _Bedford_ State _Indiana_

" Residence—Street No. _/_ City _Bedford, Ind._

Single
Widower  } _Widower_ { 1st, 2nd or 3rd marriage } _2nd_
Divorced

Name of Father _Homer Allen_

Maiden name of Mother _Jassnet Goodman_

Bride's name _Ruby Cox_

Her age _30_

" color _white_

" occupation _Seamstress_

" Birthplace—City _Indph_ State _Ind_

" Residence—Street No. City _Bedford, Ind._

Single
Widow  } _Single_ { 1st, 2nd or 3rd marriage } _1st_
Divorced

Name of Father _Clarence Allen Cox_

Maiden name of Mother _Josephine Ellen Brown_

Date of this marriage _April 10-44_

Place of this marriage _Indph Ind._

Name and title of person
Performing this marriage _Ernest V Lane, Justice of Peace_

His address _15½ East Court_

Witness { Name _Mary Jo Lane_
{ Address _3741 College Ave._

## Return this Report to County Clerk with License and Certificate

# Marriage Record for Board of Health

To Be Returned by the Minister or Other Person Performing Ceremony

*Arthur Grider* and *June Tungate*

Groom's name *Arthur Grider*

His age *26*

" color *white*

" occupation *Truck Driver*

" Birthplace—City *Brownstown* State *Ind.*

" Residence—Street No. *1446 W Ohio* City *Indpls.*

Single / Widower / Divorced } *Single*    { 1st, 2nd or 3rd marriage } *1st*

Name of Father *Charles Grider*

Maiden name of Mother *Mary Huckleberry*

Bride's name *June Tungate*

Her age *34*

" color *white*

" occupation *Housekeeper*

" Birthplace—City *Campbellville* State *Ky.*

" Residence—Street No. *1546 S Harding* City *Indpls.*

Single / Widow / Divorced } *Single*    { 1st, 2nd or 3rd marriage } *1st*

Name of Father *Jeff Tungate*

Maiden name of Mother *Mary Minor*

Date of this marriage *April 15, 1944*

Place of this marriage *Indpls. Ind.*

Name and title of person Performing this marriage *Albert Kane Justice of Peace*

His address *158½ E Court St.*

Witness { Name *Floyd M. Skile*  { Address *457 N. La Salle*

## Return this Report to County Clerk with License and Certificate

# Marriage Record for Board of Health

## To Be Returned by the Minister or Other Person Performing Ceremony

*William N. Proctor* and *Pearl Messer*

Groom's name *William N. Proctor*

His age *48*

" color *White*

" occupation *Pennsylvania R R*

" Birthplace—City *Detroit* State *Mich*

" Residence—Street No. *126 School Ave* City *Detroit*

Single / Widower / Divorced } *Single* { 1st, 2nd or 3rd marriage } *1st*

Name of Father *Wm Proctor*

Maiden name of Mother *Anna Proctor*

Bride's name *Pearl Messer*

Her age *42*

" color *white*

" occupation *Laundry Worker*

" Birthplace—City *Bedford* State *Kentucky*

" Residence—Street No. *918 Highland* City *Indpls*

Single / Widow / Divorced } *Divorced* { 1st, 2nd or 3rd marriage } *2nd*

Name of Father *Charles Miles*

Maiden name of Mother *Lula Watson*

Date of this marriage *April 10 1944*

Place of this marriage *Indianapolis Indiana*

Name and title of person Performing this marriage *Ernest T Lane, Justice of Peace*

His address *152½ East Court St*

Witness { Name *Mary Jo Lane* Address *3741 College Ave.*

## Return this Report to County Clerk with License and Certificate

# Marriage Record for Board of Health

To Be Returned by the Minister or Other Person Performing Ceremony

*Kilian Schrandt* and *Nellie Sudler*

Groom's name _Kilian Schrandt_

His age _62_

" color _White_

" occupation _Hangman_

" Birthplace—City _Germany_ State _____

" Residence—Street No. _Roosevelt Hotel Indianapolis_

Single / Widower / Divorced } _Single_    1st, 2nd or 3rd marriage } _1st_

Name of Father _Oddo Schrandt_

Maiden name of Mother _Marie Weimit_

Bride's name _Nellie Sudler_

Her age _57_

" color _White_

" occupation _Cook_

" Birthplace—City _Winchester_ State _Indiana_

" Residence—Street No. _Roosevelt Hotel_ City _Indianapolis_

Single / Widow / Divorced } _Single_    1st, 2nd or 3rd marriage } _1st_

Name of Father _Columbus Sudler_

Maiden name of Mother _Sarah E. Barnes_

Date of this marriage _April 10, 1944_

Place of this marriage _Indianapolis Ind._

Name and title of person Performing this marriage _Ernest Lowe Justice of Peace_

His address _152½ East Court St._

Witness { Name _Mary Jo Lowe_
{ Address _3741 College Ave_

**Return this Report to County Clerk with License and Certificate**

12

# Marriage Record for Board of Health

### To Be Returned by the Minister or Other Person Performing Ceremony

_Frank_ and _____

Groom's name _Frank_

His age _24_

" color _White_

" occupation _Factory worker_

" Birthplace—City _____ State _Ind._

" Residence—Street No. _310_ _____ City _____

Single
~~Widower~~
Divorced } _Divorced_ { ~~1st,~~ 2nd or 3rd marriage } _2nd_

Name of Father _____

Maiden name of Mother _____

Bride's name _____

Her age _18_

" color _White_

" occupation _____

" Birthplace—City _____ State _____

" Residence—Street No. _542_ _____ City _____

Single
~~Widow~~
~~Divorced~~ } _Single_ { 1st, 2nd or 3rd marriage } _1st_

Name of Father _____

Maiden name of Mother _____

Date of this marriage _7/18/44_

Place of this marriage _____

Name and title of person
Performing this marriage _Rev._ _____

His address _627_ _____

_____

Witness { Name _____
{ Address _____

### Return this Report to County Clerk with License and Certificate

# Marriage Record for Board of Health
### To Be Returned by the Minister or Other Person Performing Ceremony

_Ross Neely_ and _Pearl E Wright_

Groom's name _Ross Neely_

His age _39_

" color _c_

" occupation _butcher_

" Birthplace—City _DeKull_ State _Mississippi_

" Residence—Street No. _305 W 28th_ City _Indianapolis_

~~Single~~
~~Widower~~
Divorced } _divorced_   { 1st, 2nd or 3rd marriage } _3 rd_

Name of Father _Robert Neely_

Maiden name of Mother _Mary Gully_

Bride's name _Pearl E. Wright_

Her age _27_

" color _c_

" occupation _nothing_

" Birthplace—City _Carlington_ State _Kentucky_

" Residence—Street No. _805 W. 28th st_ City _Indianapolis_

Single
~~Widow~~
~~Divorced~~ } _single_   { 1st, 2nd or 3rd marriage } _first_

Name of Father _James H. Wright_

Maiden name of Mother _Annie Mae Bell_

Date of this marriage _April 11, 1944_

Place of this marriage _Indianapolis, Indiana_

Name and title of person
Performing this marriage _S. S. Thomas minister_

His address _702 S. Illinois street, Indpls, Indiana_

Witness { Name _Opal L. Tandy_
         { Address _321 W. 14th st. Indpls. Indiana_

### Return this Report to County Clerk with License and Certificate

# Marriage Record for Board of Health

## To Be Returned by the Minister or Other Person Performing Ceremony

_Charles Robert Baker_ and _Phyllis Ann Garrity_

Groom's name _Charles Robert Baker_

His age _22_

" color _white_

" occupation _U. S. Navy_

" Birthplace—City _Hamilton C_ State _Ind._

" Residence—Street No. _321 E 10_ City _Indianapolis Ind._

Single / Widower / Divorced } _Single_ 1st, 2nd or 3rd marriage } _first 1st_

Name of Father _Virgil Legran Baker_

Maiden name of Mother _Fern Hadley_

Bride's name _Phyllis Ann Garrity_

Her age _18_

" color _white_

" occupation ___

" Birthplace—City _Indianapolis_ State _Ind._

" Residence—Street No. _321 E 10_ City _Indianapolis Ind._

Single / Widow / Divorced } _Single_ 1st, 2nd or 3rd marriage } _1st_

Name of Father _Alfred Deldine Garrity_

Maiden name of Mother _Stella Ann Smith_

Date of this marriage _April 14 1944_

Place of this marriage _Indianapolis Ind._

Name and title of person Performing this marriage _Rev. Basil G. Stults_

His address _28 N Addison St_
_Indianapolis_

Witness { Name _Adrian Lee Henry_
{ Address _Westfield, Ind._

## Return this Report to County Clerk with License and Certificate

# Marriage Record for Board of Health
### To Be Returned by the Minister or Other Person Performing Ceremony

_____ Joseph _____ and _____

Groom's name _____ Joseph _____

His age _____ 26

" color _____ _____

" occupation _____ _____

" Birthplace—City _____ State _____

" Residence—Street No. _____ City _____

Single / Widower / Divorced } _____ yes       { 1st, 2nd or 3rd marriage } _____

Name of Father _____ John H _____

Maiden name of Mother _____ Josephine _____

Bride's name _____ Helen _____

Her age _____ 21

" color _____ _____ Brown

" occupation _____ _____

" Birthplace—City _____ State _____

" Residence—Street No. _____ City _____

Single / Widow / Divorced } _____       { 1st, 2nd or 3rd marriage } _____

Name of Father _____ _____

Maiden name of Mother _____ _____

Date of this marriage _____ April _____

Place of this marriage _____ Indianapolis _____

Name and title of person Performing this marriage _____ Rev _____

His address _____ _____

Witness { Name _____
{ Address _____

### Return this Report to County Clerk with License and Certificate

# Marriage Record for Board of Health

### To Be Returned by the Minister or Other Person Performing Ceremony

_Harold K. Light_ and _Jean Kline_

Groom's name _Harold K. Light_

His age _23_

" color _White_

" occupation _U. S. Army_

" Birthplace—City _Plainfield_ State _Indiana_

" Residence—Street No. _Fort Custer_ City _Michigan_ Indianapolis Indiana

Single } _Single_ { 1st, 2nd or 3rd } _First_
Widower } { marriage }
Divorced

Name of Father _Israel Light_

Maiden name of Mother _Cora Leweller_

Bride's name _Jean Kline_

Her age _21_

" color _White_

" occupation _Stenographer_

" Birthplace—City _Indianapolis_ State _Indiana_

" Residence—Street No. _346 East Morris_ street City _Indianapolis, Ind._

Single } _Single_ { 1st, 2nd or 3rd } _First_
Widow } { marriage }
Divorced

Name of Father _George W. Kline_

Maiden name of Mother _Stella Marie Galvin_

Date of this marriage _April 1, 1944_

Place of this marriage _Indianapolis, Indiana_

Name and title of person
Performing this marriage _Rev. E Robert Ansley_

His address _287 Downey Avenue_
_Indianapolis_

Witness { Name _Leon McNeely Liverett_
{ Address _520 N. Meridian St #316 Indpl's, Ind._

## Return this Report to County Clerk with License and Certificate

12

# Marriage Record for Board of Health
## To Be Returned by the Minister or Other Person Performing Ceremony

_Dallas Garfield Davis_ and _Mary Jane Manning_

Groom's name _Dallas Garfield Davis_

His age _30_

" color _White_

" occupation _Navy_

" Birthplace—City _Mt Auburn Shelby County_ State _Indiana_

" Residence—Street No. _Davisville, Rhode Island_

Single
Widower  } _single_      { 1st, 2nd or 3rd  } _first_
Divorced                   marriage

Name of Father _James Garfield Davis_

Maiden name of Mother _Ethel Mae Carvin_

---

Bride's name _Mary Jane Manning_

Her age _26_

" color _White_

" occupation _Defense worker_

" Birthplace—City _Anderson_ State _Indiana_

" Residence—Street No. _2402 Central Ave_ City _Indianapolis_

Single
Widow   } _single_      { 1st, 2nd or 3rd  } _first_
Divorced                  marriage

Name of Father _William Edward Manning_

Maiden name of Mother _Effa Ann Williams_

---

Date of this marriage _April 11, 1944_

Place of this marriage _Sutherland Presbyterian Church_

Name and title of person
Performing this marriage _Rev. Hazel A. Pfluger_

His address _3246 Winthrop Ave_
_Indianapolis 6, Ind._

Witness { Name _Mrs. Nellie M. Wigle  John L. ____
         { Address _2964 Guilford   2914 Guilford Ave._

## Return this Report to County Clerk with License and Certificate

# Marriage Record for Board of Health

### To Be Returned by the Minister or Other Person Performing Ceremony

Martin Jessie _____ and _Frances Harris_

Groom's name _Martin Jessie_

His age _25_

" color _White_

" occupation _Truck Driver_

" Birthplace—City _Dare County (Weed)_ State _Kentucky_

" Residence—Street No. _5174 W. Washington_ City _Indianapolis, Ind._

Single  
Widower } _Divorced_      { 1st, 2nd or 3rd } _Second_  
Divorced                    { marriage

Name of Father _M. D. Jessie_

Maiden name of Mother _Ethel Dixon_

Bride's name _Frances Harris_

Her age _19_

" color _White_

" occupation _Allison Eng. - Inspection_

" Birthplace—City _Farmersburg_ State _Indiana_

" Residence—Street No. _118 W. Walnut St_ City _Indianapolis, Ind._

Single  
Widow } _Single_      { 1st, 2nd or 3rd } _First_  
Divorced              { marriage

Name of Father _Elmer Harris_

Maiden name of Mother _Holdie Crapo_

Date of this marriage _April 11, 1944_

Place of this marriage _Indianapolis, Indiana_

Name and title of person  
Performing this marriage _Orrie M. McCleary, Minister_

His address _542 Holt Rd - Indianapolis, Indiana_

Witness { Name _Mrs J. W. McCleary_  
         { Address _542 Holt Rd Indianapolis, Indiana_

## Return this Report to County Clerk with License and Certificate

# Marriage Record for Board of Health
### To Be Returned by the Minister or Other Person Performing Ceremony

*King* and *Burch*

Groom's name *Robert L. King*

His age *26*

" color *White*

" occupation *Lieut. U.S. Army*

" Birthplace—City *Indpls.* State *Ind*

" Residence—Street No. *617 Tecumseh* City *Indpls*

Single / Widower / Divorced } *Single* { 1st, 2nd or 3rd marriage } *first*

Name of Father *Thomas King*

Maiden name of Mother *Ellen Bell Frantz*

Bride's name *Mary Margaret Burch*

Her age *22*

" color *White*

" occupation *Clerk U.S. Employment Service*

" Birthplace—City *Indpls* State *Ind*

" Residence—Street No. *1112 W. 28th St* City *Indpls*

Single / Widow / Divorced } *Single* { 1st, 2nd or 3rd marriage } *first*

Name of Father *Ernest H. Burch*

Maiden name of Mother *Pauline M. Samuel*

Date of this marriage *April 11, 1944*

Place of this marriage *59 N. Rural St*

Name and title of person Performing this marriage *C. A. Trinkle, D.D.*

His address *59 N. Rural St*

Witness { Name *Lawrence King / Mary O'Day*
Address *970 Middle Dr. / 40 N. Rural St* }

### Return this Report to County Clerk with License and Certificate

# Marriage Record for Board of Health

### To Be Returned by the Minister or Other Person Performing Ceremony

*Joseph Linville* and *Velma Kieninger*

Groom's name _Joseph Linville._

His age _18_

" color _white_

" occupation _United States Rubber Co._

" Birthplace—City _Indianapolis_ State _Ind._

" Residence—Street No. _1162 Cameron_ City _Indianapolis_

Single ⎫
~~Widower~~ ⎬        ⎧ 1st, ~~2nd or 3rd~~ ⎫
~~Divorced~~ ⎭        ⎩ marriage ⎭

Name of Father _Frederick Linville._

Maiden name of Mother _Clara Tanger._

Bride's name _Velma Kieninger_

Her age _16 yrs_

" color _white_

" occupation _House Keeper._

" Birthplace—City _Indianapolis_ State _Ind._

" Residence—Street No. _1243 Mc Dougal_ City _Indianapolis_

Single ⎫
~~Widow~~ ⎬        ⎧ 1st, ~~2nd or 3rd~~ ⎫
~~Divorced~~ ⎭        ⎩ marriage ⎭

Name of Father _Julius Kieninger_

Maiden name of Mother _Florence Arnold._

Date of this marriage _April 11, 1944._

Place of this marriage _1109 E. Tabor St._

Name and title of person
Performing this marriage _Rev. J. M. Downey_

His address _1109 E. Tabor St._
_Indianapolis, Ind_

Witness ⎧ Name _Harry Kieninger._
⎩ Address _Loretta Adcock_

## Return this Report to County Clerk with License and Certificate

# Marriage Record for Board of Health
### To Be Returned by the Minister or Other Person Performing Ceremony

*George Edwin Witte* and *Roberta Faye Roberts*

Groom's name _George Edwin Witt_

His age _22_

" color _White_

" occupation _Gunner in Navy_

" Birthplace—City _Decatur_ State _Illinois_

" Residence—Street No. _1674 E Johns_ City _Decatur_

Single / Widower / Divorced } _Single_     { 1st, 2nd or 3rd marriage } _First_

Name of Father _Adolph Witt_

Maiden name of Mother _Frieda Skaronski_

Bride's name _Roberta Faye Roberts_

Her age _20_

" color _White_

" occupation _Nurse_

" Birthplace—City _Decatur_ State _Illinois_

" Residence—Street No. _R R #7_ City _Decatur_

Single / Widow / Divorced } _Single_     { 1st, 2nd or 3rd marriage } _First_

Name of Father _LeRoy Roberts_

Maiden name of Mother _Frances Nichols_

Date of this marriage _Apr. 12, 1944_

Place of this marriage _Indianapolis Ind_

Name and title of person Performing this marriage _J.S. Albert, D.D. Minister_

His address _414 N. Wallace_

_Indianapolis 1, Ind_

Witness { Name _Ernest W. Dworak_
{ Address _Decatur, Ill._

## Return this Report to County Clerk with License and Certificate

# Marriage Record for Board of Health
## To Be Returned by the Minister or Other Person Performing Ceremony

George F. Rebbock and Amalia V. Miller

Groom's name _George F. Rebbock_

His age _54_

" color _White_

" occupation _Truck Driver_

" Birthplace—City _Cincinnati_ State _Ohio_

" Residence—Street No _1934 N. LaSalle_ City _Indianapolis_

Single Widower Divorced } _Single_ { 1st, 2nd or 3rd marriage } _1st_

Name of Father _Charles H. Rebbock_

Maiden name of Mother _Emma Krantz_

Bride's name _Amalia V. Miller_

Her age _50_

" color _White_

" occupation _None_

" Birthplace—City _Indianapolis_ State _Indiana_

" Residence—Street No _2518 E. 18_ City _Indianapolis_

Single Widow Divorced } _Divorced_ { 1st, 2nd or 3rd marriage } _3rd_

Name of Father _Henry R. Steinkühler_

Maiden name of Mother _Elizabeth T. Meyer_

Date of this marriage _April 12, 1944_

Place of this marriage _Indianapolis, Ind._

Name and title of person Performing this marriage _Ernest Lane, Justice of Peace._

His address _152½ East Court_

Witness { Name _Mary Jo Lane_ { Address _3741 N. College_

## Return this Report to County Clerk with License and Certificate

# Marriage Record for Board of Health
### To Be Returned by the Minister or Other Person Performing Ceremony

Ernest W Dvorak and Helen L. Kearney

Groom's name _Ernest W. Dvorak_

His age _21_

" color _White_

" occupation _Sergeant_

" Birthplace—City _Decatur_ State _Illinois_

" Residence—Street No. _R R # 2_ City _Decatur, Ill_

Single
Widower } _Single_ { 1st, 2nd or 3rd marriage } _1st_
Divorced

Name of Father _Gus Dvorak_

Maiden name of Mother _Louise Skrugina_

Bride's name _Helen L. Kearney_

Her age _19_

" color _White_

" occupation _Student Nurse_

" Birthplace—City _Lovington_ State _Illinois_

" Residence—Street No. _____ City _Lovington, Ill_

Single
Widow } _Single_ { 1st, 2nd or 3rd marriage } _First_
Divorced

Name of Father _John Kearney_

Maiden name of Mother _Zoe Foster_

Date of this marriage _Apr. 12, 1944_

Place of this marriage _Indianapolis, Ind._

Name and title of person Performing this marriage _J.S. Albert, D.D. Minister_

His address _414 N. Wallace Str._
_Indianapolis 1, Ind._

Witness { Name _Roberta Faye Witt_
{ Address _Decatur, Ill._

### Return this Report to County Clerk with License and Certificate

12

# Marriage Record for Board of Health

### To Be Returned by the Minister or Other Person Performing Ceremony

Joseph W Beavers _____ and _Georgiann Peters_

Groom's name _Joseph W Beavers_

His age _27_

" color _white_

" occupation _Service Station attendent_

" Birthplace—City _Bedford_ State _Indiana_

" Residence—Street No. _1901 N. Hel._ City _Indianapolis_

Single Widower Divorced } _Single_ { 1st, 2nd or 3rd marriage } _1st_

Name of Father _Wm. R. Beavers_

Maiden name of Mother _Leona Lake_

Bride's name _Georgiann Peters_

Her age _25_

" color _white_

" occupation _Curtis Wright - Tabulator_

" Birthplace—City _Huntington_ State _Ind_

" Residence—Street No. _1901 N Hel._ City _Indianapolis_

Single Widow Divorced } _Single_ { 1st, 2nd or 3rd marriage } _1st_

Name of Father _George Peters_

Maiden name of Mother _Ala - Boker_

Date of this marriage _April - 12 - 1944_

Place of this marriage _Indianapolis_

Name and title of person Performing this marriage _Rev John A Edwards_

His address _4335 Pennsylvania St_
_Indianapolis Indiana_

Witness { Name _Chas W. Webster_
{ Address _Indianapolis Ind. 21 - West16_

### Return this Report to County Clerk with License and Certificate

# Marriage Record for Board of Health
### To Be Returned by the Minister or Other Person Performing Ceremony

*Charles W. Holder* and *Dorothy E Jack*

Groom's name *Charles W. Holder*

His age *39*

" color *White*

" occupation *Lawyer*

" Birthplace—City *Mattoon* State *Illinois*

" Residence—Street No. *915 E. Maple Road* City *Indianapolis*

Single / Widower / Divorced } *Single*  { 1st, 2nd or 3rd marriage } *1*

Name of Father *John W. Holder*

Maiden name of Mother *Martha F. Glaser*

Bride's name *Dorothy E. Jack*

Her age *32*

" color *White*

" occupation *Comp. Opr.*

" Birthplace—City *Los Angeles* State *California*

" Residence—Street No. *3145 N. Illinois* City *Indianapolis*

Single / Widow / Divorced } *Single*  { 1st, 2nd or 3rd marriage } *1*

Name of Father *Wm. M. Jack*

Maiden name of Mother *Elizabeth Z. Waller*

Date of this marriage *April 12-1944*

Place of this marriage *Indianapolis*

Name and title of person Performing this marriage *Rev. Raymond R. Nolf*

His address *1347 N. Meridian St. Indianapolis*

Witness { Name *Ralph E. Hueber and Dorothy J. Hueber* Address *3917 N. New Jersey St - Indianapolis Ind* }

### Return this Report to County Clerk with License and Certificate

# Marriage Record for Board of Health
### To Be Returned by the Minister or Other Person Performing Ceremony

Harry T. Biehl Jr. and A. Pauline Brazendine

Groom's name _Harry T. Biehl Jr._

His age _27_

" color _White_

" occupation _Shell Car agents_

" Birthplace—City _Indianapolis_ State _Indiana_

" Residence—Street No. _2257 N. Ill St_ City _Indianapolis Ind_

Single / Widower / Divorced } _Single_   { 1st, 2nd, 3rd marriage } _First_

Name of Father _Harry T. Biehl Sr._

Maiden name of Mother _May Stanbrough_

Bride's name _A. Pauline Brazendine_

Her age _20_

" color _White_

" occupation _Machine operator_

" Birthplace—City _Indianapolis_ State _Indiana_

" Residence—Street No. _2343 English_ City _Indianapolis_

Single / Widow / Divorced } _Single_   { 1st, 2nd, 3rd marriage } _First_

Name of Father _Ellis B. Brazendine_

Maiden name of Mother _Mary Ola Rippy_

Date of this marriage _April 12 —1944_

Place of this marriage _418 So. Temple av Indpls_

Name and title of person Performing this marriage _Rev. J. E. Adams_

His address _418 So. Temple av Indianapolis Ind_

Witness { Name _Florence Spoon_
{ Address _314 Leeds av Indianapolis_

### Return this Report to County Clerk with License and Certificate

# Marriage Record for Board of Health
## To Be Returned by the Minister or Other Person Performing Ceremony

_____ and _____

Groom's name _Elmer R. Pursell_

His age _37_

" color _White_

" occupation _U. S. Army_

" Birthplace—City _Dolph_ State _Ind_

" Residence—Street No. _3330 N Meridian_ City _Dolph_

Single / Widower- / Divorced } _Divorced_ { 1st, 2nd or 3rd— marriage } _2nd_

Name of Father _Elmer M. Pursell_

Maiden name of Mother _Ida Blanche Ralph_

Bride's name _Burnelle Bailey_

Her age _27_

" color _White_

" occupation _Superin_

" Birthplace—City _Indianapolis_ State _Ind_

" Residence—Street No. _5771 Central_ City _Indps_

Single- / Widow- / Divorced } _Divorced_ { 1st, 2nd or 3rd marriage } _2nd_

Name of Father _Harry E. Bailey_

Maiden name of Mother _Beatrice Mk. Hugh_

Date of this marriage _April 12, 1944_

Place of this marriage _Indianapolis, Ind_

Name and title of person Performing this marriage _Harry E. Campbell_

His address _4750 N Drummond St_ _Indianapolis, Ind_

Witness { Name _Dorothy Letteras_
{ Address _Kenneth V. Christena_

## Return this Report to County Clerk with License and Certificate

# Marriage Record for Board of Health

### To Be Returned by the Minister or Other Person Performing Ceremony

Robert Richard Swatsenbarg and Carol Frances Wylie

Groom's name _Robert Richard Swatsenbarg_

His age _23_

" color _White_

" occupation _Soldier_

" Birthplace—City _Proctor_ State _Oklahoma_

" Residence—Street No. _Billings Gen. Hosp._ City _Ft. Benj. Harrison, Indiana_

Single / Widower / Divorced } _Single_ { 1st, 2nd or 3rd marriage } _First_

Name of Father _Elmer Wesley Swatsenbarg_

Maiden name of Mother _Janie Roberts_

Bride's name _Carol Frances Wylie_

Her age _20_

" color _White_

" occupation _None_

" Birthplace—City _Connersville_ State _Indiana_

" Residence—Street No. _1532 East Tenth_ City _Indianapolis_

Single / Widow / Divorced } _Single_ { 1st, 2nd or 3rd marriage } _First_

Name of Father _Charles Dow Wylie_

Maiden name of Mother _Matilda Jane Prather_

Date of this marriage _12 April 1944_

Place of this marriage _Ft. Benjamin Harrison, Indiana_

Name and title of person Performing this marriage _Chaplain David A. Donohoe, Lt. Col._

His address _Billings General Hospital, Ft. Benjamin Harrison, Indiana_

Witness { Name _Pfc. John P. Timmerman_ { Address _Billings General Hospital, Ft. Benjamin Harrison, Indiana_

## Return this Report to County Clerk with License and Certificate

# Marriage Record for Board of Health

To Be Returned by the Minister or Other Person Performing Ceremony

_Lee_ and _Guberman_

Groom's name _Billy Lee_

His age _23_

" color _White_

" occupation _Y.S.Navy_

" Birthplace—City _Indianapolis_ State _Indiana_

" Residence—Street No. _U.S.Navy_ City _____

Single / Widower / Divorced } _Single_ { 1st, 2nd or 3rd marriage } _First_

Name of Father _John Lee_

Maiden name of Mother _Edna Whitaker_

Bride's name _Silvia Guberman_

Her age _20_

" color _White_

" occupation _Blueprint Draftsman_

" Birthplace—City _Chicago_ State _Illinois_

" Residence—Street No. _2254 Carollton_ City _Indianapolis_

Single / Widow / Divorced } _Single_ { 1st, 2nd or 3rd marriage } _First_

Name of Father _Leo Guberman_

Maiden name of Mother _Sophie Bresont_

Date of this marriage _April 12, 1944_

Place of this marriage _Indianapolis_

Name and title of person Performing this marriage _Jean S. Milner, minister_

His address _Minister 2nd Pres. Ch. Indianapolis_

Witness { Name _Willard A. Murray_
{ Address _1815 Roosevelt Ave, Indpls Ind_

**Return this Report to County Clerk with License and Certificate**

# Marriage Record for Board of Health

### To Be Returned by the Minister or Other Person Performing Ceremony

Merrill F Thompson _____ and _____ Frances Thelma Bennett

Groom's name _____ Merrill F. Thompson

His age _____ 35

" color _____ White

" occupation _____ Apt. Care Taker

" Birthplace—City _____ Indianapolis _____ State _____ Ind

" Residence—Street No. 2869 N Illinois City _____ Indianapolis, Ind

Single / Widower / Divorced } _____ Single _____ { 1st, 2nd or 3rd marriage } _____ 1st

Name of Father _____ Millard Thompson

Maiden name of Mother _____ Patti Brown

Bride's name _____ Frances Thelma Bennett

Her age _____ 34

" color _____ White

" occupation _____ Inspector

" Birthplace—City _____ Haute _____ State _____ Kentucky

" Residence—Street No. 313 Berton Ave City _____ Indianapolis

Single / Widow / Divorced } _____ Single _____ { 1st, 2nd or 3rd marriage } _____ 1st

Name of Father _____ Benjamin Bennett

Maiden name of Mother _____ Mary Mc Cauley

Date of this marriage _____ Apr. 12, 1944

Place of this marriage _____ St Anthonys Rectory, Indianapolis Ind.

Name and title of person Performing this marriage _____ M. J. Forman Catholic Priest

His address _____ 379 N Warman Ave, Indianapolis Ind

Witness { Name _____ Mrs Annabelle Aliff _____ Mildred Aliff
{ Address _____ R.R.2 Box 100 _____ 313 Berton Ave
_____ Greenwood Ind _____ Greenwood Ind.

### Return this Report to County Clerk with License and Certificate

12

# Marriage Record for Board of Health
### To Be Returned by the Minister or Other Person Performing Ceremony

H. Leverett Jacobi _____ and _____ Anita Fleming

Groom's name _____ H. Leverett Jacobi

His age _____ 25

" color _____ White

" occupation _____ 1st Lt. Marine Aviator

" Birthplace—City _____ Kellogg _____ State _____ Idaho

" Residence—Street No. _____ Sioux City _____ City _____ Iowa

Single / Widower / Divorced } Single _____ { 1st, 2nd or 3rd marriage } First

Name of Father _____ H. R. Jacobi

Maiden name of Mother _____ Fern Leola West

Bride's name _____ Anita Fleming

Her age _____ 24

" color _____ White

" occupation _____ Advertising

" Birthplace—City _____ Mobile, Alabama _____ State _____ Alabama

" Residence—Street No. _____ 410 N. Meridian St _____ City _____ Indianapolis, Ind

Single / Widow / Divorced } Single _____ { 1st, 2nd or 3rd marriage } First

Name of Father _____ Sol Fleming

Maiden name of Mother _____ Ruby Lee Sprinkle

Date of this marriage _____ April 12th 1944

Place of this marriage _____ Christ Church, Indianapolis

Name and title of person Performing this marriage _____ Rev. E. Hargis Powell, Rector of First Church

His address _____ 126 East 43rd St

_____ Indianapolis, Ind

Witness { Name _____ Captain Roy J. High
{ Address _____ 410 N. Meridian St. Indianapolis, Ind.

### Return this Report to County Clerk with License and Certificate

# Marriage Record for Board of Health

## To Be Returned by the Minister or Other Person Performing Ceremony

Charles De Graphenreed and Lois Smith

Groom's name _Charles T. De Graphenreed_

His age _30_

" color _Coolord_

" occupation _Truck Driver_

" Birthplace—City _Springfield_ State _Tenn_

" Residence—Street No. _2619 Bulvd_ City _Indianapolis_

Single / Widower / Divorced } _Divorced_   1st, 2nd or 3rd marriage } _2nd_

Name of Father _Fort Pile Graphenreed_

Maiden name of Mother _Ida Murphy_

Bride's name _Lois Smith_

Her age _25_

" color _Colord_

" occupation _Defense Work_

" Birthplace—City _Indiapolis_ State _Ind_

" Residence—Street No. _444 W 89_ City _Indianapolis_

Single / Widow / Divorced } _Divorce_   1st, 2nd or 3rd marriage } _2nd_

Name of Father _Joseph Gardener_

Maiden name of Mother _Anvil_

Date of this marriage _April 12, 1944_

Place of this marriage _Indianapolis_

Name and title of person Performing this marriage _Rev J B. Carter_

His address _452 W 20 St_ _Indianapolis_

Witness { Name _Verona McDougle  Rogrlau_
{ Address _605 N 88 St   1247 Blvd Place_

## Return this Report to County Clerk with License and Certificate

# Marriage Record for Board of Health
### To Be Returned by the Minister or Other Person Performing Ceremony

*Burnett Conner* ___ and *Beulah I Werler*

Groom's name _Burnett Conner_

His age _47_

" color _White_

" occupation _Lathe Operator_

" Birthplace—City _Shelbyville_ State _Indiana_

" Residence—Street No. _156 W. 18th St._ City _Indpls_

~~Single~~ ~~Widower~~ Divorced } _Divorced_ { 1st, ~~2nd or 3rd~~ marriage } _2nd_

Name of Father _William C. Bennett_

Maiden name of Mother _Margaret Conner_

Bride's name _Beulah I Werler_

Her age _41_

" color _White_

" occupation _Hostess_

" Birthplace—City _Lebanon_ State _Ind_

" Residence—Street No. _156 W. 18th_ City _Indpls Ind_

~~Single~~ ~~Widow~~ Divorced } _Divorced_ { ~~1st,~~ 2nd or ~~3rd~~ marriage } _2nd_

Name of Father _Grant Hawkins_

Maiden name of Mother _Minnie Haller_

Date of this marriage _April 13-1944_

Place of this marriage _Greenfield Indiana_

Name and title of person Performing this marriage _Byron Kennerly_

His address _235 West N St Greenfield Ind_

Witness { Name _Ruth K White_ Address _656 East 21st St Indianapolis Ind_

### Return this Report to County Clerk with License and Certificate

 12

# Marriage Record for Board of Health

### To Be Returned by the Minister or Other Person Performing Ceremony

_____ and _____

Groom's name _Delman P. Wright_

His age _39_

" color _White_

" occupation _U S Army_

" Birthplace—City _Hayzi_ State _Va._

" Residence—Street No. _U. S. Army_ City _____

Single / Widower / Divorced } _Divorced_  {1st, 2nd or 3rd marriage} _2nd_

Name of Father _John Wright_

Maiden name of Mother _Lydia Sutherland_

Bride's name _Helen R. Grable_

Her age _33_

" color _White_

" occupation _Clerk_

" Birthplace—City _New Castle_ State _Ind_

" Residence—Street No. _Indpls._ City _Ind_

Single / Widow / Divorced } _Divorced_  {1st, 2nd or 3rd marriage} _3rd_

Name of Father _Carl T. Walters._

Maiden name of Mother _Anna Forbes._

Date of this marriage _April 13 1944_

Place of this marriage _Indpls. Ind._

Name and title of person Performing this marriage _Rev. Geo. G. Tymony_

His address _2424 W. St Clair St_
_Indpls. Ind_

Witness { Name _N Wayne Hunt_

{ Address _913 Congress, Indpls, Indiana_

## Return this Report to County Clerk with License and Certificate

12

# Marriage Record for Board of Health

### To Be Returned by the Minister or Other Person Performing Ceremony

*John Worland Hartman* and *Pearl Tubbs*

Groom's name _John Worland Hartman_

His age _46_

" color _White_

" occupation _Painter_

" Birthplace—City _Shelbyville_ State _Indiana_

" Residence—Street No. _247 h Gray_ City _Ind._

Single / Widower / Divorced } _Divorced_ { 1st, 2nd or 3rd marriage } _2nd_

Name of Father _George Hartman_

Maiden name of Mother _Mary Worland_

Bride's name _Pearl Tubbs_

Her age _44_

" color _White_

" occupation _None_

" Birthplace—City _Bloomfield_ State _Ind._

" Residence—Street No. _260 Richard_ City _Ind._

Single / Widow / Divorced } _Widow_ { 1st, 2nd or 3rd marriage } _2nd_

Name of Father _Robert A. Hudson_

Maiden name of Mother _Lucy Baugh_

Date of this marriage _April 13 - 44_

Place of this marriage _Ind._

Name and title of person Performing this marriage _Justice of Peace_

His address _152 ½ East Court St._

Witness { Name _Mary Jo Lane_ / Address _3741 College Ave._

## Return this Report to County Clerk with License and Certificate

# Marriage Record for Board of Health

### To Be Returned by the Minister or Other Person Performing Ceremony

Oscar Franklin Clark and Helen Louise Keller

Groom's name _Oscar Franklin Clark_

His age _20_

" color _white_

" occupation _Mechanic_

" Birthplace—City _Cleveland_ State _Tennessee_

" Residence—Street No. _1227 Bellefontain_ City _Indpls._

Single / Widower / Divorced } _Single_    { 1st, 2nd or 3rd marriage } _1st_

Name of Father _Homer Clark_

Maiden name of Mother _Annie Belle Suson_

Bride's name _Helen Louise Keller_

Her age _16_

" color _white_

" occupation _none_

" Birthplace—City _Birmingham_ State _Alabama_

" Residence—Street No. _1016 N New Jersey_ City _Indpls._

Single / Widow / Divorced } _Single_    { 1st, 2nd or 3rd marriage } _1st_

Name of Father _James Keller_

Maiden name of Mother _Mamie Osman_

Date of this marriage _April 13-44_

Place of this marriage _Indianapolis Indiana_

Name and title of person Performing this marriage _Ernest T Hane Justice of Peace_

His address _15½ East Court Street_

Witness { Name _Mary Jo Hane_ { Address _3741 College Ave._

## Return this Report to County Clerk with License and Certificate

# Marriage Record for Board of Health

To Be Returned by the Minister or Other Person Performing Ceremony

Earl Abbott and Wilma L. Brown

Groom's name _Earl Abbott_

His age _25_

" color _white_

" occupation _Elevator Operator_

" Birthplace—City _Acorn_ State _Ky_

" Residence—Street No. _1705 Ingram_ City _Indpls._

Single / Widower / Divorced } _Divorced_ { 1st, 2nd or 3rd marriage } _2nd_

Name of Father _Chester A. Abbott_

Maiden name of Mother _Mollie Bullock_

Bride's name _Wilma L. Brown_

Her age _28_

" color _white_

" occupation _Sales lady_

" Birthplace—City _Indpls._ State _Ind._

" Residence—Street No. _1062 N. Berwick_ _Indpls._

Single / Widow / Divorced } _Single_ { 1st, 2nd or 3rd marriage } _1st_

Name of Father _Milton Jane Brown_

Maiden name of Mother _Rebecca Jane Poore_

Date of this marriage _April 18-44_

Place of this marriage _Indpls. Ind._

Name and title of person Performing this marriage _Ernest Lane, Justice of Peace_

His address _152½ East Court St_

Witness { Name _Mary Jo Lane_ Address _3741 College Ave_

**Return this Report to County Clerk with License and Certificate**

# Marriage Record for Board of Health

### To Be Returned by the Minister or Other Person Performing Ceremony

*George H Woods* and *Irene Mason*

Groom's name _Geo Howard Woods._

His age _28._

" color _C._

" occupation _Labor._

" Birthplace—City _Irwoy, Paris_ State _Tenn._

" Residence—Street No. _1953 Columbia_ City _Indianapolis._

Single
Widower } _Divorced_ { 1st, 2nd or 3rd marriage } _2 nd_
Divorced

Name of Father _Geo Woods._

Maiden name of Mother _Manie Patterson_

Bride's name _Irene Mason_

Her age _21._

" color _C._

" occupation _none._

" Birthplace—City _Indianapolis_ State _Ind._

" Residence—Street No. _1909 Yandes St_ City _Indianapolis Ind_

Single
Widow } _Single_ { 1st, 2nd or 3rd marriage } _1 st._
Divorced

Name of Father _Marshall Mason._

Maiden name of Mother _Bertha Sanders_

Date of this marriage _April 13, 1944._

Place of this marriage _Indianapolis, Ind._

Name and title of person
Performing this marriage _St Thomas minister_

His address _702 S. Illinois_

Witness { Name _Mrs Bertha King_
        { Address _1909 Yandes St_

## Return this Report to County Clerk with License and Certificate

## Marriage Record for Board of Health
### To Be Returned by the Minister or Other Person Performing Ceremony

*Luke Bozeman* and *Margaret Flagg*

Groom's name _Luke Bozeman_

His age _21_

" color _C_

" occupation _Chopping_

" Birthplace—City _____ State _Ala_

" Residence—Street No. _1505 Madicoll ...., Indianapois_

Single Widower Divorced } _Single_   { 1st, 2nd or 3rd marriage } _1st_

Name of Father _Clarence Bozeman_

Maiden name of Mother _Rejora Dompson_

Bride's name _Margaret Flagg_

Her age _19_

" color _C_

" occupation _Housekeeper_

" Birthplace—City _Alberta_ State _Ga._

" Residence—Street No. _1226 Calligoune, Indianapois_

Single Widow Divorced } _Single_   { 1st, 2nd or 3rd marriage } _1st_

Name of Father _James Flagg_

Maiden name of Mother _Flagg Sarah Hill_

Date of this marriage _April 13, 1944_

Place of this marriage _Indianapolis, Ind_

Name and title of person Performing this marriage _SS Thomas, Minister_

His address _702 S. Illinois Street_

Witness { Name _E L Johnson_
{ Address _152½ E. Court St_

### Return this Report to County Clerk with License and Certificate

# Marriage Record for Board of Health

### To Be Returned by the Minister or Other Person Performing Ceremony

_Harding_ and _McGinley_

Groom's name _Warren D. Harding_

His age _23_

" color _White_

" occupation _U.S. Army_

" Birthplace—City _Shoals_ State _Ind_

" Residence—Street No. _1351 N. Gladstone_ _Indpls Ind_

Single / Widower / Divorced _Single_ { 1st, 2nd or 3rd marriage _first_

Name of Father _Thomas Harding_

Maiden name of Mother _Anna Dickerson_

Bride's name _Katherine L. McGinley_

Her age _22_

" color _White_

" occupation _Secretary_

" Birthplace—City _Indpls._ State _Ind_

" Residence—Street No. _927 N Rural_ City _Indpls. Ind_

Single / Widow / Divorced _Single_ { 1st, 2nd or 3rd marriage _first_

Name of Father _Elbert H. McGinley_

Maiden name of Mother _Edna E. Pettycrew_

Date of this marriage _April. 13 - 1944_

Place of this marriage _Indianapolis Ind_

Name and title of person . Performing this marriage _Rev A H Emsworth_

His address. _550 N. Rural_

Witness { Name _Joseph Scanlan, Marvee Breeden_
{ Address _Phyllis Mae Yaggis_

### Return this Report to County Clerk with License and Certificate

# Marriage Record for Board of Health
## To Be Returned by the Minister or Other Person Performing Ceremony

_____ and _____

Groom's name __Fred H. Hamann__

His age __29__

" color __white__

" occupation __Ship Cook - 3rd__

" Birthplace—City __Oshkosh__, State __Wis__

" Residence—Street No. __U.S. Navy__ City _____

Single Widower Divorced } __Divorced__ { 1st, 2nd or 3rd marriage } __2nd__

Name of Father __Fred G. Hamann__

Maiden name of Mother __Gertrude Robbins__

Bride's name __Mary L. Stadler__

Her age __18__

" color __white__

" occupation __Saleslady__

" Birthplace—City __Osh Kosh__ State __Wis__

" Residence—Street No. __1028 Virginia av__ City _____

Single Widow Divorced } __Single__ { 1st, 2nd or 3rd marriage } __1st__

Name of Father __John Stadler__

Maiden name of Mother __Lou Brown__

Date of this marriage __April 13, 1944__

Place of this marriage __Indianapolis__

Name and title of person Performing this marriage __Carlton W. Atwater__
__minister - 1st Baptist Church__
__Newridian & Vermont,__

His address _____

Witness { Name __Earl F. Eade - 1028 Virginia__
{ Address __Margaret Lambert - R.R #2 Coatesville, Ind.__

## Return this Report to County Clerk with License and Certificate

12

# Marriage Record for Board of Health

### To Be Returned by the Minister or Other Person Performing Ceremony

*John A. Bannister* and *Mary J. Driscoll.*

Groom's name _John Augustine Bannister._

His age _22_

" color _white_

" occupation _U.S. Army_

" Birthplace—City _Indianapolis_ State _Ind._

" Residence—Street No. _217 E. 23rd St_ City _Indianapolis, Ind._

Single ~~Widower~~ ~~Divorced~~ } { 1st, ~~2nd or 3rd~~ marriage }

Name of Father _Taborn Bannister_

Maiden name of Mother _Alleta Creekbaum_

Bride's name _Mary J. Driscoll._

Her age _20_

" color _white_

" occupation _Clerk, Lucas-Harrold_

" Birthplace—City _Indianapolis_ State _Indiana._

" Residence—Street No. _1819 E. Minn_ City _Indianapolis_

Single ~~Widow~~ ~~Divorced~~ } { 1st, ~~2nd or 3rd~~ marriage }

Name of Father _Arthur Driscoll._

Maiden name of Mother _Mary J. Griffin._

Date of this marriage _April 13, 1944,_

Place of this marriage _St. Catherines Church_

Name and title of person Performing this marriage _Rev. J. M. Downey_

His address _1109 E. Tabor St_ _Indianapolis, Indiana._

Witness { Name _Arthur Driscoll_ { Address _Ruth Heylmann_

### Return this Report to County Clerk with License and Certificate

## Marriage Record for Board of Health
### To Be Returned by the Minister or Other Person Performing Ceremony

*William R. Wilson* and *Mary Jane Henry*

Groom's name *William R. Wilson*

His age *27*

" color *White*

" occupation *Sailor*

" Birthplace—City *Ohio County* State *Ky*

" Residence—Street No. *R.R. #20 Box 854* City *Ind'p'l's*

~~Single~~ ~~Widower~~ Divorced } *Divorced* { ~~1st, 2nd or 3rd~~ marriage } *Second*

Name of Father *Thomas D. Wilson*

Maiden name of Mother *Minnie Young*

Bride's name *Mary Jane Henry*

Her age *18*

" color *White*

" occupation *at home*

" Birthplace—City *Indianapolis* State *Ind*

" Residence—Street No. *1125 Laich St* City *Ind'p'l's*

Single ~~Widow~~ ~~Divorced~~ } *Single* { 1st, ~~2nd or 3rd~~ marriage } *First*

Name of Father *Raymond R. Henry*

Maiden name of Mother *Elizabeth Dickerson*

Date of this marriage *April 13, 1944*

Place of this marriage *Heath Memorial Methodist Church*

Name and title of person Performing this marriage *Rev. Charles R. Furry*

His address *1254 Windsor St Indianapolis, Ind.*

Witness { Name *Corliss Cour* Address *3024 Central Ave City*

### Return this Report to County Clerk with License and Certificate

12

# Marriage Record for Board of Health
### To Be Returned by the Minister or Other Person Performing Ceremony

_Frederick William Bergau_ and _Margaret Agnes Morrison_

Groom's name _Frederick William Bergau_

His age __37__

" color __White__

" occupation __bank teller__

" Birthplace—City __Indianapolis__ State __Indiana__

" Residence—Street No. __701 Cottage__ City __Indianapolis__

Single Widower Divorced } __Single__  {1st, 2nd or 3rd marriage} __1st__

Name of Father __John Bergau__

Maiden name of Mother __Amelia Klabunde__

Bride's name _Margaret Agnes Morrison_

Her age __33__

" color __White__

" occupation __Stenographer__

" Birthplace—City __Florence__ State __S. Carolina__

" Residence—Street No. __701 Cottage__ City __Indianapolis__

Single Widow Divorced } __Single__  {1st, 2nd or 3rd marriage} __1st__

Name of Father __William Joseph Morrison__

Maiden name of Mother __Agnes Katherine Brodhite__

Date of this marriage __April 13 1944__

Place of this marriage __Indianapolis, Indiana__

Name and title of person Performing this marriage __Ernst A. Tegenhart__

His address __905 Sanders, Indianapolis, Ind.__

Witness { Name __Mr. Bruce Garrison__

Address __701 Cottage__

## Return this Report to County Clerk with License and Certificate

# Marriage Record for Board of Health
### To Be Returned by the Minister or Other Person Performing Ceremony

~~Verdeyne Alves Moorhead~~ and ~~Rose Marie Ford~~

Groom's name __Verdayne alves Moorhead__

His age __28__

" color __White__

" occupation __Painter__

" Birthplace—City __Terre Haute__ State __Indiana__

" Residence—Street No. __2821 E 10th St__ City __Indpls Ind__

~~Single~~
x ~~Widower~~ } { 1st, 2nd or 3rd marriage } __2 nd__
Divorced }

Name of Father __Carson Moorhead__

Maiden name of Mother __Frances ~~Moorhead~~ Devol__

Bride's name __Rose Marie Ford__

Her age __28__

" color __White__

" occupation __Marker__

" Birthplace—City __Indpls__ State __Indian__

" Residence—Street No. __247 N Fulton__ City __Indpls__

Single }
~~Widow~~ } { 1st, 2nd or 3rd marriage } __1st__
~~Divorced~~ }

Name of Father __Roy Ford__

Maiden name of Mother __Maude Tomloin__

Date of this marriage __April 13/1944__

Place of this marriage __2608 W Mich St Indpls Ind__

Name and title of person
Performing this marriage __Walter Bradford Justice of Peace__

His address __2608 W Mich Syt Indpls Ind__

Witness { Name __George T Tunning__
{ Address __1418 No. 25 th St__

## Return this Report to County Clerk with License and Certificate

12

# Marriage Record for Board of Health

### To Be Returned by the Minister or Other Person Performing Ceremony

Charles P Hurt _____ and _Ada Kathrine Griffith_

Groom's name _Charles P. Hurt_

His age _Twenty- Five (25)_

" color_ _White_

" occupation _Locomotive Fireman_

" Birthplace—City _Salem_ State _Ohio_

" Residence—Street No. _RR #11, Box 292_ City _Indianapolis, Ind_

Single Widower Divorced } _Single_ { 1st, 2nd or 3rd marriage } _1st_

Name of Father _Albert C. Hurt_

Maiden name of Mother _Reva May Sturm_

Bride's name _Ada Kathrine Griffith_

Her age _Twenty- Five (25)_

" color _White_

" occupation _None_

" Birthplace—City _Indianapolis_ State _Ind_

" Residence—Street No. _4061 Cornelius ave_ City _Indianapolis, Ind_

Single Widow Divorced } _Single_ { 1st, 2nd or 3rd marriage } _Second_

Name of Father _Willis W. Lockwood_

Maiden name of Mother _Grace Marie Watts_

Date of this marriage _April 14, 1944_

Place of this marriage _Indianapolis, Ind_

Name and title of person Performing this marriage _Roland Johnson, Minister_

His address _143 N. 40th, Indianapolis, Ind_

Witness { Name _Grace Marie Lockwood_ Address _4061 Cornelius ave, Indianapolis, Ind_

### Return this Report to County Clerk with License and Certificate

## Marriage Record for Board of Health
### To Be Returned by the Minister or Other Person Performing Ceremony

Harry K Nelson _____ and Stella Katherine Blackman

Groom's name ..................

His age _26_

" color _Colored_

" occupation _Labor_

" Birthplace—City _Indianapolis_ State _Ind_

" Residence—Street No _1061 N Belmont_ City _Indianapolis_

~~Single~~ Widower Divorced } _Divorced_ { 1st, 2nd ~~or 3rd~~ marriage } _Second_

Name of Father _Luther Nelson_

Maiden name of Mother _Hellen Branner_

Bride's name _Stella Katherine Blackman_

Her age _21_

" color _Colored_

" occupation _none_

" Birthplace—City _Indianapolis_ State _Ind_

" Residence—Street No _1063 n Pershing_ City _Indianapolis_

Single ~~Widow~~ ~~Divorced~~ } _Single_ { 1st, ~~2nd or 3rd~~ marriage } _First_

Name of Father _Frank Blackman_

Maiden name of Mother _Oclie Wadsworth_

Date of this marriage _April 14 — 44_

Place of this marriage _Indianapolis Ind_

Name and title of person Performing this marriage _Rev C J Bailey_

His address _Indianapolis Ind_

Witness { Name _Mrs Carl Blackman Pernie Barlow_
{ Address _1203 N. Pershing Ave 1828 S. Keystone ave_

### Return this Report to County Clerk with License and Certificate

## Marriage Record for Board of Health

To Be Returned by the Minister or Other Person Performing Ceremony

*Charles Ledford* and *Lillian Voyles*

Groom's name *Charles Ledford*

His age *38*

" color *White*

" occupation *Freight Agent*

" Birthplace—City *Livingston* State *Tennessee*

" Residence—Street No. *541 Longfield* City *Louisville Ky*

Single / Widower / Divorced } *Single*   1st, 2nd or 3rd marriage } *1st*

Name of Father *Isaac Ledford*

Maiden name of Mother *Mary Ledbetter*

Bride's name *Lillian Voyles*

Her age *47*

" color *White*

" occupation *None*

" Birthplace—City *Monroe Co* State *Indiana*

" Residence—Street No. *734 West 8th* City *Bloomington Ind*

Single / Widow / Divorced } *Single*   1st, 2nd or 3rd marriage } *1st*

Name of Father *Jas Voyles*

Maiden name of Mother *Elizabeth Sullivan*

Date of this marriage *April 14, 1944*

Place of this marriage *Indianapolis Ind*

Name and title of person Performing this marriage *Ernest J Lane Justice of the Peace*

His address *152½ East Court St*

Witness { Name *Mary J Lane*  { Address *374 College Ave*

## Return this Report to County Clerk with License and Certificate

# Marriage Record for Board of Health
### To Be Returned by the Minister or Other Person Performing Ceremony

Owen J. West _____ and Dorothy Killian

Groom's name _____ Owen J. West

His age _____ 21

" color _____ White

" occupation _____ Shipping Clerk

" Birthplace—City _____ Louisville _____ State _____ Kentucky

" Residence—Street No. _____ Hotel Linden _____ City _____ Indianapolis

Single / Widower / Divorced } Single     { 1st, 2nd or 3rd marriage } _____ 1st

Name of Father _____ James West

Maiden name of Mother _____ Edna M. Johnson

Bride's name _____ Dorothy Killian

Her age _____ 19

" color _____ White

" occupation _____ None

" Birthplace—City _____ Mattoon _____ State _____ Illinois

" Residence—Street No. _____ 324 E. 31st _____ City _____ Indianapolis

Single / Widow / Divorced } Single     { 1st, 2nd or 3rd marriage } _____ 1st

Name of Father _____ Benjamin Killian

Maiden name of Mother _____ Noble Heisenbuger

Date of this marriage _____ April 14, 1944

Place of this marriage _____ Indianapolis Ind

Name and title of person Performing this marriage _____ Emeri Lang Justice of the Peace

His address _____ 152½ East Court St

Witness { Name _____ Emily Lozno
{ Address _____ 116 East St. Clair

### Return this Report to County Clerk with License and Certificate

# Marriage Record for Board of Health
## To Be Returned by the Minister or Other Person Performing Ceremony

John R. White _____ and _____ Mary Vester

Groom's name __John R. White__

His age __31__

" color __C.__

" occupation __Soldier__

" Birthplace—City __Indianapolis__ State __Indiana__

" Residence—Street No. __948 N. West__ City __Indianapolis__

Single Widower Divorced } __Single__  { 1st, 2nd or 3rd marriage } __1st__

Name of Father __Ruben White__

Maiden name of Mother __Rachel Taylor__

Bride's name __Mary Vester__

Her age __35__

" color __C.__

" occupation __Housekeeper__

" Birthplace—City __Nashville__ State __Tenn__

" Residence—Street No. __2313 Paris__ City __Indianapolis__

Single Widow Divorced } __Widow__  { 1st, 2nd or 3rd marriage } __2nd__

Name of Father __Amos Warren Bryant__

Maiden name of Mother __Lula Merridith__

Date of this marriage __April 14, 1944.__

Place of this marriage __Indianapolis Indiana__

Name and title of person Performing this marriage __S. S. Thomas, minister__

His address __702 S. Ill. St Indianapolis__

Witness { Name __Henrietta Wilson__
{ Address __2313 Paris Ave Indianapolis__

## Return this Report to County Clerk with License and Certificate

12

# Marriage Record for Board of Health
## To Be Returned by the Minister or Other Person Performing Ceremony

*Kenneth B. Huisman* and *Elaine P. Schwartz*

Groom's name _Kenneth Brandt Huisman_

His age _21_

" color _White_

" occupation _U. S. Navy_

" Birthplace—City _Grand Haven_ State _Michigan_

" Residence—Street No. _____ City _Norfolk, Va._

Single Widower Divorced } _Single_ { 1st, 2nd or 3rd marriage } _First_

Name of Father _Klaas Huisman_

Maiden name of Mother _Gertrude Brandt_

Bride's name _Elaine Phyllis Schwartz_

Her age _19_

" color _White_

" occupation _Typist_

" Birthplace—City _Indianapolis_ State _Indiana_

" Residence—Street No. _447 N. Keystone_ City _Indianapolis Ind_

Single Widow Divorced } _Single_ { 1st, 2nd or 3rd marriage } _First_

Name of Father _Gilbert Henry Schwartz_

Maiden name of Mother _Dovie Marie Allison_

Date of this marriage _14th April 1944_

Place of this marriage _Indianapolis Ind_

Name and title of person Performing this marriage _Israel A. Doe, Rev. Ps. I Schw_

His address _1439 _____ St._
_Indianapolis, Ind._

Witness { Name _Gilbert Henry Schwartz_
{ Address _447-N-Keystone Indianapolis Ind._

## Return this Report to County Clerk with License and Certificate

## Marriage Record for Board of Health
### To Be Returned by the Minister or Other Person Performing Ceremony

_____ and _____

Groom's name _Harry F. Smith_

His age _53_

" color _White_

" occupation _Well drilling_

" Birthplace—City _Sardinia_ State _Indiana_

" Residence—Street No. _6333 N. Rochester_ City _Indianapolis_

Single Widower Divorced } _Divorced_   { 1st, 2nd or 3rd marriage } _Third_

Name of Father _Charles Smith_

Maiden name of Mother _Louise Jane Boyer_

Bride's name _Lorena Van Gordon_

Her age _43_

" color _White_

" occupation _House work_

" Birthplace—City _Hartford City_ State _Indiana_

" Residence—Street No. _3930 Byram_ City _Indianapolis_

Single Widow Divorced } _Divorced_   { 1st, 2nd or 3rd marriage } _Second_

Name of Father _William A. A. Baker_

Maiden name of Mother _Sarah Frances Blankenbaker_

Date of this marriage _April 14 – 1944_

Place of this marriage _Indianapolis, Ind._

Name and title of person Performing this marriage _Rev. I. N. Greene_

His address _1841 Cross Drive, Woodruff Place, Indianapolis, Indiana_

Witness { Name _Ewing M. Hamilton_
         { Address _440 Laurel Club_

### Return this Report to County Clerk with License and Certificate

12

# Marriage Record for Board of Health

### To Be Returned by the Minister or Other Person Performing Ceremony

Randall M. Clore and Alma Domrose

Groom's name _Randall M. Clore_

His age _37_

" color _White_

" occupation _Machinist_

" Birthplace—City _Alamo_ State _Indiana_

" Residence—Street No. _1205 Herbert_ City _Indpls_

Single / Widower / Divorced } _divorced_ { 1st, 2nd or 3rd marriage } _2nd_

Name of Father _James Clore_

Maiden name of Mother _Stonebreaker_

Bride's name _Alma Domrose_

Her age _35_

" color _white_

" occupation _stenographer_

" Birthplace—City _Stolppmmun_ State _Germany_

" Residence—Street No. _2420 Brookside_ City _Indpls_ (north Drive)

Single / Widow / Divorced } _divorced_ { 1st, 2nd or 3rd marriage } _2nd_

Name of Father _Eric Domrose_

Maiden name of Mother _Alma Moffke_

Date of this marriage _April 14, 1944_

Place of this marriage _St. Peter's Church ~ Indpls, Ind._

Name and title of person Performing this marriage _W. L. Barth, Minister_

His address _1014 Dudley_

_Indpls, Indiana_

Witness { Name _John W. Hodge Jr._

{ Address _5811 E. 10th St._

## Return this Report to County Clerk with License and Certificate

# Marriage Record for Board of Health
### To Be Returned by the Minister or Other Person Performing Ceremony

*Tallie H. Greenwade* and *Minnie Lee Rogers.*

Groom's name _Tallie H. Greenwade,_

His age _56_

" color _C._

" occupation _Fireman,_

" Birthplace—City _Cadiz_ State _Ky._

" Residence—Street No. _974 Sheffield_ City _Indianapolis_

Single / Widower / Divorced } _Widower_ { 1st, 2nd or 3rd marriage } _3rd._

Name of Father _James Greenwade._

Maiden name of Mother _Kittie Rogers._

Bride's name _Minnie Lee Rogers._

Her age _30_

" color _C._

" occupation _Housewife._

" Birthplace—City _Duluth_ State _Ga._

" Residence—Street No. _949 Sheffield_ City _Indianapolis,_

Single / Widow / Divorced } _Divorced._ { 1st, 2nd or 3rd marriage } _2nd._

Name of Father _Henry Rogers._

Maiden name of Mother _Josie Howard._

Date of this marriage _April 14, 1944,_

Place of this marriage _Indianapolis, Indiana,_

Name and title of person Performing this marriage _L. A. Thomas, Minister._

His address _702 So. Illinois St. Indianapolis, Indiana_

Witness { Name _Lucille Miles._
{ Address _329½ N. 12 St._

## Return this Report to County Clerk with License and Certificate

# Marriage Record for Board of Health
### To Be Returned by the Minister or Other Person Performing Ceremony

Carl Michel _and_ Mary Bivens

Groom's name _Carl Michel._

His age _27_

" color _White_

" occupation _tailor_

" Birthplace—City _Indianapolis_ State _Ind_

" Residence—Street No. _R R 12_ City _Indianapolis_

Single / Widower / Divorced } _Single_ { 1st, 2nd or 3rd marriage } _First_

Name of Father _Carl Michel_

Maiden name of Mother _Margaret Hudson_

Bride's name _Mary Bivens_

Her age _21_

" color _White_

" occupation _House wife._

" Birthplace—City _Indianapolis_ State _Ind_

" Residence—Street No. _R R 12_ City _Indianapolis_

Single / Widow / Divorced } _Single_ { 1st, 2nd or 3rd marriage } _First_

Name of Father _Harry Bivens_

Maiden name of Mother _Flossie Hastings_

Date of this marriage _April 14, 1944_

Place of this marriage _Indianapolis_

Name and title of person Performing this marriage _Carey C Dobson_ _minister_

His address _164 Belmar Indianapolis Ind_

Witness { Name _Clara J Keller_
{ Address _327 So Oxford St._

### Return this Report to County Clerk with License and Certificate

# Marriage Record for Board of Health
### To Be Returned by the Minister or Other Person Performing Ceremony

*Amos Paul Butts* and *Frances Lenora Thatcher*

Groom's name _Amos Paul Butts_

His age _25 years_

" color _White_

" occupation _Cab Driver_

" Birthplace—City _Indianapolis_ State _Indiana_

" Residence—Street No. _3710 Robson_ City _Indianapolis_

Single } Widower 
Widower } _Widower_ { 1st, 2nd or 3rd marriage } _Second_
Divorced }

Name of Father _John Butts_

Maiden name of Mother _Ida C. Horman_

Bride's name _Frances Lenora Thatcher_

Her age _29_

" color _white_

" occupation _Housewife_

" Birthplace—City _Indianapolis_ State _Indiana_

" Residence—Street No. _3829 E 13th St_ City _Indianapolis_

Single } 
Widow } _Divorced_ { 1st, 2nd or 3rd marriage } _Second_
Divorced }

Name of Father _Frank Marion Thatcher_

Maiden name of Mother _Charlotte Lancaster_

Date of this marriage _April 14 1944_

Place of this marriage _St. Mathews Lutheran Church_

Name and title of person
Performing this marriage _Rev. M. P. G. Doermann_

His address _1118 Troost Av. Forrest Park, Ill._

Witness { Name _Ralph Butts_
          { Address _U.S. Army._

### Return this Report to County Clerk with License and Certificate

# Marriage Record for Board of Health
## To Be Returned by the Minister or Other Person Performing Ceremony

Hampton Wm Rhodes and Anna Francis Adams

Groom's name Hampton Wm Rhodes

His age 22

" color White

" occupation Sailor

" Birthplace—City Indianapolis State Indiana

" Residence—Street No. N. S. Navy City _

Single / Widower / Divorced } Single

1st, 2nd or 3rd marriage } 1st

Name of Father Robert Russell Rhodes

Maiden name of Mother Florence McAuley

Bride's name Anna Francis Adams

Her age 17

" color White

" occupation Housewife

" Birthplace—City Indianapolis State Indiana

" Residence—Street No. 6455 Vintage City Indianapolis

Single / Widow / Divorced } Single

1st, 2nd or 3rd marriage } 1st

Name of Father Denzil Adams

Maiden name of Mother Sarah Clough

Date of this marriage April 14, 1944

Place of this marriage Indianapolis, Indiana

Name and title of person Performing this marriage N. C. Ball, Minister

His address 1510 East 12 St.
Indianapolis, Indiana

Witness { Name Harold R. McAuley
{ Address 1903 Lexington St.

## Return this Report to County Clerk with License and Certificate

12

# Marriage Record for Board of Health
### To Be Returned by the Minister or Other Person Performing Ceremony

George William Howard and Mary Ann Johnston

Groom's name _George William Howard_

His age _22_

" color _White_

" occupation _Navy_

" Birthplace—City _Springfield_ State _Ky_

" Residence—Street No. _2315 W. Wash._ City _Indianapolis_

Single / ~~Widower~~ / ~~Divorced~~    1st, ~~2nd or 3rd~~ marriage

Name of Father _Arch Howard_

Maiden name of Mother _Ada Hampton_

Bride's name _Mary Ann Johnston_

Her age _23_

" color _White_

" occupation _Steno._

" Birthplace—City _Indianapolis_ State _Ind_

" Residence—Street No. _257 S. Audubon_ City _Indianapolis_

Single / ~~Widow~~ / ~~Divorced~~    1st, ~~2nd or 3rd~~ marriage

Name of Father _Fred Johnston_

Maiden name of Mother _Ann Shea_

Date of this marriage _April 14, 1944_

Place of this marriage _Our Lady of Lourdes Church_

Name and title of person Performing this marriage _Rev James W. Moore, Pastor_

His address _5333 E. Wash. St._
_Indianapolis, Ind._

Witness { Name _Boris S. Dimancheff_ _Indianapolis_
{ Address _Bonnie L. Dockan_ _Indianapolis_

### Return this Report to County Clerk with License and Certificate

13

# Marriage Record for Board of Health
### To Be Returned by the Minister or Other Person Performing Ceremony

*Frank R Keshef* and *Betty ane Prot*

Groom's name _Frank R Keshe_

His age _27, Twenty seven_

" color _White_

" occupation _Teacher_

" Birthplace—City _Steubenville_ State _Ohio_

" Residence—Street No. _723 Joke_ City _Indianapolis_

Single
Widower  } _Single_   { 1st, 2nd or 3rd marriage } _1st_
Divorced

Name of Father _Harry Keshe_

Maiden name of Mother _Dena Angerman_

Bride's name _Betty Jane Prot_

Her age _25, Twenty-five_

" color _White_

" occupation _Clerk_

" Birthplace—City _Indianapolis_ State _Indiana_

" Residence—Street No. _208 Napoleon_ City _Indianapolis_

Single
Widow  } _Divorced_   { 1st, 2nd or 3rd marriage } _2nd_
Divorced

Name of Father _Clee Stransku_

Maiden name of Mother _Ettalyn Williams_

Date of this marriage _April 12 1942_

Place of this marriage _Indianapolis_

Name and title of person
Performing this marriage _Rev Jane_

His address _611 E Southern Dr - Indiana_

_Rosinai_

Witness { Name _Valentine Kelle_
        { Address _Trenton City Indiana_

### Return this Report to County Clerk with License and Certificate

# Marriage Record for Board of Health

### To Be Returned by the Minister or Other Person Performing Ceremony

Mervin C. Warrnock and Ada M. Small

Groom's name _Mervin C. Warrnock_

His age _26_

" color _White_

" occupation _Farmer_

" Birthplace—City _Danville_ State _Indiana_

" Residence—Street No. _R. 1._ City _Pittsboro_

Single / Widower / Divorced } _Single_ { 1st, 2nd or 3rd marriage } _1st._

Name of Father _Dellmar Warrnock_

Maiden name of Mother _Mary Templin_

Bride's name _Ada M. Small_

Her age _19_

" color _White_

" occupation _Clerk._

" Birthplace—City _Indianapolis_ State _Indiana_

" Residence—Street No. _1021 Tech_ City _Indianapolis_

Single / Widow / Divorced } _Single_ { 1st, 2nd or 3rd marriage } _1st_

Name of Father _Ernest Small_

Maiden name of Mother _Gladys Courtney_

Date of this marriage _April 14, 1944_

Place of this marriage _Indianapolis, Indiana_

Name and title of person Performing this marriage _H C Ball, Minister_

His address _1570 East 12 St_

_Indianapolis, Indiana_

Witness { Name _Jay F Small_
{ Address _1403 Coyner Ave._

### Return this Report to County Clerk with License and Certificate

12

# Marriage Record for Board of Health

To Be Returned by the Minister or Other Person Performing Ceremony

Paul Mires _and_ Helen Stolty

Groom's name _Paul Mires_

His age _18_

" color _White_

" occupation _Truck Driver_

" Birthplace—City _Indianapolis_ State _Indiana_

" Residence—Street No _1322 W Market_ City _Indianapolis_

Single / Widower / Divorced } _Single_  { 1st, 2nd or 3rd marriage } _First_

Name of Father _Wyatt Mires_

Maiden name of Mother _Mary Wolf_

Bride's name _Helen Stolty_

Her age _17_

" color _White_

" occupation _Swiss Cleaners_

" Birthplace—City _Vienna_ State _Illinois_

" Residence—Street No _1322 W Market_ City _Indianapolis_

Single / Widow / Divorced } _Single_  { 1st, 2nd or 3rd marriage } _First_

Name of Father _Courtney Stolty_

Maiden name of Mother _Lula Key_

Date of this marriage _April 14, 1944_

Place of this marriage _Parsonage, 762 N. Belleview Pl._

Name and title of person Performing this marriage _Rev. Charles D. Patterson_

His address _762 N. Belleview Place_

Witness { Name _Lula Mae Stolt_ { Address _1322 W. Market St._

## Return this Report to County Clerk with License and Certificate

12

# Marriage Record for Board of Health
## To Be Returned by the Minister or Other Person Performing Ceremony

Roy B. Strong and Mary Davie Neff

Groom's name _Roy B. Strong_

His age _51 years_

" color _White_

" occupation _Shipping Clerk_

" Birthplace—City _Madison_ State _Indiana_

" Residence—Street No. _1722 N. Rural St._ City _Indianapolis, Ind._

Single
Widower
Divorced } _Divorced_   1st, 2nd or 3rd marriage } _Second_

Name of Father _John G. Strong_

Maiden name of Mother _Josie M. Francisco_

Bride's name _Mary Davie Neff_

Her age _33 years_

" color _White_

" occupation _House Wife_

" Birthplace—City _Indianapolis_ State _Indiana_

" Residence—Street No. _2917 E. 18 St._ City _Indianapolis, Ind._

Single
Widow
Divorced } _Widow_   1st, 2nd or 3rd marriage } _Second_

Name of Father _John W. Sheets_

Maiden name of Mother _Emma Mary Doane_

Date of this marriage _April 14th 1944_

Place of this marriage _1729 N. Oxford St., Indianapolis, Ind._

Name and title of person Performing this marriage _Erwin E. Wright, Minister_

His address _3019 Forest Manor Ave, Indianapolis, Ind._

Witness { Name _Lawrence G. Marshall_
{ Address _1729 N. Oxford St., Indianapolis, Ind._

## Return this Report to County Clerk with License and Certificate

# Marriage Record for Board of Health
### To Be Returned by the Minister or Other Person Performing Ceremony

*George B Champion* and *Mary Ellen Bristow*

Groom's name _George B. Champion._

His age _21._

" color _white._

" occupation _U. S. Army._

" Birthplace—City _Handrum._ State _So. Car_

" Residence—Street No. _Camp Atterbury_ City _____

Single / Widower / Divorced } _____ { 1st, 2nd or 3rd marriage } _1st._

Name of Father _George Champion._

Maiden name of Mother _May Howard._

Bride's name _Mary Ellen Bristow._

Her age _19._

" color _white_

" occupation _House work_

" Birthplace—City _Paducah._ State _Ky._

" Residence—Street No. _1635—19th St._ City _Detroit_

Single / Widow / Divorced } _____ { 1st, 2nd or 3rd marriage } _1st._

Name of Father _William Bristow._

Maiden name of Mother _Lila Cosey_

Date of this marriage _April 17, 1944._

Place of this marriage _2608 W. Mich St. Indpls Ind_

Name and title of person Performing this marriage _Walter Burford Justice of Peace._

His address _2608 W. Mich St Indpls Ind_

Witness { Name _Sgt William A Benton Jr._
         { Address _Camp Atterbury, Indiana._

### Return this Report to County Clerk with License and Certificate

12

# Marriage Record for Board of Health
### To Be Returned by the Minister or Other Person Performing Ceremony

Francis F. Joslin _____ and _____ Willie Pearl Russell

Groom's name _Francis F. Joslin_

His age _73_

" color _White_

" occupation _Grocery, Properter._

" Birthplace—City _Vandalia_ State _Ill._

" Residence—Street No. _2207 Barrett_ City _Inpls Ind_

Single / Widower / Divorced } ____ { 1st, 2nd or 3rd marriage } _1st._

Name of Father _Henry Joslin_

Maiden name of Mother _Margaret Fister._

Bride's name _Willie Pearl Russell_

Her age _63_

" color _White_

" occupation _House Work_

" Birthplace—City _Johnson County_ State _Ind._

" Residence—Street No. _2222 Barrett_ City _Inpls. Ind_

Single / Widow / Divorced } ____ { 1st, 2nd or 3rd marriage } _3rd._

Name of Father _James D. Griffith._

Maiden name of Mother _Mary E Printz_

Date of this marriage _April 19, 1944._

Place of this marriage _2207 Barrett. Ave. Inpls Ind_

Name and title of person Performing this marriage _Walter Brofield Justice? Peace._

His address _2408 W. Wirt St. Inpls. Ind_

Witness { Name _Lula E. Bost_
{ Address _2220 Conrad Ave._

## Return this Report to County Clerk with License and Certificate

# Marriage Record for Board of Health
### To Be Returned by the Minister or Other Person Performing Ceremony

Weldon Alexander Beverly and Cora M. Caldwell

Groom's name _Weldon Alexander Beverly_

His age _32_

" color _Colored_

" occupation _____

" Birthplace—City _Judson_____ State _Ind_

" Residence—Street No. _632 N. Capitol_ City _Ind_

Single / Widower / Divorced } _Divorced_ { 1st, 2nd or 3rd marriage } _2_

Name of Father _Albert Beverly_

Maiden name of Mother _Ester Porter_

Bride's name _Cora M. Caldwell_

Her age _31_

" color _Colored_

" occupation _Housewife_

" Birthplace—City _Tuskee_ State _Ala._

" Residence—Street No. _215 W. Martin_ City _Ind_

Single / Widow / Divorced } _Divorced_ { 1st, 2nd or 3rd marriage } _2_

Name of Father _Wm. A. Johnson_

Maiden name of Mother _Emilie Ferguson_

Date of this marriage _April 14–1944_

Place of this marriage _Indpls_

Name and title of person Performing this marriage _George Baltimore_

His address _3055 Main St. Indpls. Ind._

Witness { Name _Scott Parker_ { Address _1222 Cornell ave_

### Return this Report to County Clerk with License and Certificate

# Marriage Record for Board of Health
## To Be Returned by the Minister or Other Person Performing Ceremony

_____ and _____

Groom's name  _Byron F. Deer_

His age  _49_

" color  _White_

" occupation  _Plumber_

" Birthplace—City _Bargersville_  Johnson Co  State _Indiana_

" Residence—Street No.  _E Raymond_ City _Indpls_

~~Single~~  
Widower  } _Widower_  { ~~1st, 2nd or 3rd~~ marriage } _Second_  
~~Divorced~~

Name of Father  _Frank Deer_

Maiden name of Mother  _Ethel Farmer_

Bride's name  _Annabelle Johnson_

Her age  _47_

" color  _White_

" occupation  _Beauty Operator_

" Birthplace—City _RFD Owensboro_  State _Kentucky_

" Residence—Street No. _2121 S East_  City _Indpls_

~~Single~~  
Widow  } _Widow_  { 1st, 2nd or 3rd marriage } _Second_  
~~Divorced~~

Name of Father  _Daniel Webster Sparks_

Maiden name of Mother  _Sarah Elizabeth Gipe_

Date of this marriage  _April 15, 1944_

Place of this marriage  _Olive Branch Christian Church_

Name and title of person  
Performing this marriage  _Rev. Wales E Smith_

His address  _101 E Raymond St_  
_Indianapolis, Ind_

Witness { Name  _Howard Deer, Evelyn Johnson_  
{ Address  _2121 S East St_

## Return this Report to County Clerk with License and Certificate

# Marriage Record for Board of Health
### To Be Returned by the Minister or Other Person Performing Ceremony

_____ and _____

Groom's name __Wallace M Finch__

His age __54__

" color __White__

" occupation __Cream grader__

" Birthplace—City __Mace__ State __Indiana__

" Residence—Street No. __838 N. New Jersey__ City __Indianap__

Single
Widower } __widower__ { 1st, 2nd or 3rd
marriage } __third__
Divorced

Name of Father __Lee Finch__

Maiden name of Mother __Carrie Gardner__

Bride's name __Mable A Goss__

Her age __50__

" color __White__

" occupation __Sales clerk__

" Birthplace—City __Indianapolis__ State __Ind__

" Residence—Street No. __1404 Broadway__ City __Indianapolis__

~~Single~~
Widow } __widow__ { ~~1st, 2nd or 3rd~~
marriage } __second__
~~Divorced~~

Name of Father __Herman Wiedenkampt__

Maiden name of Mother __Mary Schieb__

Date of this marriage __April 5, 1944__

Place of this marriage __Olive Branch Christian Church__

Name and title of person
Performing this marriage __Rev Wales E Smith__

His address __101 E Raymond St Indianapolis, Ind.__

Witness { Name __Mrs Bessie Scheit__
{ Address __1404 Broadway, New Jersey St__

### Return this Report to County Clerk with License and Certificate

# Marriage Record for Board of Health
## To Be Returned by the Minister or Other Person Performing Ceremony

*Johnnie C. Dowe* and *May M. Archer*

Groom's name _Johnnie C. Dowe_

His age _39_

" color _White_

" occupation _Press Operator_

" Birthplace—City _Bowling Green_ State _Ky_

" Residence—Street No. _1108 Hoyt St_ City _Indianapolis_

Single Widower Divorced } _Divorced_  { 1st, 2nd or 3rd marriage } _2nd_

Name of Father _Willie Dowe_

Maiden name of Mother _Maude Key_

Bride's name _May M. Archer_

Her age _34_

" color _White_

" occupation _None_

" Birthplace—City _Crawfordsville_ State _Ind_

" Residence—Street No. _1128 Hoyt St_ City _Indianapolis_

Single Widow Divorced } _Divorced_  { 1st, 2nd or 3rd marriage } _2nd_

Name of Father _Johnnie Griffin_

Maiden name of Mother _Hattie Zipper_

Date of this marriage _April 15 - 1944_

Place of this marriage _Indianapolis Ind_

Name and title of person Performing this marriage _Rev. H.L. Avery Minister_

His address _1039 Spruce St. Indianapolis Ind_

Witness { Name _Martha Avery_
Address _1039 Spruce St_

## Return this Report to County Clerk with License and Certificate

# Marriage Record for Board of Health

## To Be Returned by the Minister or Other Person Performing Ceremony

---

_____ and _____

Groom's name _Elmer Louis Wilks_

His age _30_

" color _White_

" occupation _Order clerk_

" Birthplace—City _Vincennes_ State _Indiana_

" Residence—Street No. _341 Chester_ City _Indianapolis_

Single
Widower } _Single_  { 1st, 2nd or 3rd
Divorced            marriage

Name of Father _Percy Wilks_

Maiden name of Mother _Margaret Theriac_

Bride's name _Beatrice Ryan_

Her age _26_

" color _White_

" occupation _Secretary_

" Birthplace—City _Washington_ State _Indiana_

" Residence—Street No. _261 Hendricks_ City _Indianapolis_

Single
Widow } _Single_  { 1st, 2nd or 3rd
Divorced            marriage

Name of Father _Hugh Ryan_

Maiden name of Mother _Angela Smith_

Date of this marriage _April 15, 1944_

Place of this marriage _Indianapolis, Ind_

Name and title of person
Performing this marriage _Rev. Victor L. Goossens_

His address _125 No Oriental St — Indianapolis_

Witness { Name _Raymond Monaghan_ } Witness
         { Address _Catherine Sadowski_ }

## Return this Report to County Clerk with License and Certificate

# Marriage Record for Board of Health
### To Be Returned by the Minister or Other Person Performing Ceremony

_Robert E. Agnew_ and _Jo ann. Monts_

Groom's name _Robert E. Agnew_

His age _26_

" color _White_

" occupation _Tool Engineer_

" Birthplace—City _Indianapolis_ State _Ind._

" Residence—Street No. _6301 Broadway_ City _Indianapolis_

Single / Widower / Divorced } _Single_ { 1st, 2nd or 3rd marriage } _First_

Name of Father _Eugene Agnew_

Maiden name of Mother _Elizabeth Dowd_

Bride's name _Jo ann Monts_

Her age _27_

" color _White_

" occupation _House Wife_

" Birthplace—City _Bloomington_ State _Ind._

" Residence—Street No. _6301 Broadway_ City _Indianapolis, Ind._

Single / Widow / Divorced } _Divorced_ { 1st, 2nd or 3rd marriage } _Second_

Name of Father _Leslie Peters_

Maiden name of Mother _Craig Young_

Date of this marriage _April 15th 1944_

Place of this marriage _Indianapolis, Ind._

Name and title of person Performing this marriage _J. S. Johns, Minister_

His address _955 W. 38th St._
_Indianapolis 8 Ind._

Witness { Name _Sandra Craft_
{ Address _955 West 30th St. Indianapolis Indiana_

### Return this Report to County Clerk with License and Certificate

# Marriage Record for Board of Health

## To Be Returned by the Minister or Other Person Performing Ceremony

_Aubrey White_ and _Ethel Brandes_

Groom's name _Aubrey White_

His age _44_

" color _White_

" occupation _Sales Engineer_

" Birthplace—City _Nashville_ State _Tenn_

" Residence—Street No. _2770 Barth Ave_ City _Indianapolis, Ind._

Single / Widower / Divorced } _Widower_ { 1st, 2nd or 3rd marriage } _2nd_

Name of Father _Houston C. White_

Maiden name of Mother _Martha Darrow_

Bride's name _Ethel Brandes_

Her age _35_

" color _white_

" occupation _Housewife_

" Birthplace—City _Madison_ State _Ind._

" Residence—Street No. _1333 Cornell_ City _Indianapolis, Ind._

Single / Widow / Divorced } _Widow_ { 1st, 2nd or 3rd marriage } _2nd_

Name of Father _Charles Kernan_

Maiden name of Mother _Grace Adams_

Date of this marriage _April 15_

Place of this marriage _Indianapolis, Indiana_

Name and title of person Performing this marriage _Norman H. Schultz Ordained Minister_

His address _2117 Napolean St._
_Indianapolis, Indiana_

Witness { Name _Albert H. Mayo_
{ Address _2224 Spann Ave Indianapolis Ind._

## Return this Report to County Clerk with License and Certificate

12

# Marriage Record for Board of Health
## To Be Returned by the Minister or Other Person Performing Ceremony

Britt _and_ Lester

Groom's name _Richard J. Lest_

His age _19_

" color _white_

" occupation _Laborer_

" Birthplace—City _Pikeville_ State _Kentucky_

" Residence—Street No. _427 W. horwood_ City _Indianapolis Ind_

Single / Widower / Divorced } _Single_ { 1st, 2nd or 3rd marriage } _1st_

Name of Father _B. Lester_

Maiden name of Mother _Mae Stepp_

Bride's name _Ressie B. Britt_

Her age _18_

" color _white_

" occupation _Laborer_

" Birthplace—City _Indianapolis_ State _Indiana_

" Residence—Street No. _427 W. horwood_ City _Indianapolis_

Single / Widow / Divorced } _Single_ { 1st, 2nd or 3rd marriage } _1st_

Name of Father _William Estes Britt_

Maiden name of Mother _Ruby Pearl Muse_

Date of this marriage _April 15 — 1944_

Place of this marriage _Mayer Chapel_

Name and title of person Performing this marriage _P.C. Bruker — Minist_

His address _448 W. horwood Indianapolis_

Witness { Name _Aline Metzman_  Address _424 W. horwood_

## Return this Report to County Clerk with License and Certificate

# Marriage Record for Board of Health
### To Be Returned by the Minister or Other Person Performing Ceremony

*Scott* and *Eyster*

Groom's name *Charles E. Scott*

His age *23*

" color *White*

" occupation *Dispatcher Curtis-Wright*

" Birthplace—City *Indps* State *Ind.*

" Residence—Street No. *506 S. Woodrow* City *Indps.*

Single / ~~Widower~~ / ~~Divorced~~ } *Single* { 1st, ~~2nd or 3rd~~ marriage } *first*

Name of Father *Charles Edw. Scott Jr.*

Maiden name of Mother *Bertha June Nelson Keeler*

Bride's name *Juanita E. Eyster*

Her age *20*

" color *White*

" occupation *Domestic*

" Birthplace—City *Indps* State *Ind.*

" Residence—Street No. *232 N. Belmont* City *Indps.*

Single / ~~Widow~~ / ~~Divorced~~ } *Single* { 1st, ~~2nd or 3rd~~ marriage } *first*

Name of Father *Theodore R Eyster*

Maiden name of Mother *Beatrice B. Wiggans*

Date of this marriage *April 15, 1944*

Place of this marriage *59 N. Rural St*

Name and title of person Performing this marriage *M. Linsky DD.*

His address *59 N. Rural Street*

Witness { Name *Mr. & Mrs. Otto Ruben* Address *3112 W. North St.*

## Return this Report to County Clerk with License and Certificate

# Marriage Record for Board of Health
### To Be Returned by the Minister or Other Person Performing Ceremony

_Ramsey_ and _Buchanan_

Groom's name _William M. Ramsey Jr_

His age _21_

" color _White_

" occupation _U.S.A._

" Birthplace—City _Indpls_ State _Ind_

" Residence—Street No. _Billings Hospital_ City _Ft. Harrison_

Single / ~~Widower~~ / ~~Divorced~~ } _Single_ { 1st, ~~2nd or 3rd~~ marriage } _First_

Name of Father _Wm M Ramsey Sr_

Maiden name of Mother _Dorothy Mawson_

Bride's name _Marjorie A. Buchanan_

Her age _18_

" color _White_

" occupation _Telephone Operator_

" Birthplace—City _Indpls_ State _Ind_

" Residence—Street No. _5107 Winthrop_ City _Indpls_

Single / ~~Widow~~ / ~~Divorced~~ } _Single_ { 1st, ~~2nd or 3rd~~ marriage } _First_

Name of Father _Lee H. Buchanan_

Maiden name of Mother _Alice Maude Houston_

Date of this marriage _April 15, 1944_

Place of this marriage _5107 Winthrop_

Name and title of person Performing this marriage _CH Trinkle D.D._

His address _59 N. Russel St_

Witness { Name _Wm M Ramsey_ | _Alice Lee Smith_ { Address _535 Middle Dr W?_ | _3144 N. Delaware_

### Return this Report to County Clerk with License and Certificate

# Marriage Record for Board of Health

To Be Returned by the Minister or Other Person Performing Ceremony

*Maurice A Clark* and *Elouise Walker*

Groom's name *Maurice A. Clark*

His age 21

" color white

" occupation Machine Shop

" Birthplace—City St Marie State Illinois

" Residence—Street No. 1615 N Ill City Indpls

Single / Widower / Divorced } Single { 1st, 2nd or 3rd marriage } 1st

Name of Father Geo Clark

Maiden name of Mother Sarah Effie Brigg

Bride's name Elouise Walker

Her age 18

" color white

" occupation Defense Worker

" Birthplace—City Vendat State Ky

" Residence—Street No. 1615 N Ill City Indpls

Single / Widow / Divorced } Single { 1st, 2nd or 3rd marriage } 1st

Name of Father Isaac Walker

Maiden name of Mother Emma Day

Date of this marriage April 15 – 44

Place of this marriage Indpls Ind

Name and title of person
Performing this marriage Ora A. Lane Justice of Peace

His address 153½ East Court

Witness { Name Mary J Lane
{ Address 3741 College Ave

## Return this Report to County Clerk with License and Certificate

# Marriage Record for Board of Health

### To Be Returned by the Minister or Other Person Performing Ceremony

Mickey Couie and Mary Lois Nordhoff

Groom's name _____ Mickey Couie

His age _____ 21

" color _____ white

" occupation _____ wool presser

" Birthplace—City _____ Zavalla _____ State _____ Texas

" Residence—Street No. 970 Stillwell St. City _____ Indpls

Single / Widower / Divorced } single { 1st, 2nd or 3rd marriage } 1st

Name of Father _____ Albert J. Couie

Maiden name of Mother _____ Neble Rhodes

---

Bride's name _____ Mary Lois Nordhoff

Her age _____ 19

" color _____ white

" occupation _____ war worker

" Birthplace—City _____ Huntingburg _____ State _____ Indiana

" Residence—Street No. 970 Stillwell _____ City _____ Indpls

Single / Widow / Divorced } single { 1st, 2nd or 3rd marriage } 1st

Name of Father _____ Joseph Nordhoff

Maiden name of Mother _____ Velita Walton

---

Date of this marriage _____ April 15, 1944

Place of this marriage _____ Indianapolis, Ind.

Name and title of person Performing this marriage _____ Rev. James H. Jansen, Pastor St. Joseph's Church

His address _____ 623 East North St. Indianapolis, Ind.

Witness { Name _____ Clyde McNuley
Address _____ 1306 Arrow Ave. Indianapolis, Ind.

## Return this Report to County Clerk with License and Certificate

12

# Marriage Record for Board of Health
### To Be Returned by the Minister or Other Person Performing Ceremony

_Marino Beatrice_ and _Dorothy Kruse_

Groom's name _Marino Beatrice_

His age _21_

" color _White_

" occupation _Soldier_

" Birthplace—City _Brooklyn Mass_ State _1_

" Residence—Street No. _Belling ___ Hospital U.S. army_

Single / Widower / Divorced } _single_    { 1st, 2nd or 3rd marriage } _1st_

Name of Father _Salvatore Beatrice_

Maiden name of Mother _Annie Morrella_

Bride's name _Dorothy Kruse_

Her age _21_

" color _White_

" occupation _R.C.A._

" Birthplace—City _Osgood_ State _Ind_

" Residence—Street No. _1321 College_ City _Indpls Ind_

Single / Widow / Divorced } _single_    { 1st, 2nd or 3rd marriage } _1st_

Name of Father _Fred Kruse_

Maiden name of Mother _Gladys Morrell_

Date of this marriage _April 15 '44_

Place of this marriage _Indianapolis Ind_

Name and title of person Performing this marriage _Rev R.A. Shoemaker_

His address _20 25 N, Temple_
_Indianapolis, Ind_

Witness { Name _John L. Scarfague_
Address _863-4 Ave, ___ lyon, N.Y._

### Return this Report to County Clerk with License and Certificate

# Marriage Record for Board of Health
## To Be Returned by the Minister or Other Person Performing Ceremony

Clyde L. Fenley and Katherine Manning

Groom's name _____ Clyde L. Fenley

His age _____ 19

" color _____ white

" occupation _____ wool presser

" Birthplace—City _____ Indianapoli _____ State _____ Ind.

" Residence—Street No. _____ 1306 Arrow Ave _____ City _____ Indpls

Single
Widower } _____ Single _____ { 1st, 2nd or 3rd marriage } _____ 1st
Divorced

Name of Father _____ Virgil Fenley

Maiden name of Mother _____ Violet C. Leeds

Bride's name _____ Catherine Manning

Her age _____ 19

" color _____ white

" occupation _____ war worker

" Birthplace—City _____ Carter Co. _____ State _____ Kentucky

" Residence—Street No. _____ 970 Stillwell _____ City _____ Indpls

Single
Widow } _____ single _____ { 1st, 2nd or 3rd marriage } _____ 1st
Divorced

Name of Father _____ Alvin Manning

Maiden name of Mother _____ Arlena Patton

Date of this marriage _____ April 15, 1944

Place of this marriage _____ Indianapolis, Ind.

Name and title of person
Performing this marriage _____ Rev. James F. Jansen, Pastor, St. Joseph's Church

His address _____ 623 East North St. Indianapolis Ind.

Witness { Name _____ Mickey Couie
Address _____ 970 Stillwell St Indpls, Ind.

## Return this Report to County Clerk with License and Certificate

# Marriage Record for Board of Health
### To Be Returned by the Minister or Other Person Performing Ceremony

*Melvin G. Cunningham* and *Ellen Jane Hatton*

Groom's name _Melvin G. Cunningham_

His age _22_

" color _White_

" occupation _Mechanic_

" Birthplace—City _Indianapolis_ State _Indiana_

" Residence—Street No. _1004 S. Lynhurst Dr._ City _Indianapolis Ind._

Single / Widower / Divorced } _Single_    1st, 2nd, 3rd marriage } _First_

Name of Father _Melvin G. Cunningham Sr._

Maiden name of Mother _Lilly E. Limbaugh_

Bride's name _Ellen Jane Hatton_

Her age _24_

" color _White_

" occupation _Clerk_

" Birthplace—City _Chestnut Ridge_ State _Indiana_

" Residence—Street No. _3018 Newton_ City _Indianapolis_

Single / Widow / Divorced } _Single_    1st, 2nd, 3rd marriage } _First_

Name of Father _Carson May fred Hatton_

Maiden name of Mother _Hazel Vi (Elsie Beldon_

Date of this marriage _April 15 - 1944_

Place of this marriage _Woodside Meth. Ch._

Name and title of person Performing this marriage _Rev. T. E. Adams_

His address _418 So. Temple Ave._
_Indianapolis Indiana_

Witness { Name _Charlotte Yvonne Simpson_
{ Address _Crp Lloyd Colvin_

### Return this Report to County Clerk with License and Certificate

12

## Marriage Record for Board of Health
### To Be Returned by the Minister or Other Person Performing Ceremony

RALPH WISE and JOSEPHINE DOBBS

Groom's name _Ralph wise_

His age _19_

" color _white_

" occupation _Farmer_

" Birthplace—City _Indianapolis_ State _Ind_

" Residence—Street No, _Mooresville RR # 1_ _Indiana_

Single ✓
Widower
Divorced

1st 2nd or 3rd marriage

Name of Father _Roscoe wise_

Maiden name of Mother _Minnetta Spitz_

Bride's name _Josephine Dobbs_

Her age _19_

" color _white_

" occupation _house work_

" Birthplace—City _Bartholomew Co_ State _Ind._

" Residence—Street No _Columbus RR # 5_ City

Single
Widow
Divorced

1st 2nd or 3rd marriage

Name of Father _Arthur Dobbs_

Maiden name of Mother _Goldie Whittington_

Date of this marriage _April 15 1944_

Place of this marriage _Columbus, Indiana_

Name and title of person Performing this marriage _Rev. Alfred L. Beatty_

His address _736 Ohio avenue_
_Columbus, Indiana._

Witness { Name _Mrs Morris Hawk_
{ Address _R.R.2 Columbus, Indiana_

### Return this Report to County Clerk with License and Certificate

12

## Marriage Record for Board of Health
### To Be Returned by the Minister or Other Person Performing Ceremony

Cowherd _and_ Farley

Groom's name _James Willis Cowherd_

His age _Twentyeight_

" color _Colored_

" occupation _Cleaner_

" Birthplace—City _Campbellsville_ State _Ky_

" Residence—Street No. _2421 Sherman_ City _Indpls_

Single / Widower / Divorced } _Single_ { 1st, 2nd or 3rd marriage } _1st_

Name of Father _Lee Ray Cowherd_

Maiden name of Mother _Estella Buckner_

Bride's name _Allie Mae Farley_

Her age _Twentythree_

" color _Colored_

" occupation _Housewife_

" Birthplace—City _Gallatin_ State _Tenn_

" Residence—Street No. _2718 Highland_ City _Indpls_

Single / Widow / Divorced } _Single_ { 1st, 2nd or 3rd marriage } _1st_

Name of Father _Clennis Farley_

Maiden name of Mother _Wilma Anthony_

Date of this marriage _April 15th 1944_

Place of this marriage _Indianapolis Ind_

Name and title of person Performing this marriage _Rev. C. Henry Bell_

His address _365 W. 27th St_
_Indianapolis Ind_

Witness { Name _Mattie Bingham_
{ Address _2718 Highland Pl_

### Return this Report to County Clerk with License and Certificate

# Marriage Record for Board of Health
## To Be Returned by the Minister or Other Person Performing Ceremony

Zopp _____ and _____ Filick

Groom's name _____ Gerald M. Zopp

His age _____ 26

" color _____ White

" occupation _____ U.S. Army —

" Birthplace—City _____ Chicago _____ State _____ Illinois

" Residence—Street No. _____ Fort Benj. Harrison City _____ Indianapolis

Single } _____ Single { 1st, 2nd or 3rd } _____ First
Widower }              {   marriage       }
Divorced }

Name of Father _____ John Zopp

Maiden name of Mother _____ Anna Paulina

Bride's name _____ Roma B. Filick

Her age _____ 22

" color _____ White

" occupation _____ Clerk

" Birthplace—City _____ French Lick _____ State _____ Indiana

" Residence—Street No. _____ 5902 Rawls _____ City _____ Indianapolis

Single } _____ Single { 1st, 2nd or 3rd } _____ First
Widow }               {   marriage       }
Divorced }

Name of Father _____ Charles Filick

Maiden name of Mother _____ Slitta Kellams

Date of this marriage _____ April 15, 1944

Place of this marriage _____ Sts. Peter and Paul Cathedral - Indpls.

Name and title of person
Performing this marriage _____ Cornelius B. Sweeney, asst. pastor

His address _____ 1347 N. Meridian St.
_____ Indianapolis, Indiana

Witness { Name _____ John Zopp - Marie Filick
        { Address _____ Chicago, Illinois

## Return this Report to County Clerk with License and Certificate

# Marriage Record for Board of Health

### To Be Returned by the Minister or Other Person Performing Ceremony

_Bruce W. Stenberg_ and _Eleanor May Clancy_

Groom's name _Bruce William Clancy Stenberg_

His age _33_

" color _white_

" occupation _Soldier_

" Birthplace—City _Minneapolis_ State _Minn._

" Residence—Street No. _Ft. Benj. Harrison_ City _Ind._

Single
Widower    } — { 1st, 2nd or 3rd marriage } _1st_
Divorced

Name of Father _Fred Hilding Stenberg_

Maiden name of Mother _Mable S. Peterson_

Bride's name _Eleanor May Clancy_

Her age _27_

" color _white_

" occupation _Secretary_

" Birthplace—City _Indianapolis_ State _Ind._

" Residence—Street No. _505 E. 32nd St_ City _Indianapolis_

Single
Widow    } — { 1st, 2nd or 3rd marriage } _1st_
Divorced

Name of Father _Summer Clancy_

Maiden name of Mother _May Wands_

Date of this marriage _15 April 1944_

Place of this marriage _Ft. Benjamin Harrison, Ind._

Name and title of person
Performing this marriage _Chaplain Clarence G. Wolbslager_

His address _Ft. Benjamin Harrison, Ind_

Witness { Name _Pvt. Harold Gallagher - Ft. Benj. Harrison, Ind_
{ Address _Mary Jane Saatz - 3929 Park Ave., Indianapolis, Ind._

## Return this Report to County Clerk with License and Certificate

# Marriage Record for Board of Health
### To Be Returned by the Minister or Other Person Performing Ceremony

Buford England Jr. and Lois Robbins

Groom's name _Buford England Jr._

His age _20_

" color _White_

" occupation _American Linnen Supply_

" Birthplace—City _Indianapolis_ State _Indiana_

" Residence—Street No. _2407 McClure St_ City _Indianapolis (3)_

Single / Widower / Divorced } _Single_ { 1st, 2nd or 3rd marriage } _1st_

Name of Father _Buford England_

Maiden name of Mother _Edith L. Schell_

Bride's name _Lois Marie Robbins_

Her age _17_

" color _White_

" occupation _American Linnen Supply_

" Birthplace—City _Indianapolis_ State _Indiana_

" Residence—Street No. _1116 N. Capitol_ City _Indianapolis_

Single / Widow / Divorced } _Single_ { 1st, 2nd or 3rd marriage } _1st_

Name of Father _Ralph Emory Robbins_

Maiden name of Mother _Hazel Spoon_

Date of this marriage _April 15, 1944_

Place of this marriage _Indianapolis, Ind._

Name and title of person Performing this marriage _J. Clinton Swanagan - Minister_

His address _2654 Lockburn_

_Indianapolis 3, Ind._

Witness { Name _Mrs George Bloor_
Address _2409 McClure Street Indpls, Ind._

### Return this Report to County Clerk with License and Certificate

# Marriage Record for Board of Health
To Be Returned by the Minister or Other Person Performing Ceremony

Marcus Anderson and Hazel E. Hodge

Groom's name _Marcus Anderson_

His age _33_

" color _C_

" occupation _U.S. Army_

" Birthplace—City _Ganesboro_ State _Tenn_

" Residence—Street No. _____ City _Camp Pickett Va._

Single / Widower / Divorced } _Divorced_ { 1st, 2nd or 3rd marriage } _2nd_

Name of Father _John Anderson_

Maiden name of Mother _Eliza Hobby_

Bride's name _Hazel E. Hodge_

Her age _29_

" color _C_

" occupation _Office Girl_

" Birthplace—City _Paducah_ State _Kentucky_

" Residence—Street No. _429 West Mich St_ City _Indianapolis Ind._

Single / Widow / Divorced } _Single_ { 1st, 2nd or 3rd marriage } _1st_

Name of Father _Joseph Hodge_

Maiden name of Mother _Carrie Kirk_

Date of this marriage _April - 15 - 1943_

Place of this marriage _Indianapolis Indiana_

Name and title of person Performing this marriage _S.S. Thomas, Minister_

His address _707 S. Illinois Street_

_Indianapolis, Indiana_

Witness { Name _Betty Stuckliffe_

{ Address _2336 Indianapolis Ave._

## Return this Report to County Clerk with License and Certificate

# Marriage Record for Board of Health
### To Be Returned by the Minister or Other Person Performing Ceremony

Harold L. Marcus _and_ Blanche C. Flechtner

Groom's name _Harold L. Marcus_

His age _25_

" color _White_

" occupation _Soldier_

" Birthplace—City _Patterson_ State _New Jersey_

" Residence—Street No. _Stout Field_ City _Ind'pls_

Single / Widower / Divorced } _Single_ { 1st, 2nd or 3rd marriage } _1st_

Name of Father _William A. Marcus_

Maiden name of Mother _Sophie Stern_

Bride's name _Blanche C. Flechtner_

Her age _22_

" color _White_

" occupation _none_

" Birthplace—City _Garfield_ State _New Jersey_

" Residence—Street No. _4 Burgess Place_ City _Passaic, New Jersey_

Single / Widow / Divorced } _Single_ { 1st, 2nd or 3rd marriage } _1st_

Name of Father _Joseph Flechtner_

Maiden name of Mother _Sophie Voca_

Date of this marriage _April 15 - 1944_

Place of this marriage _Indianapolis, Indiana_

Name and title of person Performing this marriage _Ernest V. Lam, Justice of Peace_

His address _152½ East Court Street_

Witness { Name _Walter C. Paugh_
{ Address _Stout Field, Ind'pls._

### Return this Report to County Clerk with License and Certificate

## Marriage Record for Board of Health

### To Be Returned by the Minister or Other Person Performing Ceremony

_____ and _____

Groom's name _Martin Elliott Ridley_

His age _29_

" color _Colored_

" occupation _U S A_

" Birthplace—City _Indianapolis_ State _Indiana_

" Residence—Street No. _2857 N Capital_ City _Indianapolis Ind_

Single
Widower } _widower_ { 1st, 2nd or 3rd } _2d_
Divorced                  marriage

Name of Father _Thomas Howard Ridley_

Maiden name of Mother _Evelyn Hazelwood_

Bride's name _Marie Morris_

Her age _26_

" color _Colored_

" occupation _Interviewer_

" Birthplace—City _Huntsboro_ State _Alabama_

" Residence—Street No. _653 N. West St_ City _Indianapolis Ind_

Single
Widow } _Single_ { 1st, 2nd or 3rd } _1st_
Divorced                  marriage

Name of Father _Robert Morris_

Maiden name of Mother _Ilma Cooper_

Date of this marriage _Apr. 15— 1944_

Place of this marriage _Indianapolis Ind_

Name and title of person
Performing this marriage _Rev J. P. Q. Wallace_

His address _1943 Carrollton Ave_
_Indianapolis Ind_

Witness { Name _Lillian M. Shea_
        { Address _653 N. West St_

## Return this Report to County Clerk with License and Certificate

## Marriage Record for Board of Health
### To Be Returned by the Minister or Other Person Performing Ceremony

_Young_ ........................... and ........... _Fisse_

Groom's name ..... _William Young_

His age ..... _40_

" color ..... _White_

" occupation ..... _Truck Driver_

" Birthplace—City _Bandalia_ ............ State _Illinois_

" Residence—Street No. ................ City ............

Single / Widower / Divorced } _Widower_ { 1st, 2nd or 3rd marriage } _2nd_

Name of Father ..... _Edgar Young_

Maiden name of Mother ..... _Louisa Metcalf_

Bride's name ..... _Jewell Fisse_

Her age ..... _22_

" color ..... _white_

" occupation ..... _Machinist_

" Birthplace—City _Versailes_ ............ State _Indiana_

" Residence—Street No. _2444 W. 10th_ City _Indianapolis_

Single / Widow / Divorced } _divorced_ { 1st, 2nd or 3rd marriage } _2nd_

Name of Father ..... _Fred B. Fisse_

Maiden name of Mother ..... _Lula Housemyere_

Date of this marriage ..... _April 15 1941_

Place of this marriage ..... _Whiteland Ind_

Name and title of person Performing this marriage ..... _Rev. A.S. Prasner_

His address ..... _Whiteland, Indiana_

Witness { Name ..... _Mrs. A.S. Prasner_
         { Address ..... _Whiteland, Ind._

### Return this Report to County Clerk with License and Certificate

## Marriage Record for Board of Health
### To Be Returned by the Minister or Other Person Performing Ceremony

Raymond Conrad Vallet ___ and ___ Norma Dale Stevenson

Groom's name _Raymond Conrad Vallet_

His age _34_

" color _White_

" occupation _Accountant_

" Birthplace—City _Callaway_ State _Neb._

" Residence—Street No. _R.R. 7 Box 54_ City _Indianapolis_

Single / Widower / Divorced } _Divorced_ { 1st, 2nd or 3rd marriage }

Name of Father _Conrad Vallet_

Maiden name of Mother _Sarah R. McCreary._

Bride's name _Norma Dale Stevenson_

Her age _21_

" color _White_

" occupation _Key punch operator_

" Birthplace—City _Springville_ State _Indiana_

" Residence—Street No. _2649 N Alabama_ City _City._

Single / Widow / Divorced } _Single_ { 1st, 2nd or 3rd marriage }

Name of Father _Chas Stevenson_

Maiden name of Mother _Ethel Hammond._

Date of this marriage _April 15 — 1944_

Place of this marriage _2414 Station St Indianapolis, Indiana_

Name and title of person Performing this marriage _Merl H. Reynolds, minister_

His address _2414 Station Street Indianapolis Indiana_

Witness { Name _Don M Hassler_
{ Address _7530 E. Northgate_

### Return this Report to County Clerk with License and Certificate

# Marriage Record for Board of Health

To Be Returned by the Minister or Other Person Performing Ceremony

_Isaac B. Hill_ and _Elizabeth Armstrong_

Groom's name _Isaac B. Hill_

His age _54_

" color _White_

" occupation _Elevator Operator_

" Birthplace—City _New Albany_ State _Indiana_

" Residence—Street No _1147 N. Ill_ City _Indianapolis_

Single / Widower / Divorced } _Divorced_ { 1st, 2nd or 3rd marriage } _2nd_

Name of Father _Benj Hill_

Maiden name of Mother _Margaret Groover_

Bride's name _Elizabeth Armstrong_

Her age _44_

" color _White_

" occupation _Clerk_

" Birthplace—City _Filesville_ State _Indiana_

" Residence—Street No _1147 N. Ill_ City _Indianapolis_

Single / Widow / Divorced } _Divorced_ { 1st, 2nd or 3rd marriage } _2nd_

Name of Father _John T. Harrison_

Maiden name of Mother _Dora Etta Doode_

Date of this marriage _April 15, 1944_

Place of this marriage _Indianapolis Ind_

Name and title of person Performing this marriage _Ermin Lane Justice of Peace_

His address _152½ East Court St._

Witness { Name _Mary Jo Lane_
{ Address _3741 College Ave_

**Return this Report to County Clerk with License and Certificate**

## Marriage Record for Board of Health
### To Be Returned by the Minister or Other Person Performing Ceremony

*Walter R. Tobin* and *Viola Carolyn Menning*

Groom's name *Walter R. Tobin*

His age *49*

" color *white*

" occupation *Physician*

" Birthplace—City *Greenriver* State *Wyoming*

" Residence—Street No. *10935 Longwood* *Chicago Ill*

Single / Widower / Divorced } *Widower* / *Single* ‹ 1st, 2nd or 3rd marriage }

Name of Father *William J. Tobin*

Maiden name of Mother *Mary Hay*

Bride's name *Viola Carolyn Menning*

Her age *30*

" color *white*

" occupation *Secretary*

" Birthplace—City *Whiting* State *Indiana*

" Residence—Street No *632 Dan Ave* City *Whiting Ind*

Single / Widow / Divorced } *Divorced* ‹ 1st, 2nd or 3rd marriage } *2nd*

Name of Father *Paul J. Dureck*

Maiden name of Mother *Anna Bishop*

Date of this marriage *April 15 44*

Place of this marriage *Joseph Ind*

Name and title of person Performing this marriage *Curtis V Lane Justice of Peace*

His address *151½ East Court St*

Witness { Name *Mary J. Lane* / Address *3741 College Ave* }

### Return this Report to County Clerk with License and Certificate

# Marriage Record for Board of Health
## To Be Returned by the Minister or Other Person Performing Ceremony

_Stump_ and _Blackwell_

Groom's name _Marion Stump_

His age _50_

" color _white_

" occupation _Real Estate_

" Birthplace—City _Elkhart Co._ State _Ind._

" Residence—Street No. _3211 Kenwood_ City _Indianapolis, Ind._

Single / Widower / Divorced } _Divorced_ { 1st, 2nd or 3rd marriage } _2nd_

Name of Father _Wm. B. Stump_

Maiden name of Mother _Clara Ella Wysong_

Bride's name _Virginia Ellen Blackwell_

Her age _19_

" color _white_

" occupation _Housewife_

" Birthplace—City _Indianapolis_ State _Ind._

" Residence—Street No. _51 N. ____ City _Indianapolis_

Single / Widow / Divorced } _Single_ { 1st, 2nd or 3rd marriage } _1st_

Name of Father _Beverly G. Blackwell_

Maiden name of Mother _Pearl Bryant_

Date of this marriage _April 13, 1944_

Place of this marriage _Southport, Ind._

Name and title of person Performing this marriage _Rev. F. M. Taylor_

His address _Southport, Ind._

Witness { Name _Ronald Fowler_   Address _73 N. 3rd Ave. Beech Grove, Ind._

## Return this Report to County Clerk with License and Certificate

# Marriage Record for Board of Health
### To Be Returned by the Minister or Other Person Performing Ceremony

David Bess _____ and _____ Bonice Plummer

Groom's name __David Bess__

His age __21 yrs__

" color __White__

" occupation __Meat Inspector__

" Birthplace—City __Indpls__ State __Ind__

" Residence—Street No. __814 N Jefferson__ City __Indpls__

Single } __Single__    1st, 2nd or 3rd } __1st__
Widower }              marriage
Divorced }

Name of Father __David Bess__

Maiden name of Mother __Grace Stapelkamper__

Bride's name __Bonice Plummer__

Her age __21 yrs__

" color __White__

" occupation __Insurance Co.__

" Birthplace—City __Indpls__ State __Ind__

" Residence—Street No. __931 Holloway__ City __Indpls__

Single } __Single__    1st, 2nd or 3rd } __1st__
Widow }                marriage
Divorced }

Name of Father __Chas Wm Plummer__

Maiden name of Mother __Mable Feliz Stamm__

Date of this marriage __April 15, 1944__

Place of this marriage __St Francis De Sales Church__

Name and title of person
Performing this marriage __Rev Joseph Vollmer__

His address __2191 Avondale Pl__
__City__

Witness { Name __Dale Armantrout__
        { Address __Victoria Todd__

### Return this Report to County Clerk with License and Certificate

# Marriage Record for Board of Health
## To Be Returned by the Minister or Other Person Performing Ceremony

*James T. Woods* and *Mary E. Donahue*

Groom's name _James T. Woods_

His age _30_

" color _White_

" occupation _Machinist_

" Birthplace—City _Atlanta_ State _Ind_

" Residence—Street No. _____ City _Atlanta, Ind._

Single
Widower } _Single_ 1st, ~~2nd or 3rd~~ } _1st_
Divorced marriage

Name of Father _Chester Chas. Woods_

Maiden name of Mother _Margaret Mae Gallagher_

Bride's name _Mary E Donahue_

Her age _36_

" color _White_

" occupation _Telephone operator_

" Birthplace—City _Indianapolis_ State _Ind_

" Residence—Street No. _324 N Tacoma_ City _Indianapolis_

Single
Widow } _Single_ 1st, ~~2nd or 3rd~~ } _1st_
Divorced marriage

Name of Father _William Donahue_

Maiden name of Mother _Mary Ann Wilker_

Date of this marriage _April 15 - 44_

Place of this marriage _St Philip Neri Church, 550 N Rural_

Name and title of person
Performing this marriage _Wilan Meny - Cath priest_

His address _550 N Rural St_

_Indianapolis Ind_

Witness { Name _Alfred Heede - 324 N Tacoma_
{ Address _Ethel Pfenning - 2018 N Lasalle_

## Return this Report to County Clerk with License and Certificate

# Marriage Record for Board of Health

To Be Returned by the Minister or Other Person Performing Ceremony

_____ and _____

Groom's name _Roy Edward Reid_

His age _22_

" color _white_

" occupation _Salesman_

" Birthplace—City _Indianapolis_ State _Ind_

" Residence—Street No. _1229 Newman_ City _Indianapolis Ind_

Single / Widower / Divorced } _Single_ {1st, 2nd or 3rd marriage} _1st_

Name of Father _John Reid_

Maiden name of Mother _Bessie Rigney_

Bride's name _Norma Jean Green_

Her age _18_

" color _white_

" occupation _none_

" Birthplace—City _Indianapolis_ State _Ind_

" Residence—Street No. _RR10 Box 83_ City _Indianapolis Ind_

Single / Widow / Divorced } _Single_ {1st, 2nd or 3rd marriage} _1st_

Name of Father _Harold Green_

Maiden name of Mother _Margaret Huber_

Date of this marriage _April 15 - 1944_

Place of this marriage _Indianapolis Ind_

Name and title of person Performing this marriage _Rev L.G. Huddleston_

His address _1613 Fletcher Ave
Indianapolis Ind_

Witness { Name _Mrs L.G. Huddleston_
Address _1613 Fletcher Ave Indianapolis Ind_

## Return this Report to County Clerk with License and Certificate

# Marriage Record for Board of Health

### To Be Returned by the Minister or Other Person Performing Ceremony

_____ and _____

Groom's name _Clyde E Clark_

His age _25_

" color _white_

" occupation _Machinist_

" Birthplace—City _Indianapolis_ State _Ind_

" Residence—Street No. _3936 E 30th_ City _Indianapolis Ind_

Single Widower Divorced } _Single_ { 1st, 2nd or 3rd marriage } _1st_

Name of Father _John L. Clark_

Maiden name of Mother _Florence Petty_

Bride's name _Helen Cundiff_

Her age _21_

" color _white_

" occupation _Plater_

" Birthplace—City _Indianapolis_ State _Ind_

" Residence—Street No. _1636 Spann_ City _Indianapolis Ind_

Single Widow Divorced } _Single_ { 1st, 2nd or 3rd marriage } _1st_

Name of Father _Samuel O Cundiff_

Maiden name of Mother _Frannie Barker_

Date of this marriage _April 13 1944_

Place of this marriage _Indianapolis Ind_

Name and title of person Performing this marriage _Rev L S Geddleisla_

His address _1813 Fletcher Ave_

_Indianapolis Ind_

Witness { Name _James Emil Tucker_
{ Address _1923 S Pershing_

## Return this Report to County Clerk with License and Certificate

# Marriage Record for Board of Health
### To Be Returned by the Minister or Other Person Performing Ceremony

_John Lee Smith_ and _____

Groom's name _John P. Smith_

His age _27_

" color _Brown_

" occupation _Labor_

" Birthplace—City _Dayton_ State _Ohio_

" Residence—Street No. _____ City _____

Single / Widower / Divorced } _Single_  { 1st, 2nd or 3rd marriage } _____

Name of Father _John Smith_

Maiden name of Mother _Mary Walker_

Bride's name _Edna Earl Jones_

Her age _18_

" color _Brown_

" occupation _none_

" Birthplace—City _____ State _____

" Residence—Street No. _____ City _____

Single / Widow / Divorced } _Single_  { 1st, 2nd or 3rd marriage } _____

Name of Father _Lionel Jones_

Maiden name of Mother _____

Date of this marriage _____

Place of this marriage _____

Name and title of person Performing this marriage _____

His address _____

_____

Witness { Name _____
         { Address _____

## Return this Report to County Clerk with License and Certificate

# Marriage Record for Board of Health
## To Be Returned by the Minister or Other Person Performing Ceremony

Charles H. Wilson and Hazel Clark

Groom's name _Charles H Wilson_

His age _19_

" color _White_

" occupation _hotel worker_

" Birthplace—City _Harlan_ State _Kentucky_

" Residence—Street No. _215 E. 10th St,_ City _Indianapolis_

Single / Widower / Divorced } _Single_    { 1st, 2nd or 3rd marriage } _1st_

Name of Father _Sylus Wilson_

Maiden name of Mother _Mallie Ward_

Bride's name _Hazel Clark_

Her age _16_

" color _White_

" occupation _P R Mallory Co._

" Birthplace—City _Berea_ State _Kentucky_

" Residence—Street No. _5135 W. 10th St_ City _Indianapolis_

Single / Widow / Divorced } _Single_    { 1st, 2nd or 3rd marriage } _1st_

Name of Father _Tom Clark_

Maiden name of Mother _Martha Robinson_

Date of this marriage _April 15, 1944_

Place of this marriage _Almon J. Coble_

Name and title of person Performing this marriage _minister_

His address _8 S Warman Ave._ _Indianapolis_

Witness { Name _Erwin Kolb_
{ Address _730 S Sheppard St Indianapolis Ind_

## Return this Report to County Clerk with License and Certificate

# Marriage Record for Board of Health
## To Be Returned by the Minister or Other Person Performing Ceremony

Kenneth M. Norris and Thelma Bishop

Groom's name _Kenneth_

His age _27_

" color _White_

" occupation _Elevator Adjuster_

" Birthplace—City _Rockdale_ State _Indiana_

" Residence—Street No. _832 Goodlock_ City _Indianapolis_

Single / Widower / Divorced } _Single_ { 1st, 2nd or 3rd marriage } _1st_

Name of Father _Carl_

Maiden name of Mother _Lucille Will_

Bride's name _Thelma Bishop_

Her age _36_

" color _White_

" occupation _Factory Worker_

" Birthplace—City _Williamson_ State _Ky_

" Residence—Street No. _1018 14th_ City _Indianapolis_

Single / Widow / Divorced } _Divorced_ { 1st, 2nd or 3rd marriage } _2nd_

Name of Father _Joseph_

Maiden name of Mother _Oga True_

Date of this marriage _April 15/44_

Place of this marriage _Indianapolis_

Name and title of person Performing this marriage _Rev. Shute_

His address _627 Division St._
_Indianapolis Ind._

Witness { Name _Harold St Cyr_
{ Address _205 N. Truck_

## Return this Report to County Clerk with License and Certificate

FILED
42 APR 2 1 1944
CLERK

# Marriage Record for Board of Health

### To Be Returned by the Minister or Other Person Performing Ceremony

_____ and _____

Groom's name _Harold Eugene Brooks_

His age _21_

" color _White_

" occupation _Soldier_

" Birthplace—City _New Augusta_ State _Ind._

" Residence—Street No. _New Augusta_ City _Indiana_

Single ✓ _Single_    { 1st, 2nd or 3rd marriage } _1st_
Widower
Divorced

Name of Father _John Almer Brooks_

Maiden name of Mother _Rachel Marie Pollard_

Bride's name _George-Anne Thrush_

Her age _19_

" color _White_

" occupation _Secretary_

" Birthplace—City _Indianapolis_ State _Ind._

" Residence—Street No. _709 Day Street_ City _Indianapolis Ind_

Single ✓ _Single_    { 1st, 2nd or 3rd marriage } _1st_
Widow
Divorced

Name of Father _Harrison Carter Thrush_

Maiden name of Mother _Eleuthie Stilhorn Thrush_

Date of this marriage _April 15th – 1944_

Place of this marriage _Indianapolis, Ind._

Name and title of person
Performing this marriage _J.A. Hollenberger – Minister_

His address _Indianapolis, Ind._

Witness { Name _Sam E. Kissel Jr._
{ Address _R.R. 17 Box 564 Indianapolis 44, Ind._

### Return this Report to County Clerk with License and Certificate

12

# Marriage Record for Board of Health
### To Be Returned by the Minister or Other Person Performing Ceremony

*Frank A. Kopis* and *Nellie Ruth Foxworthy*

Groom's name _Frank A. Kopis_

His age _51_

" color _White_

" occupation _Foreman_

" Birthplace—City _____ ~~State~~ _Austria_

" Residence—Street No. _429 S. Spencer_ County _Indianapolis_

Single
Widower } _Widower_ { 1st, 2nd or 3rd marriage } _2nd_
Divorced

Name of Father _John Kopis_

Maiden name of Mother _Barbara Kopis_

Bride's name _Nellie Ruth Foxworthy_

Her age _49_

" color _White_

" occupation _housewife_

" Birthplace—City _Warren Co._ State _Indiana_

" Residence—Street No. _40 S. Warman_ City _Indianapolis_

Single
Widow } _Divorced_ { 1st, 2nd or 3rd marriage } _2nd_
Divorced

Name of Father _Smith Cloyd_

Maiden name of Mother _Elizabeth Jane James_

Date of this marriage _April 15, 1944_

Place of this marriage _Indianapolis_

Name and title of person
Performing this marriage _Almon J. Cotle_

His address _8 S. Warman_
_Indianapolis_

Witness { Name _Frank Wray_
{ Address _1327 _____

## Return this Report to County Clerk with License and Certificate

# Marriage Record for Board of Health

## To Be Returned by the Minister or Other Person Performing Ceremony

_____ and _____

Groom's name _W<sup>m</sup> Joack Stone_

His age _29_

" color _White_

" occupation _Mechanic_

" Birthplace—City _St Joseph_ State _Missouri_

" Residence—Street No. _389 Spaceland_ City _Indianapolis_

Single Widower Divorced } _Single_ { 1st, 2nd or 3rd marriage }

Name of Father _Isack Stone_

Maiden name of Mother _Marie Eckhart_

Bride's name _Helen Rüdmann_

Her age _23_

" color _White_

" occupation _nurse_

" Birthplace—City _Millhousen_ State _Ind_

" Residence—Street No. _3831 N Capitol_ City _Indianapolis_

Single Widow Divorced } _Single_ { 1st, 2nd or 3rd marriage }

Name of Father _Anthony Rüsman_

Maiden name of Mother _Mollie Wilkurfe_

Date of this marriage _Apr 15 1945_

Place of this marriage _St Mary Church Millhousen Ind_

Name and title of person Performing this marriage _Carl E Jreber Catholic Pastor_

His address _R 2 Greensburg Ind_

Witness { Name _Joseph Mueller Ruth Koenig_ { Address _9516 S 16 St 3131 N Capitol Indianapolis Indianapolis Ind_

## Return this Report to County Clerk with License and Certificate

# Marriage Record for Board of Health
### To Be Returned by the Minister or Other Person Performing Ceremony

*Harry Dale Brown* and *ley Luise Grow*

Groom's name *Harry Dale Brown*

His age *21*

" color *White*

" occupation *Bridge Fort Brus*

" Birthplace—City _____ State _____

" Residence—Street No. *720 N. New Jersey* City *Chidinmtohis*

Single / Widower / ~~Divorced~~ } *1st* { 1st, 2nd or 3rd marriage } *First*

Name of Father *Elmer Brown*

Maiden name of Mother *Winnie Sparling*

Bride's name *Shirley Louise Grow*

Her age *17*

" color *White*

" occupation *House Work*

" Birthplace—City *Martinsville* State *Chid*

" Residence—Street No. *720 N. N. Jersey* City *Chidnmtohis*

Single / ~~Widow~~ / ~~Divorced~~ } *1st* { 1st, 2nd or 3rd marriage } *first*

Name of Father *Evert Grow*

Maiden name of Mother *Ead Oneal*

Date of this marriage *April 14th — 1924*

Place of this marriage *Indianapolis Ind*

Name and title of person Performing this marriage *Rev Charles B Riley*

His address *621-B New York St Indianapolis Ind Baptist Minister*

Witness { Name *E H McCrea   Bonnice A Murray*
Address *Martinsville   725 N New Jersey*

### Return this Report to County Clerk with License and Certificate

# Marriage Record for Board of Health
## To Be Returned by the Minister or Other Person Performing Ceremony

Joseph Phillip Price, and Zeta Shirley Anne Richardson

Groom's name _____ Joseph Phillip Price

His age _____ 18

" color _____ White

" occupation _____ U.S. Navy

" Birthplace—City _____ Bridgeport _____ State _____ Ind

" Residence—Street No. _____ 234 Eastern _____ City _____ Indianapolis

Single / Widower / Divorced } _____ Single { 1st, 2nd or 3rd marriage } _____ First

Name of Father _____ Grover C Price

Maiden name of Mother _____ Mary Caroline Henning

Bride's name _____ Zeta Shirley Anne Richardson

Her age _____ 17

" color _____ White

" occupation _____ Office Work

" Birthplace—City _____ Indianapolis _____ State _____ Ind

" Residence—Street No. _____ 249 Beville Ave _____ City _____ Indpls

Single / Widow / Divorced } _____ Single { 1st, 2nd or 3rd marriage } _____ First

Name of Father _____ Francis Marion Richardson

Maiden name of Mother _____ Florence Mae Butcher

Date of this marriage _____ April 16th, 1944

Place of this marriage _____ 249 North Beville Ave, Indpls Ind

Name and title of person Performing this marriage _____ Rev Golden A Smith

His address _____ 2609 East New York St. Indianapolis Ind

Witness { Name _____ Mr. & Mrs. Grover C. Price
{ Address _____ 234 Eastern Ave, Indpls Ind

## Return this Report to County Clerk with License and Certificate

12

# Marriage Record for Board of Health
## To Be Returned by the Minister or Other Person Performing Ceremony

_TURNER_ _____ and _EASTER_

Groom's name _William Edward Turner_

His age _25 years_

" color _White_

" occupation _U. S. Naval Reserve_

" Birthplace—City _Indianapolis_ State _Indiana_

" Residence—Street No. _2228 Lawndale_ City _Evanston, Illinois_

Single / Widower / Divorced } _Single_ { 1st, 2nd or 3rd marriage } _1st_

Name of Father _George Edgar Turner_

Maiden name of Mother _Leona Chloe Weddle_

Bride's name _Elva Marine Easter_

Her age _21 years_

" color _White_

" occupation _U. S. Naval Reserve_

" Birthplace—City _Wellington_ State _Texas_

" Residence—Street No. _/_ City _Wellington_

Single / Widow / Divorced } _Single_ { 1st, 2nd or 3rd marriage } _1st_

Name of Father _Alonzo Lee Easter_

Maiden name of Mother _Ida Newett_

Date of this marriage _16 April 1944_

Place of this marriage _Indianapolis, Indiana_

Name and title of person Performing this marriage _Carleton W. Atwater, D.D._

His address _FIRST Baptist Church—meridian at Vermont Indianapolis, Ind._

Witness { Name _George R. Turner—14800 Leonard co Lakewood_
{ Address _Ensign Rita Cull—U.S. Navy._

## Return this Report to County Clerk with License and Certificate

# Marriage Record for Board of Health
### To Be Returned by the Minister or Other Person Performing Ceremony

Carl Edward Burton _____ and Patricia Anne Glossbrenner

Groom's name ___Carl Edward Burton

His age ___20

" color____White

" occupation 2nd Lt. U.S. Army Infantry Ft. Benning, Georgia

" Birthplace—City___Tipton _____ State ___Indiana

" Residence—Street No. 333 Kentucky Ave. City Tipton, Indiana

Single / Widower / Divorced }  Single · | 1st, 2nd or 3rd marriage }  1st

Name of Father Orley C. Burton

Maiden name of Mother Coral Holman

Bride's name ___Patricia Anne Glossbrenner

Her age 20

" color___White

" occupation Chemist Assistant Eli Lilly & Company, Indianapolis,

" Birthplace—City___Indianapolis _____ State ___Indiana

" Residence—Street No. 3609 Balsam _____ City Indianapolis

Single / Widow / Divorced }  Single | 1st, 2nd or 3rd marriage }  1st

Name of Father___Frederick W. Glossbrenner

Maiden name of Mother Helene Harrison

Date of this marriage April 16, 1944

Place of this marriage McKee Chapel-Tabernacle Presbyterian Church-Indianapolis, Indiana

Name and title of person Performing this marriage _____ Minister of First Methodist Church-Bloomington, Indiana

His address _Merrill B. McFall_
414 S. College Bloomington Ind.

Witness { Name J. Robert Cole 2nd Lt Inf
{ Address 1220 N. Tuxedo St. Indianapolis, Ind.

### Return this Report to County Clerk with License and Certificate

## Marriage Record for Board of Health
### To Be Returned by the Minister or Other Person Performing Ceremony

Harold A Johnston _and_ Marjorie R Howell

Groom's name _Harold A. Johnston_

His age _28_

" color _white_

" occupation _U. S. Army_

" Birthplace—City _Meadville_ State _Penn._

" Residence—Street No. _Camp Shelby_ City _Miss._

~~Single~~
Widower
Divorced } { 1st, 2nd or 3rd marriage } _2nd._

Name of Father _Almond B. Johnston._

Maiden name of Mother _Lula Wheeler._

Bride's name _Marjorie R. Howell._

Her age _28_

" color _White_

" occupation _R.C.A._

" Birthplace—City _Bedford._ State _Ind._

" Residence—Street No. _916 N. King_ City _Indpls. Ind._

~~Single~~
Widow
Divorced } { 1st, 2nd or 3rd marriage } _2nd_

Name of Father _Jesse Scoggan._

Maiden name of Mother _Laura Waterbury._

Date of this marriage _April, 16, 1944_

Place of this marriage _2608 W. Mich St._

Name and title of person Performing this marriage _Walter Bradford Justice 'Peace_

His address _2608 W. Mich St. City_

Witness { Name _Sarah E. Hurly_
Address _3307 Ralston ave Indpls, Ind._

### Return this Report to County Clerk with License and Certificate

# Marriage Record for Board of Health

To Be Returned by the Minister or Other Person Performing Ceremony

Truman Wallace Hays. and Edna Mae Dodds.

Groom's name _Truman Wallace Hays._

His age _23_

" color _White_

" occupation _Soldier_

" Birthplace—City _Bainbridge_ State _Ind._

" Residence—Street No. _____ City _Bainbridge_

Single / Widower / Divorced } _Single_ { 1st, 2nd or 3rd marriage } _____

Name of Father _Thomas Armond Hays_

Maiden name of Mother _Ruth Mae Davis_

Bride's name _Edna Mae Dodds._

Her age _21_

" color _White_

" occupation _____

" Birthplace—City _Toronto_ State _Canada._

" Residence—Street No. _621 E 13th St._ City _Indianapolis_

Single / Widow / Divorced } _Single_ { 1st, 2nd or 3rd marriage } _____

Name of Father _William Dodds_

Maiden name of Mother _Helena Graham._

Date of this marriage _April 16th 1944_

Place of this marriage _Indianapolis Indiana_

Name and title of person Performing this marriage _Rev. John B Ferguson_

His address _312 N. Ritter an_ _Indianapolis Ind._

Witness { Name _Thomas. O. Hays._

{ Address _2611 E 18th Indianapolis Ind_

## Return this Report to County Clerk with License and Certificate

12

# Marriage Record for Board of Health
### To Be Returned by the Minister or Other Person Performing Ceremony

Bland _____ and _____ Kearney _____

Groom's name _____ Harry E. Bland _____

His age _____ 67 _____

" color _____ White _____

" occupation _____ Butcher _____

" Birthplace—City _____ Sullivan _____ State _____ Indiana _____

" Residence—Street No. _____ 2858 N. Illinois _____ City _____ Indianapolis _____

~~Single~~ / Widower / ~~Divorced~~ } _____ Widower _____ { 1st, 2nd or 3rd marriage } _____ Second _____

Name of Father _____ Wm. H. Bland _____

Maiden name of Mother _____ Mary E. Hughes _____

Bride's name _____ Mary G. Kearney _____

Her age _____ 57 _____

" color _____ White _____

" occupation _____ Cook _____

" Birthplace—City _____ Indianapolis _____ State _____ Indiana _____

" Residence—Street No. _____ 2257 N. Illinois _____ City _____ Indianapolis _____

~~Single~~ / Widow / ~~Divorced~~ } _____ Widow _____ { 1st, 2nd or 3rd marriage } _____ Second _____

Name of Father _____ Nicholas Fiemyer _____

Maiden name of Mother _____ Jennie Haney _____

Date of this marriage _____ April 16, 1944 _____

Place of this marriage _____ SS. Peter and Paul Rectory, Indianapolis, Ind _____

Name and title of person Performing this marriage _____ Cornelius B. Sweeney, asst. pastor _____

His address _____ 1347 N. Meridian _____
_____ Indianapolis, Indiana _____

Witness { Name _____ Harry Weiker – Nola Weiker _____
{ Address _____ Indianapolis, Indiana _____

### Return this Report to County Clerk with License and Certificate

# Marriage Record for Board of Health

### To Be Returned by the Minister or Other Person Performing Ceremony

*John Hottel Curran* and *Doris Elinor Tuttle*

Groom's name _John Hotel Curran_

His age _24_

" color _white_

" occupation _Army of United States_

" Birthplace—City _Indianapolis_ State _Indiana_

" Residence—Street No. _Base Detachment_ City _Hunter Field, Georgia_

Single Widower Divorced } _Single_ { 1st, 2nd or 3rd marriage } _first_

Name of Father _John B. Curran_

Maiden name of Mother _Lorena Mae Hottel_

Bride's name _Doris Elinor Tuttle_

Her age _22_

" color _White_

" occupation _unemployed_

" Birthplace—City _Chicago_ State _Illinois_

" Residence—Street No. _543 E. 56th Street_ City _Indianapolis, Ind._

Single Widow Divorced } _single_ { 1st, 2nd or 3rd marriage } _first_

Name of Father _Max A. Tuttle_

Maiden name of Mother _Mary E. Konecker_

Date of this marriage _April 16, 1944_

Place of this marriage _Indianapolis, Indiana_

Name and title of person Performing this marriage _Rev. Ernest J. Roesti_

His address _5614 Broadway_

_Indianapolis, Indiana_

Witness { Name _William H. Lewis_
Address _1055 W. Main, Franklin, Ind._

## Return this Report to County Clerk with License and Certificate

12

# Marriage Record for Board of Health
### To Be Returned by the Minister or Other Person Performing Ceremony

_William Mooneyhan_ and _Esther L Smithee_

Groom's name _William Mooneyhan_

His age _Twenty Five_

" color _White_

" occupation _Soldier · U. S. A._

" Birthplace—City _Sumner County_ State _Tennessee_

" Residence—Street No. _Whites Creek_ City _R. F. D._

Single Widower Divorced } _Single_  { 1st, 2nd or 3rd marriage } _First_

Name of Father _William Henry Mooneyhan_

Maiden name of Mother _Netty Gurtrude Gilliam_

Bride's name _Esther Louise Smithee_

Her age _Twenty Three_

" color _White_

" occupation _Nurse_

" Birthplace—City _Wabash_ State _Ind._

" Residence—Street No. _Erie St_ City _Greencastle Ind._

Single Widow Divorced } _Single_  { 1st, 2nd or 3rd marriage } _First_

Name of Father _Edward L Smithee_

Maiden name of Mother _Ena Louretta Smithee_

Date of this marriage _April 16th – 1944 –_

Place of this marriage _Ft Wayne Ind._

Name and title of person Performing this marriage _Rev Edward L Smithee_

His address _1910 West Fourth · Ft Wayne_

Witness { Name _T/Sgt Paul Hayden_

{ Address _Billings Gen Hospital_

### Return this Report to County Clerk with License and Certificate

# Marriage Record for Board of Health
## To Be Returned by the Minister or Other Person Performing Ceremony

Robert H. Moore and Vera Quirk

Groom's name _Robert H. Moore_

His age _32_

" color _C_

" occupation _Cadre maker_

" Birthplace—City _New Orleans_ State _La._

" Residence—Street No. _2119 W. Howard St._ City _Indianapolis, Ind._

Single / Widower / Divorced } _Divorced_ { 1st, 2nd or 3rd marriage } _2nd_

Name of Father _Jordan Moore_

Maiden name of Mother _Cressy Scott_

Bride's name _Vera Quirk_

Her age _28_

" color _C_

" occupation _Home Keeper_

" Birthplace—City _Blytheville_ State _Ark._

" Residence—Street No. _2117 W. Howard St., Indianapolis,_

Single / Widow / Divorced } _Single_ { 1st, 2nd or 3rd marriage } _1st_

Name of Father _Wilson Quirk_

Maiden name of Mother _Ruby Pierce_

Date of this marriage _April 17, 1944_

Place of this marriage _Indianapolis, Indiana._

Name and title of person Performing this marriage _J. S. Hensley, Minister_

His address _702 N. Illinois St._ _Indianapolis, Indiana_

Witness { Name _Lily Pierce_ { Address _2117 W. Howard St._

## Return this Report to County Clerk with License and Certificate

# Marriage Record for Board of Health

To Be Returned by the Minister or Other Person Performing Ceremony

*Lexie V Huffman* and *Robbie Lanier*

Groom's name _Lexie V Huffman_

His age _36_

" color _White_

" occupation _Crane Operator_

" Birthplace—City _Marion Co_ State _Kentucky_

" Residence—Street No _1357 Modison_ City _Indianapolis_

Single
Widower } _Single_ { 1st, 2nd or 3rd marriage } _1st_
Divorced

Name of Father _J B. Huffman_

Maiden name of Mother

Bride's name _Robbie Lanier_

Her age _30_

" color _White_

" occupation _None_

" Birthplace—City _Calhoue_ State _Georgia_

" Residence—Street No. _1357 Modison_ City _Indianapolis_

Single
Widow } _Divorced_ { 1st, 2nd or 3rd marriage } _2nd_
Divorced

Name of Father _Clifford Lanier_

Maiden name of Mother _Ollie Tate_

Date of this marriage _April 17, 1944_

Place of this marriage _Indianapolis Ind_

Name and title of person
Performing this marriage _Ernest Longe Justice of Peace_

His address _152½ East Court St_

Witness { Name _Mary J. Lane_
{ Address _3740 College_

**Return this Report to County Clerk with License and Certificate**

# Marriage Record for Board of Health

### To Be Returned by the Minister or Other Person Performing Ceremony

_____ and _____

Groom's name _William Berman_

His age _23_

" color _White_

" occupation _U. S. Army — Capt._

" Birthplace—City _Indianapolis_ State _Ind._

" Residence—Street No. _1361 S Shelby St._ City _Indianapolis._

Single | _1st._ | 1st, 2nd or 3rd
Widower | | marriage
Divorced |

Name of Father _Harry Berman_

Maiden name of Mother _Sarah Gelman_

Bride's name _Harriet Elaine Levey_

Her age _21_

" color _White_

" occupation _____

" Birthplace—City _Indianapolis_ State _Ind._

" Residence—Street No. _5606 Wash. Blvd._ City _Indianapolis._

Single | _1st_ | 1st, 2nd or 3rd
Widow | | marriage
Divorced |

Name of Father _Lewis J. Levey_

Maiden name of Mother _Ruth A. Hammerman_

Date of this marriage _April 17, 1944_

Place of this marriage _Indianapolis, Ind._

Name and title of person
Performing this marriage _Rabbi Morris M. Feuerlicht_

His address _Indianapolis, Ind._

Witness { Name _____
{ Address _____

### Return this Report to County Clerk with License and Certificate

12

# Marriage Record for Board of Health
## To Be Returned by the Minister or Other Person Performing Ceremony

_____ and _____

Groom's name _Norman I Foglison_

His age _52_

" color _White_

" occupation _Boiler Inspector_

" Birthplace—City _Oklahoma City_ State _Oklahoma_

" Residence—Street No. _1833 Foster_ City _Chicago_

Single
Widower } _Divorced_ { 1st, 2nd or 3rd } _Second_
Divorced marriage

Name of Father _John Foglison_

Maiden name of Mother _Bertha Edith Ridle_

Bride's name _Hilda Weber_

Her age _53_

" color _White_

" occupation _____

" Birthplace—City _Cincinnati_ State _Ohio_

" Residence—Street No. _4629 N. Winchester_ City _Chicago_

Single
Widow } _Divorced_ { 1st, 2nd or 3rd } _Second_
Divorced marriage

Name of Father _Gottfried Weber_

Maiden name of Mother _Louise Haus_

Date of this marriage _April 17 - 1941_

Place of this marriage _Indianapolis Indiana_

Name and title of person
Performing this marriage _Rev. J. N. Greene_

His address _1841 Cross Drive Woodruff Place_
_Indianapolis Indiana_

Witness { Name _Mrs. J. N. Greene_
{ Address _1841 Cross Dr. Woodruff Place_

## Return this Report to County Clerk with License and Certificate

# Marriage Record for Board of Health

### To Be Returned by the Minister or Other Person Performing Ceremony

_Willie Lenzy_ and _Margaret Gaines_

Groom's name _Willie Lenzy_

His age _32_

" color _negro_

" occupation _Machine operator_

" Birthplace—City _Washington County_ State _Miss_

" Residence—Street No. _226 W. 18th_ City _Indianapolis_

Single } _Single_  { 1st, 2nd or 3rd } _1st_
Widower              marriage
Divorced

Name of Father _Fozy Lenzy_

Maiden name of Mother _Nellie Nelson_

Bride's name _Margaret Gaines_

Her age _37_

" color _negro_

" occupation _Housekeeper_

" Birthplace—City _Hopkinsville_ State _Ky_

" Residence—Street No. _226 W. 18th_ City _Indianapolis_

Single } _1st Single_  { 1st, 2nd or 3rd } _1st_
Widow               marriage
Divorced

Name of Father _Joshua Gaines_

Maiden name of Mother _Clara Monjoy_

Date of this marriage _April 17th, 1944_

Place of this marriage _Indianapolis_

Name and title of person
Performing this marriage _O. A. Calhoun, Minister_

His address _2128 N. Capitol_
_Indianapolis, Ind_

Witness { Name _Lela Cavanaugh_
         { Address _324 W 21 Street #3_

### Return this Report to County Clerk with License and Certificate

12

# Marriage Record for Board of Health
## To Be Returned by the Minister or Other Person Performing Ceremony

John A. Remmetter----------- and Loretta C. Feeney.

Groom's name __John A. Remmetter,__

His age __next August 3rd, 25 years old.__

" color __White.__

" occupation __Soldier, at Fort Benning, Georgia.__

" Birthplace—City __Indianapolis,__ State __Indiana.__

" Residence—Street No. __at Fort Benning,__ City __State of Georgia.__

Single / ~~Widower~~ / ~~Divorced~~ } __Single.__   { 1st, ~~2nd or 3rd~~ marriage } __First Marriage.__

Name of Father __John Remmetter,__

Maiden name of Mother __Beatrice McDuff.__

Bride's name __Loretta Cecelia Feeney,__

Her age __next June 27th, 24 years old.__

" color __White,__

" occupation __Group Leader at Allisons.__

" Birthplace—City __Indianapolis,__ State __Indiana.__

" Residence—Street No. __1148 Beville Ave.,__ City __Indianapolis, Indiana.__

Single / ~~Widow~~ / ~~Divorced~~ } __Single;__   { 1st, ~~2nd or 3rd~~ marriage } __First Marriage.__

Name of Father __John Feeney,__

Maiden name of Mother __Helen Jonas.__

Date of this marriage __April 17, 1944.__

Place of this marriage __St.Philip Neri Church, Indianapolis, Indiana.__

Name and title of person Performing this marriage __Rev.Andrew J.Bastnagel (Catholic Priest)__

His address __550 North Rural Street, Indianapolis, Indiana.__

_Rev. Andrew J. Bastnagel_

Witness { Name __Sherman Clark,and Rita Ann Jonas,__ / Address __Both of Indianapolis, Indiana.__

## Return this Report to County Clerk with License and Certificate

12

# Marriage Record for Board of Health
### To Be Returned by the Minister or Other Person Performing Ceremony

J. Everard Gallagher and Kathryn E. Walsh

Groom's name _J. Everard Gallagher_

His age _41_

" color _white_

" occupation _Statistician_

" Birthplace—City _Shelby Co._ State _Indiana_

" Residence—Street No. _2716 N. Meridian_ City _Indianapolis_

Single / Widower / Divorced } _Divorced_ { 1st, 2nd or 3rd marriage } _Second_

Name of Father _Richard T. Gallagher_

Maiden name of Mother _Edna M. C. Biggs_

Bride's name _Kathryn E. Walsh_

Her age _37_

" color _white_

" occupation _Bookkeeper_

" Birthplace—City _Shelbyville_ State _Indiana_

" Residence—Street No. _Apt. 1, 22 W. 34th St._ City _Indianapolis_

Single / Widow / Divorced } _Divorced_ { 1st, 2nd or 3rd marriage } _Second_

Name of Father _Peter J. Lux, Sr._

Maiden name of Mother _Mary Gobel_

Date of this marriage _April 17, 1944_

Place of this marriage _Indianapolis, Marion Co., Indiana_

Name and title of person Performing this marriage _N Nathan Swaim, Judge of Supreme Court_

His address _316 N. Delaware St, Indianapolis, Indiana_

Witness { Name _Peter Lux Jr_ Address _1107 Meridian Shelbyville, Ind_

### Return this Report to County Clerk with License and Certificate

# Marriage Record for Board of Health
### To Be Returned by the Minister or Other Person Performing Ceremony

*H. Gayle Woodring* and *Eileen D. Yount*

Groom's name _H. Gayle Woodring_

His age _31_

" color _W._

" occupation _Tool Maker_

" Birthplace—City _Muncie_ State _Ind._

" Residence—Street No. _118 E. Wysor_ City _Muncie_

Single / Widower / Divorced } _Single_   { 1st, 2nd or 3rd marriage }

Name of Father _C. Guy Woodring_

Maiden name of Mother _Ethel A. Smith_

Bride's name _Eileen D. Yount_

Her age _30_

" color _W._

" occupation _Secretary_

" Birthplace—City _Hartford City_ State _Ind._

" Residence—Street No. _1427 Park_ City _Indpls, Ind._

Single / Widow / Divorced } _Single_   { 1st, 2nd or 3rd marriage }

Name of Father _Chas. Yount_

Maiden name of Mother _Delphia Larrimore_

Date of this marriage _Apr. 17 - 1944_

Place of this marriage _Indpls._

Name and title of person Performing this marriage _Judge Walter Pritchard_

His address _____

_Walter Pritchard, Judge -_
3406 Fall Creek Blvd.

Witness { Name _Lawrence L. Gammon_
{ Address _Mabel K. Larson_

### Return this Report to County Clerk with License and Certificate

## Marriage Record for Board of Health

### To Be Returned by the Minister or Other Person Performing Ceremony

*Clifford C. Brady* and *Mary Ottinger Lewis*

Groom's name _Clifford C. Brady_

His age _42_

" color _White_

" occupation _Link Belt – Screw machine Operator_

" Birthplace—City _Danville_ State _Indiana_

" Residence—Street No. _1132 S. Dennison_ City _Indianapolis_

~~Single~~ ~~Widower~~ Divorced } _Divorced_ { 1st, 2nd or 3rd marriage } _2nd_

Name of Father _Howard N. Brady_ } _Danville Ind_

Maiden name of Mother _Ada McPheeters_

Bride's name _Mary Ottinger Lewis_

Her age _23_

" color _White_

" occupation _Housekeeper_

" Birthplace—City _Hartford_ State _Michigan_

" Residence—Street No. _3324 W Wilcox_ City _Indianapolis_

~~Single~~ ~~Widow~~ Divorced } _Divorced_ { 1st, 2nd or 3rd marriage } _4th_

Name of Father _Clinton Ottinger_

Maiden name of Mother _Lucy Mae Harvey_

Date of this marriage _April 17, 1944_

Place of this marriage _242 E. Pleasant Run Parkway_

Name and title of person Performing this marriage _Roscoe Kirkman – Pastor_

His address _Same_ _West Side Christian_

Witness { Name _Everett Harvey Jr_
{ Address _27 N Greely St._

### Return this Report to County Clerk with License and Certificate

# Marriage Record for Board of Health
### To Be Returned by the Minister or Other Person Performing Ceremony

_Stanford Rogers_ and _Dorothy Mae Milne_

Groom's name _Stanford Rogers_

His age _27_

" color _C_

" occupation _Dry Cleaner_

" Birthplace—City _Indpls._ State _Ind._

" Residence—Street No. _2518 Indpls_ City _Indpls._

Single Widower Divorced } _Divorced_ { 1st, 2nd or 3rd marriage } _second_

Name of Father _William Gillon_

Maiden name of Mother _Harriet Rogers_

Bride's name _Dorothy Mae Milne_

Her age _23_

" color _C_

" occupation _none_

" Birthplace—City _Indpls._ State _Ind._

" Residence—Street No. _633 W 13th St_ City _Indpls._

Single Widow Divorced } _Single_ { 1st, 2nd or 3rd marriage } _first_

Name of Father _Justice Reginald Milne_

Maiden name of Mother _Carolyn Freddie_

Date of this marriage _April 18, 1944_

Place of this marriage _Indianapolis Indiana_

Name and title of person Performing this marriage _S S Thomas minister_

His address _707 South Illinois St_
_Indianapolis Indiana_

Witness { Name _Betty Lou Wickliffe_
{ Address _2336 Indianapolis Ind._

### Return this Report to County Clerk with License and Certificate

# Marriage Record for Board of Health

### To Be Returned by the Minister or Other Person Performing Ceremony

_____ *Luke Stanley* and *Elizabeth* _____

Groom's name _____ *Luke Stanley* _____

His age _____ *26* _____

" color _____ *White* _____

" occupation _____ *labor* _____

" Birthplace—City _____ *Louisville* _____ State _____ *Ill* _____

" Residence—Street No. _____ City _____

Single }
Widower } _____ *Single* _____  { 1st, 2nd or 3rd } _____
Divorced }                      { marriage

Name of Father _____ *Willie J. Stanley* _____

Maiden name of Mother _____ *Ida M. Linion* _____

Bride's name _____ *Elizabeth J. Prayer* _____

Her age _____ *20* _____

" color _____ *Brown* _____

" occupation _____ *family* _____

" Birthplace—City _____ *Dubuque* _____ State _____ *Iowa* _____

" Residence—Street No. _____ City _____

Single }
Widow } _____ *Single* _____  { 1st, 2nd or 3rd } _____
Divorced }                    { marriage

Name of Father _____ *J. W. Prayer* _____

Maiden name of Mother _____ *Lucille Christman* _____

Date of this marriage _____

Place of this marriage _____

Name and title of person
Performing this marriage _____

His address _____ *812 Walk St* _____

_____

Witness { Name _____
        { Address _____ *1826* _____

## Return this Report to County Clerk with License and Certificate

# Marriage Record for Board of Health

### To Be Returned by the Minister or Other Person Performing Ceremony

*James W. Davis* and *Erma Stamler*

Groom's name _James W. Davis_

His age _33_

" color _White_

" occupation _Jeweler_

" Birthplace—City _Bedford_ State _Kentucky_

" Residence—Street No. _Munroe_ City _California_

Single / Widower / Divorced } _Divorced_ { 1st, 2nd or 3rd marriage } _2nd_

Name of Father _James Davis_

Maiden name of Mother _Hattie Kent_

Bride's name _Erma Stamler_

Her age _18_

" color _White_

" occupation _None_

" Birthplace—City _Carrollton_ State _Kentucky_

" Residence—Street No. _Carrollton_ City _Kentucky_

Single / Widow / Divorced } _Single_ { 1st, 2nd or 3rd marriage } _1st_

Name of Father _Ewing Stamler_

Maiden name of Mother _Eula Bromwell_

Date of this marriage _April 18 1914_

Place of this marriage _Indianapolis Ind._

Name and title of person Performing this marriage _Ernest Line Justice of the Peace_

His address _132½ East Court_

Witness { Name _Mary Jo Lane_ { Address _3541 College_

## Return this Report to County Clerk with License and Certificate

# Marriage Record for Board of Health
### To Be Returned by the Minister or Other Person Performing Ceremony

*Earl L. Shaver* and *Jeanne Faulk,*

Groom's name _Earl L. Shaver_

His age _30_

" color _W,_

" occupation _Soldier_

" Birthplace—City _Monongah_ State _W. Va,_

" Residence—Street No. _Co. a 201 Inf,_ City _Camp Carson, Colo,_

Single / Widower / Divorced } _Single_ { 1st, 2nd or 3rd marriage } _1st,_

Name of Father _R. B. Shaver_

Maiden name of Mother _Cora Leota Crayton,_

Bride's name _Jeanne Faulk_

Her age _19_

" color _W,_

" occupation _house keeper,_

" Birthplace—City _Indpls,_ State _Ind,_

" Residence—Street No. _1232 S. Bel. a_ City _Indpls,_

Single / Widow / Divorced } _Single_ { 1st, 2nd or 3rd marriage } _1st,_

Name of Father _James H. Faulk,_

Maiden name of Mother _Mary E. Gauble_

Date of this marriage _April 12th, 1944_

Place of this marriage _Indianapolis Ind,_

Name and title of person Performing this marriage _Rev. Thomas Paino_

His address _2114 Miller St,_
_Indianapolis, Ind,_

Witness { Name _Lyda Paino_ Address _2114 Miller St_

## Return this Report to County Clerk with License and Certificate

# Marriage Record for Board of Health

To Be Returned by the Minister or Other Person Performing Ceremony

_Leonard Hardy_ and _Emma Huston_

Groom's name _Leonard Hardy_

His age _24_

" color _colored_

" occupation _Soldier_

" Birthplace—City _Little Rock Ark_ State _Arkansas_

" Residence—Street No. _____ City _____

Single / Widower / Divorced } _wife dead_ { 1st, 2nd or 3rd marriage } _2nd marriage_

Name of Father _Otis Hardy_

Maiden name of Mother _Lillie Gray_

Bride's name _Emma Huston_

Her age _17_

" color _colored_

" occupation _none_

" Birthplace—City _Indianapolis_ State _Indiana_

" Residence—Street No. _713 W 13th St_ City _Indianapolis_

Single / Widow / Divorced } _Single_ { 1st, 2nd or 3rd marriage }

Name of Father _Melvin Huston_

Maiden name of Mother _Norrea Smith_

Date of this marriage _April 18 – 1944_

Place of this marriage _925 N California Ave Indianapolis Ind_

Name and title of person Performing this marriage _Rev S. Russell_

His address _357 W 12th st Indianapolis Indiana_

_Rev S. Russell minister 357 W 12 st_

Witness { Name _Navie Huston_ Address _925 Camp St_

## Return this Report to County Clerk with License and Certificate

# Marriage Record for Board of Health

To Be Returned by the Minister or Other Person Performing Ceremony

Malcolm F. Welch and Jessica S. Lawrence

Groom's name _Malcolm F. Welch_

His age _21_

" color _White_

" occupation _Army_

" Birthplace—City _Dahlgren Va._ State _Virginia_

" Residence—Street No. _986 N. Audubon_ City _Indpls. Ind._

Single / Widower / Divorced  { 1st, 2nd or 3rd marriage }

Name of Father _Earnest L. Welch_

Maiden name of Mother _Inez Bowie_

Bride's name _Jessica Lawrence_

Her age _22_

" color _White_

" occupation _Lucas Harold_

" Birthplace—City _New Bedford_ State _Mass._

" Residence—Street No. _31 Spencer_ City _Indianapolis Ind._

Single / Widow / Divorced  { 1st, 2nd or 3rd marriage }

Name of Father _Anthony P. Lawrence_

Maiden name of Mother _Mary Mitchell_

Date of this marriage _April 18, 1944_

Place of this marriage _Our Lady of Lourdes Rectory_

Name and title of person Performing this marriage _Rev. James W. Moore_

His address _5333 E. Wash St._
_Indianapolis, Indiana_

Witness { Name _Elmo Fairfax_  986 N. Audubon
{ Address _Lucelle Weidekamp - 266 S. Audubon_

**Return this Report to County Clerk with License and Certificate**

# Marriage Record for Board of Health
## To Be Returned by the Minister or Other Person Performing Ceremony

Virgil E. Proud and Mary Molloy

Groom's name _Virgil E. Proud_

His age _51_

" color _White_

" occupation _Clerk_

" Birthplace—City _Anderson_ State _Indiana_

" Residence—Street No. _1848 N. Penn_ City _Indianapolis_

Single
~~Widower~~
~~Divorced~~ } { 1st, ~~2nd or 3rd~~ marriage }

Name of Father _Barton S. Proud_

Maiden name of Mother _Emma M. Kessler_

Bride's name _Mary Molloy_

Her age _53_

" color _White_

" occupation _Clerk_

" Birthplace—City _Cuttawa_ State _Kentucky_

" Residence—Street No. _3509 Kenwood_ City _Indianapolis_

Single
~~Widow~~
~~Divorced~~ } { 1st, ~~2nd or 3rd~~ marriage }

Name of Father _Sam C. Molloy_

Maiden name of Mother _Annie Coleman_

Date of this marriage _April 18, 1944._

Place of this marriage _Indianapolis,_

Name and title of person Performing this marriage _Rev. D. H. O'Donnell_

His address _517 East 23d St., Indpls, Ind_

Witness { Name _Mrs. Emma Proud,_
Address _Anderson, Ind_ }

## Return this Report to County Clerk with License and Certificate

# Marriage Record for Board of Health

### To Be Returned by the Minister or Other Person Performing Ceremony

*Norman Ball* and *Patty Poe*

Groom's name _Norman Ball_

His age _33_

" color _White_

" occupation _Chopper_

" Birthplace—City _Shirley_ State _Indiana_

" Residence—Street No. _3336 Stanton_ City _Indianapolis_

Single / Widower / Divorced } _Divorced_ { 1st, 2nd or 3rd marriage } _2nd_

Name of Father _Eli A. Ball_

Maiden name of Mother _Minka Morris_

Bride's name _Patty Poe_

Her age _21_

" color _White_

" occupation _Defence worker_

" Birthplace—City _Huntington_ State _Indiana_

" Residence—Street No. _815 N. Euclid_ City _Indianapolis_

Single / Widow / Divorced } _Divorced_ { 1st, 2nd or 3rd marriage } _2nd_

Name of Father _Harry G. Cross_

Maiden name of Mother _Ethel E. Payne_

Date of this marriage _April 19, 1944_

Place of this marriage _Indianapolis Ind_

Name and title of person Performing this marriage _Ernest Dow Justice of Peace_

His address _152½ East Court_

Witness { Name _May Jo Lane_ Address _3740 College Ave_

### Return this Report to County Clerk with License and Certificate

# Marriage Record for Board of Health
### To Be Returned by the Minister or Other Person Performing Ceremony

_____ and _____

Groom's name _Preston Carl Hazzard_

His age _19_

" color _White_

" occupation _R.C.A. Victor Division_

" Birthplace—City _Millington_ State _Michigan_

" Residence—Street No. _4148 Brown Ave_ City _Indianapolis, Indiana_

Single Widower Divorced } _single_ { 1st, 2nd or 3rd marriage } _first_

Name of Father _Lloyd B. Hazzard_

Maiden name of Mother _Elsie Van Wagoner_

Bride's name _Dorothy Genevieve Rubush_

Her age _20_

" color _white_

" occupation _U. S. Navy_

" Birthplace—City _Indianapolis_ State _Indiana_

" Residence—Street No. _Great Lakes_ City _Illinois_

Single Widow Divorced } _single_ { 1st, 2nd or 3rd marriage }

Name of Father _Harold Herschell Rubush_

Maiden name of Mother _Dorothy Elizabeth Negrich_

Date of this marriage _April 19 1944_

Place of this marriage _Indianapolis Ind._

Name and title of person Performing this marriage _Rev. L. A. Huddleston_

His address _1613 F_____ ave, Indianapolis Ind._

Witness { Name _Kenneth E. Bryant_
{ Address _Olivet College Kankakee Ill._

### Return this Report to County Clerk with License and Certificate

# Marriage Record for Board of Health
### To Be Returned by the Minister or Other Person Performing Ceremony

_Harold D. Davis_ and _Doris Dawson_

Groom's name _Harold D. Davis_

His age _23_

" color _white_

" occupation _Barber_

" Birthplace—City _Columbury_ State _Ind_

" Residence—Street No. _4102 Hoyt Ave_ City _Indpls_

Single Widower Divorced } _Single_ { 1st, 2nd or 3rd marriage

Name of Father _Virgil Davis_

Maiden name of Mother _Amanda Moffet_

Bride's name _Doris Dawson_

Her age _19_

" color _White_

" occupation _Laborer_

" Birthplace—City _Connersville_ State _Ind._

" Residence—Street No. _766 Clara_ City _Indpls_

Single Widow Divorced } _Single_ { 1st, 2nd or 3rd marriage

Name of Father _John Dawson_

Maiden name of Mother _Lula Edwards_

Date of this marriage _April 19, 1944_

Place of this marriage _Indianapolis_

Name and title of person Performing this marriage _Geo. E. Tillie_

His address _1410 S... Ave Minister Indianapolis Ind_

Witness { Name _Mrs. Nellie Garrett_ { Address _409 E McCarty St Indpls Ind_

### Return this Report to County Clerk with License and Certificate

_George W. Dillard_
_127 N. Sherman Dr. Indpls Ind_

# Marriage Record for Board of Health
### To Be Returned by the Minister or Other Person Performing Ceremony

*Lawrence Jones* and *Maurice D. Carr*

Groom's name *Lawrence R. Jones*

His age *215*

" color *Colored*

" occupation *Foundry*

" Birthplace—City _____ State _____

" Residence—Street No. *132 R 21 St.* City *Indianapolis*

Single Widower Divorced } *First*  { 1st, 2nd or 3rd marriage

Name of Father *Thomas Jones*

Maiden name of Mother *Lena Poleseel*

Bride's name *Maurice D. Carr.*

Her age *20*

" color *Colored*

" occupation *Maid*

" Birthplace—City *Indianapolis* State *Ind.*

" Residence—Street No. *2051 Kenwood* City *Indianapolis*

Single Widow Divorced } *First*  { 1st, 2nd or 3rd marriage

Name of Father *Leeroy Carr*

Maiden name of Mother *Mauey Johnson*

Date of this marriage *April 19,*

Place of this marriage *2051 Kenwood*

Name and title of person Performing this marriage *Rev. J. A. Saunders*

His address *2649 N. Western Ave*
*Indianapolis Indiana*

Witness { Name *Loralla Freeman*
{ Address *451 W. St. Clair St.*

### Return this Report to County Clerk with License and Certificate

# Marriage Record for Board of Health
## To Be Returned by the Minister or Other Person Performing Ceremony

Norman Bitterman _____ and _Annette Krumsiek_

Groom's name _Norman Bittermann_

His age _27_

" color _white_

" occupation _Army Air Corps_

" Birthplace—City _Joliet_ State _Illinois_

" Residence—Street No. _709 Wilcox St_ City _Joliet, Illinois_

Single / Widower / Divorced } _Single_   { 1st, 2nd or 3rd marriage } _First_

Name of Father _George P Bittermann_

Maiden name of Mother _Minnie Berlin_

Bride's name _Annette Krumsiek_

Her age _24_

" color _white_

" occupation _File clerk_

" Birthplace—City _Shelbyville_ State _Illinois_

" Residence—Street No. _____ City _Auburn, Illinois_

Single / Widow / Divorced } _Single_   { 1st, 2nd or 3rd marriage } _1st._

Name of Father _Walter Wesley Krumsiek_

Maiden name of Mother _Dorothea Jacobi_

Date of this marriage _April 19, 1944_

Place of this marriage _North Methodist Church_

Name and title of person Performing this marriage _Dallas L Browning_

His address _5530 N Delaware St_

_Indianapolis 5, Ind._

Witness { Name _Sgt. J. Ray Watson_
{ Address _Camp Lee, Virginia_

## Return this Report to County Clerk with License and Certificate

# Marriage Record for Board of Health
## To Be Returned by the Minister or Other Person Performing Ceremony

_____ and _____

Groom's name _Melvin D. Coleman_

His age _18_

" color _White_

" occupation _Soldier_

" Birthplace—City _Morgantown_ State _Indiana_

"·Residence—Street No. _Camp Shelby_ City _Miss._

Single ⎫
~~Widower~~ ⎬          ⎧ 1st, ~~2nd or 3rd~~
~~Divorced~~ ⎭          ⎨ marriage ⎬

Name of Father _Marion Colman_

Maiden name of Mother _Maude Greenley_

Bride's name _Patricia Ann. Malden_

Her age _17_

" color _White_

" occupation _Work for Ice Cream Company_

" Birthplace—City _Indianapolis_ State _Indiana_

" Residence—Street No. _213 E. Henry_ City _Indianapolis, Ind._

Single ⎫
~~Widow~~ ⎬          ⎧ 1st, 2nd ~~or 3rd~~
~~Divorced~~ ⎭          ⎨ marriage ⎬

Name of Father _John Malden_

Maiden name of Mother _Florence Killian_

Date of this marriage _April 19, 1944_

Place of this marriage _First Trinity Lutheran Parsonage_

Name and title of person
Performing this marriage _A. Steinman, Lutheran Pastor_

His address _919 E. Orange St., Indianapolis, Ind._

Witness ⎰ Name _Herbert O. Y____ & Ula L. Richmond_
        ⎱ Address _131 Harman St. N. C. Young St._

## Return this Report to County Clerk with License and Certificate

# Marriage Record for Board of Health

### To Be Returned by the Minister or Other Person Performing Ceremony

*Carl F Gierke, Jr* and *Jean Scheidler*

Groom's name _Carl F Gierke, Jr._

His age _21_

" color_ _White_

" occupation_ _United States Army Air Corps_

" Birthplace—City _Indianapolis_ State _Indiana_

" Residence—Street No. _1348 N Gale St_ City _Indianapolis, Ind_

Single / Widower / Divorced — _Single_    1st, 2nd or 3rd marriage — _1st_

Name of Father _Carl F. Gierke, Sr._

Maiden name of Mother _Mabel Kathryn Lohman_

Bride's name _Jean Scheidler_

Her age _21_

" color_ _White_

" occupation_ _None_

" Birthplace—City _Indianapolis_ State _Indiana_

" Residence—Street No. _3434 E Kessler Blvd_ City _Indianapolis, Ind_

Single / Widow / Divorced — _Single_    1st, 2nd or 3rd marriage — _1st_

Name of Father_ _Ralph R Scheidler_

Maiden name of Mother_ _Ada Wilma Fulwig_

Date of this marriage _April 19, 1944_

Place of this marriage _Indianapolis, Indiana_

Name and title of person Performing this marriage _Monroe S. Scheidler (Clergyman)_

His address _Cambridge City, Indiana_

Witness { Name _Wayne H. Brownlee_
Address _41 Bankers Lane, Indianapolis_

## Return this Report to County Clerk with License and Certificate

# Marriage Record for Board of Health

### To Be Returned by the Minister or Other Person Performing Ceremony

Robert N. McLaughlin and Hazel Marie Lipscomb

Groom's name _Robert N. McLaughlin_

His age _22_

" color _White_

" occupation _Curator_

" Birthplace—City _Indpls_ State _Ind_

" Residence—Street No. _6845 Madison_ City _Indpls_

Single / Widower / Divorced } _Single_ { 1st, 2nd or 3rd marriage } _1st_

Name of Father _Walter P. McLaughlin_

Maiden name of Mother _Lillian C. Bratton_

Bride's name _Hazel M Lipscomb_

Her age _20_

" color _White_

" occupation _Stenographer_

" Birthplace—City _Indpls_ State _Ind_

" Residence—Street No. _1105 N. Tremont_ City _Indpls_

Single / Widow / Divorced } _Single_ { 1st, 2nd or 3rd marriage } _1st_

Name of Father _Norman Lipscomb_

Maiden name of Mother _Clexia Freeman_

Date of this marriage _April 20_

Place of this marriage _Indianapolis_

Name and title of person Performing this marriage _Luther_

His address _Fort Wayne_

Witness { Name _Mrs O.L. Davis_ { Address _Southport Ind_

## Return this Report to County Clerk with License and Certificate

# Marriage Record for Board of Health
## To Be Returned by the Minister or Other Person Performing Ceremony

*William Hendricks* and *Lottie M. Robertson*

Groom's name *Guy William Hendricks*

His age 41

" color White

" occupation Mechanic

" Birthplace—City Hardensburg State Kentucky

" Residence—Street No. 824 Lexington City Indpls

Single / Widower / Divorced } Divorced

1st, 2nd or 3rd marriage } 2nd

Name of Father Alvin Hendricks (deceased)

Maiden name of Mother Myrtle McCoy ( " )

Bride's name Lottie M. Robertson

Her age 38

" color White

" occupation Housekeeper

" Birthplace—City Louisville State Ill.

" Residence—Street No. 2085 English City Indpls

Single / Widow / Divorced } Widow

1st, 2nd or 3rd marriage } 2nd

Name of Father Edward C. Maskley

Maiden name of Mother Maude Wilson

Date of this marriage April 20-44

Place of this marriage Indianapolis Indiana

Name and title of person / Performing this marriage Mary J. Lane Justice of Peace

His address 152½ East Court Street

Witness { Name Mary J. Lane

{ Address 3741 College Ave.

## Return this Report to County Clerk with License and Certificate

# Marriage Record for Board of Health
## To Be Returned by the Minister or Other Person Performing Ceremony

*Harold A. Crail* and *Edith M. Perry*

Groom's name *Harold A. Crail*

His age 22

" color *white*

" occupation *Police Dept.*

" Birthplace—City *Indpls* State *Ind.*

" Residence—Street No. *737 N. Noble* City *Indpls.*

Single / Widower / Divorced } *Divorced* { 1st, 2nd or 3rd marriage } *3rd*

Name of Father *Walter Crail*

Maiden name of Mother *Linnie Mae Moore*

Bride's name *Edith M. Perry*

Her age 21

" color *white*

" occupation *none*

" Birthplace—City *Indpls* State *Ind.*

" Residence—Street No. *3180 N. Gale* City *Indpls.*

Single / Widow / Divorced } *Single* { 1st, 2nd or 3rd marriage } *1st*

Name of Father *Ensley Perry*

Maiden name of Mother *Elsie Mae Banks*

Date of this marriage *April 20, 44*

Place of this marriage *Joseph, Ind.*

Name and title of person Performing this marriage *Everett Lane Justice of Peace*

His address *153½ E. Court St.*

Witness { Name *Mary Jo Lane* Address *3741 College Ave.*

## Return this Report to County Clerk with License and Certificate

# Marriage Record for Board of Health
## To Be Returned by the Minister or Other Person Performing Ceremony

Albert N. Roberts _____ and Catherine E. Hollis

Groom's name _Albert N. Roberts_

His age __26__

" color __Negro__

" occupation __Truck Driver__

" Birthplace—City __Lovelaceville__ State __Ky.__

" Residence—Street No. _7325 S. Ill. St_ City _Indianapolis, Ind._

Single / Widower / Divorced } _Divorced_   { 1st, 2nd or 3rd marriage } __2nd__

Name of Father __Alvatin Roberts__

Maiden name of Mother __Mattie Easton__

Bride's name __Catherine E. Hollis__

Her age __26__

" color __Negro__

" occupation __Grid Operator__

" Birthplace—City __Henderson__ State __Ky.__

" Residence—Street No. _7325 S. Ill. St_ City _Indianapolis, Ind._

Single / Widow / Divorced } _Divorced_   { 1st, 2nd or 3rd marriage } __2nd__

Name of Father __William Durville__

Maiden name of Mother __Goldie Crowe__

Date of this marriage _April 20, 1944_

Place of this marriage _Indianapolis_

Name and title of person Performing this marriage _Al Thomas, Minister_

His address _702 S. Illinois_

Witness { Name _Betty Wickliffe_
         { Address _2336 Indianapolis_

## Return this Report to County Clerk with License and Certificate

12

# Marriage Record for Board of Health
### To Be Returned by the Minister or Other Person Performing Ceremony

Elmer Watkins and Ora Boyce

Groom's name _____ Elmer Watkins

His age _____ 16

" color _____ c

" occupation _____ Porter

" Birthplace—City _____ Indianapolis State _____ Ind

" Residence—Street No. _____ 117 E 19 St City _____ Indianapolis

Single Widower Divorced } _____ Single { 1st, 2nd or 3rd marriage } _____ 1st

Name of Father _____ Elmore Watkins

Maiden name of Mother _____ Dunkerson

Bride's name _____ Ora Boyce

Her age _____ 15

" color _____ c

" occupation _____ none

" Birthplace—City _____ Indianapolis State _____ Ind

" Residence—Street No. _____ 2806 Howey City _____ Indianapolis

Single Widow Divorced } _____ Single { 1st, 2nd or 3rd marriage } _____ 1st

Name of Father _____ Henry Jameson

Maiden name of Mother _____ Julia Ann Brown

Date of this marriage _____ April 20, 1944

Place of this marriage _____ Indianapolis, Ind

Name and title of person Performing this marriage _____ S S Thomas, Minister

His address _____ 702 S. Illinois St Indianapolis, Inde

Witness { Name _____ Lillian Brown
Address _____ 2051 Tipton St

### Return this Report to County Clerk with License and Certificate

## Marriage Record for Board of Health

To Be Returned by the Minister or Other Person Performing Ceremony

_____ and _____

Groom's name _Edward Burton Payne_

His age _20_

" color _White_

" occupation _U.S. Army_

" Birthplace—City _Goley,_ State _Tenn._

" Residence—Street No. _____ City _____

Single
~~Widower~~  } _Single_   { 1st, ~~2nd or 3rd~~ } _1st_
~~Divorced~~       { marriage

Name of Father _James Arvine Payne_

Maiden name of Mother _Emma Jones_

Bride's name _Mary Jayne Long_

Her age _19_

" color _White_

" occupation _House Keeper_

" Birthplace—City _Indpls._ State _Ind._

" Residence—Street No. _____ City _____

Single
~~Widow~~  } _Single_   { 1st, ~~2nd or 3rd~~ } _1st_
~~Divorced~~      { marriage

Name of Father _Allen L. Long_

Maiden name of Mother _Velda Tolbert_

Date of this marriage _April 29, 1944_

Place of this marriage _Indpls. Ind._

Name and title of person
Performing this marriage _Rev Geo. G. Rimmer_

His address _2424 W. Claude? Indpls. Ind._

Witness { Name _Artie B Payne_
         { Address _U.S. Army_

## Return this Report to County Clerk with License and Certificate

# Marriage Record for Board of Health

## To Be Returned by the Minister or Other Person Performing Ceremony

*Oliver Maggard Jr.* and *Beth P. Anderson*

Groom's name _Oliver Maggard Jr._

His age _20_

" color _White_

" occupation _Lieutenant army air corps_

" Birthplace—City _Memphis_ State _Tennessee_

" Residence—Street No. _3644 N. Penn St_ City _Indianapolis, Ind_

Single / Widower / Divorced } _Single_   { 1st, 2nd or 3rd marriage } _1st_

Name of Father _Oliver Maggard_

Maiden name of Mother _Mary Yates nee Liffert_

Bride's name _Beth P. Anderson_

Her age _20_

" color _White_

" occupation _none_

" Birthplace—City _Buffalo_ State _New York_

" Residence—Street No. _344 N. Penn St_ City _Indianapolis, Ind_

Single / Widow / Divorced } _Single_   { 1st, 2nd or 3rd marriage } _1st_

Name of Father _James Main Anderson Jr._

Maiden name of Mother _Helen Marie Praeger_

Date of this marriage _April 20, 1844_

Place of this marriage _Church of the Advent_

Name and title of person Performing this marriage _James G. Jones  Priest_

His address _3504 Winthrop Ave._

Witness { Name _Helen P. Anderson_
         { Address _3444 N. Penn St. Indianapolis_

## Return this Report to County Clerk with License and Certificate

# Marriage Record for Board of Health
### To Be Returned by the Minister or Other Person Performing Ceremony

Virgil O Scott _____ and _____ Hazel M Austin

Groom's name _____ Virgil O Scott

His age _____ 44

" color _____ White

" occupation _____ Work inspector – R.R.

" Birthplace—City _____ Lytton _____ State _____ Indiana

" Residence—Street No. 7332 Pendleton Pike City _____ Indianapolis, Ind

Single / Widower / Divorced } Divorced { 1st, 2nd or 3rd marriage } 2nd

Name of Father _____ J. H. M. Scott

Maiden name of Mother _____ Ella (Armstrong) Scott

Bride's name _____ Hazel M Austin

Her age _____ 36

" color _____ white

" occupation _____ housewife

" Birthplace—City _____ Bedford _____ State _____ Indiana

" Residence—Street No. 2019 Broadway City _____ Indianapolis, Ind

Single / Widow / Divorced } Divorced { 1st, 2nd or 3rd marriage } 2nd

Name of Father _____ H. A. Mc Gowen

Maiden name of Mother _____ Clara (Miles) Mc Gowen

Date of this marriage _____ April 20, 1944

Place of this marriage _____ Lawrence, Indiana

Name and title of person Performing this marriage _____ Bernard J. Renner, Minister

His address _____ 4444 Franklin Road _____ Lawrence, Indiana

Witness { Name _____ Mr and Mrs Donald Comer
{ Address _____ 440 East Vermont Street

### Return this Report to County Clerk with License and Certificate

FILED
42 APR 2 2. 1944

CLERK

# Marriage Record for Board of Health

## To Be Returned by the Minister or Other Person Performing Ceremony

Ralph S. Decker _____ and Margaret M. Clark _____

Groom's name Ralph S. Decker

His age 53

" color White

" occupation Insurance-108 E. 9th Street, Indianapolis, Indiana

" Birthplace—City Ligonier _____ State Indiana

" Residence—Street No. 120 W. 41st St. City Indianapolis

Single ⎫
Widower ⎬ Widower    { 1st, 2nd or 3rd    Second
Divorced ⎭              marriage

Name of Father William D. Decker (Deceased)

Maiden name of Mother Martha Scoles (Deceased)

Bride's name Margaret M. Clark

Her age 46

" color White

" occupation Saleswoman-Adams Furniture Inc.-Indianapolis, Indiana

" Birthplace—City Logansport _____ State Indiana

" Residence—Street No. 2019 N. Penn St. City Indianapolis

Single ⎫
W'dow ⎬ Divorced    { 1st, 2nd or 3rd    Second
Divorced ⎭              marriage

Name of Father Walter Maiben (Deceased)

Maiden name of Mother Blanche Collett

Date of this marriage April 20, 1944

Place of this marriage McKee Chapel-Tabernacle Presbyterian Church-Indiana-
Name and title of person                          polis, Indiana
Performing this marriage _____ Minister of the above Church

His address 418 East 34th Street

_____ Indianapolis 5, Indiana

Witness { Name William C Kessebaun
         { Address 3561 College Ave Indianapolis, Ind.

## Return this Report to County Clerk with License and Certificate

12

# Marriage Record for Board of Health

To Be Returned by the Minister or Other Person Performing Ceremony

Donald Butcher and Sibyl Hollingsworth

Groom's name __Donald Butcher__

His age __47__

" color __White__

" occupation __Sunnyside Sanatorium__

" Birthplace—City __Bryant__ State __Ind.__

" Residence—Street No. __Sunnyside Sanatorium R.R.12__ City __Indianapolis, Ind__

Single Widower Divorced } __Single__ { 1st, 2nd or 3rd marriage } __1st__

Name of Father __S Erwin Butcher__

Maiden name of Mother __Gertrude Williams__

Bride's name __Sibyl Hollingsworth__

Her age __42__

" color __White__

" occupation __Waitress Sunnyside Sanatorium__

" Birthplace—City __Manchester__ State __Kentucky__

" Residence—Street No. __Sunnyside Sanatorium R.R.12__ City __Indianapolis, Ind__

Single Widow Divorced } __single__ { 1st, 2nd or 3rd marriage } __1st__

Name of Father __John Hollingsworth__

Maiden name of Mother __Emma Rice__

Date of this marriage __April 20, 1944__

Place of this marriage __Indianapolis, Ind.__

Name and title of person Performing this marriage __Rev. George F. King__

His address __609 N. Riley Ave., Indianapolis, Ind.__

Witness { Name __Raymond King__
{ Address __Indianapolis, Ind.__

## Return this Report to County Clerk with License and Certificate

# Marriage Record for Board of Health

### To Be Returned by the Minister or Other Person Performing Ceremony

_Ted B. Lewis_ and _Freda W. Simmons_

Groom's name _Ted B. Lewis._

His age _24_

" color _White_

" occupation _Army Officer_

" Birthplace—City _Noblesville_ State _Ind._

" Residence—Street No. _128 S. 7th St._ City _Beech Grove,_

Single / Widower / Divorced } _Single_   1st, 2nd or 3rd marriage } _1st._

Name of Father _John B. Lewis_

Maiden name of Mother _Charlie Jackson_

Bride's name _Freda W. Simmons,_

Her age _22_

" color _White_

" occupation _Housewife_

" Birthplace—City _Kurthwood_ State _La.,_

" Residence—Street No. _703 N. 2nd St._ City _Lufkin, Texas_

Single / Widow / Divorced } _Single_   1st, 2nd or 3rd marriage } _1st_

Name of Father _George W. Simmons._

Maiden name of Mother _Ida E. Howden,_

Date of this marriage _April 20, 1944_

Place of this marriage _Indianapolis, Ind._

Name and title of person Performing this marriage _Rev. George Y. King_

His address _609 N. Riley Ave._
_Indianapolis, Ind._

Witness { Name _Wm. R. Waggoner — Mrs. Bertrice Stanford_
{ Address _Indianapolis, Ind._

### Return this Report to County Clerk with License and Certificate

# Marriage Record for Board of Health
### To Be Returned by the Minister or Other Person Performing Ceremony

Robert W. Weber and Emma L. Richie.

Groom's name ___ Robert W. Weber

His age ___ 29 yrs

" color ___ white

" occupation ___ Sales Clerk

" Birthplace—City ___ Indianapolis ___ State ___ Indiana

" Residence—Street No. 2160 Singleton St City ___ Indianapolis

Single / Widower / Divorced ___ { 1st, 2nd or 3rd marriage

Name of Father ___ Harry Weber

Maiden name of Mother ___ Ottilia Kuhm.

Bride's name ___ Emma Louise Richie

Her age ___ 21

" color ___ white

" occupation ___ Clerk.

" Birthplace—City ___ Hazleton ___ State ___ Indiana.

" Residence—Street No. 1271 W. 30th St City ___ Indianapolis

Single / Widow / Divorced ___ { 1st, 2nd or 3rd marriage

Name of Father ___ Walter Richie

Maiden name of Mother ___ Mary Ross.

Date of this marriage ___ April 20, 1944

Place of this marriage ___ 1109 E Tabor St.

Name and title of person Performing this marriage ___ Rev. J. M. Downey

His address ___ 1109 E. Tabor St. Indianapolis, Ind.

Witness { Name ___ Edward B. Niehaus

{ Address ___ Marjoire Richie.

### Return this Report to County Clerk with License and Certificate

12

# Marriage Record for Board of Health
### To Be Returned by the Minister or Other Person Performing Ceremony

Charley Kirkendall and Flavia Cox

Groom's name ..... Charley Kirkendall

His age ..... 39

" color ..... White

" occupation ..... Apartment House Owner

" Birthplace—City ..... Howard County ..... State ..... Indiana

" Residence—Street No. ..... 2366 College Ave ..... City ..... Indianapolis

Single / Widower / Divorced } ..... Widower ..... { 1st, 2nd or 3rd marriage } ..... 2nd

Name of Father ..... Omar Kirkendall

Maiden name of Mother ..... Muriel Rawlings

Bride's name ..... Flavia Cox

Her age ..... 27

" color ..... White

" occupation ..... Waitress

" Birthplace—City ..... Columbus ..... State ..... Ohio

" Residence—Street No. ..... 1210 Carrolton ..... City ..... Indianapolis

Single / Widow / Divorced } ..... Single ..... { 1st, 2nd or 3rd marriage } ..... 1st

Name of Father ..... Norvin Grady Cox

Maiden name of Mother ..... Goldie Huston

Date of this marriage ..... April 20, 1944

Place of this marriage ..... Lebanon, Indiana

Name and title of person Performing this marriage ..... Minister

His address ..... 312 E. South Street, Lebanon, Indiana

Witness { Name ..... George W. Hornaday.
{ Address ..... Lebanon, Indiana

## Return this Report to County Clerk with License and Certificate

# Marriage Record for Board of Health

To Be Returned by the Minister or Other Person Performing Ceremony

Charles Kendrick Eaves and Dorothy Ann Peirce

Groom's name ___Charles Kendrick Eaves___

His age __24__

" color __White__

" occupation __Engineering Clerk__

" Birthplace—City __Indianapolis__ State __Indiana__

" Residence—Street No. __1431 N. Meridian__ City __Indianapolis__

Single / Widower / Divorced } __Single__ { 1st, 2nd or 3rd marriage } __First__

Name of Father ___Walter C Eaves___

Maiden name of Mother ___Edith Strassner (deceased)___

Bride's name __Dorothy Ann Peirce__

Her age __23__

" color __White__

" occupation __None__

" Birthplace—City __Indianapolis__ State __Indiana__

" Residence—Street No. __1606 Fisher__ City __Indianapolis__

Single / Widow / Divorced } __Divorced__ { 1st, 2nd or 3rd marriage } __Second__

Name of Father ___Vern E. Peirce___

Maiden name of Mother ___Gertrude Reynolds___

Date of this marriage __April 20, 1944__

Place of this marriage __Speedway Christian Church__

Name and title of person Performing this marriage __Rev. Howard E. Anderson__

His address __5215 W 15 Street__
__Indianapolis 8 Indiana__

Witness { Name __Mary Lucille Hughes__
{ Address __1203 Allison St__

## Return this Report to County Clerk with License and Certificate

# Marriage Record for Board of Health
### To Be Returned by the Minister or Other Person Performing Ceremony

Benjamin F Larkin and Margaret Glenn

Groom's name _Benjamin F. Larkin_

His age _21_

" color _negro_

" occupation _Shipping Clerk_

" Birthplace—City _Hopkinsville_ State _Ky_

" Residence—Street No. _1615 Northwestern_ City _Indianapolis_

Single Widower Divorced } _Single_   1st, 2nd or 3rd marriage } _1st_

Name of Father _Benjamin F Larkin_

Maiden name of Mother _Ophelia Spencer_

Bride's name _Margaret Glenn_

Her age _18_

" color _negro_

" occupation _Seamstress_

" Birthplace—City _Indianapolis_ State _Ind_

" Residence—Street No. _518 W. 12th St_ City _Indianapolis_

Single Widow Divorced } _Single_   1st, 2nd or 3rd marriage } _1st_

Name of Father _Plush Elder Glenn_

Maiden name of Mother _Anna L. Spence_

Date of this marriage _21st day of April_

Place of this marriage _Indianapolis, Ind_

Name and title of person Performing this marriage _Rev O. H. Calhoun_

His address _2128 N. Capitol_

_Indianapolis, Ind._

Witness { Name _Elizabeth Glenn_
         { Address _518 W. 12th Street_

## Return this Report to County Clerk with License and Certificate

# Marriage Record for Board of Health
### To Be Returned by the Minister or Other Person Performing Ceremony

Robert Ellis Marquess _and_ Laura V. Mullinix

Groom's name ___Robert Ellis Marquess.___

His age ___21___

" color ___White___

" occupation ___Test Operator Allison Eng. Co.___

" Birthplace—City ___Williamsport___ State ___Ind.___

" Residence—Street No. ___2308 Park Ave___ City ___Indianapolis___

Single / Widower / Divorced } ___Divorced___ { 1st, 2nd or 3rd marriage } ___Second.___

Name of Father ___William Marquess.___

Maiden name of Mother ___Lola Bush___

Bride's name ___Laura V. Mullinix___

Her age ___17___

" color ___White.___

" occupation ___Housewife.___

" Birthplace—City ___Shelby Co___ State ___Ind.___

" Residence—Street No. ___2308 Park Ave___ City ___Indianapolis.___

Single / Widow / Divorced } ___Single.___ { 1st, 2nd or 3rd marriage } ___1st___

Name of Father ___William Mullinix___

Maiden name of Mother ___Lillie Lawson.___

Date of this marriage ___April 21, 1944___

Place of this marriage ___Indianapolis, Ind.___

Name and title of person Performing this marriage ___Rev. George J. King.___

His address ___609 N. Riley Ave. Indianapolis, Ind.___

Witness { Name ___Wm. Harvey Myers.– Sarah Myers.___ Address ___Indianapolis, Ind.___

### Return this Report to County Clerk with License and Certificate

# Marriage Record for Board of Health
## To Be Returned by the Minister or Other Person Performing Ceremony

*Paul J. Worrell* and *Mary Ellen Johns*

Groom's name ___ *Paul J. Worrell*

His age ___ 23

" color ___ White

" occupation ___ U. S. Navy Coast Guard

" Birthplace—City ___ Danville ___ State ___ Indiana

" Residence—Street No. ___ R. R. 2 ___ City ___ Indianapolis, Indiana

Single / Widower / Divorced } ___ Single ___ { 1st, 2nd or 3rd marriage } ___ 1st

Name of Father ___ Lee Worrell

Maiden name of Mother ___ Opal Kittleson

Bride's name ___ Mary Ellen Johns

Her age ___ 24

" color ___ White

" occupation ___ Book Keeper

" Birthplace—City ___ Indianapolis ___ State ___ Indiana

" Residence—Street No. ___ 610 Exter Ave ___ City ___ Indianapolis, Ind

Single / Widow / Divorced } ___ Single ___ { 1st, 2nd or 3rd marriage } ___ 1st

Name of Father ___ Wm Warner Johns

Maiden name of Mother ___ Cora Mae Wood

Date of this marriage ___ April 21, 1944

Place of this marriage ___ Indianapolis, Indiana

Name and title of person Performing this marriage ___ Leon K. Weatherman, Minister

His address ___ 443 Alton Ave

___ Indianapolis 8, Indiana

Witness { Name ___ Charles L. Worrell
{ Address ___ Indianapolis, Ind. Route 2

## Return this Report to County Clerk with License and Certificate

# Marriage Record for Board of Health
To Be Returned by the Minister or Other Person Performing Ceremony

Jerry F. Daniels _____ and _Una B. White_

Groom's name _Jerry F. Daniels_

His age _28_

" color _Brown, Negro_

" occupation _Soldier_

" Birthplace—City _Indianapolis_ State _Ind._

" Residence—Street No. _441 W. 12th_ City _Indianapolis_

Single Widower Divorced } — { 1st, 2nd or 3rd marriage } _1st,_

Name of Father _Jerry P. Daniels_

Maiden name of Mother _Anna Franklin_

Bride's name _Una B. White_

Her age _18_

" color _Brown - Negro_

" occupation _School._

" Birthplace—City _Paris_ State _Texas_

" Residence—Street No. _1077 22nd_ City _Paris_

Single Widow Divorced } — { 1st, 2nd or 3rd marriage } _1st,_

Name of Father _Jessie White,_

Maiden name of Mother _Jessie C. King_

Date of this marriage _April 21st, 1944_

Place of this marriage _Indianapolis Ind._

Name and title of person Performing this marriage _Rev. Charles E. Winston_

His address _348 W. Madison St._
_Franklin Ind._

Witness { Name _Irene Joyner_
{ Address _2629 Blvd. Place_

## Return this Report to County Clerk with License and Certificate

12

# Marriage Record for Board of Health

### To Be Returned by the Minister or Other Person Performing Ceremony

Frank Orrell _____ and Wanda _____

Groom's name _Frank Orrell_

His age _21_

" color _White_

" occupation _filling Station att_

" Birthplace—City _Clayton_ State _Indiana_

" Residence—Street No. _2448 N Talbot_ City _Indianapolis_

Single / Widower / Divorced } _Single_ { 1st, 2nd or 3rd marriage } _1st._

Name of Father _Frank Orrell_

Maiden name of Mother _Emma Jayne Myers_

Bride's name _Wanda Roe_

Her age _18_

" color _White_

" occupation _Sales Clerk_

" Birthplace—City _Indianapolis_ State _Indiana_

" Residence—Street No. _3403 E Wash St_ City _Indianapolis_

Single / Widow / Divorced } _Single_ { 1st, 2nd or 3rd marriage } _1st._

Name of Father _James Wesley Roe Sr._

Maiden name of Mother _Aurie Ruff_

Date of this marriage _April 21st 1944_

Place of this marriage _3403 E. Washington St. Indpls. Ind_

Name and title of person Performing this marriage _Licensed Minister_

His address _R. R. 1 Box 618 Indianapolis 42nd_

Witness { Name _Essie Mae — Lyman L. May_  { Address _29 S Winona, Indianapolis Ind_

## Return this Report to County Clerk with License and Certificate

## Marriage Record for Board of Health
### To Be Returned by the Minister or Other Person Performing Ceremony

Groom's name _Paul Edward Boyer_ and

His age _26_

" color _White_

" occupation _Machinist_

" Birthplace—City _Clifford_ State _Ind_

" Residence—Street No _Indpls_ City _Ind_

Single } _Single_ { 1st, 2nd or 3rd } _1st_
Widower     marriage
Divorced

Name of Father _Roscoe L. Boyer_

Maiden name of Mother _Angeline Lawson_

Bride's name _Mary Louise Jarrett_

Her age _29_

" color _White_

" occupation _Tool Clerk_

" Birthplace—City _New Castle_ State _Ind_

" Residence—Street No. _____ City _____

Single } _Divorced_ { 1st, 2nd or 3rd } _2nd_
Widow      marriage
Divorced

Name of Father _Chs. L. Holtzel_

Maiden name of Mother _Dorothy Wagoner_

Date of this marriage _April 21, 1944_

Place of this marriage _Indpls. Ind_

Name and title of person Performing this marriage _Rev Geo G Kimmey_

His address _2425 W. St Clair st Indpls Ind_

Witness { Name _Chas W. Dittow_
{ Address _2030 N Emerson - City_

### Return this Report to County Clerk with License and Certificate

12

# Marriage Record for Board of Health

## To Be Returned by the Minister or Other Person Performing Ceremony

_____ and _____

Groom's name _John Henry Bryant_

His age _36_

" color _Colored_

" occupation _Labor_

" Birthplace—City _Trenton Tenn._ State _Tenn._

" Residence—Street No. _2019 Cornell_ City _Indianapolis_

Single
Widower } _Single_    { 1st, 2nd or 3rd marriage } _1st._
Divorced

Name of Father _Jim Bryant_

Maiden name of Mother _Mary Doke_

Bride's name _Mattie B. Stepp_

Her age _42_

" color _Colored_

" occupation _House Keeper_

" Birthplace—City _Trenton_ State _Ky—_

" Residence—Street No. _2019 Cornell_ City _Indianapolis_

Single
Widow } _Widow_    { 1st, 2nd or 3rd marriage } _2nd._
Divorced

Name of Father _John Allen Shaw_

Maiden name of Mother _Elizabeth Harper_

Date of this marriage _April 21, 1944._

Place of this marriage _Indianapolis Ind._

Name and title of person
Performing this marriage _SS Thomas, Minister_

His address _702 South Illinois_

Witness { Name _Emma Williams_
{ Address _616 E. Miami_

## Return this Report to County Clerk with License and Certificate

# Marriage Record for Board of Health

### To Be Returned by the Minister or Other Person Performing Ceremony

*Victor Eugene Walters* and *Anna Louise Bales*

Groom's name _Victor Eugene Walters_

His age _24_

" color _White_

" occupation _Soldier_

" Birthplace—City _Dover_ State _Ohio_

" Residence—Street No. _Ft Stewart_ City _Georgia_

Single / Widower / Divorced } _Single_ { 1st, 2nd or 3rd marriage } _1st_

Name of Father _Harry W. Walters_

Maiden name of Mother _Margaret Hall_

Bride's name _Anna Louise Bales_

Her age _20_

" color _White_

" occupation _Housewife_

" Birthplace—City _Denison_ State _Ohio_

" Residence—Street No. _372 Spring_ City _Indianapolis_

Single / Widow / Divorced } _Divorced_ { 1st, 2nd or 3rd marriage } _2nd_

Name of Father _Ralph Dickson_

Maiden name of Mother _Mary E. Gowens_

Date of this marriage _April 21, 1944_

Place of this marriage _Indianapolis_

Name and title of person Performing this marriage _Emma Louise Justice Peace_

His address _152½ E. South St_

Witness { Name _Mary J. Love_
{ Address _3741 College Ave_

## Return this Report to County Clerk with License and Certificate

# Marriage Record for Board of Health

To Be Returned by the Minister or Other Person Performing Ceremony

*John H. Stopp* and *Rose Roempke*

Groom's name _John H. Stopp_

His age _47_

" color _White_

" occupation _Neon Sign Co_

" Birthplace—City _Bloomington_ State _Indiana_

" Residence—Street No. _1010 Virginia_ City _Indianapolis_

Single / Widower / Divorced } _Divorced_ { 1st, 2nd or 3rd marriage } _2nd_

Name of Father _Frank Stopp_

Maiden name of Mother _Mary Cartwright_

Bride's name _Rose Roempke_

Her age _32_

" color _White_

" occupation _Religion Shop_

" Birthplace—City _Indianapolis_ State _Indiana_

" Residence—Street No. _1022 Virginia_ City _Indianapolis_

Single / Widow / Divorced } _Divorced_ { 1st, 2nd or 3rd marriage } _2nd_

Name of Father _Samuel Monroe_

Maiden name of Mother _Margaret Abeynu_

Date of this marriage _April 21, 1944_

Place of this marriage _Indianapolis Ind_

Name and title of person Performing this marriage _Emmit Long Justice of Peace_

His address _152½ East Court_

Witness { Name _Mary Jo Lowe_ { Address _3741 College Ave_

## Return this Report to County Clerk with License and Certificate

# Marriage Record for Board of Health
## To Be Returned by the Minister or Other Person Performing Ceremony

Claude F. Case ___ and ___ Ruth H. Flohr

Groom's name ___ Claude F. Case

His age ___ 36

" color ___ White

" occupation ___ Armed Services

" Birthplace—City ___ Estelle Co. Ky. ___ State ___ Kentucky.

" Residence—Street No. ___ 121 Hancock ___ City ___ Indianapolis, Ind.

Single
Widower } ___ divorced ___ { 1st, 2nd or 3rd marriage } ___ second
Divorced

Name of Father ___ John A. Case

Maiden name of Mother ___ Maud A. Wierman

Bride's name ___ Ruth H. Flohr.

Her age ___ 24

" color ___ White

" occupation ___ Clerk.

" Birthplace—City ___ Washington Court House ___ State ___ Ohio.

" Residence—Street No. ___ 1114 S. Belmont ___ City ___ Indianapolis

Single
Widow } ___ divorced ___ { 1st, 2nd or 3rd marriage } ___ second
Divorced

Name of Father ___ L. E. Hard

Maiden name of Mother ___ Sarah Jane Buckley

Date of this marriage ___ April 21, 1944

Place of this marriage ___ Indianapolis, Indiana

Name and title of person
Performing this marriage ___ Albertow Clarke, Minister

His address ___ 1153 Blaine Avenue

___ Indianapolis, Indiana.

Witness { Name ___ Oscar Blau
{ Address ___ 1114 So Belmont ave
___ Indianapolis, Ind.

## Return this Report to County Clerk with License and Certificate

12

# Marriage Record for Board of Health
## To Be Returned by the Minister or Other Person Performing Ceremony

........................................................ and ........................................................

Groom's name _Chester L. Rogers_

His age _31_

" color _White_

" occupation _Labor_

" Birthplace—City _Gosport_ State _Indiana_

" Residence—Street No. _531 S. Capitol St_ City _Indianapolis_

Single  
Widower  } ........................................ { 1st, 2nd or 3rd marriage ........................................  
Divorced

Name of Father _Ottie F. Rogers_

Maiden name of Mother _Dovey May Simms_

Bride's name _Lola M. Sparks_

Her age _16_

" color _White_

" occupation _Labor_

" Birthplace—City _Indianapolis_ State _Indiana_

" Residence—Street No. _1343 S. Tremont_ City _Indianapolis_

Single  
Widow  } ........................................ { 1st, 2nd or 3rd marriage ........................................  
Divorced

Name of Father _Albert A. Sparks_

Maiden name of Mother _Clara Jane Finch_

Date of this marriage _April 22, 1919_

Place of this marriage _437 N. Raymond Street_

Name and title of person  
Performing this marriage _Arizona Hodges – Minister_

His address _437 N. Raymond Street_

_Clara Jane Sparks Mother_

Witness { Name _Edith Sirk_  
{ Address _1343 S. Tremont_

## Return this Report to County Clerk with License and Certificate

# Marriage Record for Board of Health

### To Be Returned by the Minister or Other Person Performing Ceremony

Theodore M. Englehart and Nancy Campbell

Groom's name _Theodore M. Englehart_

His age _23_

" color _White_

" occupation _Army First_

" Birthplace—City _Brazil_ State _Indiana_

" Residence—Street No. _18 E. Church St_ City _Brazil, Ind._

Single Widower Divorced } _Single_    1st, 2nd or 3rd marriage } _First_

Name of Father _D. H. Englehart_

Maiden name of Mother _Virginia McNutt_

Bride's name _Nancy Campbell_

Her age _24_

" color _White_

" occupation _____

" Birthplace—City _Indianapolis_ State _Indiana_

" Residence—Street No. _3332 Wash Blvd_ City _Indianapolis_

Single Widow Divorced } _Single_    1st, 2nd or 3rd marriage } _First_

Name of Father _Leonard L. Campbell_

Maiden name of Mother _Irene Peck_

Date of this marriage _April 22nd 1944_

Place of this marriage _Indianapolis Indiana_

Name and title of person Performing this marriage _Benjamin Marsh, Minister_

His address _1315 E. 2nd St Bloomington, Indiana_

Witness { Name _Elizabeth D. Woodue_
{ Address _549 N. Pennsylvania St. Indianapolis, Ind._

### Return this Report to County Clerk with License and Certificate

# Marriage Record for Board of Health

### To Be Returned by the Minister or Other Person Performing Ceremony

James A. Spychalski and Dorothy S Gray

Groom's name _James A Spychalski_

His age _25_

" color _White_

" occupation _Chemical Engineer_

" Birthplace—City _Michigan City_ State _Indiana_

" Residence—Street No. _1901 N. Delaware_ City _Indianapolis_

Single
Widower } _Single_ 1st, 2nd or 3rd } _1st_
Divorced marriage

Name of Father _Andrew A Spychalski_

Maiden name of Mother _Anna Tieffer_

Bride's name _Dorothy S Gray_

Her age _30_

" color _White_

" occupation _Clerk_

" Birthplace—City _Wabash_ State _Indiana_

" Residence—Street No. _1901 N. Delaware_ City _Indianapolis_

Single
Widow } _Single_ 1st, 2nd or 3rd } _1st_
Divorced marriage

Name of Father _Harry L Gray_

Maiden name of Mother _Jessie Irene Gunder Rhoades_

Date of this marriage _April 22, 1944_

Place of this marriage _Indianapolis, Indiana_

Name and title of person _R R hill Pastor_
Performing this marriage

His address _1347 N. Meridian_
_Indianapolis, Indiana_

Witness { Name _Charles Greene and Dorothy Spychalski_
{ Address _Indianapolis - Indiana_

## Return this Report to County Clerk with License and Certificate

# Marriage Record for Board of Health

## To Be Returned by the Minister or Other Person Performing Ceremony

*Howard Leon Buchanan* and *Bertha Geraldine Davis*

Groom's name __Howard Leon Buchanan__

His age __35__

" color __White__

" occupation __Inspector__

" Birthplace—City __Jefferson Cabell__ State __Indiana__

" Residence—Street No. _____ City _____

Single / Widower / Divorced } __Divorced__  { 1st, 2nd or 3rd marriage } __2nd__

Name of Father __Irvin Wesley Buchanan__

Maiden name of Mother __Zoe Risk__

Bride's name __Bertha Geraldine Davis__

Her age __23__

" color __White__

" occupation __Housewife__

" Birthplace—City __Trimble Co__ State __Ky__

" Residence—Street No. _____ City _____

Single / Widow / Divorced } __Single__  { 1st, 2nd or 3rd marriage } __1st__

Name of Father __Manuel Davis__

Maiden name of Mother __Hallie Craig__

Date of this marriage __April 22nd 1944__

Place of this marriage __Greenfield Indiana__

Name and title of person Performing this marriage __Rev. Clark W Myers__

His address __105 East South Street Greenfield Indiana__

Witness { Name __Mrs Clark W Myers__
{ Address __Greenfield Indiana__

## Return this Report to County Clerk with License and Certificate

# Marriage Record for Board of Health

### To Be Returned by the Minister or Other Person Performing Ceremony

*Gene Allen Cowgill* and *Phyllis Maxine Lloyd*

Groom's name _Gene Allen Cowgill_

His age _17_

" color _white_

" occupation _Sailor_

" Birthplace—City _Indpls_ State _Indiana_

" Residence—Street No. _Great Lake_ City _Illinois_

Single / Widower / Divorced } _Single_ { 1st, 2nd or 3rd marriage } _1st_

Name of Father _William Henry_

Maiden name of Mother _Nancy Jane Sullivan_

Bride's name _Phyllis Maxine Lloyd_

Her age _14_

" color _white_

" occupation _none_

" Birthplace—City _Frankfort_ State _Indiana_

" Residence—Street No. _1842 Howard St_ City _Indpls_

Single / Widow / Divorced } _Single_ { 1st, 2nd or 3rd marriage } _1st_

Name of Father _John James Lloyd_

Maiden name of Mother _Sophia Mae Hunter_

Date of this marriage _April 22-44_

Place of this marriage _Indianapolis Indiana_

Name and title of person Performing this marriage _Ernest Cope Justice of Peace_

His address _152 East Court St_

Witness { Name _Mary Jo Cope_ / Address _3741 College Ave._

## Return this Report to County Clerk with License and Certificate

# Marriage Record for Board of Health
### To Be Returned by the Minister or Other Person Performing Ceremony

Arnold L. Kizzee and Virginia G. Burgin

Groom's name _Arnold L. Kizzee_

His age _30_

" color _White_

" occupation _none_

" Birthplace—City _Johnson County_ State _Indiana_

" Residence—Street No. _1212 Timber_ City _Indpls._

Single / Widower / Divorced } _Divorced_   { 1st, 2nd or 3rd marriage } _2nd_

Name of Father _Eugene Kizzee_

Maiden name of Mother _maudie Pearl Carlile (deceased)_

Bride's name _Virginia G. Bergin_

Her age _33_

" color _White_

" occupation _George Mayer employee_

" Birthplace—City _Bedford_ State _Indiana_

" Residence—Street No. _974 Elm_ City _Indpls._

Single / Widow / Divorced } _Divorced_   { 1st, 2nd or 3rd marriage } _2nd_

Name of Father _Joseph Duncan_

Maiden name of Mother _Nora Hoopingarner_

Date of this marriage _April 22-44_

Place of this marriage _Indianapolis Indiana_

Name and title of person Performing this marriage _Cane H. Cane Justice of Peace_

His address _457½ East County Street_

Witness { Name _Mary J. Cane_  { Address _3741 College Ave._

### Return this Report to County Clerk with License and Certificate

# Marriage Record for Board of Health

### To Be Returned by the Minister or Other Person Performing Ceremony

Donald, Hackett _____ and _Martha Smith_

Groom's name _Donald Hackett_

His age _24_

" color _White_

" occupation _Farmer_

" Birthplace—City _Greenfield_ State _Indiana_

" Residence—Street No. _RR16_ City _Maple_

Single
Widower } _Single_ { 1st, 2nd or 3rd marriage } _1st_
Divorced

Name of Father _Jim Hackett_

Maiden name of Mother _Sylvia Mae Trowbridge_

Bride's name _Martha Smith_

Her age _18_

" color _White_

" occupation _Wire Worker_

" Birthplace—City _Maple_ State _Ind._

" Residence—Street No. _RR16_ City _Maple_

Single
Widow } _Single_ { 1st, 2nd or 3rd marriage } _1st_
Divorced

Name of Father _Paul Smith_

Maiden name of Mother _Ella Goodman_

Date of this marriage _April 22-44_

Place of this marriage _Maple, Ind._

Name and title of person
Performing this marriage _Wm E Court Jr._

His address _184 E Court_

Witness { Name _Mary Stone_
{ Address _3741 Valley Ave_

## Return this Report to County Clerk with License and Certificate

# Marriage Record for Board of Health

### To Be Returned by the Minister or Other Person Performing Ceremony

*George B Armstrong* and *Mary M. Sawyer*,

Groom's name _George B Armstrong_

His age _28_

" color _White_

" occupation _Soldier_

" Birthplace—City _Kearny_ State _New Jersey_

" Residence—Street No. _Camp Atterbury Indiana_

Single / Widower / Divorced } _Single_  { 1st, 2nd or 3rd marriage } _1st_

Name of Father _Thomas J Armstrong_

Maiden name of Mother _Mable Bennett_

Bride's name _Mary M Sawyer_

Her age _32_

" color _White_

" occupation _Adjusting Clerk_

" Birthplace—City _Carteret_ State _New Jersey_

" Residence—Street No. _1610 S Broad_ City _Elizabeth, New Jersey_

Single / Widow / Divorced } _Single_  { 1st, 2nd or 3rd marriage } _1st_

Name of Father _Thomas Sawyer_

Maiden name of Mother _Mary Zarilla_

Date of this marriage _April 22-44_

Place of this marriage _Delphi, Ind._

Name and title of person Performing this marriage _Ernest Adams Justice of Peace_

His address _15½ E Court_

Witness { Name _Mary Jo Kane_
{ Address _334 College Ave_

### Return this Report to County Clerk with License and Certificate

42

# Marriage Record for Board of Health
## To Be Returned by the Minister or Other Person Performing Ceremony

*Lester R. Gilbreath* and *Goldie W. Warrenburg*

Groom's name *Lester R. Gilbreath*

His age 57

" color white

" occupation Wood worker

" Birthplace—City Indianapolis State Indiana

" Residence—Street No. 2260 Reformer City Indpls.

Single / Widower / Divorced } Widower  { 1st, 2nd or 3rd marriage } 2nd

Name of Father Robert S. Gilbreath

Maiden name of Mother Sarah Whitford

Bride's name Goldie W. Warrenburg

Her age 48

" color white

" occupation Defense Worker

" Birthplace—City Indpls State Indiana

" Residence—Street No. 2319 Beecher City Indpls.

Single / Widow / Divorced } Divorced  { 1st, 2nd or 3rd marriage } 3rd

Name of Father William Fult

Maiden name of Mother Elizabeth McClanlan

Date of this marriage April 22 44

Place of this marriage Indpls Ind

Name and title of person Performing this marriage Knight Cane Justice of Peace

His address 152½ E Court St.

Witness { Name Harold Lembaugh
{ Address 2538 Prospect

## Return this Report to County Clerk with License and Certificate

# Marriage Record for Board of Health

### To Be Returned by the Minister or Other Person Performing Ceremony

John Thomas Becklehimer and Helen E. Pence

Groom's name _John Thomas Becklehimer_

His age _48_

" color _White_

" occupation _Mechanical_

" Birthplace—City _Pittman_ State _Indiana_

" Residence—Street No. _1522 Jones_ City _Indianapolis_

Single
Widower } _Divorced_   1st, 2nd or 3rd marriage } _3rd_
Divorced

Name of Father _Isaac Becklehimer_

Maiden name of Mother _Olive Scott_

Bride's name _Helen E. Pence_

Her age _48_

" color _White_

" occupation _None_

" Birthplace—City _Indianapolis_ State _Indiana_

" Residence—Street No. _52 Jones_ City _Indianapolis_

Single
Widow } _Widow_   1st, 2nd or 3rd marriage } _2nd_
Divorced

Name of Father _Samuel Scott_

Maiden name of Mother _Cora McCallister_

Date of this marriage _April 22, 1944_

Place of this marriage _Indianapolis, Ind._

Name and title of person
Performing this marriage _Ernest Lane, Justice of Peace_

His address _152 East Court St._

Witness { Name _Mary Jo Lane_
         { Address _3741 College Ave._

### Return this Report to County Clerk with License and Certificate

# Marriage Record for Board of Health
## To Be Returned by the Minister or Other Person Performing Ceremony

*Robert L. Brown* and *Louise George*

Groom's name _Robert L. Brown_

His age _31_

" color _white_

" occupation _keeper_

" Birthplace—City _Alton_ State _Illinois_

" Residence—Street No. _Ft Knox_ City

Single / Widower / Divorced } _Divorced_ { 1st, 2nd or 3rd marriage } _2_

Name of Father _Roy Brown_

Maiden name of Mother _Bertha Holmes_

Bride's name _Louise George_

Her age _27_

" color _white_

" occupation _Stenographer_

" Birthplace—City _Indianapolis_ State _Indiana_

" Residence—Street No. _1612 W Morris_ City _Indianapolis_

Single / Widow / Divorced } _Single_ { 1st, 2nd or 3rd marriage } _1_

Name of Father _Thomas E. George_

Maiden name of Mother _Lillie Midkiff_

Date of this marriage _April 22, 1944_

Place of this marriage _Indianapolis_

Name and title of person Performing this marriage _Ferns Lowe Justice of the Peace_

His address _152½ East Court St_

Witness { Name _Harold E. Stevens_ Address _Ft Knox Ky_

## Return this Report to County Clerk with License and Certificate

# Marriage Record for Board of Health
## To Be Returned by the Minister or Other Person Performing Ceremony

*Garald Hayne Starr* and *Cathrine Ellen Gallagher*

Groom's name *Gerald Hayne Starr*

His age *21*

" color *White*

" occupation *Machinist*

" Birthplace—City *Bedford* State *Ind*

" Residence—Street No. *713 N. Ala* City *Indianapolis*

Single / Widower / Divorced } *Single*    { 1st, 2nd or 3rd marriage } *1st*

Name of Father *Wm. A. Starr*

Maiden name of Mother *Lillie May Howe*

Bride's name *Catherine Ellen Gallagher*

Her age *24*

" color *White*

" occupation *Inspector*

" Birthplace—City *Marion Co* State *Ind*

" Residence—Street No. *3035 W. Ill* City *Indianapolis*

Single / Widow / Divorced } *Divorced*    { 1st, 2nd or 3rd marriage } *4th*

Name of Father *Bernard David Cole*

Maiden name of Mother *Harriet Margaret Peterson*

Date of this marriage *April 22, 1944*

Place of this marriage *Indianapolis, Ind.*

Name and title of person Performing this marriage *Rev. K. L. M. Brown*

His address *834 E. Drake Ave*

*Indianapolis, Ind.*

Witness { Name ............... Address ...............

## Return this Report to County Clerk with License and Certificate

# Marriage Record for Board of Health
### To Be Returned by the Minister or Other Person Performing Ceremony

John Francis Hanafee and Margaret Frances Scott

Groom's name _John Francis Hanafee_

His age _24_

" color _White_

" occupation _Ensign in U.S. Navy_

" Birthplace—City _Louisville_ State _Ky_

" Residence—Street No. _1025 N. Oakland_ City _Indianapolis_

Single / Widower / Divorced } _Single_ { 1st, 2nd or 3rd marriage }

Name of Father _John Hanafee_

Maiden name of Mother _Mary Christ Hanafee_

Bride's name _Margaret Frances Scott_

Her age _22_

" color _White_

" occupation _Clerk at Allison's_

" Birthplace—City _Shelby Co_ State _Ind._

" Residence—Street No. _____ City _Indianapolis_

Single / Widow / Divorced } _Single_ { 1st, 2nd or 3rd marriage }

Name of Father _Paul G. Scott_

Maiden name of Mother _Pauline Thomas_

Date of this marriage _April 22, 1944_

Place of this marriage _1025 N. Oakland_

Name and title of person Performing this marriage _(Rev.) Richard Kavanagh, Catholic Priest_

His address _2613 West St. Clair St._

_Indianapolis, Ind._

Witness { Name _William Hanafee_ Ena Clark

Address _1025 N Oakland_ 1825 Kawland Ave

### Return this Report to County Clerk with License and Certificate

# Marriage Record for Board of Health
### To Be Returned by the Minister or Other Person Performing Ceremony

George Cleage _____ and Mildred Mallory

Groom's name _George Cleage_

His age _40_

" color _C_

" occupation _Cook_

" Birthplace—City _Athens_ State _Tenn_

" Residence—Street No. _1014 West Mich_ City _Indianaplos_

Single / Widower / Divorced } _Divorced_ { 1st, 2nd or 3rd marriage } _2nd_

Name of Father _George Cleage_

Maiden name of Mother _Carlin Tucker_

Bride's name _Mildred Mallory_

Her age _30_

" color _C_

" occupation _Defense_

" Birthplace—City _Birmingham_ State _Ala_

" Residence—Street No. _531 Agnes_ City _Indianaplos_

Single / Widow / Divorced } _Widow_ { 1st, 2nd or 3rd marriage } _2nd_

Name of Father _Bob Mallory_

Maiden name of Mother _Mary Mallory_

Date of this marriage _April 23, 1944_

Place of this marriage _Indianapolis, Ind_

Name and title of person Performing this marriage _SS Thomas Minister_

His address _702 S Illinois_

Witness { Name _Betty Winkliffe_ Address _2336 Indianapolis Ave._

### Return this Report to County Clerk with License and Certificate

# Marriage Record for Board of Health
## To Be Returned by the Minister or Other Person Performing Ceremony

_Arnold Lewis Page_ and _Norma Jean Otts_

Groom's name _Arnold Lewis Page_

His age _22_

" color _White_

" occupation _U.S. Army_

" Birthplace—City _Linton_ State _Indiana_

" Residence—Street No. _U.S. Army_ City _—_

Single Widower Divorced } _Single_ { 1st, 2nd or 3rd marriage } _First_

Name of Father _Erman Page_

Maiden name of Mother _Florence Duncan_

Bride's name _Norma Jean Otts_

Her age _18_

" color _White_

" occupation _Inspector in Defense Plant_

" Birthplace—City _Coal City_ State _Indiana_

" Residence—Street No. _431 N. Gray St_ City _Indianapolis, Ind._

Single Widow Divorced } _Single_ { 1st, 2nd or 3rd marriage } _First_

Name of Father _Bernard Otts_

Maiden name of Mother _Fay Stantz_

Date of this marriage _April 23, 1944_

Place of this marriage _Indianapolis, Ind._

Name and title of person Performing this marriage _Rev. E. Robert Andry_

His address _287 Downey Ave._
_Indianapolis, Ind._

Witness { Name _Fred F. Beckelheimer_
{ Address _431 N. Gray St_

## Return this Report to County Clerk with License and Certificate

# Marriage Record for Board of Health
## To Be Returned by the Minister or Other Person Performing Ceremony

Paul Herman Lewellyn Jr and Irene Joy Jacobs

Groom's name _Paul Herman Lewellyn Jr_

His age _19_

" color _white_

" occupation _mechanic_

" Birthplace—City _Sullivan_ State _Indiana_

" Residence—Street No. _Berry St_ City _Lawrence_

Single / Widower / Divorced } _single_   { 1st, 2nd or 3rd marriage } _First_

Name of Father _Paul H Lewellyn Sr_

Maiden name of Mother _Audrey Ruth White (Deceased)_

Bride's name _Irene Joy Jacobs_

Her age _17_

" color _white_

" occupation _Machine operator at R.C.A._

" Birthplace—City _Indianapolis_ State _Indiana_

" Residence—Street No. _5623 Bonna_ City _Indianapolis_

Single / Widow / Divorced } _single_   { 1st, 2nd or 3rd marriage } _First_

Name of Father _Vita Lee Jacobs (Deceased)_

Maiden name of Mother _Viola Jenkins Jacobs_

Date of this marriage _April 22, 1944_

Place of this marriage _Lawrence, Indiana_

Name and title of person Performing this marriage _Reverend Bernard J. Penner_

His address _4444 Franklin Road_
_Lawrence, Indiana_

Witness { Name _William Spaulding_ / _Bonnie Hay_
{ Address _Lawrence, Ind_ / _Oaklandon, Ind._

## Return this Report to County Clerk with License and Certificate

# Marriage Record for Board of Health

To Be Returned by the Minister or Other Person Performing Ceremony

Henry C. Faus _and_ Nettie M. Phillips

Groom's name _Henry C. Faus_

His age _34_

" color _White_

" occupation _U. S. Service_

" Birthplace—City _Bolingreen_ State _Ind. Ky._

" Residence—Street No. _1035 S North_ City _Indianapolis, Ind._

Single
~~Widower~~
~~Divorced~~ } ---- { 1st, ~~2nd or 3rd~~ marriage } ----

Name of Father _John Faus_

Maiden name of Mother _Anna Holley_

Bride's name _Nettie M. Phillips_

Her age _18_

" color _White_

" occupation _Crown Products - Machine operator_

" Birthplace—City _Clarksville_ State _Ind._

" Residence—Street No. _244 N. La Salle_ City _Indianapolis, Ind._

Single
~~Widow~~
~~Divorced~~ } ---- { 1st, ~~2nd or 3rd~~ marriage } ----

Name of Father _Harry Phillips_

Maiden name of Mother _Ruby Bennett_

Date of this marriage _April 22-44_

Place of this marriage _Indianapolis Ind._

Name and title of person Performing this marriage _C. H. Scherch, Pastor_

His address _5726 Chelsea Rd., Indianapolis, 8, Ind._

Witness { Name _Wayne A. Faus_
{ Address _1035 S. Worth St._

## Return this Report to County Clerk with License and Certificate

# Marriage Record for Board of Health

To Be Returned by the Minister or Other Person Performing Ceremony

*Albert Karl Henning* and *Maxine Elizabeth Sanders*

Groom's name *Albert Karl Henning Jr*

His age ~~22~~ 23

" color White

" occupation Cadet Soldier

" Birthplace—City Akron  State Ohio

" Residence—Street No. Butler University  City Indianapolis

Single / Widower / Divorced } Single  { 1st, 2nd or 3rd marriage } 1st

Name of Father Albert Karl Henning Sr.

Maiden name of Mother Helen Munni Patrick.

Bride's name *Maxine Elizabeth Sanders*

Her age 25

" color White

" occupation Clerk Army Air Force

" Birthplace—City Vance burg  State Kentucky

" Residence—Street No. 3965 W Tacoma  City Indianapolis

Single / Widow / Divorced } Single  { 1st, 2nd or 3rd marriage } 1st

Name of Father Gray Sanders

Maiden name of Mother Minnie Bell

Date of this marriage April 22 - 1944

Place of this marriage Indianapolis

Name and title of person Performing this marriage Rev. John F. Edwards

His address 4335 N. Pennsylvania Indianapolis Ind

Witness { Name Donald Frank  { Address Kearney Neb.

## Return this Report to County Clerk with License and Certificate

# Marriage Record for Board of Health
### To Be Returned by the Minister or Other Person Performing Ceremony

---

———————————————— and ————————————————

Groom's name _____ William Griffith

His age _____ 36

" color _____ White

" occupation _____ Chevrolet Commercial Body

" Birthplace—City _____ Indpls _____ State _____ Ind.

" Residence—Street No. _____ 1131 N. Capitol _____ City _____ Indianapolis

Single Widower Divorced } _____ Single _____ { 1st, 2nd or 3rd marriage } _____ First

Name of Father _____ Frank Griffith

Maiden name of Mother _____ Mary E. Orme

---

Bride's name _____ Rena Koehler

Her age _____ 37

" color _____ White

" occupation _____ at home

" Birthplace—City _____ Pase County _____ State _____ Kentucky

" Residence—Street No. _____ 1116 N. Capitol _____ City _____ Indianapolis

Single Widow Divorced } _____ divorced _____ { 1st, 2nd or 3rd marriage } _____ third

*r stated she*
*on the*
*aller or*
*S—*
*Smith*

Name of Father _____

Maiden name of Mother _____

---

Date of this marriage _____ April 22, 1944

Place of this marriage _____ Olive Branch Christian Church

Name and title of person
Performing this marriage _____ Rev. W des E. Smith

His address _____ 1816 E Raymond St

_____ Indianapolis, Ind.

Witness { Name _____ Alfred Clark
{ Address _____ 1130 N. Capitol

---

## Return this Report to County Clerk with License and Certificate

## Marriage Record for Board of Health
### To Be Returned by the Minister or Other Person Performing Ceremony

_Edwin D Hicks_ and _Norma J. Maschino_

Groom's name _Edwin D. Hicks_

His age _24_

" color _White_

" occupation _Inspector_

" Birthplace—City _Indianapolis_ State _Indiana_

" Residence—Street No. _70 N Taft_ City _Indianapolis_

Single
~~Widower~~
~~Divorced~~ } _Single_   { 1st, ~~2nd or 3rd~~ marriage } _1st._

Name of Father _Edwin D. Hicks_

Maiden name of Mother _Rose Elizabeth Botzum_

Bride's name _Norma J. Maschino_

Her age _18_

" color _White_

" occupation _House-Keeper_

" Birthplace—City _Indianapolis_ State _Ind._

" Residence—Street No. _Michigan St.,_ City _Indianapolis_

Single
~~Widow~~
~~Divorced~~ } _Single_   { 1st, ~~2nd or 3rd~~ marriage } _1st_

Name of Father _Theodore Wm Maschino_

Maiden name of Mother _Clara Rose Marie Miller_

Date of this marriage _April 22 1944._

Place of this marriage _2424 W. St Clair St., Indianapolis, In_

Name and title of person Performing this marriage _Rev. Geo G Kinney_

His address _2424 W. St. Clair St._
_Indpls. Ind._

Witness { Name _Donald H. Hicks_
{ Address _2023 W. New York St._

### Return this Report to County Clerk with License and Certificate

# Marriage Record for Board of Health
## To Be Returned by the Minister or Other Person Performing Ceremony

*Lawrence M Brust* and *Ruth Anne Branam*

Groom's name *Lawrence M Brust*

His age *25*

" color *White*

" occupation *Army*

" Birthplace—City *Indiana Co.* State *Pennsylvania*

" Residence—Street No. *2447 N Talbot* City *Indianapolis*

Single
~~Widower~~ } *1st*  { 1st, 2nd or 3rd
~~Divorced~~        marriage

Name of Father *Arilla Brust*

Maiden name of Mother *Rose L Nibert*

Bride's name *Ruth Anne Branam*

Her age *19*

" color *White*

" occupation *Secretary*

" Birthplace—City *Indianapolis* State *Ind*

" Residence—Street No. *2447 N Talbot* City *Indianapolis*

Single
~~Widow~~ } *1st*  { 1st, 2nd or 3rd
~~Divorced~~       marriage

Name of Father *Daniel Voorhees*

Maiden name of Mother *Edith Henderson*

Date of this marriage *April x x 1944*

Place of this marriage *Indianapolis*

Name and title of person
Performing this marriage *George F Snyder*

His address *846 N Dr Woodruff*
*Indianapolis Indiana*

Witness { Name *James E Hegwood*
        { Address *Fort Knox, Ky. 345 8 715 2*

## Return this Report to County Clerk with License and Certificate

# Marriage Record for Board of Health
### To Be Returned by the Minister or Other Person Performing Ceremony

*Paul R. Harding* and *Mary E. Shulswick*

Groom's name __Paul__

His age __55__

" color __White__

" occupation __Tailor__

" Birthplace—City __Dayton__ State __Ohio__

" Residence—Street No. __1325 Oliver__ City __Indianapolis__

~~Single~~ Widower ~~Divorced~~ } __Widower__ { ~~1st,~~ 2nd or ~~3rd~~ marriage } __2nd__

Name of Father __Wm__

Maiden name of Mother __Clara Parker__

Bride's name __Mary__

Her age __64__

" color __White__

" occupation __Housewife__

" Birthplace—City __Flemsburg__ State __Ky__

" Residence—Street No. __1325 Oliver__ City __Indianapolis__

~~Single~~ Widow ~~Divorced~~ } __Widow__ { ~~1st,~~ 2nd or ~~3rd~~ marriage } __2nd__

Name of Father __John Parker__

Maiden name of Mother __Sally Hull__

Date of this marriage __4/22/44__

Place of this marriage __Indianapolis Ind.__

Name and title of person Performing this marriage __Rev. C.P. White__

His address __627 Division St. Indianapolis__

Witness { Name __Mrs. C.P. White__
Address __627 Division St. Indianapolis__

### Return this Report to County Clerk with License and Certificate

# Marriage Record for Board of Health
### To Be Returned by the Minister or Other Person Performing Ceremony

Robert P Bryant and Ruby C Barton

Groom's name _Robert P Bryant_

His age _35_

" color _white_

" occupation _U.S.A. Service Command_

" Birthplace—City _Terre Haute_ State _Indiana_

" Residence—Street No. _2132 Beech_ City _Terre Haute_

Single / Widower / Divorced _Single_ { 1st, 2nd or 3rd marriage } _First_

Name of Father _Herbert Bryant_

Maiden name of Mother _Josephine Bonham_

Bride's name _Ruby C. Barton_

Her age _30_

" color _White_

" occupation _Allison's Div. of Y M C_

" Birthplace—City _Muncie_ State _Indiana_

" Residence—Street No. _R. R. 3 Box 33_ City _Muncie_

Single / Widow / Divorced _Divorced_ { 1st, 2nd or 3rd marriage } _Second_

Name of Father _Walter Wilmer Clevenger_

Maiden name of Mother _Eva McCorkle_

Date of this marriage _April 22, 1944_

Place of this marriage _5822 E. New York, Indianapolis_

Name and title of person Performing this marriage _C L Roy Williams – Minister_

His address _R. R. 17 Box 571_
_Indianapolis, Indiana_

Witness { Name _Victor R Morris_
{ Address _5822 East New York St_

### Return this Report to County Clerk with License and Certificate

# Marriage Record for Board of Health
## To Be Returned by the Minister or Other Person Performing Ceremony

_____ and _____

Groom's name _____ *Albert D. Hillock* _____

His age _____ *36* _____

" color _____ *W.* _____

" occupation _____ *Cook* _____

" Birthplace—City _____ *Kempton* _____ State _____ *Indiana* _____

" Residence—Street No. *729 Greer* City _____ *Indpls, Ind.* _____

Single / Widower / Divorced } _____ *Widower* _____ { 1st, 2nd or 3rd marriage } _____ *2nd* _____

Name of Father _____ *John Hillock* _____

Maiden name of Mother _____ *Authie (Woods)* _____

Bride's name _____ *Esther Barnett* _____

Her age _____ *35* _____

" color _____ *W.* _____

" occupation _____ *None* _____

" Birthplace—City _____ *Arthur* _____ State _____ *Illinois* _____

" Residence—Street No. *729 Greer St* City _____ *Indpls, Ind.* _____

Single / Widow / Divorced } _____ *Divorced* _____ { 1st, 2nd or 3rd marriage } _____ *2nd* _____

Name of Father _____ *Charles Browne* _____

Maiden name of Mother _____ *Della (Henderson)* _____

Date of this marriage _____ *April 22 - 1944* _____

Place of this marriage _____ *Indpls Ind.* _____

Name and title of person Performing this marriage _____ *Wm E. Nelson, Minister* _____

His address _____ *1035 So. New Jersey* _____
_____ *Indianapolis Ind.* _____

Witness { Name _____ *Mrs E. Hillock* _____
{ Address _____ *525 Weghorst St* _____

## Return this Report to County Clerk with License and Certificate

# Marriage Record for Board of Health
## To Be Returned by the Minister or Other Person Performing Ceremony

_Henry Roach_ and _Jaunita Daniell_

Groom's name _Henry Roach_

His age _23_

" color _White_

" occupation _(Medical Discharge from U.S. Army)_

" Birthplace—City _Rochester_ State _Kentucky_

" Residence—Street No. _1917 Arrow Ave._ City _Indianapolis_

Single Widower Divorced } _Single_ { 1st, 2nd or 3rd marriage } _1st_

Name of Father _Sidney Wayne Roach_

Maiden name of Mother _Vadie Pendley_

Bride's name _Jaunita Daniell_

Her age _23_

" color _White_

" occupation _R.C.A. - Mounter_

" Birthplace—City _Indianapolis_ State _Indiana_

" Residence—Street No. _1917 Arrow_ City _Indianapolis_

Single Widow Divorced } _Single_ { 1st, 2nd or 3rd marriage } _1st_

Name of Father _Hansford Daniell_

Maiden name of Mother _Allie McEndree_

Date of this marriage _April 22, 1944_

Place of this marriage _Indianapolis, Ind._

Name and title of person Performing this marriage _Hoyt S. Canary, Minister_

His address _1931 Ingram St._ _Indianapolis, Ind._

Witness { Name _Catherine Swhear_ Address _518 Eastern Avenue_

## Return this Report to County Clerk with License and Certificate

# Marriage Record for Board of Health

To Be Returned by the Minister or Other Person Performing Ceremony

_John Douglas_ and _Alice Strauser_

Groom's name _John Douglas_

His age _22_

" color _white_

" occupation _Factory work_

" Birthplace—City _Bloomington_ State _Indiana_

" Residence—Street No. _____ City _____

Single Widower Divorced } _Single_ 1st, 2nd or 3rd marriage } _1st._

Name of Father _Walter Russel Douglas_

Maiden name of Mother _Alpha Rush_

Bride's name _Alice Strauser._

Her age _21_

" color _white_

" occupation _defined_

" Birthplace—City _Bloomfield_ State _Indiana_

" Residence—Street No. _____ City _____

Single Widow Divorced } _Single_ 1st, 2nd or 3rd marriage } _1st_

Name of Father _Joel Strauser_

Maiden name of Mother _Philena Strauser_

Date of this marriage _April 22, 1944_

Place of this marriage _Bloomfield Indiana_

Name and title of person Performing this marriage _Minister_

His address _Bloomfield Ind._

Witness { Name _Mrs. C. H. Layton — Mrs. A. R. English_
        { Address _____

## Return this Report to County Clerk with License and Certificate

12

# Marriage Record for Board of Health

## To Be Returned by the Minister or Other Person Performing Ceremony

Mose McCauley and Pauline Dinwiddie

Groom's name _Mose McCauley_

His age _26_

" color _C_

" occupation _soilder_

" Birthplace—City _Lacenter_ State _Ky_

" Residence—Street No. _825 Odgon_ City _Indianapolis Ind_

Single / Widower / Divorced } _Single_ { 1st, 2nd or 3rd marriage } _one st_

Name of Father _Will McCauley_

Maiden name of Mother _Mattis Coal_

Bride's name _Pauline Dinwiddie_

Her age _37_

" color _C_

" occupation _Meat Cutter_

" Birthplace—City _Paris Tenn_ State

" Residence—Street No. _825 Odgon_ City _Indianapolis_

Single / Widow / Divorced } _Widow_ { 1st, 2nd or 3rd marriage } _Second_

Name of Father _Lincoln woods_

Maiden name of Mother _Emmer Mojors_

Date of this marriage _April 22 1944_

Place of this marriage _Indianapolis Ind_

Name and title of person Performing this marriage _SS Thomas Minister_

His address _702 S. Illinos st Indianapolis Ind_

Witness { Name _Stella muse_

{ Address _825 Odgon St_

## Return this Report to County Clerk with License and Certificate

# Marriage Record for Board of Health

## To Be Returned by the Minister or Other Person Performing Ceremony

*Isaiah Burse* and *Clarissa Jones*

Groom's name _____ Isaiah Burse

His age _____ 26

" color _____ Colored

" occupation _____ In United State Army

" Birthplace—City _____ Guthrie _____ State _____ Kentucky

" Residence—Street No. _____ Camp Van Dorn, Miss. City

Single
Widower } _____ Divorced { 1st, ~~2nd~~ or 3rd } _____ Second
~~Divorced~~         marriage

Name of Father _____ Rodger Cornell

Maiden name of Mother _____ Katie Harris

Bride's name _____ Clarissa Jones

Her age _____ 21

" color _____ Colored

" occupation _____ Defence worker

" Birthplace—City _____ Indianapolis _____ State _____ Indiana

" Residence—Street No. _____ 2910 Martindale ave City _____ Indianapolis

~~Single~~
Widow } _____ Single { ~~1st,~~ 2nd or 3rd } _____ First
Divorced         marriage

Name of Father _____ Clarence L. Jones

Maiden name of Mother _____ Eliza Vaughn

Date of this marriage _____ April 22nd 1944

Place of this marriage _____ 2118 N. Capitol Ave. Apt #19

Name and title of person
Performing this marriage _____ Rev. John J. Weeden

His address _____ 2805 Boulevard Place
_____ Indianapolis, Indiana.

Witness { Name _____ Josephine Jackson
{ Address _____ 2118 N. Capitol Ave

## Return this Report to County Clerk with License and Certificate

12

# Marriage Record for Board of Health
### To Be Returned by the Minister or Other Person Performing Ceremony

Richard Cullen Gustin _____ and Donna Norene Draper _____

Groom's name ___ Richard Cullen Gustin _____

His age __ 21

" color___ White _____

" occupation Junior Accountant-P.R. Mallory-Indianapolis, Ind. ___

" Birthplace—City Lafayette _____ State ___ Indiana ___

" Residence—Street No. 1327 W. 33rd St. ___ City Indianapolis, Ind.

Single / Widower / Divorced } Single { 1st, 2nd or 3rd marriage } 1st

Name of Father Howard Emerson Gustin (Deceased)

Maiden name of Mother___ Ruth Cullen

Bride's name ___ Donna Norene Draper

Her age ___ 20

" color___ White _____

" occupation Student-Butler University-Indianapolis, Indiana

" Birthplace—City___ Gary _____ State ___ Indiana ___

" Residence—Street No. 831 W. Hampton Dr. City ___ Indianapolis

Single / Widow / Divorced } Single { 1st, 2nd or 3rd marriage } 1st

Name of Father___ Alfred Pearman Draper

Maiden name of Mother___ Leontine Porter

Date of this marriage___ April 22, 1944

Place of this marriage McKee Chapel-Tabernacle Presbyterian Church- Indiana
polis, Indiana
Name and title of person *(signature)* ___ Minister of above Church
Performing this marriage

His address___ 418 East Thirty-Fourth Street

___ Indianapolis 5, Ind.

Witness { Name *(signature)* / Address *(signature)*

### Return this Report to County Clerk with License and Certificate

# Marriage Record for Board of Health
### To Be Returned by the Minister or Other Person Performing Ceremony

_Granville Alexander_ and _Lucille Craig_

Groom's name _Granville Alexander_

His age _49_

" color _Col._

" occupation _Machonist_

" Birthplace—City _Richmond_ State _Va_

" Residence—Street No _946 N. California_ City _Mpls. Md_

Single / Widower / Divorced } _Divorced_  1st, 2nd or 3rd marriage } _2nd._

Name of Father _Johnnie Alexander_

Maiden name of Mother _Henritta Swilley_

Bride's name _Lucille Craig_

Her age _39_

" color _Col_

" occupation _Housewife_

" Birthplace—City _Lexington_ State _Ky._

" Residence—Street No. _946 N Calif St_ City _Mpls_

Single / Widow / Divorced } _Widow_  1st, 2nd or 3rd marriage } _3rd._

Name of Father _Sanford Jackson_

Maiden name of Mother _Hettie Strider_

Date of this marriage _4/22/44_

Place of this marriage _Minneapolis Md._

Name and title of person Performing this marriage _Plummer D. Jacobs Minister_

His address _941 W. 25th Street Minneapolis Md._

Witness { Name _Ella Orps_  Address _456 West 13th Street_

### Return this Report to County Clerk with License and Certificate

# Marriage Record for Board of Health

### To Be Returned by the Minister or Other Person Performing Ceremony

William S. Witsman _____ and _____ Betty Lavonn Williams

Groom's name _William Witsman_

His age _23_

" color _White_

" occupation _U.S. Marines_

" Birthplace—City _Knox County_ State _Indiana_

" Residence—Street No. _1602 Washington Ave_ City _Vincennes, Ind._

Single } _Single_    { 1st, 2nd or 3rd } _First_
Widower            marriage
Divorced

Name of Father _Odes Witsman_

Maiden name of Mother _Flora Smith_

Bride's name _Betty Lavonn Williams_

Her age _18_

" color _White_

" occupation _Machine Operator Jukes Howel_

" Birthplace—City _Indianapolis_ State _Ind._

" Residence—Street No. _1120 N. Keystone_ City _Indianapolis, Ind._

Single } _Single_    { 1st, 2nd or 3rd } _First_
Widow            marriage
Divorced

Name of Father _Franklin D. Williams_

Maiden name of Mother _Opal M. Hatley_

Date of this marriage _April 22 1944_

Place of this marriage _937 W. Dr. Woodruff Pl. Indianapolis, Ind._

Name and title of person
Performing this marriage _Reverend Archibus M. Brown_

His address _937 W. Dr. Woodruff Pl._
_Indianapolis, Ind._

Witness { Name _Delmar Clawson_
        { Address _407 N. State St. City_

## Return this Report to County Clerk with License and Certificate

# Marriage Record for Board of Health
### To Be Returned by the Minister or Other Person Performing Ceremony

_John V. Steeb_ and _Catherine M. Jackson_

Groom's name _John V. Steeb_    _May 26 1898_

His age _45_

" color _White_

" occupation _Printer_

" Birthplace—City _Indianapolis_ State _Indiana_

" Residence—Street No. _1721 Albany_ City _Beech Grove_

~~Single~~
Widower
~~Divorced~~ } _____ { ~~1st,~~ 2nd or ~~3rd~~ marriage }

Name of Father _John Steeb_

Maiden name of Mother _Sena Berkel_

Bride's name _Catherine Maxine Jackson_

Her age _39_   _May 20 1904_

" color _White_

" occupation _Store Keeper_

" Birthplace—City _Kokomo_ State _Indiana_

" Residence—Street No. _531 E. N. York_ City _Indianapolis_

~~Single~~
~~Widow~~
Divorced } _____ { ~~1st,~~ 2nd or ~~3rd~~ marriage }

Name of Father _Samuel Wiley_

Maiden name of Mother _Allie Taylor_

Date of this marriage _Apr. 22 - 44_

Place of this marriage _Holy Name Church Beech Grove Ind._

Name and title of person Performing this marriage _John F. Patterson Catholic Priest_

His address _R.R. 5 Box 160 Indianapolis Indiana_

Witness { Name _Leo J. Milli_
        { Address _Catherine Louise Milli_

### Return this Report to County Clerk with License and Certificate

# Marriage Record for Board of Health

### To Be Returned by the Minister or Other Person Performing Ceremony

_____ and _____

Groom's name _Robert F Cantlon_

His age _23_

" color _White_

" occupation _bookkeeper_

" Birthplace—City _Indianapolis_ State _Indiana_

" Residence—Street No. _1736 Union_ City _Indianapolis Ind._

Single } _Single_ { 1st, 2nd or 3rd } _first_
Widower } marriage }
Divorced }

Name of Father _Leo Cantlon_

Maiden name of Mother _Clara Puller_

Bride's name _Lorraine E. Leanty_

Her age _23_

" color _White_

" occupation _beautician_

" Birthplace—City _Indianapolis_ State _Indiana_

" Residence—Street No. _326 E. Minn._ City _Indianapolis Ind._

Single } _Single_ { 1st, 2nd or 3rd } _first_
Widow } marriage }
Divorced }

Name of Father _Charles Leanty_

Maiden name of Mother _Elis. Johannes._

Date of this marriage _April 22 1944_

Place of this marriage _Indianapolis Indiana_

Name and title of person
Performing this marriage _Ephrem Wuench - Priest_

His address _1530 Milton St. Indianapolis Indiana_

Witness { Name _Helen Leanty 326 E. Minn._
{ Address _Indianapolis Ind._

## Return this Report to County Clerk with License and Certificate

# Marriage Record for Board of Health
### To Be Returned by the Minister or Other Person Performing Ceremony

........................................... and ...........................................

Groom's name _Carlo Raymond Parker_

His age _Forty_

" color _White_

" occupation _House Representative_

" Birthplace—City _Delaware Co_ State _Ind_

" Residence—Street No. _Hartford City_ City _R.R. 4 Ind_

Single / Widower / Divorced } _Single_ { 1st, 2nd or 3rd marriage } _First_

Name of Father _Thomas E. Parker_

Maiden name of Mother _Clara May Kinnard_

Bride's name _Minnie L. Harris_

Her age _Thirty-nine_

" color _White_

" occupation ...........................................

" Birthplace—City _Hillham_ State _Ind_

" Residence—Street No. _508 E. Michigan_ City _Indianapolis_

Single / Widow / Divorced } _Widow_ { 1st, 2nd or 3rd marriage } _3rd._

Name of Father _Nelson Kinnger_

Maiden name of Mother _Margaret Harris_

Date of this marriage _Apr 22 1944_

Place of this marriage _Indianapolis_

Name and title of person Performing this marriage _E. R. Cross Minister_

His address _1122 N. Libby_

Witness { Name _Ora Harris Jr._ { Address _5650 Terrell Ave._

---

## Return this Report to County Clerk with License and Certificate

12

# Marriage Record for Board of Health
## To Be Returned by the Minister or Other Person Performing Ceremony

Warren A. Seaborg and Betty Jane Ward

Groom's name ...... Warren A. Seaborg

His age ...... 23

" color ...... white

" occupation ...... U. S. Army

" Birthplace—City South Bend ...... State Indiana

" Residence—Street No. 314 Franklin ...... City South Bend

Single / Widower / Divorced } Single { 1st, 2nd or 3rd marriage } 1st.

Name of Father ...... Charles Seaborg

Maiden name of Mother ...... Alma Nelson

Bride's name ...... Betty Jane Ward

Her age ...... 22

" color ...... White

" occupation ...... Personnel Office

" Birthplace—City Indianapolis ...... State Indiana

" Residence—Street No. 337 Layman Ave. ...... City Indianapolis

Single / Widow / Divorced } Single { 1st, 2nd or 3rd marriage } 1st.

Name of Father ...... Irwin A. Ward

Maiden name of Mother ...... Zelma V. Simpson

Date of this marriage ...... April 27th 1944

Place of this marriage ...... Indianapolis Ind

Name and title of person Performing this marriage ...... Rev. Clarence A. Shaky

His address ...... 28 N. Audubon Rd

Indianapolis Ind

Witness { Name ...... Irwin A. Ward
{ Address ...... 337 Layman ave. Indpls Ind.

## Return this Report to County Clerk with License and Certificate

12

# Marriage Record for Board of Health
### To Be Returned by the Minister or Other Person Performing Ceremony

*Berdean E. Oldroyd* and *Elsa Leavitt*

Groom's name _Berdean E. Oldroyd_

His age _25_

" color _White_

" occupation _Special Agent, F B I_

" Birthplace—City _Kenwood_ State _Utah_

" Residence—Street No. _223 Forest_ City _Inapls, Indiana_

Single / Widower / Divorced } ✓ { 1st, 2nd or 3rd marriage } _1st marriage_

Name of Father _Andrew Oldroyd_

Maiden name of Mother _Celia Sorenson (Oldroyd)_

Bride's name _Elsa Leavitt_

Her age _19_

" color _White_

" occupation _Clerk, Railroadmen's Fed. Sav & Loan_

" Birthplace—City _Samoan Isles_ State _Tonga_

" Residence—Street No. _223 Forest_ City _Inapls. Indiana_

Single / Widow / Divorced } { 1st, 2nd or 3rd marriage } _1st marriage_

Name of Father _Lawrence Clark Leavitt_

Maiden name of Mother _Mary Ann Davies (Leavitt)_

Date of this marriage _April 23 (22 ?) 1944_

Place of this marriage _Indianapolis_

Name and title of person Performing this marriage _L. C. Leavitt, Minister_

His address _1406 E. New York Street_
_Indianapolis, Ind_

Witness { Name _Sibyl S. Sullivan_
{ Address _1015 N. Burillo_

### Return this Report to County Clerk with License and Certificate

## Marriage Record for Board of Health
### To Be Returned by the Minister or Other Person Performing Ceremony

Robert L. Patterson and Sarah J. Johnson

Groom's name _Robert L. Patterson_

His age _22_

" color _white_

" occupation _Laborer – Kingan & Co._

" Birthplace—City _Indianapolis_ State _Ind._

" Residence—Street No. _1631 Leonard_ City _Indianapolis, Ind._

Single / Widower / Divorced } _Single_ { 1st, 2nd or 3rd marriage } _1st_

Name of Father _William George Patterson_

Maiden name of Mother _Delia Keaton_

Bride's name _Sarah J. Johnson_

Her age _19_

" color _white_

" occupation _Kingan & Co._

" Birthplace—City _Theodo_ State _Indiana_

" Residence—Street No. _3157 E. Wash._ City _Indianapolis, Ind._

Single / Widow / Divorced } _Single_ { 1st, 2nd or 3rd marriage } _1st_

Name of Father _Carl Henry Johnson_

Maiden name of Mother _Margaret Tedran_

Date of this marriage _April 22, 1944_

Place of this marriage _Indianapolis, Ind._

Name and title of person Performing this marriage _Norman H. Schmit – Ordained Minister_

His address _2117 Napoleon St._

_Indianapolis, Indiana_

Witness { Name _Philip Ford_

{ Address _1631 Leonard st Indpls Ind_

### Return this Report to County Clerk with License and Certificate

# Marriage Record for Board of Health
## To Be Returned by the Minister or Other Person Performing Ceremony

_____ Joseph R. Hodge _____ and _____ Rosemary Deilkes _____

Groom's name _____ Joseph R. Hodge

His age _____ 19

" color _____ white

" occupation _____ truck driver

" Birthplace—City _____ Indianapolis, _____ State _____ Indiana

" Residence—Street No. _____ 303 S. State _____ City _____ Indianapolis, Ind.

Single / Widower / Divorced _____ single _____ { 1st, 2nd or 3rd marriage _____ 1st

Name of Father _____ Joseph I. Hodge

Maiden name of Mother _____ Letha Judd

Bride's name _____ Rosemary Deilkes

Her age _____ 18

" color _____ white

" occupation _____ lathe operator

" Birthplace—City _____ Indianapolis, _____ State _____ Indiana.

" Residence—Street No. _____ 705 N. New Jersey _____ City _____ Indianapolis, Ind.

Single / Widow / Divorced _____ single _____ { 1st, 2nd or 3rd marriage _____ 1st

Name of Father _____ Hershbel Deilker

Maiden name of Mother _____ Alta Mary Tickner

Date of this marriage _____ April 22, 1944

Place of this marriage _____ Indianapolis, Ind.

Name and title of person Performing this marriage _____ Rev. James H. Jensen, pastor St. Joseph Church

His address _____ 623 East North St. Indianapolis, Ind.

Witness { Name _____ Clifford L. Mitchell
{ Address _____ U.S. Army Camp Blanding, Fla.

## Return this Report to County Clerk with License and Certificate

# Marriage Record for Board of Health

## To Be Returned by the Minister or Other Person Performing Ceremony

William Nathaniel Scott _____ and _Joanne F. Krouse_

Groom's name _William Nathaniel Scott_

His age _nineteen (19)_

" color _White_

" occupation _Lieutenant U.S. Army Air Forces_

" Birthplace—City _Denver_ State _Colorado_

" Residence—Street No. _Eagle Pass Army Air Field_ City _Eagle Pass, Texas_

Single
Widower } _Single_   1st, 2nd or 3rd } _first_
Divorced         marriage

Name of Father _James Scott_

Maiden name of Mother _Jean Thomson_

Bride's name _Joanne F. Krouse_

Her age _Twenty-one (21)_

" color _White_

" occupation _____

" Birthplace—City _Logansport_ State _Indiana_

" Residence—Street No. _4651 North Capitol_ City _Indpls, Indiana_

Single
Widow } _Single_   1st, 2nd or 3rd } _first_
Divorced         marriage

Name of Father _Boyd Gustavus Krouse_

Maiden name of Mother _Marvel Adelade Fuller_

Date of this marriage _April 22nd, 1944_

Place of this marriage _Indianapolis, Indiana_

Name and title of person
Performing this marriage _S. Grundy Fisher, Minister_

His address _2101 Park Ave, Indianapolis 2, Indiana_

Witness { Name _Jane Hyde_
          Address _4444 Carrollton Avenue_
                  _Indianapolis, Indiana_

## Return this Report to County Clerk with License and Certificate

12

# Marriage Record for Board of Health
### To Be Returned by the Minister or Other Person Performing Ceremony

*Frank C. Boyer* and *Frances E. Sims*

Groom's name __FRANK C. BOYER__

His age __44__

" color __White__

" occupation __RECEIVING CLERK__

" Birthplace—City __INDIANAPOLIS__ State __INDIANA__

" Residence—Street No. __2624 E. North__ City __INDIANAPOLIS__

Single / Widower / Divorced } __DIVORCED__ { 1st, 2nd or 3rd marriage } __3rd.__

Name of Father __Charles Boyer__

Maiden name of Mother __Sarah Duffy__

Bride's name __Francis E. Sims__

Her age __46__

" color __White__

" occupation __house work.__

" Birthplace—City __Bloomington__ State __Indiana__

" Residence—Street No. __1115 North Alabama__ City __Indianapolis__

Single / Widow / Divorced } __divorced__ { 1st, 2nd or 3rd marriage } __3rd__

Name of Father __Joseph Sims__

Maiden name of Mother __Salina Monhorn__

Date of this marriage __April 23, 1944__

Place of this marriage __Indianapolis Indiana__

Name and title of person Performing this marriage __Ernest Lane, Justice of Peace__

His address __152½ East Court Street__

Witness { Name __Mary Jo Lane__ { Address __374 ? College Ave__

### Return this Report to County Clerk with License and Certificate

# Marriage Record for Board of Health

### To Be Returned by the Minister or Other Person Performing Ceremony

7 _____ and _____

Groom's name _Frederick Hulsmann III_

His age _20_

" color _White_

" occupation _Lt. in Army Air Force_

" Birthplace—City _Brooklyn_ State _New York_

" Residence—Street No. _3540 N. Penn._ City _Indianapolis, Ind._

Single Widower Divorced } _First_  { 1st, 2nd or 3rd marriage } _____

Name of Father _Frederick Hulsmann Jr. or II_

Maiden name of Mother _Florence Brown_

Bride's name _Mary Jane Hackemeyer_

Her age _21_

" color _White_

" occupation _Sales clerk_

" Birthplace—City _Indianapolis_ State _Indiana_

" Residence—Street No. _3403 Ruckle_ City _Indianapolis, Ind._

Single Widow Divorced } _First_  { 1st, 2nd or 3rd marriage } _____

Name of Father _Oliver H. Hackemeyer_

Maiden name of Mother _Margaret Eata Ferguson_

Date of this marriage _April 23, 1944_

Place of this marriage _Indianapolis, Indiana_

Name and title of person Performing this marriage _Judson L. Stark, Judge Marion_

His address _Indianapolis, Ind._ _Superior Court_

Witness { Name _John O. Hulsmann_,
{ Address _3403 Ruckle Ave., Indianapolis, Ind._

### Return this Report to County Clerk with License and Certificate

12

## Marriage Record for Board of Health
### To Be Returned by the Minister or Other Person Performing Ceremony

*Beverly Edith Barker* and *David Cullen Beck*

Groom's name _David Cullen Beck_

His age _20_

" color _White_

" occupation _In Navy_

" Birthplace—City _Michigan City_ State _Ind_

" Residence—Street No. _2923 Wrobel Ave_ City _Michigan City, Ind_

Single ⎫
Widower ⎬ _Single_     { 1st, 2nd or 3rd marriage } _first_
Divorced ⎭

Name of Father _Russell L. Beck_

Maiden name of Mother _Florence L. Biskel_

Bride's name _Beverly Edith Barker_

Her age _21_

" color _White_

" occupation _School Teacher_

" Birthplace—City _Hillisburg_ State _Ind_

" Residence—Street No. _Scircleville_ City _Ind_

Single ⎫
Widow ⎬ _Single_     { 1st, 2nd or 3rd marriage } _first_
Divorced ⎭

Name of Father _Paul Scott Barker_

Maiden name of Mother _Edith Marine Cripe_

Date of this marriage _April 23 - 1944_

Place of this marriage _Scircleville, Ind_

Name and title of person Performing this marriage _Rev J. E. Douglas_

His address _Scircleville, Ind_

Witness { Name _Joseph A. Beck - Paula Barker_
{ Address _2923 Wrobel Ave. michigan City Ind. - Scircleville, Ind_

### Return this Report to County Clerk with License and Certificate

# Marriage Record for Board of Health
## To Be Returned by the Minister or Other Person Performing Ceremony

*Patrick B. Knox* and *Ellamae Scheffel*

Groom's name _Patrick B. Knox_

His age _27_

" color _white_

" occupation _Production Control R C A_

" Birthplace—City _Ayrshire_ State _Scotland_

" Residence—Street No. _1431 N. Delaware_ City _Indianapolis, Ind_

Single Widower Divorced } _single_ { 1st, 2nd or 3rd marriage } _first_

Name of Father _Peter Knox_

Maiden name of Mother _Jessie_

Bride's name _Ellamae Scheffel_

Her age _27_

" color _white_

" occupation _assistant Manager Tea Room_

" Birthplace—City _Ponca_ State _Nebraska_

" Residence—Street No. _1431 N. Delaware_ City _Indianapolis, Ind_

Single Widow Divorced } _single_ { 1st, 2nd or 3rd marriage } _first_

Name of Father _Harry Edward Scheffel_

Maiden name of Mother _Myrtle Virginia Patterson_

Date of this marriage _April 23, 1944_

Place of this marriage _Terre Haute Indiana_

Name and title of person Performing this marriage _James W Davis_

His address _916 N. 7th St._
_Terre Haute Indiana_

Witness { Name _Jack Cochrane - Mary Cochrane_
{ Address _317½ W. Clinton St. Napoleon Ohio_

## Return this Report to County Clerk with License and Certificate

## Marriage Record for Board of Health
### To Be Returned by the Minister or Other Person Performing Ceremony

James A. Wisehart and Mary Virginia Turner

Groom's name __James A. Wisehart__

His age __23__

" color __White__

" occupation __Army Air Corp__

" Birthplace—City __Union City__ State __Indiana__

" Residence—Street No. __502 E. Third__ City __Bloomington, Ind__

Single / Widower / Divorced } __Single__ { 1st, 2nd or 3rd marriage } __First__

Name of Father __Roy Parker Wisehart__

Maiden name of Mother __Mary Frederica Gustin__

Bride's name __Mary Virginia Turner__

Her age __20__

" color __White__

" occupation __Student__

" Birthplace—City __Bloomington__ State __Indiana__

" Residence—Street No. __502 E. Third__ City __Bloomington, Ind.__

Single / Widow / Divorced } __Single__ { 1st, 2nd or 3rd marriage } __First__

Name of Father __Norman Booth Turner__

Maiden name of Mother __Grace Elizabeth Davis__

Date of this marriage __April 23, 1944__

Place of this marriage __First Presbyterian Church, Bloomington Ind.__

Name and title of person Performing this marriage __Rev. Charles Brant__

His address __527 E. Kirkwood Ave.__
__Bloomington, Indiana__

Witness { Name __Mrs. J Lewis__
{ Address __Frankfort, Ind.__

### Return this Report to County Clerk with License and Certificate

12

# Marriage Record for Board of Health

## To Be Returned by the Minister or Other Person Performing Ceremony

*Jacob Alinkoff* and *Katie Bohard*

Groom's name _Jacob Alinkoff_

His age _55 years_

" color _Dark_

" occupation _Butcher_

" Birthplace—City _____ State _Russia_

" Residence—Street No. _717 S. Illinois_ City _Indianapolis 2nd_

Single / Widower / Divorced

1st, 2nd or 3rd marriage _2nd_

Name of Father _Summer_

Maiden name of Mother _Sittel_

Bride's name _Katie Bohard_

Her age _48_

" color _Dark_

" occupation _Poultry Business_

" Birthplace—City _Russia_ State _____

" Residence—Street No. _1226 Union_ City _Indianapolis Ind_

Single / Widow / Divorced

1st, 2nd or 3rd marriage _2nd_

Name of Father _Abraham_

Maiden name of Mother _Ida_

Date of this marriage _April 23 - 1944_

Place of this marriage _Chicago, Ill._

Name and title of person Performing this marriage _Rabbi H. Goldstein_

His address _3444 Douglas Blvd_

Witness Name _I. Siegel_
Address _1821 S. ____ ___

## Return this Report to County Clerk with License and Certificate

# Marriage Record for Board of Health
### To Be Returned by the Minister or Other Person Performing Ceremony

Joseph A. Hooper _____ and _____ Florence Sigler

Groom's name _____ Joseph A. Hooper

His age _____ 31

" color _____ white

" occupation _____ soldier

" Birthplace—City _____ Glouster, Ohio _____ State _____

" Residence—Street No. _____ Ft. Harrison _____ City _____ Indianapolis

Single / Widower / Divorced } _____ divorced _____ { 1st, 2nd or 3rd marriage } _____ second

Name of Father _____ John Hooper

Maiden name of Mother _____ Nellie Judson

Bride's name _____ Florence Sigler

Her age _____ 21

" color _____ white

" occupation _____ House-Keeper

" Birthplace—City _____ Boiling Springs _____ State _____ Penn.

" Residence—Street No. _____ R.D. 3 Roate Ave. N. City _____ Canton, Ohio

Single / Widow / Divorced } _____ single _____ { 1st, 2nd or 3rd marriage } _____ first

Name of Father _____ Albert Sigler

Maiden name of Mother _____ Mary Yost

Date of this marriage _____ April 22, 1944

Place of this marriage _____ Post Chapel, Ft. Harrison, Ind.

Name and title of person Performing this marriage _____ Chaplain Albert M B Snapp, A.U.S.

His address _____ Ft. Benjamin Harrison, Ind chapel

Witness { Name _____ Grend L Taylor - T/4 M M Elyestone

{ Address _____ 2520 E. Walnut, New Castle, Ind. Post

### Return this Report to County Clerk with License and Certificate

# Marriage Record for Board of Health
## To Be Returned by the Minister or Other Person Performing Ceremony

Charles Benedict and Carolyn Davis

Groom's name _Charles Benedict_

His age _21_

" color _White_

" occupation _In armed forces_

" Birthplace—City _Vevay_ State _Indiana_

" Residence—Street No. _____ City _____

Single / Widower / Divorced } _Single_    1st, 2nd or 3rd marriage } _1_

Name of Father _Dale_

Maiden name of Mother _Loretta Dittgen_

Bride's name _Carolyn Davis_

Her age _22_

" color _White_

" occupation _Librarian_

" Birthplace—City _Crawfordsville_ State _Indiana_

" Residence—Street No. _904 W. Main_ City _Crawfordsville In_

Single / Widow / Divorced } _Single_    1st, 2nd or 3rd marriage } _1st_

Name of Father _Warren Davis_

Maiden name of Mother _Mabel Todd Davis_

Date of this marriage _April 23 - 1944_

Place of this marriage _Crawfordsville - Ind_

Name and title of person Performing this marriage _Paul E. Millim_

His address _Crawfordsville - Ind -_

Witness { Name _Will Hays_
{ Address _204 W. Pike St_

## Return this Report to County Clerk with License and Certificate

# Marriage Record for Board of Health
### To Be Returned by the Minister or Other Person Performing Ceremony

Robert R. Keenan _and_ Bettie Harritt

Groom's name __Robert R. Keenan__

His age __21__

" color __White__

" occupation __U.S. Army__

" Birthplace—City __Denver__ State __Col__

" Residence—Street No. __U.S. Army__ City _____

Single / Widower / Divorced } __Single__ { 1st, 2nd or 3rd marriage } __1st__

Name of Father __Walter E.__

Maiden name of Mother __Pearl Rahn__

Bride's name __Betty Harritt__

Her age __21__

" color __White__

" occupation __Pay roll Clerk__

" Birthplace—City __Indianapolis__ State __Ind__

" Residence—Street No. __5310 E. 9th__ City __Indpls__

Single / Widow / Divorced } __Single__ { 1st, 2nd or 3rd marriage } __1st__

Name of Father __Frank M.__

Maiden name of Mother __Hazel Barrett__

Date of this marriage __April 23, 1944__

Place of this marriage __Indianapolis__

Name and title of person Performing this marriage __Rev. W. R. Montgomery, _____

His address __1516 N. Arley St. Indpls Ind.__

Witness { Name __Virginia Lee Worrell__ { Address __Clayton, Indiana__

### Return this Report to County Clerk with License and Certificate

# FILED

42 APR 25 1944

CLERK

# Marriage Record for Board of Health
### To Be Returned by the Minister or Other Person Performing Ceremony

_Philmer F. Real_ and _Grace Crowder_

Groom's name _Philmer F. Real_

His age _47_

" color _White_

" occupation _Time Study Engineer_

" Birthplace—City _Freelandville_ State _Indiana_

" Residence—Street No. _250 S. Meu_ City _Indpls Ind_

Single / Widower / Divorced } _Divorced_ { 1st, 2nd or 3rd marriage } _3rd_

Name of Father _Charles Real_

Maiden name of Mother _Cleo Stanley_

Bride's name _Grace Crowder_

Her age _37_

" color _White_

" occupation _Pantry Lady, Severin Hotel_

" Birthplace—City _Linton_ State _Indiana_

" Residence—Street No. _250 S. Meu_ City _Indpls Ind_

Single / Widow / Divorced } _widow_ { 1st, 2nd or 3rd marriage } _3rd_

Name of Father _John Randall_

Maiden name of Mother _Nancy Frances Hunter_

Date of this marriage _April 23 1944_

Place of this marriage _319 Fulton Street_

Name and title of person Performing this marriage _Rev. Stanley Stevens_

His address _1627 Asbury Street_

Witness { Name _Mr. & Mrs. Jesse McClure_
{ Address _319 Fulton St. Indpls Ind_

### Return this Report to County Clerk with License and Certificate

# Marriage Record for Board of Health
### To Be Returned by the Minister or Other Person Performing Ceremony

Raymond Edward Fields and Helen Marceil Aspy

Groom's name _Raymond Edward Fields_

His age _27_

" color _white_

" occupation _U. S. Army_

" Birthplace—City _Geneva_ State _Indiana_

" Residence—Street No. _____ City _Geneva_

Single Widower Divorced } _Single_ { 1st, 2nd or 3rd marriage } _first_

Name of Father _Perry C. Fields_

Maiden name of Mother _Marietta Stettler_

Bride's name _Helen Marceil Aspy_

Her age _22_

" color _white_

" occupation _____

" Birthplace—City _Geneva_ State _Indiana_

" Residence—Street No. _____ City _Geneva_

Single Widow Divorced } _Single_ { 1st, 2nd or 3rd marriage } _first_

Name of Father _Roy Aspy_

Maiden name of Mother _Mearl Burris_

Date of this marriage _April 23, 1944_

Place of this marriage _Geneva, Indiana_

Name and title of person Performing this marriage _Rev. Claude M. Favus_

His address _Geneva, Indiana_

Witness { Name _Ethel Confer, Ossian, Indiana_
{ Address _____

### Return this Report to County Clerk with License and Certificate

# Marriage Record for Board of Health

### To Be Returned by the Minister or Other Person Performing Ceremony

*David S. Powers* and *Nellie M. Dickmeyer*

Groom's name _David_

His age _70_

" color _White_

" occupation _Railroader_

" Birthplace—City _Ill_ State _Kansas_

" Residence—Street No. _2446 Holt Rd_ City _Indianapolis_

~~Single~~
Widower
~~Divorced~~ } _Widower_ { 1st, 2nd or 3rd marriage } _2nd_

Name of Father _Calvey Jackson_

Maiden name of Mother _Martha Meyer_

Bride's name _Nellie M. Dickmeyer_

Her age _63_

" color _White_

" occupation _Housewife_

" Birthplace—City _312 W. Linwood_ State _Indianapolis_

" Residence—Street No. _Hillymille_ City _Ill._

~~Single~~
~~Widow~~
Divorced } _Divorced_ { 1st, 2nd or 3rd marriage } _3.nd_

Name of Father _James W. Tibbets_

Maiden name of Mother _Ada Tyler_

Date of this marriage _Rev. E White_ _4/28/44_

Place of this marriage _Indianapolis_

Name and title of person
Performing this marriage _Rev. E White_

His address _627 Division St._
_Indianapolis Ind._

Witness { Name _Mrs Mary Eakin_
{ Address _553 Marion Ave City_

### Return this Report to County Clerk with License and Certificate

# Marriage Record for Board of Health
### To Be Returned by the Minister or Other Person Performing Ceremony

_____ and _____

Groom's name _Henry Lewis_

His age _28_

" color _Colored_

" occupation _Porter_

" Birthplace—City _Joshua_ , _Tenn_ State _Tenn_

" Residence—Street No. _1729 Bellmont_ City _Nashville_

Single
Widower } _Widower_ { 1st, 2nd or 3rd marriage } _2 nd_
Divorced

Name of Father _Anthony Lewis_

Maiden name of Mother _Rosa Robinson_

═══════════════════════════════════════════

Bride's name _Melvina Mosely_

Her age _22_

" color _C_

" occupation _____

" Birthplace—City _Louisville_ State _Ky_

" Residence—Street No. _____ City _____

Single
Widow } _Single_ { 1st, 2nd or 3rd marriage } _____
Divorced

Name of Father _W_

Maiden name of Mother _____

═══════════════════════════════════════════

Date of this marriage _____

Place of this marriage _____

Name and title of person
Performing this marriage _Rev. Barr_

His address _____

Witness { Name _____
          { Address _1729_

## Return this Report to County Clerk with License and Certificate

# Marriage Record for Board of Health

To Be Returned by the Minister or Other Person Performing Ceremony

_Jones_ and _Roberts_

Groom's name _Alonzo Jones_

His age _43 yrs_

" color _Colored_

" occupation _defense work_

" Birthplace—City _Edwards_ State _Miss_

" Residence—Street No. _2051 Kenwood_ City _Indpls_

Single / Widower / Divorced _Widower_ { 1st, 2nd or 3rd marriage } _2nd_

Name of Father _Hartigee Jones_

Maiden name of Mother _Ella Griggs_

Bride's name _Blossom Mae Roberts_

Her age _41_

" color _Colored_

" occupation _Housewife_

" Birthplace—City _Bloomington_ State _Ind_

" Residence—Street No. _____ City _____

Single / Widow / Divorced _Divorced_ { 1st, 2nd or 3rd marriage } _2nd_

Name of Father _Sam Brewer_

Maiden name of Mother _Ola Matthews_

Date of this marriage _April 23rd 1944_

Place of this marriage _Indianapolis Ind_

Name and title of person Performing this marriage _Rev C Henry Bell_

His address _365 W. 28th Indianapolis Ind_

Witness { Name _Catherine Charleston_ Address _2412 N. Capitol_

**Return this Report to County Clerk with License and Certificate**

# Marriage Record for Board of Health

## To Be Returned by the Minister or Other Person Performing Ceremony

*Alva Franklin Motto* and *Betty Louise Dunn*

Groom's name _Alva Franklin Motto_

His age _37_

" color _White_

" occupation _Laborer_

" Birthplace—City _Clermont_ State _Ind._

" Residence—Street No. _232 n. Miley_ City _Indpls, Ind._

Single Widower Divorced } _Single_ { 1st, 2nd or 3rd marriage } _1st_

Name of Father _Elzia Motto_

Maiden name of Mother _Minnie Starkey_

Bride's name _Betty Louise Dunn_

Her age _18_

" color _White_

" occupation _House wife_

" Birthplace—City _Paris_ State _Illinois_

" Residence—Street No. _2434 n. Miley_ City _Indianapolis_

Single Widow Divorced } _Single_ { 1st, 2nd or 3rd marriage } _1st_

Name of Father _Walter Clinton Dunn_

Maiden name of Mother _Fannie Meeks_

Date of this marriage _April 23rd 1944_

Place of this marriage _West Side Mission 1520 W. Ohio_

Name and title of person Performing this marriage _Jacob Friesen PASTOR_

His address _242 E. Pleasant Run (West Side Mission) Indianapolis_

Witness { Name _Mrs Goldia M Heininger_  Address _232 n. Miley_

## Return this Report to County Clerk with License and Certificate

# Marriage Record for Board of Health

### To Be Returned by the Minister or Other Person Performing Ceremony

John S. Visher _and_ Peggy Anne Stein

Groom's name _John S. Visher_

His age _23_

" color _white_

" occupation _medical student_

" Birthplace—City _Waukesha_ State _Wisconsin_

" Residence—Street No. _____ City _____

Single / Widower / Divorced } _single_ {1st, 2nd or 3rd marriage} _1st_

Name of Father _John W. Visher_

Maiden name of Mother _Marguerite Miller_

Bride's name _Peggy Anne Stein_

Her age _20_

" color _white_

" occupation _student_

" Birthplace—City _Indianapolis_ State _Indiana_

" Residence—Street No. _353 Burgess Ave._ City _Indianapolis_

Single / Widow / Divorced } _single_ {1st, 2nd or 3rd marriage} _1st_

Name of Father _Schley Dewey Stein_

Maiden name of Mother _Esther Gayle Engstrom_

Date of this marriage _April 23 1944_

Place of this marriage _Sweeney Chapel, Butler University, Indpls Ind._

Name and title of person Performing this marriage _Dr. Frank C. Beck_

His address _Indiana University Bloomington, Indiana_

Witness { Name _Dr John W. Visher_ Address _1066 Madison Ave, Evansville, Ind._

### Return this Report to County Clerk with License and Certificate

12

# Marriage Record for Board of Health
## To Be Returned by the Minister or Other Person Performing Ceremony

*James Lane Borders* and *Betty Jeannette Burckes*

Groom's name _James Lane Borders_

His age _22_

" color _white_

" occupation _Physician_

" Birthplace—City _Jacksonville_ State _Florida_

" Residence—Street No. _3239 Illinois_ City _Indianapolis Ind_

Single / Widower / Divorced } _single_ { 1st, 2nd or 3rd marriage } _first_

Name of Father _James Arnold Borders_

Maiden name of Mother _Edith Lane_

Bride's name _Betty Jeannette Burckes_

Her age _23_

" color _white_

" occupation _Teacher_

" Birthplace—City _Elyria_ State _Ohio_

" Residence—Street No. _6133 Park Ave_ City _Indianapolis_

Single / Widow / Divorced } _single_ { 1st, 2nd or 3rd marriage } _first_

Name of Father _Frederick Burckes_

Maiden name of Mother _Vivian Watts_

Date of this marriage _April 23rd, 1944_

Place of this marriage _Indianapolis, Indiana_

Name and title of person Performing this marriage _S. Grundy Fisher_

His address _2101 Park Ave, Indianapolis, Ind_

Witness { Name _Lewis N. Walker_
{ Address _3104 W. Jackson St., Indpls._

## Return this Report to County Clerk with License and Certificate

12

# Marriage Record for Board of Health

### To Be Returned by the Minister or Other Person Performing Ceremony

_Robert Earl Moses_ and _Betty Jo Dyar_

Groom's name _Robert Earl Moses_

His age _21_

" color _White_

" occupation _Army - Medical Student_

" Birthplace—City _Switz City_ State _Ind._

" Residence—Street No. _462 N. Meridian_ City _Indianapolis, Ind._

Single / Widower / Divorced } _Single_ { 1st, 2nd or 3rd marriage } _1st_

Name of Father _Dr. George E. Moses_

Maiden name of Mother _Nelle Meridith Switz_

Bride's name _Betty Jo Dyar_

Her age _21_

" color _White_

" occupation _Nurse_

" Birthplace—City _Worthington_ State _Ind._

" Residence—Street No. _City Hospital_ City _Indianapolis, Ind._

Single / Widow / Divorced } _Single_ { 1st, 2nd or 3rd marriage } _1st_

Name of Father _Jessie Ray Dyar_

Maiden name of Mother _Amy Hines_

Date of this marriage _4-23-44_ _April 23, 1944_

Place of this marriage _Worthington, Indiana_

Name and title of person Performing this marriage _P. E. Roll - Minister_

His address _Worthington, Ind._

Witness { Name _Virginia Jean Ploda_ _F. I. Hayne_
{ Address _George E. Moss m.d._ _Worthington_

### Return this Report to County Clerk with License and Certificate

# Marriage Record for Board of Health
### To Be Returned by the Minister or Other Person Performing Ceremony

James Baker Jr. and Marjorie Jean Norman

Groom's name James Baker Jr.

His age 20 years

" color white

" occupation U. S. Army

" Birthplace—City Morristown State Indiana

" Residence—Street No. Fresno City California

Single Widower Divorced } Yes.      { 1st, 2nd or 3rd marriage } 1st.

Name of Father Rev. James M. Baker

Maiden name of Mother Caroline S. Gipe

Bride's name Marjorie Jean Norman

Her age 20 years

" color white

" occupation Nurse

" Birthplace—City Marion State Indiana

" Residence—Street No. 1812 N. Capitol City Indianapolis Ind.

Single Widow Divorced } Yes.      { 1st, 2nd or 3rd marriage } 1st.

Name of Father Nolan C. Norman

Maiden name of Mother Leora Phillips

Date of this marriage April 23 1944

Place of this marriage 10 5 S. S. St. Marion Ind.

Name and title of person Performing this marriage Rev. James M. Baker

His address Fowlerton, Indiana

Witness { Name Mrs. Wm E. Whitsell   Robert Webster
{ Address 1812 No. Capitol Ave.   Fowlerton. Indiana
    Indianapolis 7, Ind.

### Return this Report to County Clerk with License and Certificate

# Marriage Record for Board of Health

To Be Returned by the Minister or Other Person Performing Ceremony

*Harry Leon Bixler* and *Mary Alice Burns*

Groom's name *Harry Leon Bixler*

His age *47*

" color *White*

" occupation *Engineer*

" Birthplace—City *Indianapolis* State *Indiana*

" Residence—Street No. *Ansonia* City *Ohio*

Single / Widower / Divorced } *Widower* { 1st, 2nd or 3rd marriage } *2nd*

Name of Father *William H. Bixler*

Maiden name of Mother *Anna Radcliff*

Bride's name *Mary Alice Burns*

Her age *29*

" color *White*

" occupation *Leisure Worker*

" Birthplace—City *Union City* State *Ohio*

" Residence—Street No. City *Union City, O*

Single / Widow / Divorced } *Divorced* { 1st, 2nd or 3rd marriage } *2nd*

Name of Father *Samuel K. Myers*

Maiden name of Mother *Susan Stable*

Date of this marriage *April 24, 1944*

Place of this marriage *Indianapolis, Ind.*

Name and title of person Performing this marriage *Evart Lane Justice of Peace*

His address *152½ East Court St.*

Witness { Name *Mary J. Long* Address *3740 College Ave* }

## Return this Report to County Clerk with License and Certificate

# Marriage Record for Board of Health
### To Be Returned by the Minister or Other Person Performing Ceremony

*Henry J. Galloway* and *Thurza Louise Bright*

Groom's name _Henry J. Galloway_

His age _24_

" color _white_

" occupation _Soldier_

" Birthplace—City _Hartford_ State _Alabama_

" Residence—Street No. _Fort Harrison_ City _Indiana_

Single Widower Divorced } _Single_ { 1st, 2nd or 3rd marriage } _1st_

Name of Father _Robert Isaac Galloway_

Maiden name of Mother _Lucille Shepheard_

Bride's name _Thurza Louise Bright_

Her age _22_

" color _white_

" occupation _Waitress_

" Birthplace—City _Hickory_ State _North Carolina_

" Residence—Street No. _1128 N Illinois_ City _Indpls_

Single Widow Divorced } _Single_ { 1st, 2nd or 3rd marriage } _1st_

Name of Father _Carl C Bright_

Maiden name of Mother _Beatrice Kogan_

Date of this marriage _April 24 - 44_

Place of this marriage _Indpls. Ind._

Name and title of person Performing this marriage _Gerald T Kane, Justice of Peace_

His address _153½ E Court_

Witness { Name _Mary J Kane_

Address _3741 College Ave._

### Return this Report to County Clerk with License and Certificate

# Marriage Record for Board of Health

## To Be Returned by the Minister or Other Person Performing Ceremony

Kenneth Plunkett Jr. and Murline Irene Wooten

Groom's name _Emmett Kenneth Plunkett Jr._

His age _57_

" color _white_

" occupation _Druggist_

" Birthplace—City _Forest_ State _Indiana_

" Residence—Street No. _1325 N. Randel_ City _Indpls._

Single Widower Divorced } _Divorced_  { 1st, 2nd or 3rd marriage } _2nd_

Name of Father _John William Plunkett_

Maiden name of Mother _Rebecca Jane Nutter_

Bride's name _Murline Irene Wooten_

Her age _43_

" color _white_

" occupation _Housekeeper_

" Birthplace—City _Shelby County_ State _Indiana_

" Residence—Street No. _3916 E. 18th_ City _Indpls._

Single Widow Divorced } _Divorced_  { 1st, 2nd or 3rd marriage } _2nd_

Name of Father _Jessie Hayes Dye_

Maiden name of Mother _Lola Belle Plummer_

Date of this marriage _April 24-44_

Place of this marriage _Franklin Ind._

Name and title of person Performing this marriage _Gilbert King Minister of Peace_

His address _1502 East Court_

Witness { Name _Mary Jane_ { Address _3741 College Ave._

## Return this Report to County Clerk with License and Certificate

# Marriage Record for Board of Health

### To Be Returned by the Minister or Other Person Performing Ceremony

Will Smith and Etheridge Gilbert

Groom's name _Will Smith_

His age _21_

" color _Colored_

" occupation _Laborer_

" Birthplace—City _Elkmond_ State _Alabama_

" Residence—Street No. _1525 Cornell_ City _Indianapolis_

Single / Widower / Divorced _Single_ { 1st, 2nd or 3rd marriage } _1st_

Name of Father _Lovett Smith_

Maiden name of Mother _Addie Brown_

Bride's name _Etheridge Gilbert_

Her age _18_

" color _Colored_

" occupation _None_

" Birthplace—City _Gile Co_ State _Tennessee_

" Residence—Street No. _2819 Hovey_ City _Indianapolis_

Single / Widow / Divorced _Single_ { 1st, 2nd or 3rd marriage } _1st_

Name of Father _Philips Gilbert_

Maiden name of Mother _Lizzie Gilbert_

Date of this marriage _April 24, 1944_

Place of this marriage _Indianapolis Ind_

Name and title of person Performing this marriage _Ernest Lane Justice of Peace_

His address _152½ East Court St_

Witness { Name _Mor J Lane_ Address _3740 College Ave_

### Return this Report to County Clerk with License and Certificate

# Marriage Record for Board of Health

To Be Returned by the Minister or Other Person Performing Ceremony

*PAUL WILLIAMS* and *GRACE L THORPE*

Groom's name ___ PAUL WILLIAMS

His age ___ 34 YRS OLD

" color ___ NEGRO

" occupation ___ ENGINEER (AERO)

" Birthplace—City ___ YOUNGSTOWN State OHIO

" Residence—Street No. 2314 LAKEVIEW City DAYTON OHIO

Single ✗ / Widower / Divorced } SINGLE    1st, 2nd or 3rd marriage } _____

Name of Father ___ CHARLES JAMES WILLIAMS

Maiden name of Mother ___ ALYCE E GASKEEN WILLIAMS

Bride's name ___ Grace L. Thorpe

Her age ___ 24

" color ___ Negro

" occupation ___ Clerk

" Birthplace—City ___ Custer State Oua

" Residence—Street No. 2240 Lakeview City Dayton, O.

Single / Widow / Divorced } Single    1st, 2nd or 3rd marriage } 1st

Name of Father ___ James W. Thorpe

Maiden name of Mother ___ Grace L. Feldham

Date of this marriage ___ April 24, 1944

Place of this marriage ___ Indianapolis, Ind

Name and title of person Performing this marriage ___ S.S. Thomas, minister

His address ___ 702 L. Illinois

Witness { Name ___ Bettie Wickliffe
        { Address ___ 2336 Indianapolis Ave

## Return this Report to County Clerk with License and Certificate

12

# Marriage Record for Board of Health
## To Be Returned by the Minister or Other Person Performing Ceremony

Irene Smith Holmes and Leland James Terrell

Groom's name _Leland James Terrell_

His age _25_

" color _White_

" occupation _U.S. Army_

" Birthplace—City _Crawfordsville_ State _Indiana_

" Residence—Street No. _1815 15th St_ City _Bedford, Indiana_

Single
Widower   } _since_   { 1st, 2nd or 3rd   } _1st_
Divorced          marriage

Name of Father _Enoch E. Terrell_

Maiden name of Mother _Nella Ruth Fields_

Bride's name _Irene Smith Holmes_

Her age _25_

" color _White_

" occupation _Stenographer_

" Birthplace—City _Glasgow_ State _Kentucky_

" Residence—Street No. _429 N. Chester_ City _Indianapolis, Ind._

Single
Widow   } _single_   { 1st, 2nd or 3rd   } _1st_
Divorced          marriage

Name of Father _Ed. Holmes_

Maiden name of Mother _Maud C. _____

Date of this marriage _April 24, 1944_

Place of this marriage _429 N. Chester, Indianapolis, Ind._

Name and title of person
Performing this marriage _Earl West, minister, Irvington Church of Christ_

His address _34 N. _____ Ave._

Witness { Name _____
         { Address _2332 ___ st., Indpls, Ind._

## Return this Report to County Clerk with License and Certificate

FILED
42 APR 25 1944

CLERK

# Marriage Record for Board of Health

### To Be Returned by the Minister or Other Person Performing Ceremony

Herbert F. Waldhier _____ and Mary M. Haselmire

Groom's name _____ Herbert F. Waldhier

His age _____ 21

" color _____ White

" occupation _____ Student of Dentistry

" Birthplace—City _____ New Boston _____ State _____ Indiana

" Residence—Street No. _____ — _____ City _____ New Boston, P.O. Troy

Single / Widower / Divorced } _____ Single _____ { 1st, 2nd or 3rd marriage } _____ First

Name of Father _____ Edward Waldhier

Maiden name of Mother _____ Frances Hildenbrand

Bride's name _____ Mary Margaret Haselmire

Her age _____ 19

" color _____ White

" occupation _____ Nurse

" Birthplace—City _____ Union City _____ State _____ Indiana

" Residence—Street No. _____ 508 N. High St. _____ City _____ Union City

Single / Widow / Divorced } _____ Single _____ { 1st, 2nd or 3rd marriage } _____ First

Name of Father _____ John J. Haselmire

Maiden name of Mother _____ Margaret Stack

Date of this marriage _____ April 24, 1944

Place of this marriage _____ New Boston, Indiana

Name and title of person Performing this marriage _____ Rev. Bernard Beck, O.S.B
Pastor - St. John Chrysostom Cath. Ch.

His address _____ St. Meinrad Abbey
St. Meinrad, Indiana

Witness { Name _____ John W. Hohe, 972 Oak St. Huntington, Ind.
{ Address _____ Thomas Waldhier, New Boston, P.O. Troy, Ind.

### Return this Report to County Clerk with License and Certificate

12

# Marriage Record for Board of Health
## To Be Returned by the Minister or Other Person Performing Ceremony

Jerman J. Weaver and Virginia D. Lynch

Groom's name _Jerman J. Weaver_

His age _23_

" color _White_

" occupation _Soldier_

" Birthplace—City _Jefferson_ State _North Carolina_

" Residence—Street No. _Ft. Harrison_ City _Indianapolis_

Single / Widower / Divorced } _Single_ { 1st, 2nd or 3rd marriage } _first_

Name of Father _Robert L. Weaver_

Maiden name of Mother _Mallie Stamper_

Bride's name _Virginia D. Lynch_

Her age _20_

" color _White_

" occupation _Typist_

" Birthplace—City _Roncevert_ State _West Virginia_

" Residence—Street No. _902 Pocahontas_ City _Roncevert_

Single / Widow / Divorced } _Divorced_ { 1st, 2nd or 3rd marriage } _second_

Name of Father _Charles_

Maiden name of Mother _Claudie Givens_

Date of this marriage _April 24, 1944_

Place of this marriage _Ft. Ben. Harrison_

Name and title of person Performing this marriage _Francis J. Harkum, Chaplain_

His address _Ft. Benjamin Harrison Indianapolis_

Witness { Name _Sgt. John Shelleme_ Address _Ft. Ben. Harrison_

## Return this Report to County Clerk with License and Certificate

# Marriage Record for Board of Health

### To Be Returned by the Minister or Other Person Performing Ceremony

_Robert G. Claeys_ and _Mary Wanda Mitchell_

Groom's name _Robert George Claeys_

His age _22_

" color _white_

" occupation _U.S. Army_

" Birthplace—City _Mishawaka_ State _Indiana_

" Residence—Street No. _6149 N. Alabama_ City _Indianapolis, Ind._

Single / Widower / Divorced } _single_ { 1st, 2nd or 3rd marriage } _first_

Name of Father _Raymond Claeys_

Maiden name of Mother _Caroline Probst_

Bride's name _Mary Wanda Mitchell_

Her age _23_

" color _white_

" occupation _student_

" Birthplace—City _Vincennes_ State _Indiana_

" Residence—Street No. _423 S. Woodlawn_ City _Bloomington, Ind._

Single / Widow / Divorced } _single_ { 1st, 2nd or 3rd marriage } _first_

Name of Father _John H. Mitchell_

Maiden name of Mother _Mildred Briscoe_

Date of this marriage _April 27 1944_

Place of this marriage _Bloomington, Ind._

Name and title of person Performing this marriage _Rev. Thomas J. Kilfoil_

His address _213 S. ____ Bloomington, Ind._

Witness { Name _June Sanders — Richard Claeys_ Address _Shoals, Ind. — Mishawaka, Ind._

### Return this Report to County Clerk with License and Certificate

12

# Marriage Record for Board of Health
## To Be Returned by the Minister or Other Person Performing Ceremony

Oren C. Sowers and Eva Belle Keen

Groom's name _Oren C. Sowers_

His age _26_

" color _White_

" occupation _U S Army_

" Birthplace—City _Castleton_ State _Indiana_

" Residence—Street No. _3525 Kenwood_ City _Indianapolis, Indiana_

Single / Widower / Divorced } _Single_   1st, 2nd or 3rd marriage } _1st_

Name of Father _Truman Sowers_

Maiden name of Mother _Daisy Meldrum_

Bride's name _Eva Belle Keen_

Her age _19_

" color _White_

" occupation _—_

" Birthplace—City _Harpsville_ State _Tenn._

" Residence—Street No. _Sunnyside Sanatorium_ City _Indianapolis, Ind_

Single / Widow / Divorced } _Single_   1st, 2nd or 3rd marriage } _1st_

Name of Father _Alonzo M Keen_

Maiden name of Mother _Ollie Mae Gregory_

Date of this marriage _April 24, 1944_

Place of this marriage _Sunnyside Sanatorium_

Name and title of person Performing this marriage _Rev John Reidy, Catholic Priest_

His address _Ladywood School, Indianapolis, Indiana_

Witness { Name _George Sears_
{ Address _Sunnyside Sanatorium_

## Return this Report to County Clerk with License and Certificate

# Marriage Record for Board of Health

### To Be Returned by the Minister or Other Person Performing Ceremony

William James Boroman and Laura Neal

Groom's name _William James Boroman_

His age _62_

" color _Col._

" occupation _Pastor_

" Birthplace—City _Indianapolis_ State _Ind._

" Residence—Street No _1418 Mills St._ City _____

Single / Widower / Divorced } _Divorced_     1st, 2nd or 3rd marriage } _2nd_

Name of Father _John Boroman_

Maiden name of Mother _Ankn_

Bride's name _Laura Neal_

Her age _54_

" color _Col_

" occupation _Maid_

" Birthplace—City _Gallatin_ State _Tenn_

" Residence—Street No _1418 Mills St_ City _Ind_

Single / Widow / Divorced } _Divorced_     1st, 2nd or 3rd marriage } _2nd._

Name of Father _Edward Barr_

Maiden name of Mother _Petsie Paster._

Date of this marriage _April 24th 1944_

Place of this marriage _Indianapolis, Indiana_

Name and title of person Performing this marriage _Plummer D. Jacobs - Minister_

His address _941 W. 25th Street_

_Indianapolis, Indiana._

Witness { Name _____ Address _Celester J. Barr_ _1418 Mill St_

### Return this Report to County Clerk with License and Certificate

12

# Marriage Record for Board of Health
## To Be Returned by the Minister or Other Person Performing Ceremony

Marcell L Robinson _____ and _____ Lucille Tyler

Groom's name _____ Marcell L Robinson

His age _____ 23

" color _____ C

" occupation _____ Soldier

" Birthplace—City _____ Clanubia _____ State _____ Ala.

" Residence—Street No. _____ City _____ Camp Ellis Ill

Single Widower Divorced } _____ Single _____ 1st, 2nd or 3rd marriage } _____ First

Name of Father _____ Irvin Robinson

Maiden name of Mother _____ Nonie Leath

Bride's name _____ Lucille Tyler

Her age _____ 22

" color _____ C

" occupation _____ None

" Birthplace—City _____ Indianapolis _____ State _____ Indiana

" Residence—Street No. _____ 1531 Northdale Ave _____ City _____ Indianapolis Ind.

Single Widow Divorced } _____ Single _____ 1st, 2nd or 3rd marriage } _____ Second

Name of Father _____ Aaron Tyler

Maiden name of Mother _____ Willie Mae Kemp

Date of this marriage _____ April 25, 1944

Place of this marriage _____ Indianapolis, Indiana.

Name and title of person Performing this marriage _____ S. S. Thomas, Minister

His address _____ 702 N. Illinois St
_____ Indianapolis, Indiana.

Witness { Name _____ Rosa L. Thomas.
{ Address _____ 702 N. Illinois St

## Return this Report to County Clerk with License and Certificate

FILED

42 APR 25 1944

*Jno Kean*
CLERK

# Marriage Record for Board of Health

### To Be Returned by the Minister or Other Person Performing Ceremony

*Ivory A. Ferguson* and *Marion Oppenlander*

Groom's name *Ivory A. Ferguson*

His age *56*

" color *white*

" occupation *Jewler*

" Birthplace—City *New Bethel* State *Penn.*

" Residence—Street No. *90 Dodge St.* City *Buffalo, New York*

Single Widower Divorced } *Widower* { 1st, 2nd or 3rd marriage *3rd*

Name of Father *John Elmer Ferguson*

Maiden name of Mother *Sadie Jay Seanor*

Bride's name *Marion Oppenlander*

Her age *31*

" color *white*

" occupation *Telephone Operator*

" Birthplace—City *Buffalo* State *New York*

" Residence—Street No. *112 Winslow* City *Buffalo, New York*

Single Widow Divorced } *Single* { 1st, 2nd or 3rd marriage *1st*

Name of Father *Herman Oppenlander*

Maiden name of Mother *Mary Hafner*

Date of this marriage *April 25-44*

Place of this marriage *Indianapolis, Indiana*

Name and title of person Performing this marriage *Ernest Dane Leslie of there*

His address *1525 E East St*

Witness { Name *Herman Dahl*
{ Address *1145 W 37th St*

### Return this Report to County Clerk with License and Certificate

# Marriage Record for Board of Health

### To Be Returned by the Minister or Other Person Performing Ceremony

*Reeves* — and — *Elswick*

Groom's name _Hobert Lee Reeves_

His age _18_

" color _White_

" occupation _Army_

" Birthplace—City _Chilton_ State _Kentucky_

" Residence—Street No. _1926 S. Belmont_ City _Indpls Ind._

Single / Widower / Divorced _Single_    1st, 2nd or 3rd marriage _First_

Name of Father _Omar Reeves_

Maiden name of Mother _Dessie Taylor_

Bride's name _Hazel L. Elswick_

Her age _18_

" color _White_

" occupation _Clerk Std mkt._

" Birthplace—City _Raven_ State _Virginia_

" Residence—Street No. _2306 Barrett_ City _Indpls Ind_

Single / Widow / Divorced _Single_    1st, 2nd or 3rd marriage _First_

Name of Father _James Walter Elswick_

Maiden name of Mother _Lily Harris_

Date of this marriage _April 25 1944_

Place of this marriage _M.B. Parsonage 1509 S Belmont Indpls_

Name and title of person Performing this marriage _I. C. Alderton – Minister_

His address _1509 S. Belmont Ave, Indpls, Indiana._

Witness { Name _Leota H. Alderton_
{ Address _1509 S. Belmont Ave, Indpls, Ind_

## Return this Report to County Clerk with License and Certificate.

13

# Marriage Record for Board of Health

### To Be Returned by the Minister or Other Person Performing Ceremony

*Harry Messersmith* and *Kathryn Parrish*

Groom's name _Harry A. Messersmith, Sr._

His age _62_

" color _White_

" occupation _Farmer_

" Birthplace—City _Southport_ State _Indiana_

" Residence—Street No. _R.R. 13_ City _Indpls., Ind_

Single / Widower / Divorced } _Widower_ { 1st, 2nd or 3rd marriage } _2nd_

Name of Father _John Messersmith_

Maiden name of Mother _Margaret Hankins_

Bride's name _Kathryn Parrish_

Her age _56_

" color _White_

" occupation _____

" Birthplace—City _Millstadt_ State _Illinois_

" Residence—Street No. _Indianapolis_ City _Indiana_

Single / Widow / Divorced } _Widow_ { 1st, 2nd or 3rd marriage } _2nd_

Name of Father _John Christian Fauth_

Maiden name of Mother _Elizabeth Leppert_

Date of this marriage _April 25, 1944_

Place of this marriage _Castleton, Indiana_

Name and title of person Performing this marriage _Rev. Charles Tyler_

His address _P. O. Box 6_ _Castleton, Ind_

Witness { Name _Margaret C. Alyea_ Address _Castleton, Indiana_

## Return this Report to County Clerk with License and Certificate

12

# Marriage Record for Board of Health
## To Be Returned by the Minister or Other Person Performing Ceremony

Walter N. Collins _____ and Frances M. Teepe

Groom's name _____ Walter N. Collins

His age _____ 22

" color _____ White

" occupation _____ U.S. Navy

" Birthplace—City _____ Jeffersonville _____ State _____ Indiana

" Residence—Street No. _____ 1349 Barth _____ City _____ Indianapolis

Single / Widower / Divorced } single { 1st, 2nd or 3rd marriage } 1st

Name of Father _____ James C. Collins

Maiden name of Mother _____ Margaret Dobson

Bride's name _____ Frances M. Teepe

Her age _____ 18

" color _____ White

" occupation _____ uncomp Coupl

" Birthplace—City _____ Indianapolis _____ State _____ Indiana

" Residence—Street No. _____ 1629 Harlan _____ City _____ Indianapolis

Single / Widow / Divorced } single { 1st, 2nd or 3rd marriage } 1st

Name of Father _____ William C. Teepe

Maiden name of Mother _____ Irene D. Lockwood

Date of this marriage _____ April 25, 1944

Place of this marriage _____ Indianapolis, Indiana

Name and title of person Performing this marriage _____ Smith Tujentok

His address _____ 902 Sanders, Indianapolis

Witness { Name _____ Ora Baxter

Address _____ 1605 Asbury, Indianapolis

## Return this Report to County Clerk with License and Certificate

12

# Marriage Record for Board of Health
## To Be Returned by the Minister or Other Person Performing Ceremony

Paul Wayne Plymate and Virginia Elizabeth Rand

Groom's name _____ Paul Wayne Plymate

His age _____ 21

" color _____ White

" occupation _____ Soldier

" Birthplace—City _____ Indianapolis _____ State _____ Indiana

" Residence—Street No. 101 S. 9th Ave City Beech Grove, Ind.

Single Widower Divorced } Single    { 1st, 2nd or 3rd marriage } 1st

Name of Father _____ Carold Arthur Plymate

Maiden name of Mother _____ Emma Lena Shaw

Bride's name _____ Virginia Elizabeth Rand

Her age _____ 20

" color _____ White

" occupation _____ Typist

" Birthplace—City _____ Lawrenceburg _____ State _____ Indiana

" Residence—Street No. 90 So. 4th Ave City Beech Grove

Single Widow Divorced } Single    { 1st, 2nd or 3rd marriage } 1st

Name of Father _____ Ralph LeRoy Rand

Maiden name of Mother _____ Grace Florence Kennedy

Date of this marriage _____ April 25, 1944

Place of this marriage _____ Princeton, Indiana

Name and title of person Performing this marriage _____

His address _____

Witness { Name _____ Mrs. Sylvia Carlson
         { Address _____ 417 E. Pinkney Street

## Return this Report to County Clerk with License and Certificate

# Marriage Record for Board of Health
### To Be Returned by the Minister or Other Person Performing Ceremony

_Scott E. Henry_ and _Hannah G. Dunne_

Groom's name _Scott E. Henry_

His age _41_

" color _White_

" occupation _Tool Maker_

" Birthplace—City _Athens County_ State _Indiana_

" Residence—Street No. _1602 Broadway_ City _Indpls._

Single / Widower / Divorced } _Divorced_ { 1st, 2nd or 3rd marriage } _3rd_

Name of Father _Clarence L. Henry_

Maiden name of Mother _Nancy Jane Board_

Bride's name _Hannah G. Dunne_

Her age _33_

" color _white_

" occupation _none_

" Birthplace—City _Indpls_ State _Ind._

" Residence—Street No. _160 Carrollton_ City _Indpls._

Single / Widow / Divorced } _Single_ { 1st, 2nd or 3rd marriage } _1st_

Name of Father _Titus Patrick Dunne_

Maiden name of Mother _Mary Theresa Twohig_

Date of this marriage _April 25-44_

Place of this marriage _Indpls Ind_

Name and title of person Performing this marriage _John H. Kane, Justice of Peace_

His address _1502 E. Court_

Witness { Name _Mary J. Kane_

Address _3741 College Ave._

### Return this Report to County Clerk with License and Certificate

# Marriage Record for Board of Health
### To Be Returned by the Minister or Other Person Performing Ceremony

Emil Dale Wilson and Mary Ellen Brummett

Groom's name _Emil Dale Wilson_

His age _23_

" color _White_

" occupation _Railroader_

" Birthplace—City _Olney_ State _Ill_

" Residence—Street No. _2402 Sherman_ City _Indianapolis In_

Single Widower Divorced } _Single_   { 1st, 2nd or 3rd marriage } _1st_

Name of Father _Uriah Jeff Wilson_

Maiden name of Mother _Clara Edith Hannah_

---

Bride's name _Mary Ellen Brummett_

Her age _23_

" color _White_

" occupation _House Keeper_

" Birthplace—City _____ State _____

" Residence—Street No. _Scotland_ City _Ind_

Single Widow Divorced } _Widow_   { 1st, 2nd or 3rd marriage } _2nd_

Name of Father _Ballie Hill_

Maiden name of Mother _Lewis Shane_

---

Date of this marriage _April 25 — 1944_

Place of this marriage _2414 Station Street Indianapolis Ind_

Name and title of person Performing this marriage _M. E. Reynolds minister_

His address _2414 Station Street Indianapolis Indiana_

Witness { Name _Frank C Dabney_
Address _3513 E 25 st Indianapolis Ind_

### Return this Report to County Clerk with License and Certificate

# Marriage Record for Board of Health
## To Be Returned by the Minister or Other Person Performing Ceremony

Joseph Sales _ and _ Mary M. Finch

Groom's name _ Joseph Sales

His age _ 24 yrs old

" color _ C

" occupation _ Soldier

" Birthplace—City _ Moundsville _ State _ Ala.

" Residence—Street No. _ Soldiers Home _ City _ Dayton, Ohio

Single Widower Divorced } _ Single _ { 1st, 2nd or 3rd marriage } _ first

Name of Father _ Sam Sales

Maiden name of Mother _ Sarah Sanders

Bride's name _ Mary M. Finch

Her age _ 20 yrs old

" color _ C

" occupation _ Laundress

" Birthplace—City _ Tuscaloosa _ State _ Ala.

" Residence—Street No. 2357-N-Rural City _ Indianapolis, Ind.

Single Widow Divorced } _ Single _ { 1st, 2nd or 3rd marriage } _ first

Name of Father _ Zeak Finch

Maiden name of Mother _ Bessie Richardson

Date of this marriage _ April 25, 1944

Place of this marriage _ Indianapolis

Name and title of person Performing this marriage _ L. S. Thomas, Minister

His address _ 702-S-Illinois Street _ Indianapolis, Ind.

Witness { Name _ Thelma Howell _ Address 2357-N-Rural St.

## Return this Report to County Clerk with License and Certificate

## Marriage Record for Board of Health
### To Be Returned by the Minister or Other Person Performing Ceremony

_____ and _____

Groom's name _Wayne J. Jones_

His age _22_

" color _White_

" occupation _Soldier_

" Birthplace—City _Indianapolis_ State _Ind_

" Residence—Street No. _2240 Hoyt_ City _Indpls_

Single Widower Divorced } _Single_ { 1st, 2nd or 3rd marriage } _1st_

Name of Father _Ernes E. Jones_

Maiden name of Mother _Ulalia Erff_

Bride's name _Bettie M. Lull_

Her age _18_

" color _White_

" occupation _Homekeeper_

" Birthplace—City _Indianapolis_ State _Ind_

" Residence—Street No. _2361 Hoyt St_ City _Indpls_

Single Widow Divorced } _Single_ { 1st, 2nd or 3rd marriage } _1st_

Name of Father _Edward Lull_

Maiden name of Mother _Rosa M Mitchell_

Date of this marriage _4—25——1944_

Place of this marriage _Greenfield Ind_

Name and title of person Performing this marriage _Minister_

His address _23 West South Street_

Witness { Name _Indianapolis_ { Address _Mr—Mrs Robert Jones_

### Return this Report to County Clerk with License and Certificate

# Marriage Record for Board of Health
## To Be Returned by the Minister or Other Person Performing Ceremony

Wilford A. Pyle _____ and _Lillian M. King_

Groom's name _Wilford A. Pyle_

His age _27_

" color _White_

" occupation _U.S. Army Air Force_

" Birthplace—City _Indianapolis_ State _Ind._

" Residence—Street No. _Army_ City _____

Single / Widower / Divorced } _Single_ { 1st, 2nd or 3rd marriage } _1st_

Name of Father _Lora Pyle_

Maiden name of Mother _Lora Allison_

Bride's name _Lillian King_

Her age _21_

" color _White_

" occupation _Indiana Weaving Co_

" Birthplace—City _Frankfort_ State _Ky._

" Residence—Street No. _R.R. 11 Box 476_ City _____

Single / Widow / Divorced } _Single_ { 1st, 2nd or 3rd marriage } _1st_

Name of Father _Alfred King_

Maiden name of Mother _Ethel Hulett_

Date of this marriage _April 26 1942_

Place of this marriage _Indianapolis Ind_

Name and title of person Performing this marriage _Rev. R.R. Shumaker_

His address _2025 N. Temple_ _Indianapolis Ind._

Witness { Name _Virgil Ferguson_ Address _1135 W. Johnson_

## Return this Report to County Clerk with License and Certificate

# Marriage Record for Board of Health

### To Be Returned by the Minister or Other Person Performing Ceremony

Millard G. McClain and Edna Hill

Groom's name ___Millard G. McClain___

His age ___44 years___

" color ___White___

" occupation ___Soldier___

" Birthplace—City ___Franklin___ State ___Indiana___

" Residence—Street No. ___ City ___Camp Chaffe, Arkansas___

Single / Widower / Divorced } ___Divorced___ { 1st, 2nd or 3rd marriage } ___Second___

Name of Father ___Guy McClain___

Maiden name of Mother ___Mary Ann Voris___

Bride's name ___Edna Hill___

Her age ___26 years___

" color ___White___

" occupation ___Domestic___

" Birthplace—City ___Mt. Pisga___ State ___Ky.___

" Residence—Street No. ___ City ___Mt. Pisga, Ky.___

Single / Widow / Divorced } ___Divorced___ { 1st, 2nd or 3rd marriage } ___Second___

Name of Father ___Jeff Davis___

Maiden name of Mother ___Mary Foster___

Date of this marriage ___April 26, 1944.___

Place of this marriage ___Post Chapel, Ft. Benj. Harrison, Ind.___

Name and title of person Performing this marriage ___Minister, Chaplain Albert M.B. Snapp AUS___

His address ___Post Chapel Office, Ft. Benj. Harrison, Ind.___

Witness { Name ___Effie Hill___ ___Mearl McVay___
{ Address ___Mt. Pisga, Ky.___ ___Indianapolis, Ind.___

## Return this Report to County Clerk with License and Certificate

12

# Marriage Record for Board of Health
## To Be Returned by the Minister or Other Person Performing Ceremony

_____ Quinn _____ and _____ Pollard _____

Groom's name _John Charles Quinn_

His age _24_

" color _white_

" occupation _soldier_

" Birthplace—City _Decatur_ State _Illinois_

" Residence—Street No. _Stout Field_ City _Indianapolis_

Single Widower Divorced } _single_    1st, 2nd or 3rd marriage } _1st marriage_

Name of Father _William John Quinn_

Maiden name of Mother _Mary Frances McLaughlin_

Bride's name _Katherine Pollard_

Her age _21_

" color _white_

" occupation _nurse U.S. Army_

" Birthplace—City _Cerro Gordo_ State _Illinois_

" Residence—Street No. _Percy Jones General Hospital_ City _Battle Creek Michigan_

Single Widow Divorced } _single_    1st, 2nd or 3rd marriage } _1st marriage_

Name of Father _James E. Pollard_

Maiden name of Mother _Marguerite Lang_

Date of this marriage _April 26, 1944_

Place of this marriage _Stout Field - Indianapolis Indiana_

Name and title of person Performing this marriage _Alden J Bell - Chaplain-U.S. Army_

His address _Stout Field Indianapolis Indiana_

Witness { Name _Sgt Paul Gardner — Stout Field Indianapolis_
{ Address _S/Sgt Stephany Kowal " " " Ind._

## Return this Report to County Clerk with License and Certificate

12

# Marriage Record for Board of Health

## To Be Returned by the Minister or Other Person Performing Ceremony

*Earl Allison Holwager* and *Alice Louise Leep*

Groom's name _Earl Allison Holwager_

His age _38_

" color _White_

" occupation _Cook_

" Birthplace—City _Madison, R._ State _Indiana_

" Residence—Street No. _1538 N. Wilcox_ City _Indianapolis_

Single / Widower / Divorced } _Divorced_    { 1st, 2nd or 3rd marriage } _3rd_

Name of Father _Lealdus J. Holwager_

Maiden name of Mother _E Amy B Lichlyter_

Bride's name _Alice Louise Leep_

Her age _38_

" color _White_

" occupation _Housekeeper_

" Birthplace—City _Madison_ State _Indiana_

" Residence—Street No. _1538 N. Wilcox_ City _Indianapolis_

Single / Widow / Divorced } _Divorced_    { 1st, 2nd or 3rd marriage } _2nd_

Name of Father _William Dowell_

Maiden name of Mother _Nancy Bear_

Date of this marriage _April 26 1944_

Place of this marriage _Vernon, Ind_

Name and title of person Performing this marriage _Rev. Chesley Holmes_

His address _Vernon, Ind._

Witness { Name _Gertrude F. Holmes_    Address _Vernon, Ind_

## Return this Report to County Clerk with License and Certificate

42

# Marriage Record for Board of Health
### To Be Returned by the Minister or Other Person Performing Ceremony

Eugene A. Carver and Mary Lou Carver

Groom's name _Eugene A. Carver_

His age _33_

" color _White_

" occupation _Store manager_

" Birthplace—City _Crawfordsville_ State _Indiana_

" Residence—Street No. _1224 Norman Ave_ City _Indianapolis, Ind_

Single / Widower / Divorced } _Divorced_   { 1st, 2nd or 3rd marriage } _Second_

Name of Father _Ora Carver_

Maiden name of Mother _Wannetia Sink_

Bride's name _Mary Lou Carver_

Her age _31_

" color _White_

" occupation _Curtis Wright Employee_

" Birthplace—City _Wingate_ State _Indiana_

" Residence—Street No. _1224 Norman Ave_ City _Indianapolis, Ind._

Single / Widow / Divorced } _Divorced_   { 1st, 2nd or 3rd marriage } _Second_

Name of Father _Clarence L. Hatton_

Maiden name of Mother _Bessie M. Davidson_

Date of this marriage _April 26, 1944_

Place of this marriage _Indianapolis, Indiana_

Name and title of person Performing this marriage _minister_

His address _1821 N. Lambert St, Indianapolis, Ind._

Witness { Name _Dorothy Shanks_
        { Address _828 Manhattan St_

## Return this Report to County Clerk with License and Certificate

# Marriage Record for Board of Health

### To Be Returned by the Minister or Other Person Performing Ceremony

Ralph Eugene Sharkey _____ and ____ Barbara Jeanne May

Groom's name ____ Ralph Eugene Sharkey

His age _____ 22

" color ____ White

" occupation ____ U.S. Army

" Birthplace—City Detroit _____ State ____ Michigan

" Residence—Street No. 16615 Blackstone Ave ____ City ____ Detroit, Mich.

Single / Widower / Divorced } Single   { 1st, 2nd or 3rd marriage } ____ 1st

Name of Father _____ James Vernon Sharkey

Maiden name of Mother ____ Lois Rix

Bride's name ____ Barbara Jeanne May

Her age _____ 21

" color _____ White

" occupation ____ Home Owners Loan Corp. U.S. Government

" Birthplace—City Detroit _____ State ____ Mich.

" Residence—Street No. Marot Hotel (Temp.) ____ City Indianapolis, Ind.

Single / Widow / Divorced } Single   { 1st, 2nd or 3rd marriage } ____ 1st

Name of Father _____ Arthur Anson May

Maiden name of Mother ____ Ora Owen

Date of this marriage _____ April 26, 1944

Place of this marriage Christ Episcopal Church, Monument Circle, Indianapolis 4, Ind

Name and title of person Performing this marriage _____ Rector, Christ Episcopal Church, Indianapolis, Ind.

His address _____ 126 E 43rd St.,

_____ Indianapolis, Ind.

Witness { Name ____ Mrs Arthur Anson May
{ Address #1 Ascan Ave, Forrest Hills, Long Island, N.Y.

## Return this Report to County Clerk with License and Certificate

# Marriage Record for Board of Health
To Be Returned by the Minister or Other Person Performing Ceremony

James W. Edwards and Virginia A. Glass

Groom's name _James W. Edwards_

His age _18_

" color _C_

" occupation _Filling Station attendant_

" Birthplace—City _Indianapolis_ State _Indiana_

" Residence—Street No. _627 Maxwell St._ City _Indianapolis_

Single
Widower } _Single_  { 1st, 2nd or 3rd marriage } _1st_
Divorced

Name of Father _James Edwards_

Maiden name of Mother _Mary E. Beard_

Bride's name _Virginia A. Glass_

Her age _17_

" color _C._

" occupation _— None_

" Birthplace—City _Paducah_ State _Kentucky_

" Residence—Street No. _627 Maxwell St._ City _Indianapolis_

Single
Widow } _Single_  { 1st, 2nd or 3rd marriage } _1st_
Divorced

Name of Father _Clarence G. Glass_

Maiden name of Mother _Addie B. Glass Garey_

Date of this marriage _April 26, 1944_

Place of this marriage _Indianapolis Ind_

Name and title of person Performing this marriage _H. Thomas, Minister_

His address _708 S. Illinois Indianapolis Ind_

Witness { Name _Addie B. Glass_
          Address _627 Maxwell St._

## Return this Report to County Clerk with License and Certificate

# Marriage Record for Board of Health

## To Be Returned by the Minister or Other Person Performing Ceremony

*Donald C. Eggers* and *Marjorie Robinson*

Groom's name _Donald C. Eggers_

His age _23_

" color _White_

" occupation _Sheetmetal_

" Birthplace—City _Crawfordsville_ State _Indiana_

" Residence—Street No. _W Wabash_ City _n/a_

Single
Widower } _Single_    { 1st, 2nd or 3rd } _1st_
Divorced              { marriage

Name of Father _Frank Eggers_

Maiden name of Mother _Mary A White_

Bride's name _Marjorie Robinson_

Her age _18_

" color _White_

" occupation _None_

" Birthplace—City _Plainfield_ State _Indiana_

" Residence—Street No. _137 Blaine_ City _Indianapolis_

Single
Widow } _Single_     { 1st, 2nd or 3rd } _1st_
Divorced             { marriage

Name of Father _Harvey Robinson_

Maiden name of Mother _Doris McKnight_

Date of this marriage _April 26, 1944_

Place of this marriage _Indianapolis_

Name and title of person
Performing this marriage _Ernest Lane Justice of the Peace_

His address _152½ East County St_

Witness { Name _Nora M. Lane_
        { Address _3741 College Ave_

## Return this Report to County Clerk with License and Certificate

12

# Marriage Record for Board of Health
### To Be Returned by the Minister or Other Person Performing Ceremony

*Ernest C. Richardson* and *Helen L. Zipoff*

Groom's name *Ernest C. Richardson*

His age *39*

" color *White*

" occupation *New York Central Railroad Employee*

" Birthplace—City *Bloomington* State *Indiana*

" Residence—Street No. *940 Pleasant Run Blvd Indpls*

Single
Widower } *Divorced*  { 1st, 2nd or 3rd } *4th*
Divorced        marriage

Name of Father *Abraham Richardson*

Maiden name of Mother *Hulda Steidl*

Bride's name *Helen L. Zipoff*

Her age *23*

" color *White*

" occupation *Elevator operator*

" Birthplace—City *Indpls* State *Indiana*

" Residence—Street No. *829 English* City *Indpls*

Single
Widow } *Divorced*  { 1st, 2nd or 3rd } *2nd*
Divorced        marriage

Name of Father *Stephen P. Zipoff*

Maiden name of Mother *Florence Evelyn Ferguson*

Date of this marriage *April 26 - 44*

Place of this marriage *Indianapolis Indiana*

Name and title of person
Performing this marriage *Ernest Lang Justice of Peace*

His address *1525 East Court Street*

Witness { Name *Florence Evelyn Zipoff*
         { Address *829 English Ave*

## Return this Report to County Clerk with License and Certificate

 12

# Marriage Record for Board of Health
### To Be Returned by the Minister or Other Person Performing Ceremony

_John F. Finley_ and _Frances M. Freeman_

Groom's name _John F. Finley_

His age _26_

" color _White_

" occupation _U.S. Army_

" Birthplace—City _Harrisburg_ State _Pa._

" Residence—Street No. _1623 North ST._ City _Harrisburg, Pa._

Single / Widower / Divorced } _Single_ { 1st, 2nd or 3rd marriage } _1st_

Name of Father _John N. Finley_

Maiden name of Mother _Leora Fryer_

Bride's name _Frances M. Freeman_

Her age _26_

" color _White_

" occupation _Clerk_

" Birthplace—City _Terre Haute_ State _Indiana_

" Residence—Street No. _1920 Eighth Ave_ City _Terre Haute, Ind._

Single / Widow / Divorced } _Divorced_ { 1st, 2nd or 3rd marriage } _2nd_

Name of Father _Francis D. Freeman_

Maiden name of Mother _Pearl O. Reeves_

Date of this marriage _26 April 1944_

Place of this marriage _Post Chapel, Fort Benjamin Harrison, Indiana_

Name and title of person Performing this marriage _Chaplain Albert M.B. Snapp AUS_

His address _Post Chapel Office, Ft. Benj. Harrison, Ind._

Witness { Name _Maxine Pound_ _John N. Finley_

Address _Terra Haut, Ind._ _Harrisburg, Pa._

### Return this Report to County Clerk with License and Certificate

13

# Marriage Record for Board of Health
## To Be Returned by the Minister or Other Person Performing Ceremony

*Clement Charles Morloch* and *Mary Cathrine Cullen*

Groom's name _Clement Charles Morloch_

His age _23_

" color _White_

" occupation _Navy_

" Birthplace—City _Selestat_ ~~State~~ _France_

" Residence—Street No. _3343 N Kenyon_ City _Indianapolis_

Single } _Single_    { 1st, ~~2nd or 3rd~~ } _First_
~~Widower~~                {  marriage
~~Divorced~~

Name of Father _Charles Joseph Morloch_

Maiden name of Mother _Jeanne Andre_

Bride's name _Mary Cathrine Cullen_

Her age _19_

" color _White_

" occupation _Defense Worker_

" Birthplace—City _Chicago_ State _Ill_

" Residence—Street No. _1037 Shannon_ City _Indianapolis_

Single } _Single_    { 1st, ~~2nd or 3rd~~ } _First_
~~Widow~~                {  marriage
~~Divorced~~

Name of Father _Paul Aubrey Cullen_

Maiden name of Mother _Ruth Viola Reissenzehn_

Date of this marriage _April 26 – 1944_

Place of this marriage _Church of the Little Flower_

Name and title of person
Performing this marriage _Rev Stanley J Ryan Assistant Pastor_

His address _1310 N Wallace St_
_Indianapolis – Ind_

Witness { Name _Harold Braun – 1115 Linwood Ave Indiana_
{ Address _Margaret Braun 1115 Linwood Ave Indianapolis_

## Return this Report to County Clerk with License and Certificate

# Marriage Record for Board of Health
### To Be Returned by the Minister or Other Person Performing Ceremony

_Rink_ and _Danna_

Groom's name _Ralph G._

His age _32_

" color _White_

" occupation _George Hitz & Co. Laborer_

" Birthplace—City _Mitchel_ State _Indiana_

" Residence—Street No. _925 High St_ City _Indianapolis_

Single / Widower / Divorced } _Divorced_ { 1st, 2nd or 3rd marriage } _Second_

Name of Father _Ransom Rink_

Maiden name of Mother _Dr Kora Mc Drew_

Bride's name _Lena_

Her age _25_

" color _White_

" occupation _City Market_

" Birthplace—City _Indianapolis_ State _Indiana_

" Residence—Street No. _918 South East St_ City _Indianapolis_

Single / Widow / Divorced } _Single_ { 1st, 2nd or 3rd marriage } _First_

Name of Father _Joseph Danna_

Maiden name of Mother _Rose Piazza_

Date of this marriage _April 28, 1944_

Place of this marriage _Holy Rosary Church, 616 S East St, Indianapolis_

Name and title of person Performing this marriage _Rev. William Knapp, Catholic Priest_

His address _616 South East Street_

_Indianapolis 2, Indiana_

Witness { Name _Salvatore Piazza, 538 E. Merrill St, Indianapolis_

{ Address _Wilma Piazza, 538 E. Merrill St, Indianapolis_

### Return this Report to County Clerk with License and Certificate

# Marriage Record for Board of Health
### To Be Returned by the Minister or Other Person Performing Ceremony

*James J. Melvin* and *Jean Goss*

Groom's name _James J. Melvin_

His age _22_

" color _White_

" occupation _Soldier_

" Birthplace—City _Indianapolis_ State _Ind_

" Residence—Street No _Fort Knox_ City _Ky_

Single / Widower / Divorced } _Single_ 　 { 1st, 2nd or 3rd marriage } _1st._

Name of Father _Henry Melvin_

Maiden name of Mother _Carol Bertha Carol_

Bride's name _Jean Goss_

Her age _19_

" color _White_

" occupation _Eli Lilly_

" Birthplace—City _Osgood_ State _Ind._

" Residence—Street No _838 Fletcher_ City _Indianapolis_

Single / Widow / Divorced } _Single_ 　 { 1st, 2nd or 3rd marriage } _1st._

Name of Father _William Goss_

Maiden name of Mother _Elma Roark_

Date of this marriage _April 26 - 1944_

Place of this marriage _Indianapolis Ind_

Name and title of person Performing this marriage _Rev N. R. Alvey, Minister_

His address _1037 Spruce St. Indianapolis_

Witness { Name _Mary Lucille Goss_ Address _838 Fletcher Avenue_

### Return this Report to County Clerk with License and Certificate

# Marriage Record for Board of Health
### To Be Returned by the Minister or Other Person Performing Ceremony

William Thomas Caldwell and Martha Jean Dale

Groom's name _William Thomas Caldwell_

His age _25_

" color _White_

" occupation _Soldier_

" Birthplace—City _Advance_ State _Ind_

" Residence—Street No. _____ City _Camp Stewart Georgia_

Single
~~Widower~~
~~Divorced~~ } _____ { 1st, 2nd or 3rd marriage }

Name of Father _Ross Caldwell_

Maiden name of Mother _Lucas_

Bride's name _Martha Jean Dale_

Her age _20_

" color _white_

" occupation _Nurse_

" Birthplace—City _Thorntown_ State _Indiana_

" Residence—Street No. _1740 N. Capitol_ City _Indianapolis_

Single
~~Widow~~
~~Divorced~~ } _____ { 1st, 2nd or 3rd marriage }

Name of Father _Paul Dale_

Maiden name of Mother _McDonald_

Date of this marriage _April 26, 1944_

Place of this marriage _Noblesville Indiana_

Name and title of person
Performing this marriage _Rev. E. J. Wreckershour_

His address _239 N. 16th Noblesville Ind_

Witness { Name _May H. Wreckershour_
{ Address _239 N. 10 Noblesville_

### Return this Report to County Clerk with License and Certificate

12

# Marriage Record for Board of Health

### To Be Returned by the Minister or Other Person Performing Ceremony

_____ and _____

Groom's name _____

His age _____

" color _____

" occupation _____

" Birthplace—City _____ State _____

" Residence—Street No. _____ City _____

Single / Widower / Divorced } _____ { 1st, 2nd or 3rd marriage } _____

Name of Father _____

Maiden name of Mother _____

Bride's name _____

Her age _____

" color _____

" occupation _____

" Birthplace—City _____ State _____

" Residence—Street No. _____ City _____

Single / Widow / Divorced } _____ { 1st, 2nd or 3rd marriage } _____

Name of Father _____

Maiden name of Mother _____

Date of this marriage _____

Place of this marriage _____

Name and title of person Performing this marriage _____

His address _____

Witness { Name _____
{ Address _____

## Return this Report to County Clerk with License and Certificate

# Marriage Record for Board of Health

### To Be Returned by the Minister or Other Person Performing Ceremony

*Opal S Booker* and *Ruth Lyon*

Groom's name _Opal S Booker_

His age _49_

" color _White_

" occupation _Barber_

" Birthplace—City _Montgomery C_ State _Indiana_

" Residence—Street No. _3713 E 30_ City _Indianapolis_

Single
Widower } _Divorced_ { 1st, 2nd or 3rd
Divorced } marriage } _2nd_

Name of Father _Elwood Booker_

Maiden name of Mother _Dora Booker_

Bride's name _Ruth Lyon_

Her age _37_

" color _White_

" occupation _Housekeeper_

" Birthplace—City _Indianapolis_ State _Indiana_

" Residence—Street No. _719 N. Bevill_ City _Indianapolis_

Single
Widow } _Divorced_ { 1st, 2nd or 3rd
Divorced } marriage } _2nd_

Name of Father _William Davisson_

Maiden name of Mother _Bessie Alderson_

Date of this marriage _April 27, 1944_

Place of this marriage _Indianapolis_

Name and title of person
Performing this marriage _Everin Lane Justice Peace_

His address _157½ East Court_

Witness { Name _Mary Jo Lane_
{ Address _3741 College_

### Return this Report to County Clerk with License and Certificate

12

## Marriage Record for Board of Health
### To Be Returned by the Minister or Other Person Performing Ceremony

_Garret A Beall_ and _Effie Mae Moore_

Groom's name _Garret A Beall_

His age _41_

" color _White_

" occupation _Electrical_

" Birthplace—City _Cicero_ State _Ind_

" Residence—Street No. _527 N Del_ City _Indianapolis_

Single / Widower / Divorced } _Divorced_ { 1st, 2nd or 3rd marriage } _3_

Name of Father _John Albert Beall_

Maiden name of Mother _Sadie Havens_

Bride's name _Effie Mae Moore_

Her age _35_

" color _White_

" occupation _Drill Press operator_

" Birthplace—City _Mapleville_ State _Alabama_

" Residence—Street No. _527 N Del_ City _Indianapolis_

Single / Widow / Divorced } _single_ { 1st, 2nd or 3rd marriage }

Name of Father _John Joseph Moore_

Maiden name of Mother _Sarah Elizabeth Webb_

Date of this marriage _April 27 - 1944_

Place of this marriage _Indianapolis Ind_

Name and title of person Performing this marriage _Rev F B Edwards Pastor_

His address _1821 S Meridian St Indianapolis Ind Indianapolis indiana_

Witness { Name _Alice Edwards_ { Address _1821 S Meridian St Indianapolis ind_

### Return this Report to County Clerk with License and Certificate

# Marriage Record for Board of Health
### To Be Returned by the Minister or Other Person Performing Ceremony

Harold R. Bligan _____ and Aimee Redman

Groom's name _____ Harold R. Bligan

His age _____ 22

" color _____ White

" occupation _____ U.S.A

" Birthplace—City _____ Pine Grove _____ State _____ Pa

" Residence—Street No. 36 S Main _____ City _____ Pine Grove

Single / Widower / Divorced } _____ Single _____ { 1st, 2nd or 3rd marriage } _____ 1st

Name of Father _____ James Bligan

Maiden name of Mother _____ Mary Rhinehart

Bride's name _____ Aimee M Redman

Her age _____ 19

" color _____ White

" occupation _____ Typist

" Birthplace—City _____ Cape garde _____ State _____ Ill

" Residence—Street No. 1703 N Del #4 City _____ Indianapolis Ind

Single / Widow / Divorced } _____ Single _____ { 1st, 2nd or 3rd marriage } _____ 1st

Name of Father _____ Herbert Paul Redman

Maiden name of Mother _____ Ethel Marie Mellinger

Date of this marriage _____ April 27 1944

Place of this marriage _____ Jamestown Methodist Church

Name and title of person Performing this marriage _____ Rev Ernest F. Peer

His address _____ Jamestown Ind

Witness { Name _____ Victor E. Drake
{ Address _____ 18th AAFTD Allison Div, Indianapolis 6 Ind

### Return this Report to County Clerk with License and Certificate

12

# Marriage Record for Board of Health
### To Be Returned by the Minister or Other Person Performing Ceremony

_____ and _____

Groom's name _Leonidas H. McClellan_

His age _34_

" color _W_

" occupation _Inspector, Burdos-Harold Corp._

" Birthplace—City _Frankfort_ State _Ind._

" Residence—Street No. _829 S. Noble_ City _Indianapolis, Ind._

Single / Widower / Divorced { _____ { 1st, 2nd or 3rd marriage { _____

Name of Father _Leonidas McClellan_

Maiden name of Mother _Carie Petit_

Bride's name _Margaret Elizabeth Barker_

Her age _36_

" color _W_

" occupation _Leather + Luggage Work at Gansepohl Co._

" Birthplace—City _Mexico_ State _Mo._

" Residence—Street No. _440 Oxford_ City _Indianapolis, Ind._

Single / Widow / Divorced { _____ { 1st, 2nd or 3rd marriage { _____

Name of Father _Henry Albus_

Maiden name of Mother _Harriet Burns_

Date of this marriage _April 27, 1944_

Place of this marriage _829 S. Noble St. Indianapolis Ind._

Name and title of person Performing this marriage _Rev. Harry R. Smecan_

His address _5647 N. Illinois St., Indianapolis, Ind._

Witness { Name _Mrs. Jean M. La Rosa_ { Address _829 S. Noble Street_

### Return this Report to County Clerk with License and Certificate

# Marriage Record for Board of Health

### To Be Returned by the Minister or Other Person Performing Ceremony

_Russell_ and _Mueller_

Groom's name _Clifford B Russell_

His age _38_

" color _White_

" occupation _Railroad Dispatcher_

" Birthplace—City _Indianapolis_ State _Ind_

" Residence—Street No. _West Newton_ City _Ind_

Single / Widower / Divorced } _Widower_  1st, 2nd or 3rd marriage } _2nd_

Name of Father _George N Russell_

Maiden name of Mother _Anna Weaver_

Bride's name _Bessie Mueller_

Her age _36_

" color _White_

" occupation _Clerk_

" Birthplace—City _Indianapolis_ State _Ind_

" Residence—Street No. _1833 White_ City _Indianapolis_

Single / Widow / Divorced } _Widow_  1st, 2nd or 3rd marriage } _2nd_

Name of Father _Adolph Mueller_

Maiden name of Mother _Carey Davis_

Date of this marriage _Apr 27, 44_

Place of this marriage _2614 Sutherland ave, City_

Name and title of person Performing this marriage _Samuel Coat, Minister_

His address _2614 Sutherland ave, City_

Witness { Name _____  Address _____

## Return this Report to County Clerk with License and Certificate

# Marriage Record for Board of Health
### To Be Returned by the Minister or Other Person Performing Ceremony

*Philip A. Boyd* and *Mary G. Milliner*

Groom's name _Philip A. Boyd_

His age _21_

" color _white_

" occupation _In Navy_

" Birthplace—City _Indianapolis_ State _Indiana_

" Residence—Street No. _1437 Reisner_ City _Indianapolis, Ind._

Single ⎱
~~Widower,~~ ⎰          ⎱ 1st, ~~2nd or 3rd~~
~~Divorced~~              ⎰ marriage

Name of Father _Raleigh Boyd_

Maiden name of Mother _Georgia Hybarger_

Bride's name _Mary G. Milliner_

Her age _22_

" color _White_

" occupation _Factory worker_

" Birthplace—City _Mammoth Cave_ State _Kentucky_

" Residence—Street No. _1764 Morgan_ City _Indianapolis, Ind._

Single ⎱
~~Widow~~ ⎰          ⎱ 1st, ~~2nd or 3rd~~
~~Divorced~~              ⎰ marriage

Name of Father _Felix W. Milliner_

Maiden name of Mother _Ella Casey_

Date of this marriage _April 27, 1944._

Place of this marriage _Indianapolis_

Name and title of person
Performing this marriage _Rev. S. H. O'Donnell_

His address _517 E. 23rd, Indianapolis, Ind._

Witness ⎱ Name _Mrs. Sus. B. Welch._
        ⎰ Address _2136 Central_

### Return this Report to County Clerk with License and Certificate

# Marriage Record for Board of Health
## To Be Returned by the Minister or Other Person Performing Ceremony

_William E. Skiver_ and _Christine G. Smith_

Groom's name _William E. Skiver_

His age _19 years_

" color _white_

" occupation _Disk Cutter_

" Birthplace—City _Indianapolis_ State _Indiana_

" Residence—Street No. _114 E. 23rd St._ City _Indianapolis_

Single / Widower / Divorced } _Single_ { 1st, 2nd or 3rd marriage } _1st marriage_

Name of Father _Edward William Skiver_

Maiden name of Mother _Helen Sanders_

Bride's name _Christine G. Smith_

Her age _21 years_

" color _white_

" occupation _Beauty operator_

" Birthplace—City _Science Hill_ State _Kentucky_

" Residence—Street No. _909 Villa Ave_ City _Indianapolis_

Single / Widow / Divorced } _Divorced_ { 1st, 2nd or 3rd marriage } _2nd marriage_

Name of Father _Berlin Thurman_

Maiden name of Mother _Bell Thurman_

Date of this marriage _April 27, 1944_

Place of this marriage _Indianapolis, Indiana_

Name and title of person Performing this marriage _William O. Bain, Judge_

His address _1232 Parkland Ave._
_Indianapolis, Indiana_

Witness { Name _Thomas F. Snyder_
{ Address _114 E. 23rd St., Indpls._

## Return this Report to County Clerk with License and Certificate

12

# Marriage Record for Board of Health
To Be Returned by the Minister or Other Person Performing Ceremony

Haywood Rice _____ and _Minnie Etta Bell_

Groom's name _Haywood Rice_

His age _52_

" color _Colored_

" occupation _Labor_

" Birthplace—City _Campbellville_ State _Ky._

" Residence—Street No. _626 Indiana Ave._ City _Ind'pls_

Single
Widower } _Widower_ { 1st, 2nd or 3rd marriage } _3rd_
Divorced

Name of Father _Kane Rice_

Maiden name of Mother _Ellen Johnson_

Bride's name _Minnie Etta Bell_

Her age _40_

" color _Colored_

" occupation _Housekeeper_

" Birthplace—City _Lawrence_ State _Tenn._

" Residence—Street No. _626 Ind. Ave._ City _Ind'pls_

Single
Widow } _Widow_ { 1st, 2nd or 3rd marriage } _3rd_
Divorced

Name of Father _Lacey Langford_

Maiden name of Mother _Mildita Harper_

Date of this marriage _April 29, 1944_

Place of this marriage _Ind'pls, Ind._

Name and title of person
Performing this marriage _J. J. Thomas, minister_

His address _712 South 11 St._
_Ind'pls, Ind_

Witness { Name _Alva Langford_
{ Address _626 S. J. Ave._

## Return this Report to County Clerk with License and Certificate

# Marriage Record for Board of Health
## To Be Returned by the Minister or Other Person Performing Ceremony

_Smith_ and _Parrott_

Groom's name _Ira Smith_

His age _35_

" color _Negro_

" occupation _soldier_

" Birthplace—City _Clarksdale_ State _Mississippi_

" Residence—Street No. _Camp Ellis_ City _Illinois_

Single / Widower / Divorced } _Single_ { 1st, 2nd or 3rd marriage } _1st marriage_

Name of Father _James H. Smith_

Maiden name of Mother _Bessie Smith_

Bride's name _Elizabeth Bernice Parrott_

Her age _21_

" color _Negro_

" occupation _Defense worker_

" Birthplace—City _Indianapolis_ State _Indiana_

" Residence—Street No. _2018 Yandes_ City _Indianapolis_

Single / Widow / Divorced } _Single_ { 1st, 2nd or 3rd marriage } _1st marriage_

Name of Father _George Parrott_

Maiden name of Mother _Amda Ellery_

Date of this marriage _April 27 1944_

Place of this marriage _Indianapolis Indiana_

Name and title of person Performing this marriage _Bernard H. Gerdon — Priest_

His address _1816 N. Alward Ave_
_Indianapolis, Indiana_

Witness { Name _Thomas Parrott_
{ Address _2018 Yandes_

## Return this Report to County Clerk with License and Certificate

12

# Marriage Record for Board of Health

### To Be Returned by the Minister or Other Person Performing Ceremony

*Bicknell K. Beckwith* and *Jean Ellen Boyer*

Groom's name ___Bicknell K Beckwith___

His age ___18___

" color ___White___

" occupation ___U. S. Army___

" Birthplace—City ___Pawhuska___ State ___Okla.___

" Residence—Street No. ___52nd C.T.D. Butler U___ City ___Indianapolis___

Single / ~~Widower~~ / ~~Divorced~~   {  1st, ~~2nd or 3rd~~ marriage

Name of Father ___Glen W. Beckwith___

Maiden name of Mother ___Hazel M. Bicknell___

Bride's name ___Jean Ellen Boyer___

Her age ___18___

" color ___White___

" occupation _____

" Birthplace—City ___Hartford___ State ___Mich.___

" Residence—Street No. ___4283 Blvd Pl___ City ___Indianapolis___

Single / ~~Widow~~ / ~~Divorced~~   {  1st, ~~2nd or 3rd~~ marriage

Name of Father ___Flector Boyer___

Maiden name of Mother ___Olive L. Simpson___

Date of this marriage ___Jan 27 1944.___

Place of this marriage ___Indianapolis___

Name and title of person Performing this marriage ___Rev J A Ragan___

His address ___129 W – 44th St___
___Indianapolis, Indiana___

Witness {  Name ___Mr. Mrs. Albert B Duckworth___
         {  Address ___233 Buckingham drive, City___

## Return this Report to County Clerk with License and Certificate

12

# Marriage Record for Board of Health

## To Be Returned by the Minister or Other Person Performing Ceremony

*Margaret Mae Owens* and *Raymond Varrett Hill*

Groom's name _Raymond Varrett Hill_

His age _18_

" color _White_

" occupation _U. S. Rubber Co – Utility Man_

" Birthplace—City _Providence_ State _Ky_

" Residence—Street No. _3344 Polson_ City _Indianapolis_

Single / Widower / Divorced } _Single_  { 1st, 2nd or 3rd marriage } _1st_

Name of Father _Walter Franklin Hill_

Maiden name of Mother _Bessie Grable_

Bride's name _Margaret Mae Owens_

Her age _16_

" color _white_

" occupation _none_

" Birthplace—City _Indianapolis_ State _Indiana_

" Residence—Street No. _1434 W Ohio_ City _Indianapolis_

Single / Widow / Divorced } _Single_ { 1st, 2nd or 3rd marriage } _1st_

Name of Father _Arnold Owens_

Maiden name of Mother _Bessie Matlock_

Date of this marriage _April 27 - 1944_

Place of this marriage _West Side Christian Mission_

Name and title of person Performing this marriage _Roscoe Kirkman, Pastor_

His address _242 E Pleasant Run Pkwy_ _Indianapolis Ind._

Witness { Name _Curtis Heady_  Address _1816 W. Vermont_

## Return this Report to County Clerk with License and Certificate

12

# Marriage Record for Board of Health
## To Be Returned by the Minister or Other Person Performing Ceremony

Edward B. Jones. _____ and _Willie B. Gardner._

Groom's name _Edward B. Jones._

His age _25_

" color _C._

" occupation _U.S.N_

" Birthplace—City _Fenton_ _____ State _Ky._

" Residence—Street No. _____ City _Bainbridge md._

Single / Widower / Divorced } _Single_ { 1st, 2nd or 3rd marriage } _first._

Name of Father _Sanford. Jones._

Maiden name of Mother _Goldia Brandon._

Bride's name _Willie B. Gardner._

Her age _nineteen_

" color _C._

" occupation _None_

" Birthplace—City _Dresden._ _____ State _Tenn._

" Residence—Street No. _1003 Edgemont_ City _Indianapolis_

Single / Widow / Divorced } _Single_ { 1st, 2nd or 3rd marriage } _first._

Name of Father _Will Gardner._

Maiden name of Mother _Bessie rages._

Date of this marriage _April 25 – 1944._

Place of this marriage _Indianapolis, Indiana_

Name and title of person Performing this marriage _S.A. Thomas, Minist._

His address _792 So. Illinois St._ _Indianapolis, Indiana._

Witness { Name _Jaynelle Collins_ Address _769 Indiana Ave_

## Return this Report to County Clerk with License and Certificate

# Marriage Record for Board of Health

To Be Returned by the Minister or Other Person Performing Ceremony

_Alton Jones_ and _Gaynelle Collins_

Groom's name _Alton J. Jones_

His age _21_

" color _C._

" occupation _U.S. Navy_

" Birthplace—City _Indpls, I_ State _Ind._

" Residence—Street No. _____ City _United Crossd_

Single / Widower / Divorced } _single_    1st, 2nd or 3rd marriage } _1st._

Name of Father _Walter Jones_

Maiden name of Mother _Claudia Algernon_

Bride's name _Gaynelle Collins_

Her age _22_

" color _C_

" occupation _none_

" Birthplace—City _Portland_ State _Tenn._

" Residence—Street No. _769 Indiana Ave_ City _Indpls._

Single / Widow / Divorced } _widow_    1st, 2nd or 3rd marriage } _2nd_

Name of Father _Aaron Moore_

Maiden name of Mother _Callie Mae Winning_

Date of this marriage _April 28, 44_

Place of this marriage _Indpls, Ind_

Name and title of person Performing this marriage _S. S. Thomas, Minister_

His address _702 So. Illinois St_

_Indianapolis, Indiana_

Witness { Name _Willie B. Gardner_
{ Address _1003 Edgemont St._

## Return this Report to County Clerk with License and Certificate

12

# Marriage Record for Board of Health

To Be Returned by the Minister or Other Person Performing Ceremony

*Thomas E. Dunn* and *Lelia Eileen Coble*

Groom's name _Thomas E. Dunn_

His age _22_

" color _white_

" occupation _Defense Worker_

" Birthplace—City _Patterson_ State _New Jersey_

" Residence—Street No. _1302 W 34_ City _Indpls._

Single Widower Divorced } _Single_ { 1st, 2nd or 3rd marriage } _1st_

Name of Father _George Dunn_

Maiden name of Mother _Margaret Hall_

Bride's name _Lelia Eileen Coble_

Her age _18_

" color _White_

" occupation _Maid_

" Birthplace—City _Indianapolis_ State _Indiana_

" Residence—Street No. _211 Bluff Road_ City _Indpls._

Single Widow Divorced } _Single_ { 1st, 2nd or 3rd marriage } _1st_

Name of Father _Harry Coble_

Maiden name of Mother _Mabelle Cronley_

Date of this marriage _April 28-44_

Place of this marriage _Indpls Ind._

Name and title of person Performing this marriage _Fred Kane Justice of Peace_

His address _1524 E Court St_

Witness { Name _Mary Kane_ { Address _3741 College Ave_

## Return this Report to County Clerk with License and Certificate

# Marriage Record for Board of Health
### To Be Returned by the Minister or Other Person Performing Ceremony

_Johnston_ and _Rash_

Groom's name _David J. Johnston_

His age _37_

" color _white_

" occupation _U.S. Army._

" Birthplace—City _Fort Worth_ State _Texas_

" Residence—Street No. _U.S. Army 1004 Gilbert_ City _Indianapolis_

Single Widower Divorced } _Divorced_ { 1st, 2nd or 3rd marriage } _2nd_

Name of Father _Marion Wilbur Johnston_

Maiden name of Mother _Emma Jane Weltzheimer_

Bride's name _Wilma Rash_

Her age _27_

" color _white_

" occupation _–_

" Birthplace—City _Clinton_ State _Ill._

" Residence—Street No. _1004 Gilbert_ City _Indianapolis_

Single Widow Divorced } _Single_ { 1st, 2nd or 3rd marriage } _1st_

Name of Father _William Evans Rash_

Maiden name of Mother _Dora Elizabeth Ray_

Date of this marriage _April 28, 1944_

Place of this marriage _Indianapolis_

Name and title of person Performing this marriage _Garfield W. Alwater_

His address _First Baptist Church, Indianapolis_

Witness { Name _Alma Wolford - 2122 N. Delaware_
{ Address _Minnie Burkhardt - Chicago_

### Return this Report to County Clerk with License and Certificate

12

# Marriage Record for Board of Health

To Be Returned by the Minister or Other Person Performing Ceremony

_____ and _____

Groom's name _Meddie, James Demming_

His age _Thirty_

" color _Colored_

" occupation _Labarer_

" Birthplace—City _Luverne_ State _Ala._

" Residence—Street No. _706 Edgemont_ City _Indianapolis, Ind._

Single }
Widower } _Divorced_        { 1st, 2nd or 3rd } _2nd_
Divorced }                  { marriage

Name of Father _John Demming_

Maiden name of Mother _Louise Davis_

Bride's name _Elouise Starks_

Her age _19_

" color _Colored_

" occupation _none_

" Birthplace—City _Montgomery_ State _Ala._

" Residence—Street No. _706 Edgemont_ City _Indpls., Ind._

Single }
Widow } _Single_          { 1st, 2nd or 3rd } _1st_
Divorced }                { marriage

Name of Father _Lee, Roy Starks_

Maiden name of Mother _Lillen Cooks_

Date of this marriage _4 — 28th — 44_

Place of this marriage _706 Edgemont, Indpls, Ind_

Name and title of person
Performing this marriage _S. C. Richards, Minister_

His address _118 W. 27th St., Indpls 8, Ind_

Witness { Name _Louise Starks_
         { Address _706 Edgemont St Indpls, Ind._

## Return this Report to County Clerk with License and Certificate

12

# Marriage Record for Board of Health

### To Be Returned by the Minister or Other Person Performing Ceremony

_____ and _____

Groom's name _Glenn M. Frapwith_

His age _30_

" color _White_

" occupation _Baker_

" Birthplace—City _Indianapolis_ State _Ind._

" Residence—Street No. _Try___ City _Indiana_

Single } _Single_ { 1st, 2nd or 3rd } _1st_
~~Widower~~ } { marriage }
~~Divorced~~ }

Name of Father _____

Maiden name of Mother _____

Bride's name _____ M. _____

Her age _18_

" color _White_

" occupation _None_

" Birthplace—City _Indianapolis_ State _Ind._

" Residence—Street No. _1735_ _____ City _Indianapolis_

Single } _Single_ { 1st, ~~2nd or 3rd~~ } _1st_
~~Widow~~ } { marriage }
~~Divorced~~ }

Name of Father _____

Maiden name of Mother _____

Date of this marriage _____

Place of this marriage _____

Name and title of person
Performing this marriage _____

His address _____

Witness { Name _____
{ Address _____

## Return this Report to County Clerk with License and Certificate

12

# Marriage Record for Board of Health

To Be Returned by the Minister or Other Person Performing Ceremony

*Lewis R Bridges Jr* and *Bernice Rose Hatfield*

Groom's name _____ *Lewis R Bridges Jr*

His age _____ 20

" color _____ white

" occupation _____ *M S Marine*

" Birthplace—City _____ *Indpls* State _____ *Ind*

" Residence—Street No. 619 N Houston City _____ *Indpls*

Single ✓
Widower _____ 1st, 2nd or 3rd marriage _____ 1st
Divorced

Name of Father _____ *Lewis Bridges Sr*

Maiden name of Mother _____ *Ethel Minkemer*

Bride's name _____ *Bernice Rose Hatfield*

Her age _____ 18

" color _____ white

" occupation _____ *at home*

" Birthplace—City _____ *Indpls* State _____ *Ind*

" Residence—Street No. 427 W McCarty City _____ *Indpls Ind*

Single ✓
Widow _____ 1st, 2nd or 3rd marriage _____ 1st
Divorced

Name of Father _____ *James Hatfield*

Maiden name of Mother _____ *Margaret Steel*

Date of this marriage _____ *Apr 26 - 44*

Place of this marriage _____ *Indpls Ind*

Name and title of person
Performing this marriage _____ *E Lewis Clegg, minister*

His address _____ *Indpls Ind*

Witness ⎰ Name _____
        ⎱ Address _____

**Return this Report to County Clerk with License and Certificate**

# Marriage Record for Board of Health

### To Be Returned by the Minister or Other Person Performing Ceremony

Lewis G. Williams and Myrtle B. Derringer

Groom's name _Lewis G. Williams_

His age _48_

" color _White_

" occupation _Interior Decorator_

" Birthplace—City _Washington_ State _Indiana_

" Residence—Street No. _1031 S. West_ City _Indpls, Ind_

Single
~~Widower~~
~~Divorced~~ } _Single_ { 1st, ~~2nd or 3rd~~ marriage } _1st_

Name of Father _Wm G. Williams_

Maiden name of Mother _Otie Shaw_

Bride's name _Myrtle B. Derringer_

Her age _39_

" color _White_

" occupation _Bridgeport Brass (Inspector)_

" Birthplace—City _Anderson Co._ State _Kentucky_

" Residence—Street No. _1038 S. Holmes_ City _Indpls, Ind_

~~Single~~
~~Widow~~
Divorced } _Divorced_ { 1st, 2nd or 3rd marriage } _4th_

Name of Father _Ezekial Derringer_

Maiden name of Mother _Lucy Kayse_

Date of this marriage _April 28, 1944_

Place of this marriage _Indpls, Ind_

Name and title of person
Performing this marriage _Rev John Ray Clark_

His address _1452 Pleasant St_
_Indpls, Ind_

Witness { Name _Lee Ramsey Clark_
{ Address _Indianapolis, Ind_

## Return this Report to County Clerk with License and Certificate

12

# Marriage Record for Board of Health
### To Be Returned by the Minister or Other Person Performing Ceremony

Warren Raymond Bess _____ and _Jacqueline Glenn Wills_

Groom's name ____Warren Raymond Bess

His age 20

" color___White

" occupation_U.S. Army-Signal Corp. -Ft. Mommouth, New Jersey

" Birthplace—City_Indianapolis_____State _Indiana

" Residence—Street No. 644 E. 32nd_____City Indianapolis

Single / Single     1st, 2nd or 3rd     1st
Widower             marriage
Divorced

Name of Father____William Raymond Bess (Deceased)

Maiden name of Mother____Ruth Giesendorff

Bride's name __Jacqueline Glenn Wills

Her age _____19

" color___White

" occupation_None

" Birthplace—City_Indianapolis_____State _Indiana

" Residence—Street No. 2304 Park Ave. #12 City Indianapolis

Single / Single     1st, 2nd or 3rd     1st
Widow               marriage
Divorced

Name of Father____John Wheeler Wills

Maiden name of Mother___Irene Colman

Date of this marriage___April 28, 1944

Place of this marriage_McKee Chapel-Tabernacle Presbyterian Church-Indiana-
Name and title of person _____polis, Indiana
Performing this marriage_Oey during Hile___Minister of above Church

His address___418 East 34th Street

_____Indianapolis 5, Indiana

Witness { Name _John W Will
         { Address 2304 N. Park ave., Indianapolis, Ind.

## Return this Report to County Clerk with License and Certificate

# Marriage Record for Board of Health

## To Be Returned by the Minister or Other Person Performing Ceremony

*Ira Clinton Nelson* and *Maxine Crook*

Groom's name _Ira Clinton Nelson_

His age _24_

" color _White_

" occupation _Armour & Co_

" Birthplace—City _Crawfordsville_ State _Indiana_

" Residence—Street No. _N259 Alabama_ City _Indianapolis_

Single / Widower / Divorced } _1st_     { 1st, 2nd or 3rd marriage }

Name of Father _David B Nelson_

Maiden name of Mother _Bertha Laye Swank_

Bride's name _Maxine Crook_

Her age _22_

" color _White_

" occupation _Morrison_

" Birthplace—City _Peru_ State _Indiana_

" Residence—Street No. _673 Auk_ City _Indianapolis_

Single / Widow / Divorced } _1st_     { 1st, 2nd or 3rd marriage }

Name of Father _Frank Crook_

Maiden name of Mother _Martha Sharmon_

Date of this marriage _April 28th 1944_

Place of this marriage _Indianapolis_

Name and title of person Performing this marriage _George F Snyder_

His address _846 N W Woodruff Indianapolis_

Witness { Name _Alvin M Mordoh_

{ Address _1118 S Capitol_

## Return this Report to County Clerk with License and Certificate

# Marriage Record for Board of Health

### To Be Returned by the Minister or Other Person Performing Ceremony

*Lloyd Wayne Reed* and *Florence Trilling Collins*

Groom's name _Lloyd Wayne Reed_

His age _21_

" color _White_

" occupation _In Navy_

" Birthplace—City _Lexington_ State _Nebraska_

" Residence—Street No. _New York_ City _New York_

Single ⎫
~~Widower~~ ⎬  { 1st, ~~2nd or 3rd~~ marriage }
~~Divorced~~ ⎭

Name of Father _Joshua C. Reed_

Maiden name of Mother _Dollie Scott_

Bride's name _Florence Trilling Collins_

Her age _20_

" color _White_

" occupation _Commonwealth Loan Co._

" Birthplace—City _Cleveland_ State _Ohio_

" Residence—Street No. _2206 New Jersey Indianapolis_

Single ⎫
Widow ⎬  { 1st, ~~2nd or 3rd~~ marriage }
~~Divorced~~ ⎭

Name of Father _Arthur Mason Collins_

Maiden name of Mother _Florence Trilling_

Date of this marriage _April 28 1944_

Place of this marriage _Indianapolis, Ind._

Name and title of person Performing this marriage _Rev. G. H. O'Donnell_

His address _517 East 23rd St., Indianapolis, Ind._

Witness ⎰ Name, _Victoria Caldwell - 937 South Capitol Ave._
         ⎱ Name, _Prof. Charles R. De Zano - 3402 Sutherland Ave._

### Return this Report to County Clerk with License and Certificate

12

St. 69

# Marriage Record for Board of Health

### To Be Returned by the Minister or Other Person Performing Ceremony

*Howard E Cooper* and *Grace E Harris*

Groom's name _Howard E Cooper_

His age _37_

" color _White_

" occupation _U S Army_

" Birthplace—City _Knox Co Indiana_ State _Indiana_

" Residence—Street No _1949 College_ City _Indianapolis_

Single Widower Divorced } _Divorced_ { 1st 2nd or 3rd marriage } _Second_

Name of Father _Phillip Cooper_

Maiden name of Mother _Albirdia Adams_

Bride's name _Grace E Harris_

Her age _35_

" color _White_

" occupation _____

" Birthplace—City _Hillsville_ State _Virginia_

" Residence—Street No _1949 College_ City _Indianapolis_

Single Widow Divorced } _Divorced_ { 1st 2nd or 3rd marriage } _Second_

Name of Father _William Edward Harris_

Maiden name of Mother _Lucinda Ellen Webb_

Date of this marriage _April 28 1944_

Place of this marriage _First Christian Church, Indianapolis_

Name and title of person Performing this marriage _C C Brooks, Minister_

His address _3853 Washington Blvd_

_Indianapolis, Indiana_

Witness { Name _Livia D Hurley_ _Lorin E Campbell_ Address _1949 College Ave_ _559 N Randolph_

### Return this Report to County Clerk with License and Certificate

12

FILED
42 MAY 5 1944

CLERK

# Marriage Record for Board of Health
## To Be Returned by the Minister or Other Person Performing Ceremony

_____ and _____

Groom's name _Joseph Winchester_

His age _60_

" color _White_

" occupation _Packing & Shipping_

" Birthplace—City _Monticello_ State _Ky_

" Residence—Street No. _____ City _____

~~Single~~
Widower
~~Divorced~~ } _____ { 1st, 2nd or 3rd marriage _X_ } _Second Marriage_

Name of Father _James Winchester_

Maiden name of Mother _Elisabeth Dixon_

Bride's name _Helen E. Dewitt_

Her age _44_

" color _White_

" occupation _Nurse_

" Birthplace—City _Marco_ State _Ind_

" Residence—Street No. _____ City _____

~~Single~~
Widow
~~Divorced~~ } _____ { 1st, 2nd or 3rd marriage _X_ } _Second Marriage_

Name of Father _L. W Maddox_

Maiden name of Mother _Dora Stalcup_

Date of this marriage _April 29—1944 Indianapolis Ind_

Place of this marriage _639 E Market st_

Name and title of person
Performing this marriage _Cal. Charles W Richards._

His address _639 E Market st._

Witness { Name _Robert Wilkerson_
{ Address _1105 S State Indianapolis Ind_

## Return this Report to County Clerk with License and Certificate

# Marriage Record for Board of Health

### To Be Returned by the Minister or Other Person Performing Ceremony

_Johnny Mulinaro_ and _Clara McCall_

Groom's name _Johnny Mulinaro_

His age _19_

" color _White_

" occupation _Produce receiver_

" Birthplace—City _Indianapolis_ State _Indiana_

" Residence—Street No. _519 E. Warren_ City _Indianapolis, Ind._

Single Widower Divorced } _Single_ { 1st, 2nd or 3rd marriage } _First_

Name of Father _Joseph Mulinaro_

Maiden name of Mother _Leva Murello_

Bride's name _Clara McCall_

Her age _16_

" color _White_

" occupation _Housewife_

" Birthplace—City _Indianapolis_ State _Indiana_

" Residence—Street No. _922 Sanders_ City _Indianapolis, Ind._

Single Widow Divorced } _Single_ { 1st, 2nd or 3rd marriage } _First_

Name of Father _Lafayette McCall_

Maiden name of Mother _Jennie McIntosh_

Date of this marriage _April 29, 1944_

Place of this marriage _St. Patrick Rectory Indianapolis Indiana_

Name and title of person Performing this marriage _Rev. Edward C. Bauer, asst pastor_

His address _St. Patrick's Rectory 950 Prospect St._ _Indianapolis, Indiana_

Witness { Name _Rosie Harris, Jane E. Walker & Dorothy A. Walker_

{ Address _922 Sanders. 922 Sanders_

## Return this Report to County Clerk with License and Certificate

12

# Marriage Record for Board of Health

### To Be Returned by the Minister or Other Person Performing Ceremony

Edgar E. Raymond _and_ Ruth E. Bailey.

Groom's name _Edgar E. Raymond_

His age _20_

" color _White_

" occupation _U. S. Army_

" Birthplace—City _Indianapolis_ State _Indiana_

" Residence—Street No. _1582 Penn._ City _Shelbyville_

Single / Widower / Divorced } _Single_    { 1st, 2nd or 3rd marriage } _1st_

Name of Father _Paul Leslie Raymond_

Maiden name of Mother _Margaret Elda Baker_

Bride's name _Ruth E. Bailey_

Her age _20_

" color _White_

" occupation _At home_

" Birthplace—City _Straughn_ State _Ind._

" Residence—Street No. _Indianapolis_ City _R. 3._

Single / Widow / Divorced } _Single_    { 1st, 2nd or 3rd marriage } _1st_

Name of Father _Angus Bailey_

Maiden name of Mother _Pauline States_

Date of this marriage _April 29 - 1944_

Place of this marriage _West Newton, Ind._

Name and title of person Performing this marriage _Rev. Lena Cox_

His address _West Newton, Ind._

Witness { Name _Rowena Frances Williams_
{ Address _R. 3 Box 837, Ind'pls 44, Ind._

## Return this Report to County Clerk with License and Certificate

12

# Marriage Record for Board of Health

To Be Returned by the Minister or Other Person Performing Ceremony

_Hidding_ and _Ruddick_

Groom's name _Paul J. Hidding_

His age _25_

" color _White_

" occupation _United States Navy_

" Birthplace—City _Cedar Rapids_ State _Iowa_

" Residence—Street No. _Morehead City_ City _North Carolina_

Single / Widower / Divorced } _Single_  { 1st, 2nd or 3rd— marriage } _First_

Name of Father _Clarence Martin Hidding_

Maiden name of Mother _Marie Klebenow_

Bride's name _Elizabeth L. Ruddick_

Her age _26_

" color _White_

" occupation _✓_

" Birthplace—City _Columbus_ State _Indiana_

" Residence—Street No. _5 N Park Place_ City _Keokuk, Iowa_

Single / Widow / Divorced } _Single_ { 1st, 2nd or 3rd— marriage } _First_

Name of Father _Charles Ruddick_

Maiden name of Mother _Louise Keyes_

Date of this marriage _April 29, 1944_

Place of this marriage _Indianapolis, Indiana_

Name and title of person Performing this marriage _Cornelius B. Sweeney, asst. pastor_

His address _1347 N. Meridian_
_Indianapolis, Indiana_

Witness { Name _William and Martha Howell_
{ Address _Indianapolis, Indiana_

## Return this Report to County Clerk with License and Certificate

12

# Marriage Record for Board of Health
## To Be Returned by the Minister or Other Person Performing Ceremony

_Dayton Johnson_ and _Emma Johnson Rhodes_

Groom's name _Dayton Johnson_

His age _43_

" color _C_

" occupation _Allison_

" Birthplace—City _Orlinda_ State _Tenn_

" Residence—Street No. _419 Blackford St_ City

Single
Widower } _Single_
Divorced

1st, 2nd or 3rd marriage

Name of Father _Frank Johnson_

Maiden name of Mother _Hattie Huffman_

Bride's name _Emma Johnson_

Her age _38_

" color _C_

" occupation _Maid_

" Birthplace—City _Indianapolis_ State _Ind_

" Residence—Street No. _526 Patterson St_ City

Single
Widow }
Divorced ✓

1st, 2nd or 3rd marriage

Name of Father _Albert Burt. Rhodes_

Maiden name of Mother _Eliza Jane Thurman_

Date of this marriage _April 29_

Place of this marriage _747 N California St_

Name and title of person Performing this marriage _Rev R H Willingham_

His address _747 N California, Indianapolis Ind_

Witness { Name _Mrs. R Willingham # 747 N California St_
{ Address _Mrs. Hay H Thurman # 523 Patterson St_

## Return this Report to County Clerk with License and Certificate

# Marriage Record for Board of Health
### To Be Returned by the Minister or Other Person Performing Ceremony

*Rev. Alonzo F. Gardner* _____ and _____ *Alberta Ellis*

Groom's name _Rev. Alonzo F. Gardner_

His age __37_

" color __C

" occupation __Minister

" Birthplace—City __Tenn__ State __Miss

" Residence—Street No. _811 Paca_ City __Ind.pls

Single
Widower
Divorced } _____ { 1st, 2nd or 3rd marriage }

Name of Father __dead

Maiden name of Mother __Sarah L. Clark.

Bride's name _Alberta Ellis_

Her age __29

" color __C

" occupation __Housewife

" Birthplace—City __Tenn__ State __Illinois

" Residence—Street No. _1418 E maryld_ City __Indianapolis

Single
Widow
Divorced } _____ { 1st, 2nd or 3rd marriage }

Name of Father __Frank Ellis

Maiden name of Mother __Mollie Terrell

Date of this marriage ___April 29, 1944

Place of this marriage ___1412 E Maryland

Name and title of person
Performing this marriage ___Rev. W. L. Boyd

His address ___807½ Indiana Ave.
___Indianapolis, Ind

Witness { Name ___Mrs Mary E Boyd
         { Address ___807½ Indiana Ave, Indpls, Ind.

### Return this Report to County Clerk with License and Certificate

# Marriage Record for Board of Health
### To Be Returned by the Minister or Other Person Performing Ceremony

_Leroy George Haley_ and _Beatrice Ann Kranolis_

Groom's name _Leroy George Haley_

His age _36_

" color _white_

" occupation _car builder_

" Birthplace—City _Indianapolis_ State _Indiana_

" Residence—Street No. _1410 Franklin_ City _Michigan City, Indiana_

Single / Widower / Divorced } _divorced_ { 1st, 2nd or 3rd marriage } _second_

Name of Father _Alva Haley_

Maiden name of Mother _Alma Day_

Bride's name _Beatrice Ann Kranolis_

Her age _32_

" color _white_

" occupation _saleslady_

" Birthplace—City _McLennan Co.,_ State _Texas_

" Residence—Street No. _123 Greene St_ City _Michigan City_

Single / Widow / Divorced } _single_ { 1st, 2nd or 3rd marriage } _first_

Name of Father _Michael Kranolis_

Maiden name of Mother _Mary Stepan_

Date of this marriage _April 29, 1944_

Place of this marriage _Indianapolis, Indiana_

Name and title of person Performing this marriage _A. Berton Clarke, minister_

His address _1153 Blaine Ave._
_Indianapolis, Ind._

Witness { Name _Mrs. Lora Haley_
{ Address _220 N Pershing ave. Indianapolis_

## Return this Report to County Clerk with License and Certificate

FILED

42 MAY 1 1944

Jack Kleam
CLERK

# Marriage Record for Board of Health

## To Be Returned by the Minister or Other Person Performing Ceremony

Harry Kirk Blake ___ and ___ Margaret Lissa Casey

Groom's name _Harry Kirk Blake_

His age _24_

" color _White_

" occupation _U.S. Air Corps_

" Birthplace—City _Indianapolis_ State _Indiana_

" Residence—Street No. _Murfreesborough_ City _Tennessee_

Single Widower Divorced } _Single_   1st, 2nd or 3rd marriage } _First_

Name of Father _Harry F Blake_

Maiden name of Mother _Jonette Haase_

Bride's name _Margaret Lissa Casey_

Her age _21_

" color _White_

" occupation _Curtis Wright_

" Birthplace—City _Hollister_ State _California_

" Residence—Street No. _1034 N. Hamilton_ City _Indianapolis, Ind_

Single Widow Divorced } _Single_   1st, 2nd or 3rd marriage } _First_

Name of Father _Roscoe Casey_

Maiden name of Mother _Melvina V Washer_

Date of this marriage _April 29 1944_

Place of this marriage _East Tenth St Methodist Church, Indianapolis, Ind._

Name and title of person Performing this marriage _Reverend Archiles M. Brown_

His address _937 W. Dr. Woodruff Pl_
_Indianapolis, Ind._

Witness { Name _Harold E Gentry_
{ Address _Lebanon Indiana_

## Return this Report to County Clerk with License and Certificate

## Marriage Record for Board of Health
### To Be Returned by the Minister or Other Person Performing Ceremony

and

Groom's name _Raymond Ralph Komara_

His age _22 — Feb. 15, 1922_

" color _White_

" occupation _U. S. Army_

" Birthplace—City _Youngstown_ State _Ohio_

" Residence—Street No. _1434 Humbolt_ City _Youngstown_

Single / Widower / Divorced } _Single_ 1st, 2nd or 3rd marriage } _1 St._

Name of Father _Florian Komara_

Maiden name of Mother _Kathryn Baytas_

Bride's name _Mary Louise Welsh_

Her age _17 yrs._

" color _White_

" occupation _none_

" Birthplace—City _Indianapolis_ State _Indiana_

" Residence—Street No. _339 Hanson St._ City _Indianapolis_

Single / Widow / Divorced } _Single_ 1st, 2nd or 3rd marriage } _1 St._

Name of Father _Walter Joseph Welsh_

Maiden name of Mother _Margaret Marie Hollis_

Date of this marriage _April 29th 1944_

Place of this marriage _St. Bridgits Church, Indianapolis Ind._

Name and title of person Performing this marriage _Rev. John F. McShane, Pastor, St. Bridgits Church_

His address _801 N. West St., Indianapolis Indiana._

Witness { Name _George Martin_ _Kathryn Komara_
{ Address _Youngstown, Ohio._ _Youngstown, Ohio._

### Return this Report to County Clerk with License and Certificate

12

## Marriage Record for Board of Health

### To Be Returned by the Minister or Other Person Performing Ceremony

_____ and _____

Groom's name _Edward John Swets_

His age _adult_

" color _white_

" occupation _Plumber_

" Birthplace—City _Hartsdale_ State _Indiana_

" Residence—Street No. _925-175th Place_ City _Hammond Ind_

Single Widower Divorced } _Single_ { 1st, 2nd or 3rd marriage } _1st_

Name of Father _Simon Swets_

Maiden name of Mother _Marie M. Nuss._

Bride's name _Eileen Newby_

Her age _adult_

" color _white_

" occupation _Teacher_

" Birthplace—City _Indianapolis_ State _Ind_

" Residence—Street No. _258 N Bever Pl_ City _Ind'p'ls_

Single Widow Divorced } _Single_ { 1st, 2nd or 3rd marriage } _1st_

Name of Father _Leonard R. Newby_

Maiden name of Mother _Lily Leaf._

Date of this marriage _April 29, 1944_

Place of this marriage _Indianapolis Ind_

Name and title of person Performing this marriage _Harry E. Crumpler_

His address _4750 N. Meridian St._
_Indianapolis, Ind_

Witness { Name _Fred George Brommer Diebold_
{ ×Address _Beulah Belle Murff, Richmond Indiana_

### Return this Report to County Clerk with License and Certificate

12

# Marriage Record for Board of Health
### To Be Returned by the Minister or Other Person Performing Ceremony

_Malcolm E Burton_ and _Ocie Virginia Edging_

Groom's name _Malcolm E. Burton_

His age _28_

" color _White_

" occupation _Freight Checker_

" Birthplace—City _Union Ind_ State _Ind_

" Residence—Street No. _631 S Emerson_ City _Indianapolis_

Single / Widower / Divorced } _Single_     1st, 2nd or 3rd marriage } _Second_

Name of Father _Homer Burton_

Maiden name of Mother _Gladys Thomas_

Bride's name _Ocie Virginia Edging_

Her age _32_

" color _White_

" occupation _Clerk._

" Birthplace—City _Indianapolis_ State _Indiana_

" Residence—Street No. _1429 Churchman_ City _Indpls Ind_

Single / Widow / Divorced } _Divorced_     1st, 2nd or 3rd marriage } _Third._

Name of Father _James W Bosley_

Maiden name of Mother _Florence Mamie Weddle_

Date of this marriage _April 29 1944_

Place of this marriage _1515 Harlan St._

Name and title of person Performing this marriage _Rev. Clifford Mathews_

His address _1515 Harlan St. Indianapolis Ind._

Witness { Name _Chas R Bosley_
{ Address _827 Weyhmist_

### Return this Report to County Clerk with License and Certificate

# Marriage Record for Board of Health

### To Be Returned by the Minister or Other Person Performing Ceremony

*Lowell L. Moffitt* and *Mary Emma Wills*

Groom's name _Lowell L. Moffitt_

His age _48_

" color _White_

" occupation _Chief of Plant Production — Ingersoll Stal + Dis._

" Birthplace—City _Knightstown_ State _Indiana_

" Residence—Street No. _1104 Spring Street_ City _Newcastle_

Single
~~Widower~~ } _Divorced_   { 1st, 2nd or 3rd marriage } _Second_
Divorced

Name of Father _A. C. Moffitt_

Maiden name of Mother _Gertrude Mary McMur_

Bride's name _Mary Emma Wills_

Her age _40_

" color _White_

" occupation _housekeeper_

" Birthplace—City _Cato_ State _Indiana_

" Residence—Street No. _419 N. Euclid_ City _Indianapolis_

Single
Widow } _Divorced_   { 1st, 2nd or 3rd marriage } _Second_
Divorced

Name of Father _Robert L. Kershner_

Maiden name of Mother _Mary Etta Neal_

Date of this marriage _April 25, 1944_

Place of this marriage _Indianapolis, Ind._

Name and title of person Performing this marriage _Rev. Raphael L. Mills Jr._

His address _519 N. Wallace, Indianapolis, Ind._

Witness { Name _Samuel Hiner_
         { Address _Knightstown Ind_

## Return this Report to County Clerk with License and Certificate

12

# Marriage Record for Board of Health
### To Be Returned by the Minister or Other Person Performing Ceremony

*Willie Stewart* and *Elevena Whittaker*

Groom's name _Willie Stewart_

His age _35_

" color _C_

" occupation _malde_

" Birthplace—City _hapting rule_ State _Ky_

" Residence—Street No. _311 meneua_ City _Indianapolis_

Single Widower Divorced } _Single_ { 1st, 2nd or 3rd marriage } _1 st_

Name of Father _ledford stewart_

Maiden name of Mother _drew harris_

Bride's name _Elevenor Whittaker_

Her age _31_

" color _C_

" occupation _house Keep_

" Birthplace—City _mayfield_ State _Ky_

" Residence—Street No. _311 menean_ City _Indianapilis_

Single Widow Divorced } _Unmarried_ { 1st, 2nd or 3rd marriage } _2 und_

Name of Father _Side Huffin_

Maiden name of Mother _Oala neal_

Date of this marriage _April 29 1944_

Place of this marriage _Indianapolis Ind._

Name and title of person Performing this marriage _L L Thomas Minister_

His address _708 S. Illinois Inpls Ind._

Witness { Name _Oala Brand_ Address _2336 Inpls Ave_

### Return this Report to County Clerk with License and Certificate

# Marriage Record for Board of Health

### To Be Returned by the Minister or Other Person Performing Ceremony

_____ and _____

Groom's name _Leroy Ronald Beach_

His age _26_

" color _Colored_

" occupation _Kingan's Packing Co_

" Birthplace—City _Indianapolis_ State _Indiana_

" Residence—Street No. _1125 north State_ City _Indianapolis Indiana_

Single / Widower / Divorced } _Divorced_   { 1st, 2nd or 3rd marriage } _2nd_

Name of Father _Beach Beach_

Maiden name of Mother _Mrs E. Betty Wright_

Bride's name _Gazola Pinson_

Her age _25_

" color _Colored_

" occupation _Maid at Wm H. Blocks Co_

" Birthplace—City _Rock Hill_ State _Ky_

" Residence—Street No. _1125 N. State_ City _Indianapolis Indiana_

Single / Widow / Divorced } _Single_   { 1st, 2nd or 3rd marriage } _1st_

Name of Father _Bennie Pinson_

Maiden name of Mother _Mrs Mamie Hawkins_

Date of this marriage _April 29, 1944_

Place of this marriage _945 Roache St_

Name and title of person Performing this marriage _Rev. Samuel Swancey_

His address _945 Roache St_

Witness { Name _Mrs Alma Ruth M Kissick_
{ Address _Mrs Christina Pinson_

### Return this Report to County Clerk with License and Certificate

# Marriage Record for Board of Health

### To Be Returned by the Minister or Other Person Performing Ceremony

Fred John Schmidt _and_ Geneva Shenwell

Groom's name _Fred John Schmidt_

His age _36_

" color _white_

" occupation _Sheet Metal Worker_

" Birthplace—City _Cleveland_ State _Ohio_

" Residence—Street No. _RR 9 Box 56_ City _Indpls_

Single
Widower
Divorced } _Divorced_   { 1st, 2nd or 3rd marriage } _3rd_

Name of Father _Morris C. Schmidt_

Maiden name of Mother _Mary Kendzian_

Bride's name _Geneva Shenwell_

Her age _23_

" color _white_

" occupation _Railroad Employee_

" Birthplace—City _Lumber_ State _Kentucky_

" Residence—Street No. _126 S 3rd_ City _Beech Grove_

Single
Widow
Divorced } _Divorced_   { 1st, 2nd or 3rd marriage } _2nd_

Name of Father _Samuel C. Shenwell_

Maiden name of Mother _Birdie Hinton_

Date of this marriage _April 29, 1944_

Place of this marriage _Indianapolis Indiana_

Name and title of person
Performing this marriage _Ernest Hans Justice of Peace_

His address _152½ E Court Street_

Witness { Name _Mary Crane_
         { Address _3741 College Ave_

## Return this Report to County Clerk with License and Certificate

# Marriage Record for Board of Health

### To Be Returned by the Minister or Other Person Performing Ceremony

*Leonard H. Phillips* and *Dessye A. White*

Groom's name *Leonard H. Phillips*

His age 46

" color White

" occupation Cook

" Birthplace—City Hillham State Indiana

" Residence—Street No. 715 So. Meridian City Indianapolis

Single / Widower / Divorced } Divorced  { 1st, 2nd or 3rd marriage } 2nd

Name of Father Morton J. Phillips

Maiden name of Mother Sarah Hoil

Bride's name *Dessye A. White*

Her age 48

" color White

" occupation None

" Birthplace—City Martin Co. State Indiana

" Residence—Street No. 2820 English City Indianapolis

Single / Widow / Divorced } Divorced  { 1st, 2nd or 3rd marriage } 2nd

Name of Father Thomas L. Ledrow

Maiden name of Mother Etta Abel

Date of this marriage April 29, 1944

Place of this marriage Indianapolis

Name and title of person Performing this marriage Emery S. Lane Justice of Peace

His address 152½ East Cohen St.

Witness { Name Mary M. Lane  { Address 3741 N. College Ave

### Return this Report to County Clerk with License and Certificate

# Marriage Record for Board of Health

### To Be Returned by the Minister or Other Person Performing Ceremony

Grant Shepp _and_ Laurel Virginia Leonard

Groom's name _Grant Shepp_

His age _58_

" color _White_

" occupation _Repair Man_

" Birthplace—City _Selina_ State _Ohio_

" Residence—Street No. _1912 Meeker_ City _Muncie Ind._

Single Widower Divorced } _Single_ { 1st, 2nd or 3rd marriage } _1st_

Name of Father _Charles C. Shepp_

Maiden name of Mother _Rachel Pottschin_

Bride's name _Laurel Virginia Leonard_

Her age _28_

" color _White_

" occupation _Inspector_

" Birthplace—City _Anderson_ State _Indiana_

" Residence—Street No. _1709½ E Wilbur_ City _Muncie Ind._

Single Widow Divorced } _Single_ { 1st, 2nd or 3rd marriage } _1st_

Name of Father _Leonard Frank Leonard_

Maiden name of Mother _Evelyn Clevenger_

Date of this marriage _April 29 - 44_

Place of this marriage _Indianapolis Indiana_

Name and title of person Performing this marriage _Grant Howe justice of Peace_

His address _15½ E Court_

Witness { Name _Mary Jo Rene_
         { Address _3741 College Ave_

## Return this Report to County Clerk with License and Certificate

# Marriage Record for Board of Health
## To Be Returned by the Minister or Other Person Performing Ceremony

James W. Hill and Frances Whitehead Brown

Groom's name _James W. Hill_

His age _Twenty-six_

" color _Brown_

" occupation _Housing manager_

" Birthplace—City _Indianapolis_ State _Ind_

" Residence—Street No. _1905 Barlow Pl._ City _Indianapolis Ind_

Single / ~~Widower~~ / ~~Divorced~~ } _Single_   { 1st, ~~2nd or 3rd~~ marriage } _First_

Name of Father _Walter Hill_

Maiden name of Mother _Buleah Coleman_

Bride's name _Frances Whitehead Brown_

Her age _Twenty four_

" color _Brown_

" occupation _Machinist_

" Birthplace—City _Mobile_ State _Ala_

" Residence—Street No. _1510 N. Senate_ City _Indianapolis Ind_

Single / ~~Widow~~ / ~~Divorced~~ } _Single_   { 1st, ~~2nd or 3rd~~ marriage } _First_

Name of Father _John Whitehead._

Maiden name of Mother _Lottie Dudley_

Date of this marriage _April 29th 1944_

Place of this marriage _235 W 25th Indianapolis Ind._

Name and title of person Performing this marriage _R. J. Andrews S. Minister_

His address _1235 W 25th St. Indianapolis Ind_

Witness { Name _Johnnie Wilson, Jimmy C. Tiffin_   Address _224 W 28th St., 74th ..._

## Return this Report to County Clerk with License and Certificate

12

# Marriage Record for Board of Health
### To Be Returned by the Minister or Other Person Performing Ceremony

*Roy S Griffith* and *Camolean Schwartz*

Groom's name _Roy S. Griffith_

His age _57_

" color _White_

" occupation _Salesman_

" Birthplace—City _Johnson County_ State _Indiana_

" Residence—Street No. _330 N. Keystone_ City _Indianapolis_

Single
Widower
Divorced _Widower_ 1st, 2nd or 3rd marriage _2nd_

Name of Father _Wm S. Griffith_

Maiden name of Mother _Mary E. Treon_

Bride's name _Camolean Schwartz_

Her age _54_

" color _White_

" occupation _Labor_

" Birthplace—City _Shelby Co_ State _Indiana_

" Residence—Street No. _316 Virginia Ave_ City _Indiana_

Single
Widow
Divorced _Divorced_ 1st, 2nd or 3rd marriage _2nd_

Name of Father _Lewis Griffith_

Maiden name of Mother _Rosie Herren_

Date of this marriage _April 29, 1944_

Place of this marriage _332 N. Keystone Ave_

Name and title of person Performing this marriage _Rev. Wm O. Breedlove_

His address _232 Steuart St_ _Indianapolis, Ind_

Witness { Name _Harry H Vandivier Selah Vandivier_
{ Address _330 N. Keystone ave. 330 No. Keystone av._

### Return this Report to County Clerk with License and Certificate

# Marriage Record for Board of Health

### To Be Returned by the Minister or Other Person Performing Ceremony

Earl Robertson _and_ Marie Jones

Groom's name _Earl Robertson_

His age _39_

" color _White_

" occupation _Operator_

" Birthplace—City _Bloomington_ State _Ind._

" Residence—Street No. _1419 N. Gale_ City _Indianapolis_

~~Single~~ ~~Widower~~ Divorced } _divorced_ { ~~1st,~~ 2nd ~~or 3rd~~ marriage } _Second_

Name of Father _Foster E. Robertson_

Maiden name of Mother _Essie J. Adams_

Bride's name _Marie Jones_

Her age _37_

" color _White_

" occupation _Clinical worker_

" Birthplace—City _Monticello_ State _Kentucky_

" Residence—Street No. _1419 N. Gale_ City _Indianapolis_

~~Single~~ ~~Widow~~ Divorced } _divorced_ { ~~1st,~~ 2nd ~~or 3rd~~ marriage } _Second_

Name of Father _Robert Stafford_

Maiden name of Mother _Ella Denton_

Date of this marriage _April 29, 1944_

Place of this marriage _Indianapolis Ind._

Name and title of person Performing this marriage _Rev. Elzie W. Hay, S.S._

His address _1842 N. Delaware_ _Indianapolis Ind._

Witness { Name _Mrs. F. D. Heimlich_ { Address _6237 North Delaware._

### Return this Report to County Clerk with License and Certificate

# Marriage Record for Board of Health
### To Be Returned by the Minister or Other Person Performing Ceremony

_John J. Bell_ and _Grace E. Miles_

Groom's name _John J. Bell_

His age _60_

" color _wht_

" occupation _Refrigerating Engr._

" Birthplace—City _Raymond_ State _Nebraska_

" Residence—Street No. _1147 S. Kenwood_ City _Indianapolis_

Single / Widower / Divorced } _Widower_ { 1st, 2nd or 3rd marriage } _2nd_

Name of Father _Geo. T. Bell_

Maiden name of Mother _Jane Atkin_

Bride's name _Grace E. Miles_

Her age _48_

" color _wht_

" occupation _House keeper_

" Birthplace—City _Worthington_ State _Indiana_

" Residence—Street No. _1147 S. Kenwood_ City _Indianapolis_

Single / Widow / Divorced } _Widow_ { 1st, 2nd or 3rd marriage } _3rd_

Name of Father _Rev. Geo. W. Lewis_

Maiden name of Mother _Rachel E. Baker_

Date of this marriage _4/29/44_

Place of this marriage _Indianapolis_

Name and title of person Performing this marriage _Rev. Manno Shatto_

His address _1045 Church St._
_Indianapolis, Ind._

Witness { Name _Mrs. Manno Shatts_
Address _1045 Church Street_

## Return this Report to County Clerk with License and Certificate

# Marriage Record for Board of Health

### To Be Returned by the Minister or Other Person Performing Ceremony

Maurice G. Wolfred _and_ Audrey D. Dietz

Groom's name _Maurice G. Wolfred_

His age _30_

" color _White_

" occupation _Traffic Representative_

" Birthplace—City _Indianapolis_ State _Ind._

" Residence—Street No. _2215 Brookside Parkway_ City _Indianapolis, Ind_

Single / Widower / Divorced } _Single_    { 1st, 2nd or 3rd marriage } _1st._

Name of Father _Robert Wolfred_

Maiden name of Mother _Annabelle Ellis_

Bride's name _Audrey D. Dietz_

Her age _22_

" color _White_

" occupation

" Birthplace—City _Indianapolis_ State _Ind._

" Residence—Street No. _364 Park Ave_ City _Indianapolis Ind_

Single / Widow / Divorced } _Single_    { 1st, 2nd or 3rd marriage } _1st._

Name of Father _Henry Dietz_

Maiden name of Mother _Helen Rohr_

Date of this marriage _April - 29 - 1944_

Place of this marriage _Indianapolis Ind._

Name and title of person Performing this marriage _Rev. C. M. Bosler._

His address _4217 Central Ave._ _Indianapolis Ind_

Witness { Name _Wilford Russell - Elizabeth Ann Moore_ { Address _2866 Station St_

### Return this Report to County Clerk with License and Certificate

# Marriage Record for Board of Health
### To Be Returned by the Minister or Other Person Performing Ceremony

Benton U. DeVore Jr. and Mildred P. Rumple

Groom's name _Benton U. DeVore_

His age _29_

" color _White_

" occupation _Foreman in Colonial Bakery_

" Birthplace—City _Indianapolis_ State _Ind_

" Residence—Street No. _2823 N. Meridian_ City _Indianapolis_

Single / Widower / Divorced } _Divorced_   { 1st, 2nd or 3rd marriage } _second_

Name of Father _Benton U. DeVore_

Maiden name of Mother _Olive Naomi Grubb_

Bride's name _Mildred P. Rumple_

Her age _28_

" color _White_

" occupation _____

" Birthplace—City _Gwinn County_ State _Indiana_

" Residence—Street No. _628 Cole St_ City _Indianapolis_

Single / Widow / Divorced } _Divorced_   { 1st, 2nd or 3rd marriage } _second_

Name of Father _Floyd Morrow_

Maiden name of Mother _Isla Arthur_

Date of this marriage _April 29, 1944_

Place of this marriage _Kokomo, Indiana_

Name and title of person Performing this marriage _Rev. Katie P. Brown, minister_

His address _408 W. Taylor St, Kokomo, Ind_

Witness { Name _Elmer B. Davis_
{ Address _217 - E - 25th Street Indpls Ind_

### Return this Report to County Clerk with License and Certificate

# Marriage Record for Board of Health
## To Be Returned by the Minister or Other Person Performing Ceremony

_Herselle Richmond_ and _Lorraine McCrimman_

Groom's name _Herselle Richmond_

His age _34_

" color _Negro_

" occupation _Farming_

" Birthplace—City _Indpls_ State _Ind._

" Residence—Street No. _R.R.5_ City _Noblesville Ind._

Single
Widower } _2nd_ { 1st, 2nd or 3rd marriage }
Divorced

Name of Father _Claude Richmond_

Maiden name of Mother _Marie Johnson_

Bride's name _Lorraine McCrimman_

Her age _30_

" color _Negro_

" occupation _House work_

" Birthplace—City _Indianapolis_ State _Ind._

" Residence—Street No. _____ City _____

Single
Widow } _1st_ { 1st, 2nd or 3rd marriage }
Divorced

Name of Father _John McCrimman_

Maiden name of Mother _Lena Edwards_

Date of this marriage _April 29, 1944_

Place of this marriage _Indianapolis_

Name and title of person
Performing this marriage _S.D. Hardrick_

His address _2439 Manlove Ave. Indpls Ind._

Witness { Name _Lena McCrimman 2523 Ethel St_
{ Address _____

## Return this Report to County Clerk with License and Certificate

# Marriage Record for Board of Health
### To Be Returned by the Minister or Other Person Performing Ceremony

_____ Poore _____ and _____ Howell _____

Groom's name _____ John L. Poore _____

His age _____ 19 _____

" color _____ White _____

" occupation _____ US. Army _____

" Birthplace—City _____ Anderson _____ State _____ Indiana _____

" Residence—Street No. 1208 Polk St _____ City _____ Indianapolis, Ind. _____

Single
Widower } _____ Single _____ { 1st, 2nd or 3rd marriage } _____ First _____
Divorced

Name of Father _____ Sanford Isaac Poore _____

Maiden name of Mother _____ Rebecca Myrtle Kemper _____

Bride's name _____ Thelma Darlene Howell _____

Her age _____ 17 _____

" color _____ White _____

" occupation _____ Housekeeper _____

" Birthplace—City _____ Fairbury _____ State _____ Illinois _____

" Residence—Street No. 811 N. New Jersey _____ City _____ Indianapolis, Ind. _____

Single
Widow } _____ Single _____ { 1st, 2nd or 3rd marriage } _____ First _____
Divorced

Name of Father _____ George Floyd Howell _____

Maiden name of Mother _____ Pearl Arbuckle _____

Date of this marriage _____ April 29, 1944 _____

Place of this marriage _____ 1208 Polk Street, Indianapolis, Ind. _____

Name and title of person
Performing this marriage _____ Rev. Ralph L. O'Dell, _____

His address _____ 4319 Carrollton Ave., Indianapolis, Ind. _____

Witness { Name _____ Floyd Howell _____
Address _____ 811 N new Jersey St _____

## Return this Report to County Clerk with License and Certificate

# Marriage Record for Board of Health
### To Be Returned, by the Minister or Other Person Performing Ceremony

_Jack Russell_ and _Wanda L. Hughes_

Groom's name _Jack Russell_

His age _22_

" color _White_

" occupation _Soldier_

" Birthplace—City _Anderson_ State _Indiana_

" Residence—Street No. _116½ Main St_ City _Anderson_

~~Single~~ ~~Widower~~ Divorced } _Divorced_ { ~~1st~~, 2nd or ~~3rd~~ marriage } _Second_

Name of Father _Lester_

Maiden name of Mother _Jewel Hall_

Bride's name _Wanda L. Hughes_

Her age _20_

" color _White_

" occupation _Stock Clerk_

" Birthplace—City _2441 E. Michigan_ State _Indiana_

" Residence—Street No. _Indianapolis_ City _Indiana_

Single ~~Widow~~ ~~Divorced~~ } _Single_ { 1st, ~~2nd or 3rd~~ marriage } _1st_

Name of Father _Clyde_

Maiden name of Mother _Mary Hughes_

Date of this marriage _4/29/44_

Place of this marriage _Indianapolis Ind._

Name and title of person Performing this marriage _Rev. C. White_

His address _627 Division St, Indianapolis_

Witness { Name _Mrs Jewel Turner_ Address _116½ Main St_ }

### Return this Report to County Clerk with License and Certificate

# Marriage Record for Board of Health

### To Be Returned by the Minister or Other Person Performing Ceremony

Robert E Jenkins _and_ Nancy Jane Kegley

Groom's name _Robert E. Jenkins_

His age _23_

" color _white_

" occupation _Doctor of Medicine_

" Birthplace—City _Noblesville_ State _Ind_

" Residence—Street No. _3536 N. Mer._ City _Indpols_

Single / Widower / Divorced _Single_ { 1st, 2nd or 3rd marriage } _1st_

Name of Father _Ray B. Jenkins_

Maiden name of Mother _Nell Souerwine._

Bride's name _Nancy Jane Kegley_

Her age _23_

" color _White_

" occupation _none_

" Birthplace—City _Indianapolis_ State _Ind_

" Residence—Street No. _36 E 5th St_ City _Indpols_

Single / Widow / Divorced _Single_ { 1st, 2nd or 3rd marriage } _2nd_

Name of Father _Wm F. Kegley_

Maiden name of Mother _Mary A. Tripp_

Date of this marriage _April - 29 - 1944_

Place of this marriage _Indianapolis_

Name and title of person Performing this marriage _Dr. John E. Edwards_

His address _4385 N. Penn._
_Indianapolis_

Witness { Name _Dr Harold Martin_
{ Address _West Lafayette Ind_

### Return this Report to County Clerk with License and Certificate

# Marriage Record for Board of Health
## To Be Returned by the Minister or Other Person Performing Ceremony

*Frank C Myles* and *Carolyn J Broome*

Groom's name _Frank J. Myles_

His age _28_

" color _White_

" occupation _Machinist_

" Birthplace—City _Clinton_ State _Indiana_

" Residence—Street No. _Linden Hotel_ City _Indpls._

Single Widower Divorced } _Single_ {1st, 2nd or 3rd marriage} _1st_

Name of Father _Wickie Myles_

Maiden name of Mother _Florence Fisher_

Bride's name _Carolyn Jean Broome_

Her age _27_

" color _White_

" occupation _Machine Operator_

" Birthplace—City _Marion_ State _Indiana_

" Residence—Street No. _1260 W. 30th_ City _Indpls._

Single Widow Divorced } _Divorced_ {1st, 2nd or 3rd marriage} _2nd_

Name of Father _Victor L. Peavy_

Maiden name of Mother _Lucille Johnson_

Date of this marriage _April 29th 1944_

Place of this marriage _Parsonage_

Name and title of person Performing this marriage _Minister_

His address _3135 Northwestern Ave._
_Indianapolis (8), Ind._

Witness { Name _Mrs. E.W. Nugent_
{ Address _3135 NorthWestern Ave. Indpls._

## Return this Report to County Clerk with License and Certificate

## Marriage Record for Board of Health
### To Be Returned by the Minister or Other Person Performing Ceremony

and

Groom's name _John Franklin Booye_

His age _23_

" color _White_

" occupation _Soldier_

" Birthplace—City _Bloomfield_ State _Ind_

" Residence—Street No. _U.S. Army air force_ City _Miami Fla_

Single Widower Divorced } _Single_ { 1st, 2nd or 3rd marriage } _first_

Name of Father _Frank Booye_

Maiden name of Mother _Pearl Hudson_

Bride's name _Helen Marjorie Hash_

Her age _22_

" color _White_

" occupation _Diamond Chain Co._

" Birthplace—City _Bloomfield_ State _Ind._

" Residence—Street No. _713 N. Delaware_ City _Indianapolis_

Single Widow Divorced } _Single_ { 1st, 2nd or 3rd marriage } _first_

Name of Father _Amie Hash_

Maiden name of Mother _Lillie Hanson_

Date of this marriage _April 29, 1944_

Place of this marriage _Olive Branch Christian Church_

Name and title of person Performing this marriage _Rev. Wales E. Smith_

His address _10  E Raymond St_
_Indianapolis Ind_

Witness { Name _Hallie West_
{ Address _1618 Cord St_

### Return this Report to County Clerk with License and Certificate

12

# Marriage Record for Board of Health
### To Be Returned by the Minister or Other Person Performing Ceremony

Richard Dickinson and Margie Goolsby

Groom's name _Richard Dickinson_

His age _34_

" color _white_

" occupation _Home Insulator_

" Birthplace—City _Ingalls_ State _Ind._

" Residence—Street No. _517 East 10th_ City _Indpls_

~~Single~~ Widower ~~Divorced~~ } _Second_ { 1st, 2nd ~~or 3rd~~ marriage } _Second_

Name of Father _Theo. Dickinson_

Maiden name of Mother _Mary Rosella Ryan_

Bride's name _Margie Goolsby_

Her age _19_

" color _white_

" occupation _Book Keeper_

" Birthplace—City _Indianapolis_ State _Ind._

" Residence—Street No. _706 Brookside_ City _Indpls_

Single Widow Divorced } _Single_ { 1st, ~~2nd or 3rd~~ marriage } _First_

Name of Father _Robert Goolsby_

Maiden name of Mother _Maragret Simpson_

Date of this marriage _April 29th, 1944_

Place of this marriage _East Park Methodist Parsonage_

Name and title of person Performing this marriage _Rev. Golden G. Smith_

His address _2609 East New York St, Indianapolis Ind_

Witness { Name _Doris Wise_ { Address _1706 Brookside Ave, Indpls Ind_

### Return this Report to County Clerk with License and Certificate

# Marriage Record for Board of Health

### To Be Returned by the Minister or Other Person Performing Ceremony

*James M. Russell* and *Willie Mae Tuggle*

Groom's name _James M. Russell_

His age _32_

" color _White_

" occupation _Tavern Owner_

" Birthplace—City _Raven_ State _Kentucky_

" Residence—Street No. _231/2 S Ward St_ City _Indpls._

Single Widower Divorced } _Single_ { 1st, 2nd or 3rd marriage } _1st_

Name of Father _Charle David Russell_

Maiden name of Mother _Mary Mitchell_

Bride's name _Willie Mae Tuggle_

Her age _29_

" color _White_

" occupation _Defense Worker_

" Birthplace—City _Ila_ State _Ky_

" Residence—Street No. _2322 1/2 E Wash St_ City _Indpls._

Single Widow Divorced } _Divorced_ { 1st, 2nd or 3rd marriage } _3rd_

Name of Father _John Adair_

Maiden name of Mother _Emila Upchurch_

Date of this marriage _April 29 44_

Place of this marriage _Indpls Ind_

Name and title of person Performing this marriage _Cecil H Reese J P_

His address _152 E Court St._

Witness { Name _Georgia Walter_ Address _570 Keystone_

### Return this Report to County Clerk with License and Certificate

# Marriage Record for Board of Health
## To Be Returned by the Minister or Other Person Performing Ceremony

James W. Johnson and Mildred E. Furnhas

Groom's name James W. Johnson

His age 21

" color White

" occupation Chauffeur

" Birthplace—City Indianapolis State Indiana

" Residence—Street No. 1354 Blaine City Indianapolis, Ind.

Single / Widower / Divorced } Single   { 1st, 2nd or 3rd marriage } 1st

Name of Father Jerry Johnson

Maiden name of Mother Margaret Payne

Bride's name Mildred E. Furnhas

Her age 18

" color White

" occupation none

" Birthplace—City Indianapolis State Indiana, Ind

" Residence—Street No. 1261 Oliver Ave City Indianapolis

Single / Widow / Divorced } Single   { 1st, 2nd or 3rd marriage } 1st

Name of Father Andrew J. Furnhas

Maiden name of Mother Bessie Shuvard

Date of this marriage April 29, 1944

Place of this marriage Indianapolis, Indiana.

Name and title of person Performing this marriage C. A. Wade,

His address 1821 N. Lambert Street, Indianapolis Ind.

Witness { Name Gerald Dunn Phillips Sr.
{ Address 1361 Blaine Ave.

## Return this Report to County Clerk with License and Certificate

12

# Marriage Record for Board of Health
### To Be Returned by the Minister or Other Person Performing Ceremony

George L. *Fraternus* 3rd and Elizabeth *Stevens*

Groom's name _George L. Fraternus III_

His age _19_

" color _W_

" occupation _Soldier_

" Birthplace—City _New Haven_ State _Conn._

" Residence—Street No. _Camp Atterbury_ City _Indiana_

Single / Widower / Divorced } _Single_    { 1st, 2nd or 3rd marriage } _1st_

Name of Father _George L. Fraternus Jr._

Maiden name of Mother _Elsie May Churchill_

Bride's name _Elizabeth Stevens_

Her age _19_

" color _W_

" occupation

" Birthplace—City _New Haven_ State _Conn._

" Residence—Street No. _16 Filton St._ City _New Haven, Conn._

Single / Widow / Divorced } _Single_    { 1st, 2nd or 3rd marriage } _1st_

Name of Father _James M. Stevens_

Maiden name of Mother _Genevieve McQuay_

Date of this marriage _April 29, 1944_

Place of this marriage _St. Philip's Rectory, Indianapolis_

Name and title of person Performing this marriage _Rev. Richard J. Rosser_

His address _126 N. George St._
_Indianapolis, Indiana_

Witness { Name _Elsie Stewart_
        { Address _Katherine Stevens_

## Return this Report to County Clerk with License and Certificate

# Marriage Record for Board of Health

### To Be Returned by the Minister or Other Person Performing Ceremony

_Hughes_ and _Underwood_

Groom's name _John F. Hughes_

His age _20_

" color _W_

" occupation _Sailor_

" Birthplace—City _River Rouge_ State _Mich._

" Residence—Street No. _Naval Armory_ City _Indianapolis, Ind._

Single
Widower,
Divorced } _Single_   { 1st, 2nd or 3rd
marriage } _1st_

Name of Father _____

Maiden name of Mother _____

---

Bride's name _Eileen Underwood_

Her age _19_

" color _W_

" occupation _____

" Birthplace—City _River Rouge_ State _Mich._

" Residence—Street No. _117 Bstric St._ City _River Rouge, Mich._

Single
Widow
Divorced } _Single_   { 1st, 2nd or 3rd
marriage } _First_

Name of Father _____

Maiden name of Mother _____

---

Date of this marriage _April 29 – 1944_

Place of this marriage _St. John R. C. Church_

Name and title of person
Performing this marriage _Rev. Richard B. Cryan_

His address _126 N. Terin St._
_Indianapolis, Ind._

Witness { Name _George Underwood_
{ Address _Eileen McIntire_

### Return this Report to County Clerk with License and Certificate

## Marriage Record for Board of Health
### To Be Returned by the Minister or Other Person Performing Ceremony

_____ and _____

Groom's name _Roy Verl Wise_

His age _47_

" color _White_

" occupation _Sheet metal worker_

" Birthplace—City _Putnam Co._ State _Ind._

" Residence—Street No. _770 Mass. Av._ City _Indianapolis, Ind._

Single ✓ \
Widower } _Single_     { 1st, 2nd or 3rd } _1st_ \
Divorced                { marriage

Name of Father _Simeon A. Wise_

Maiden name of Mother _Ella Hubbard_

Bride's name _Mabel J. Klopp_

Her age _38_

" color _White_

" occupation _Office work_

" Birthplace—City _Montezuma_ State _Ind._

" Residence—Street No. _815 Fairfield_ City _Indianapolis, Ind._

Single ✓ \
Widow } _Single_     { 1st, 2nd or 3rd } _1st_ \
Divorced                { marriage

Name of Father _Herman F. Klopp_

Maiden name of Mother _Myrtle May Fortner_

Date of this marriage _April 29, 1944_

Place of this marriage _Indianapolis, Ind._

Name and title of person \
Performing this marriage _W.D. Shallenberger - Minister_

His address _Indianapolis, Ind._

Witness { Name _Fred R. Klopp_     _Alice E. Klopp_ \
{ Address _1709 Beeler St._ _1709 Beeler St._ \
_Indianapolis_     _Indianapolis_

### Return this Report to County Clerk with License and Certificate

# Marriage Record for Board of Health
### To Be Returned by the Minister or Other Person Performing Ceremony

*Gillis Imrie* and *Kathryn Crowl*

Groom's name _Gillis Imrie_

His age _27_

" color _white_

" occupation _Machinist machanic_

" Birthplace—City _Dugger_ State _Ind_

" Residence—Street No. _1463 Broadway_ City _Indianapolis_

Single
Widower } _Second_    { 1st/2nd or 3rd } _Second_
Divorced } _Divorced_    { marriage }

Name of Father _Oley Imrie_

Maiden name of Mother _Effie Grimes_

Bride's name _Kathryn Crowl_

Her age _28_

" color _white_

" occupation _Army dept_

" Birthplace—City _Dugger_ State _Indiana_

" Residence—Street No. _1638 Bellau_ City _Indianapolis_

Single
Widow } _Second_    { 1st, 2nd or 3rd } _Second_
Divorced } _Divorced_    { marriage }

Name of Father _Halley Roberts_

Maiden name of Mother _Mergy Brewer Roberts_

Date of this marriage _April 29 1944_

Place of this marriage _Indianapolis_

Name and title of person
Performing this marriage _Rev. Thomas J Luke_

His address _1300 winfield Ave city_

Witness { Name _Mrs. Thomas J Luke_
{ Address _1300 winfield Ave, Indianapolis_

### Return this Report to County Clerk with License and Certificate

12

# Marriage Record for Board of Health
### To Be Returned by the Minister or Other Person Performing Ceremony

_____ Irving F. Folkening _____ and _____ Charlotte C. Maas

Groom's name _____ Irving F. Folkening _____

His age _____ 26

" color_____ white

" occupation_____ U. S. Army

" Birthplace—City___ Indianapolis _____ State ___ Indiana

" Residence—Street No. 5251 Singleton _____ City ___ Indianapolis, Ind.

Single
Widower }_____ Single _____ { 1st, 2nd or 3rd }___ First
Divorced         marriage

Name of Father_____ Edmund Folkening

Maiden name of Mother____ Ida Brinkman

Bride's name _____ Charlotte C. Maas

Her age _____ 23

" color_____ white

" occupation_____ Cashier - H. P. Wasson & Co.

" Birthplace—City_____ Indianapolis _____ State ___ Indiana

" Residence—Street No. 1501 English Ave. City ___ Indianapolis, Ind.

Single
Widow }_____ Single _____ { 1st, 2nd or 3rd }___ First
Divorced         marriage

Name of Father_____ Walter C. Maas, Sr.

Maiden name of Mother__ Minnie Meixner

Date of this marriage__ April 29, 1944

Place of this marriage____ Emmaus Lutheran Church

Name and title of person
Performing this marriage__ Walter C. Maas, Pastor, Trinity Lutheran Ch.

His address__ 5444 Carrollton Ave., Indianapolis, Ind.

Witness { Name Miss Dorothy Maas, 1501 English Ave. Indpls.
         { Address Mr. LaVaughn Brabender, Edgewood Ave. "

## Return this Report to County Clerk with License and Certificate

FILED

42 MAY 6 1944

CLERK

# Marriage Record for Board of Health

## To Be Returned by the Minister or Other Person Performing Ceremony

*Stanley H. Barrere* and *Gretchen Middleton*

Groom's name *Stanley H. Barrere*

His age *53*

" color *White*

" occupation *Mechanic*

" Birthplace—City *St Louis* State *Missouri*

" Residence—Street No. *315 East 30th* City *Indianapolis*

Single / Widower / Divorced } *Divorced* { 1st, 2nd or 3rd marriage } *2nd*

Name of Father *Wm H Barrere*

Maiden name of Mother *Katherine Bell Cady*

Bride's name *Gretchen Middleton*

Her age *51*

" color *White*

" occupation *Sales Lady*

" Birthplace—City *Kokomo* State *Indiana*

" Residence—Street No. *315 East 30th* City *Indianapolis*

Single / Widow / Divorced } *Divorced* { 1st, 2nd or 3rd marriage } *2nd*

Name of Father *Lewis Mark Springer*

Maiden name of Mother *Daisy Patterson*

Date of this marriage *April 29, 1944*

Place of this marriage *Indianapolis Indiana*

Name and title of person Performing this marriage *Rev. J. Floyd Seely*

His address *2956 North Capitol Avenue Indianapolis 8, Indiana*

Witness { Name *Mr & Mrs Forrest A Swank* { Address *5208 Rinview Drive*

## Return this Report to County Clerk with License and Certificate

12

# Marriage Record for Board of Health
## To Be Returned by the Minister or Other Person Performing Ceremony

*Lovell Nash* and *Madeline Maners*

Groom's name _Lovell Nash_

His age _20_

" color _White_

" occupation _Marine_

" Birthplace—City _Bloomington_ State _Ind._

" Residence—Street No. _316 S Parker_ City _Indianapolis_

✓ Single
Widower
Divorced } _Single_    {1st, 2nd or 3rd marriage} _First_

Name of Father _William C. Nash_

Maiden name of Mother _Elizabeth Hughes_

Bride's name _Madeline Maners_

Her age _20_

" color _White_

" occupation _War worker_

" Birthplace—City _Spencer_ State _Ind._

" Residence—Street No. _1606 E Washington_ City _Indianapolis_

✓ Single
Widow
Divorced } _Single_    {1st, 2nd or 3rd marriage} _First_

Name of Father _Abner Franklin Maners_

Maiden name of Mother _Minnie Lena McKee_

Date of this marriage _April 30, 1944_

Place of this marriage _Spencer, Ind._

Name and title of person Performing this marriage _O. S. Hawkins, Minister_

His address _R. 3, Spencer, Ind._

Witness { Name _Minnie L. Maners_
Address _Spencer, Ind._

## Return this Report to County Clerk with License and Certificate

# Marriage Record for Board of Health
## To Be Returned by the Minister or Other Person Performing Ceremony

Brown Payne _____ and Rosy James

Groom's name _Brown Payne_

His age _21_

" color _Colored_

" occupation _laborer_

" Birthplace—City _Prospect_ State _Tenn._

" Residence—Street No._2037 Highland Pl._ City _Indpls._

Single
Widower } _Single_ { 1st, 2nd or 3rd marriage } _1st._
Divorced

Name of Father _Mack Payne_

Maiden name of Mother _Mabel Brown_

Bride's name _Rosie Lee James_

Her age _21_

" color _Colored_

" occupation _Housework_

" Birthplace—City _Canton_ State _Miss._

" Residence—Street No._1056 Hoborn St._ City _Indpls._

Single
Widow } _Single_ { 1st, 2nd or 3rd marriage } _1st_
Divorced

Name of Father _Jessie James_

Maiden name of Mother _Nora Young_

Date of this marriage _4-30-44_

Place of this marriage _Indpls._

Name and title of person Performing this marriage _Rev. H. T. Toaliver_

His address _823 W. 27th St._
_Indpls. Ind._

Witness { Name _Lena Chandler_
{ Address _746 W. Walnut St_

## Return this Report to County Clerk with License and Certificate

# Marriage Record for Board of Health
## To Be Returned by the Minister or Other Person Performing Ceremony

*Willie W. Harris* and *Mary Grooms*

Groom's name *Willie Woodrow Harris*

His age *25*

" color *Colored*

" occupation *Laborer*

" Birthplace—City *Union City* State *Tenn.*

" Residence—Street No. *419 Blake St* City *Indpls.*

Single / Widower / Divorced } *Divorced*   { 1st, 2nd or 3rd marriage } *2nd*

Name of Father *Joe B. Harris*

Maiden name of Mother *Annie Dickey*

Bride's name *Mary Louise Grooms*

Her age *19*

" color *Colored*

" occupation *Laundress*

" Birthplace—City *Indpls.* State *Ind.*

" Residence—Street No. *2053 Highland Pl.* City *Indpls.*

Single / Widow / Divorced } *Divorced*   { 1st, 2nd or 3rd marriage } *2nd.*

Name of Father *Oliver Grooms*

Maiden name of Mother *Charlene Cummings*

Date of this marriage *4 — 30 — 44*

Place of this marriage *Indianapolis Indiana*

Name and title of person Performing this marriage *Rev. H. T. Toliver minister*

His address *823 W. 27th St*

*Indpls. Ind.*

Witness { Name *Rev. H Ruyter*
         { Address *2957 Indianapolis Ave.*

## Return this Report to County Clerk with License and Certificate

# Marriage Record for Board of Health
## To Be Returned by the Minister or Other Person Performing Ceremony

_Jack M. Pollard_ and _Sara Frances Denton_

Groom's name _Jack M. Pollard_

His age _17_

" color _White_

" occupation _Golf Course Worker_

" Birthplace—City _Marion Co_ State _Ind_

" Residence—Street No. _RR 16 Box 562_ City _Indianapolis, Ind_

Single } _Single_ { 1st, 2nd or 3rd } _first_
Widower    marriage
Divorced

Name of Father _Leslie Pollard_

Maiden name of Mother _Grethel Isenhour_

Bride's name _Sara Frances Denton_

Her age _16_

" color _White_

" occupation _Student_

" Birthplace—City _Marion Co_ State _Ind_

" Residence—Street No. _RR 16 Box 563 D_ City _Indianapolis, Ind_

Single } _Single_ { 1st, 2nd or 3rd } _first_
Widow     marriage
Divorced

Name of Father _Albert Denton_

Maiden name of Mother _Mary Hogue_

Date of this marriage _April 30, 1944_

Place of this marriage _Terre Haute, Ind_

Name and title of person
Performing this marriage _Minister of the Gospel_

His address _2424 Maple Ave. Terre Haute, Ind_

Witness { Name _Ada Funkhouser_
          { Address _2014-N-26 Terre Haute Ind_

## Return this Report to County Clerk with License and Certificate

12

# Marriage Record for Board of Health
### To Be Returned by the Minister or Other Person Performing Ceremony

*Orval H Brown* and *Mable M Taylor*

Groom's name *Orval H Brown*

His age _53_

" color _White_

" occupation _Clerk_

" Birthplace—City _Vermillion Co_ State _Illinois_

" Residence—Street No. _1610 Carrollton_ City _Indianapolis_

~~Single~~
~~Widower~~
Divorced } _2nd._ { 1st, 2nd or 3rd marriage }

Name of Father _Brazier H Brown_

Maiden name of Mother _Sarah Seals_

Bride's name _Mabel M Taylor._

Her age _42_

" color _White_

" occupation _Clerk_

" Birthplace—City _White Co._ State _Indiana_

" Residence—Street No. _721 E 11th_ City _Indianapolis_

~~Single~~
~~Widow~~
Divorced } _2nd._ { 1st, 2nd or 3rd marriage }

Name of Father _Charles F Gruggel_

Maiden name of Mother _Louisa Enz_

Date of this marriage _April 30 1944_

Place of this marriage _Indianapolis_

Name and title of person Performing this marriage _George A Snyder Minister_

His address _846 N Dr. Woodruff Place_
_Indianapolis Ind_

Witness { Name _Esther Snyder_
{ Address _846 middle Dr. Woodruff Pl. Indianapolis_

### Return this Report to County Clerk with License and Certificate

# Marriage Record for Board of Health
### To Be Returned by the Minister or Other Person Performing Ceremony

*Harlan E. Woodrum* and *Helen Marie Kerr*

Groom's name *Harlan E. Woodrum*

His age __23__

" color __White__

" occupation __Air corps__

" Birthplace—City __State line, Ind__ State __

" Residence—Street No. __Henning__ City __Ill__

Single
Widower } __Single__   { 1st, 2nd or 3rd   } __1st__
Divorced          marriage

Name of Father __Berkley Woodrum__

Maiden name of Mother __Blanch M. Childs__

Bride's name __Helen Marie Kerr__

Her age __20__

" color __White__

" occupation __Comptometer clerk__

" Birthplace—City __Indianapolis__ State __Indiana__

" Residence—Street No. __1015 E. Raymond__ City __Indianapolis__

Single
Widow } __Single__   { 1st, 2nd or 3rd   } __1st__
Divorced          marriage

Name of Father __deceased__

Maiden name of Mother __Margaret nee Rizzo__

Date of this marriage __April 30 1944__

Place of this marriage __Indianapolis, Indiana__

Name and title of person
Performing this marriage __Smith, priest__

His address __802 Dowden, Indianapolis, Indiana__

Witness { Name __H. Stanley Mathews__
        { Address __Cincinnati, Ohio.__

### Return this Report to County Clerk with License and Certificate

# Marriage Record for Board of Health
To Be Returned by the Minister or Other Person Performing Ceremony

*Allen G. Wagner* and *Wylda Elliot*

Groom's name *Allen G Wagner*

His age *33*

" color *White*

" occupation *Machann*

" Birthplace—City *West Terre/Haute* State *Ind.*

" Residence—Street No. *1935 N School Rd* City *Indianapolis*

Single Widower Divorced } *Single*   1st, 2nd or 3rd marriage } *1st*

Name of Father *William Frederick Wagner*

Maiden name of Mother *Ella Grace Bennett*

Bride's name *Wylda Elliot*

Her age *30*

" color *White*

" occupation *Beautician*

" Birthplace—City *Plainfield* State *Ind.*

" Residence—Street No. *R.R. 3 Box 122* City *Indianapolis*

Single Widow Divorced } *Single*   1st, 2nd or 3rd marriage } *1st*

Name of Father *Asher W. Elliot*

Maiden name of Mother *By Anna Byarlay*

Date of this marriage *9 01944*

Place of this marriage *Mt Olive Methodist Church*

Name and title of person Performing this marriage *Rev. C. H. Loveland*

His address *1447 S. High School Rd.* *City.*

Witness { Name *J E Vandivier* Address *Franklin, Ind.*

## Return this Report to County Clerk with License and Certificate

# Marriage Record for Board of Health

## To Be Returned by the Minister or Other Person Performing Ceremony

*Willis Pitman* and *Elnora Eatokins*

Groom's name _Willis Pitman_

His age _29_

" color _white_

" occupation _Steel worker_

" Birthplace—City _Camelltore_ State _Kentucky_

" Residence—Street No. _2210 Madison ave_ City _Indpls_

Single / Widower / Divorced — _Single_    1st, 2nd or 3rd marriage — _1st_

Name of Father _Millard Pitman_

Maiden name of Mother _Martha Pitman_

Bride's name _Elnora Eatokins_

Her age _24_

" color _white_

" occupation _Steel worker_

" Birthplace—City _Decatur_ State _Illinois_

" Residence—Street No. _R#6. Box 509_ City _Indpls Ind._

Single / Widow / Divorced — _Single_    1st, 2nd or 3rd marriage — _1st_

Name of Father _Anton Eatokins_

Maiden name of Mother _Ruby Duncan_

Date of this marriage _April 30, 1947_

Place of this marriage _The brides home_

Name and title of person Performing this marriage _Everett Atkinson, Minister_

His address _1049 King ave, Indianapolis, Ind._

Witness { Name _James Patrick Eustace_
{ Address _407½ main St Beech Grove Ind._

## Return this Report to County Clerk with License and Certificate

# Marriage Record for Board of Health
## To Be Returned by the Minister or Other Person Performing Ceremony

_William A. Van Horn_ and _Margaret Ann Morrison_

Groom's name _William A. Van Horn_

His age _23_

" color _White_

" occupation _U.S. Army Dental Corps_

" Birthplace—City _Terre Haute_ State _Ind_

" Residence—Street No. _"_ _"_ City _"_

Single Widower Divorced } _Single_  { 1st, 2nd or 3rd marriage } _1st_

Name of Father _Eugene Van Horn_

Maiden name of Mother _Ruth Heaton_

Bride's name _Margaret Ann Morrison_

Her age _24_

" color _White_

" occupation _Teacher_

" Birthplace—City _Huntington Co_ State _Indiana_

" Residence—Street No. _413 Conrad x ave_ City _Kokomo, Ind_

Single Widow Divorced } _Single_  { 1st, 2nd or 3rd marriage } _1st_

Name of Father _William Robert Morrison_

Maiden name of Mother _Vivian Clarke_

Date of this marriage _April 30, 1944_

Place of this marriage _Kokomo, Indiana_

Name and title of person Performing this marriage _Rev. F. E. Tribley (minister)_

His address _811 So. Washington St_

_Kokomo, Indiana._

Witness { Name _Dr. Edward A. Brown_

{ Address _625 So. Willow Rd Evansville, Ind_

## Return this Report to County Clerk with License and Certificate

# Marriage Record for Board of Health

### To Be Returned by the Minister or Other Person Performing Ceremony

Harold J Perkins and Lillian Phyllis Metz

Groom's name _Harold J Perkins_

His age _30_

" color _white_

" occupation _trucking_

" Birthplace—City _Indianapolis_ State _Indiana_

" Residence—Street No. _5206 W. Washington_ City _Indianapolis, Ind_

Single / Widower / Divorced } _Divorced_   1st, 2nd or 3rd marriage } _Second_

Name of Father _Francis Roy Perkins_

Maiden name of Mother _Helen Lucille Cherry_

Bride's name _Lillian Phyllis Metz_

Her age _28_

" color _white_

" occupation _housewife_

" Birthplace—City _Plumpton_ State _England_

" Residence—Street No. _5206 W. Washington_ City _Indianapolis_

Single / Widow / Divorced } _Divorced_   1st, 2nd or 3rd marriage } _Second_

Name of Father _Geo. Henry Washington Metz_

Maiden name of Mother _Ann Rourke_

Date of this marriage _April 30, 1944_

Place of this marriage _North Methodist Church_

Name and title of person Performing this marriage _Dallas L. Browning, Minister_

His address _5530 N. Delaware St._
_Indianapolis, Indiana_

Witness { Name _Mrs. F. R. Perkins_
{ Address _5206 W. Washington St_

### Return this Report to County Clerk with License and Certificate

# Marriage Record for Board of Health
### To Be Returned by the Minister or Other Person Performing Ceremony

_Russell A. Hibbard_ and _Irma Brooks_

Groom's name _Russell A. Hibbard_

His age _39_

" color _W. lite_

" occupation _Officer U. S. Army._

" Birthplace—City _Medford_ State _Oregon_

" Residence—Street No. _____ City _Camp Atterbury, Ind._

Single—
Widower— } _Divorced_ { 1st, 2nd or 3rd marriage } _Third_
Divorced

Name of Father _Joshua Gibson Hibbard_

Maiden name of Mother _Bertha Ellen Davis_

Bride's name _Irma Brooks_

Her age _36_

" color _White_

" occupation _none_

" Birthplace—City _Boone County_ State _Indiana_

" Residence—Street No. _1034 W. 34th_ City _Indianapolis_

Single—
Widow— } _Divorced_ { 1st, 2nd or 3rd marriage } _Second_
Divorced

Name of Father _John Thomas Bruce_

Maiden name of Mother _Louesa Miller_

Date of this marriage _April 30th 1944_

Place of this marriage _Chapel 13177, Camp Atterbury, Ind._

Name and title of person
Performing this marriage _Chaplain (1st Lt) James R. Dewey_

His address _Post Headquarters_
_Camp Atterbury, Ind._

Witness { Name _Mrs. Roy E. Mason_
{ Address _915 Roy St. So. Bend, Ind._

## Return this Report to County Clerk with License and Certificate

FILED

42 MAY 3 1944

CLERK

# Marriage Record for Board of Health
### To Be Returned by the Minister or Other Person Performing Ceremony

*Raymond H Chapman* and *Lucile Moore*

Groom's name _Raymond H Chapman_

His age _5'6_

" color _White_

" occupation _Rr Emp._

" Birthplace—City _Washington_ State _Ont_

" Residence—Street No. _221 E 9_ City _Indianapolis_

Single Widower Divorced } _Widower_  {1st, 2nd or 3rd marriage} _2nd_

Name of Father _Fayette Chapman_

Maiden name of Mother _Jennie Zeiter_

Bride's name _Lucile Moore_

Her age _43_

" color _White_

" occupation _Nurse_

" Birthplace—City _Wheeling W Va_ State _W. Va._

" Residence—Street No. _221 E 9_ City _Indianapolis_

Single Widow Divorced } _Widow_  {1st, 2nd or 3rd marriage} _2nd_

Name of Father _William H Brown_

Maiden name of Mother _Sarah Ely Clark_

Date of this marriage _April 30 1944_

Place of this marriage _Franklin_

Name and title of person Performing this marriage _Rev O T Marlin_

His address _248 E Madison St Franklin Ind_

Witness { Name _Edward Brennan Mj. C.M.S._
Address _Camp Atterbury_ }

### Return this Report to County Clerk with License and Certificate

# Marriage Record for Board of Health
### To Be Returned by the Minister or Other Person Performing Ceremony

Walter N. Maddox _____ and Bessye Lou Herring

Groom's name _Walter N. Maddox_

His age _28_

" color _W._

" occupation _Lt U.S. Army_

" Birthplace—City _Billings_ State _Montana_

" Residence—Street No. _1504 E. Hamilton_ City _Flint Mich_

Single Widower Divorced } _Second_    { 1st, 2nd or 3rd marriage } _____

Name of Father _Newton M. Maddox_

Maiden name of Mother _Winifred Joy White_

Bride's name _Bessye Lou Herring_

Her age _28_

" color _W._

" occupation _Teacher of deaf_

" Birthplace—City _Sylvarena_ State _Miss_

" Residence—Street No. _1054 S-42_ City _Indpls, Ind_

Single Widow Divorced } _____    { 1st, 2nd or 3rd marriage } _First—_

Name of Father _Oscar Herring_

Maiden name of Mother _Ada Coleman_

Date of this marriage _April 30/44_

Place of this marriage _Indianapolis, Ind_

Name and title of person Performing this marriage _Alexander Sharp_

His address _5150 College Ave_
_Indianapolis, Ind_

Witness { Name _Lester C. Stanfield_
        { Address _5033 Evanston, Indpls, Ind_

### Return this Report to County Clerk with License and Certificate

# Marriage Record for Board of Health
## To Be Returned by the Minister or Other Person Performing Ceremony

---

_____ and _____

Groom's name _Allen E. Smith_

His age _21_

" color _White_

" occupation _U.S. Navy_

" Birthplace—City _Gothersville_ State _Indiana_

" Residence—Street No. _463 Kansas_ City _Indianapolis_

Single Widower Divorced } _Single_   { 1st, 2nd or 3rd marriage } _first_

Name of Father _Laurence Smith_

Maiden name of Mother _Louise Peters_

Bride's name _Mary Ethel Balding_

Her age _21_

" color _White_

" occupation _Stenographer_

" Birthplace—City _Vincennes_ State _Indiana_

" Residence—Street No. _2273 Madison_ City _Indianapolis_

Single Widow Divorced } _Single_   { 1st, 2nd or 3rd marriage } _first_

Name of Father _Harry Balding_

Maiden name of Mother _Hazel Hicks_

Date of this marriage _April 30, 1944_

Place of this marriage _Olive Branch Christian Church_

Name and title of person Performing this marriage _Rev. Wm. S. Smith_

His address _101 E. Raymond St_ _Indianapolis - Ind_

Witness { Name _Betty Ferguson_   Address _101 E. Raymond St._

---

## Return this Report to County Clerk with License and Certificate

12

# Marriage Record for Board of Health
### To Be Returned by the Minister or Other Person Performing Ceremony

_____ and _____

Groom's name _Stewart Parsons_

His age _39_

" color _White_

" occupation _Treas. English Theatre_

" Birthplace—City _Muskegon_ State _Michigan_

" Residence—Street No. _200 N. Talbot_ City _Indpls_

Single / Widower / Divorced } _Widower_ { 1st, 2nd or 3rd marriage } _second_

Name of Father _William Parsons_

Maiden name of Mother _Harriett Eller_

Bride's name _Mildred Babb_

Her age _28_

" color _White_

" occupation _none — at home_

" Birthplace—City _Indianapolis_ State _Ind_

" Residence—Street No. _6 W. Mich_ City _Indpls_

Single / Widow / Divorced } _single_ { 1st, 2nd or 3rd marriage } _first_

Name of Father _Bruce Babb_

Maiden name of Mother _Bernice Brinson_

Date of this marriage _April 30, 1944_

Place of this marriage _6 W. Mich St Indpls_

Name and title of person Performing this marriage _Rev. Wade Smith_

His address _104 E Raymond St_
_Indianapolis, Ind_

Witness { Name _Mrs. Ira Parks_
{ Address _6 W. Mich_

### Return this Report to County Clerk with License and Certificate

## Marriage Record for Board of Health
### To Be Returned by the Minister or Other Person Performing Ceremony

_Fred S Bates_ and _Sylvia V. Achey_

Groom's name _Fred S. Bates_

His age _40_

" color _White_

" occupation _Wholesale produce_

" Birthplace—City _Charles Hill_ State _Indiana_

" Residence—Street No. _1528 Montcalm_ City _Indianapolis_

Single / Widower / Divorced | 1st, 2nd or 3rd marriage _Second_

Name of Father _Joseph Albert Bates_

Maiden name of Mother _Alice Ellen Crosby_

Bride's name _Sylvia V. Achey_

Her age _35_

" color _White_

" occupation _Typist_

" Birthplace—City _Indianapolis_ State _Indiana_

" Residence—Street No. _1635 Montcalm_ City _Indianapolis_

Single / Widow / Divorced | 1st, 2nd or 3rd marriage _Second_

Name of Father _Christopher Graham_

Maiden name of Mother _Anna Dow_

Date of this marriage _Apr. 30, 1944_

Place of this marriage _Lebanon, Indiana_

Name and title of person Performing this marriage _Curtis C. Fruth_

His address _510 S. Lebanon St., Lebanon, Indiana_

Witness { Name _Gladys Germaine — Ferdinand Wolfe_
{ Address

### Return this Report to County Clerk with License and Certificate

# Marriage Record for Board of Health
### To Be Returned by the Minister or Other Person Performing Ceremony

_William J Smith_ and _Maria J Guarino_

Groom's name _Willie J Smith_

His age _Twenty four_

" color _White_

" occupation _Labour Curtis Wrights_

" Birthplace—City _Bann Co_ State _Ky_

" Residence—Street No. _219 Soto_ City _Indianapolis_

Single / Widower / Divorced } _Single_ { 1st, 2nd or 3rd marriage } _First time_

Name of Father _Benton Smith_

Maiden name of Mother _Omie Corner_

---

Bride's name _Maria J Guarino_

Her age _Twenty years old_

" color _White_

" occupation _Machine operator_

" Birthplace—City _James Town_ State _New York_

" Residence—Street No. _271 Trowbridge_ City _Indianapolis_

Single / Widow / Divorced } _Single_ { 1st, 2nd or 3rd marriage } _first time_

Name of Father _Peter Gruano_

Maiden name of Mother _Carlina Gruano_

---

Date of this marriage _April 30 1944_

Place of this marriage _330 N Randolph St Indianapolis_

Name and title of person Performing this marriage _Rev J B Douglass_

His address _330 N Randolph St Indianapolis Ind_

Witness { Name _Mrs Virginia Trainer_
{ Address _330 N Randolph St Indpls. Ind_

### Return this Report to County Clerk with License and Certificate

# Marriage Record for Board of Health

### To Be Returned by the Minister or Other Person Performing Ceremony

_____ and _____

Groom's name _La Mar Jones_

His age _44_

" color _Colored_

" occupation _Janitor_

" Birthplace—City _Atlanta_ State _Ga_

" Residence—Street No. _Dayton_ City _Ohio_

Single
~~Widower~~
~~Divorced~~ } _____ { 1st, ~~2nd or 3rd~~ marriage }

Name of Father _William Jones_

Maiden name of Mother _Maggie Paige_

Bride's name _Jewell Majors_

Her age _34_

" color _Colored_

" occupation _domestic_

" Birthplace—City _Louisville_ State _Ky_

" Residence—Street No. _2072 Cornell ave_ City _Indianapolis Ind_

~~Single~~
~~Widow~~
Divorced } _____ { 1st, 2nd ~~or 3rd~~ marriage }

Name of Father _Edward Majors_

Maiden name of Mother _Millie Humphreis_

Date of this marriage _April 30th_

Place of this marriage _Indianapolis Ind_

Name and title of person
Performing this marriage _W. L. Barr (Bishop)_

His address _1918 Martindale ave_

Witness { Name _B. W. McLeod_
          Address _908 Cornell ave._

## Return this Report to County Clerk with License and Certificate

12

# Marriage Record for Board of Health
### To Be Returned by the Minister or Other Person Performing Ceremony

David Earl Baker and Marjorie C. Sigmund

Groom's name David Earl Baker

His age 21

" color White

" occupation General Assembly P. R. Mallory

" Birthplace—City Richmond State Indiana

" Residence—Street No. 33 S. Hawthorne Lane City Indianapolis, Ind.

Single
Widower } Single    { 1st, 2nd or 3rd marriage } First
Divorced

Name of Father Everett E. Baker

Maiden name of Mother Gladys Estell

Bride's name Marjorie C. Sigmund

Her age 22

" color White

" occupation Inspector P. R. Mallory

" Birthplace—City Terre Haute State Indiana

" Residence—Street No. 1902 Milburn City Indianapolis, Ind.

Single
Widow } Single    { 1st, 2nd or 3rd marriage } First
Divorced

Name of Father Charles Sigmund

Maiden name of Mother Jessie Florence Reece

Date of this marriage

Place of this marriage

Name and title of person
Performing this marriage

His address

Witness { Name Orla J. Steele
       { Address 1310 N. Drexel, Indianapolis, Ind.

### Return this Report to County Clerk with License and Certificate

FILED
42 APR 11 1944
CLERK

Lightning Source UK Ltd.
Milton Keynes UK
UKHW051036221118
332624UK00012BA/1684/P